'The acuity of his insights makes the books a wholly
compelling read'
Geraldine Bedell, *Observer*

'He has lots of fun and gives the reader lots of fun'
New Statesmen

'To his credit, Hastings is very much his own man'
Anthony Howard, *Sunday Times*

'Hastings is a brilliant reporter . . . and the access an editor gets
– the seat in the front stalls – gives him an extra edge'
Peter Preston, *Observer*

'He comes across in this book as fiercely ambitious,
supremely self-confident, opiniated and a bit of a snob.
But he is also loyal, brave and dedicated'
Philip Knightley, the *Oldie*

'A gripping book, unflinchingly honest'
Literary Review

'Required reading for anyone interested in newspapers'
Kim Fletcher, *Daily Telegraph*

'He has produced an outstanding example . . .
of the Fleet Street memoir'
Alan Watkins, *Spectator*

'Much excellent gossip, some of it wildly indiscreet . . . Above
everything else, ''

D1354071

'Gripping . . . Mr Ha   an just
an editor, more even th   ble hack'

Country Life

EDITOR

MAX HASTINGS was editor and editor-in-chief of the *Daily Telegraph* in the late 80s and early 90s. In 1996 he became editor of the *Evening Standard*. He has won many awards for his journalism, including Journalist of the Year, *What the Papers Say* Reporter of the Year – for his work in the South Atlantic in 1982 – and Editor of the Year in 1988. He is the author of fifteen books, two of which were named as *Yorkshire Post* Books of the Year and one of which won the Somerset Maugham Prize. He was knighted in 2002 in the Queen's birthday honours list.

MAX HASTINGS

EDITOR

An Inside Story of Newspapers

PAN BOOKS

First published 2002 by Macmillan

This edition published 2014 by Pan Books
an imprint of Pan Macmillan, a division of Macmillan Publishers Limited
Pan Macmillan, 20 New Wharf Road, London N1 9RR
Basingstoke and Oxford
Associated companies throughout the world
www.panmacmillan.com

ISBN 978-1-4472-6980-9

Grateful acknowledgement is made to Nicholas Garland and the *Daily Telegraph*
for permission to reproduce the cartoon on page 300, courtesy of the Centre for the
Study of Cartoons and Caricature, University of Kent, Canterbury.

A CIP catalogue record for this book is available from
the British Library.

Typeset by SetSystems Ltd, Saffron Walden, Essex

Printed and bound by CPI Group (UK) Ltd, Croydon, CR0 4YY

FOR MY MOTHER

ANNE SCOTT-JAMES

'I suppose history never lies, does it?' said Mr Dick, with a gleam of hope.

'Oh dear, no, sir!' I replied, most decisively. I was ingenuous and young, and I thought so.

– *David Copperfield*

" The editor will see you now "

Contents

LIST OF ILLUSTRATIONS

FOREWORD

Journalism is a self-indulgent trade, on the margin of great affairs. In the midst of one of the Tory government's endemic crises of the early 1990s, at lunch one day I asked Michael Portillo, Chief Secretary to the Treasury, how he could endure a minister's life: little money, dreadful hours, no family life, relentless public humiliations. People like me, I said, have more fun and are better paid. 'Maybe,' said Portillo drily, 'but you are on the touchline while we are on the pitch.' He was right. Journalists are privileged spectators of the divine comedy. I mistrust writers and editors who wish to perceive themselves as players, rather than as recorders and critics. This is a book about what it is like to be a privileged spectator. I have written it chiefly to please myself and some old colleagues with whom I shared a wonderful relationship – on my side anyway. I asked Don Berry, who worked with me for sixteen years at the *Daily Telegraph* and later at the *Evening Standard,* whether he thought there was a book in what happened to us. He answered: 'Somebody ought to tell the story.'

Back in the mid-1980s, when all this started, I seemed an implausible national newspaper editor. I was appointed to the *Daily Telegraph* when the paper and its parent company were on their knees. With some 300 colleagues, many of whom I recruited, our team spent almost ten years transforming the title, creating a modern newspaper. It was a period fraught with storms: commercial, personal, political. It was the most exciting phase of my life, not excluding a few wars. This is not a history of the *Telegraph* from 1986 through 1995. It is a personal account of what happened to me there. Others – Conrad Black, Andrew Knight, the working journalists – would tell different tales. Theirs would be no less valid than mine. They saw things and knew things which I did not, and vice versa. It is simply a matter of perspectives.

This is, above all, a story about what a wonderful experience it was, bumps and all. Soon after Harold Evans was forced to resign as a Murdoch editor back in 1982, he wrote a memoir entitled *Good Times, Bad Times*. I admired Harry as helmsman of *The Sunday Times* in its great years, but I was disappointed by his book. It reflects considerable bitterness towards his proprietor. It seemed odd that the author should have allowed himself to be surprised that he and Rupert Murdoch did not get on. Most newspaper proprietors are extravagant figures. Many end up as monsters, even if they do not start that way. Not infrequently, they come to regard their titles as private rifle ranges, where they can select at will targets for persecution or protected species status. They are spoilt and indulged by people who should know better, from Prime Ministers downwards. I once asked John Major why he bothered to entertain Rupert Murdoch, when it was obvious that News International's editorial hostility would not be diminished one iota by a Chequers lunch. I received no good answer. Tony Blair cultivates even the most disreputable proprietors and editors. It somewhat diminishes any sense of privilege attaching to an encounter with the Prime Minister, if on the way out one encounters entering the hall the pornography tycoon Mr Richard Desmond, who also happens to own the *Daily Express*. A senior member of the Major government asked me if I thought that Conrad Black, then as now the *Telegraph*'s chairman, would be less antagonistic to the government's European policy if he was given a peerage. For about five minutes, I said. Whatever the professed convictions of proprietors, most are moneylogues rather than ideologues. Their decisions are driven by commercial imperatives which are not susceptible to ministerial blandishments. Lord Beaverbrook, with his explicit commitment to using his newspapers to make propaganda, was the exception rather than the rule. Stripped of their own rhetoric, the political convictions of most British proprietors throughout history add up to an uncomplicated desire to make the world a safe place for rich men to live in. Few trouble to profess much concern for the plight of the dispossessed, at home or abroad. Now that I am no longer one of their editors, I can say that the Lords Rothermere, *père et fils*, are the only newspaper owners I have worked for who have shown themselves sincerely committed to the doctrine of editorial independence.

If one chooses to climb into the cage with a proprietor, as does anyone who accepts an editorship, it is reasonable to be angered, frustrated, dismayed; but one should never be surprised by what happens, or by occasional maulings. In this story there are a good many rows, some parochial and some of wider importance. Several involved our chairman. There were plenty of moments when Conrad Black was cross with me, or I with him. How could it be otherwise, when I was a journalist of liberal Tory inclinations, running a newspaper for a proprietor of avowedly right-wing conservative convictions? I have always found the views of the Right on Europe, Northern Ireland, white Africa, capital punishment and the underclass unsympathetic, even repugnant. In the light of my own opinions it seems remarkable to me, as it did to the media and the political world, that I maintained my position at the *Telegraph* for so long. Between 1986 and 1995, conservative columnists such as Paul Johnson and Stephen Glover frequently poured scorn on my ideological shortcomings, and predicted my imminent demise. What a pleasure it was to disappoint them! But also, I think, my longish tenure reflected well on Conrad Black. He continued to employ me, amid much shot and shell, until David English offered me the *Evening Standard* and I decided it was time to move on. Today, I feel nothing but gratitude to Conrad and to Andrew Knight, who gave me such opportunities, and with whom I shared so many dramas. To edit a national newspaper is the greatest privilege our business has to offer. Although for the last five years at the *Telegraph* I possessed a grand title as Group Editor-in-Chief, that of Editor is the only one which counts. Whatever my shortcomings in the role, after completing sixteen years in editors' chairs, I feel like a functionary who somehow retained continuous employment in the upper reaches of the French government between 1789 and 1805. I often twist my head on my shoulders for reassurance. In recent times only Donald Trelford, David English and Peter Preston have run major newspaper titles for longer.

Fleet Street readers may be entertained by an inside story of the *Telegraph* in its most tumultuous years. I hope there is also a public outside our business, curious about how a newspaper is run and put together, about what an editor does all day. I suspect most people's image of our activities is not dissimilar from that of Evelyn Waugh's William Boot, who once saw a film about newspaper life in which 'neurotic men in shirt sleeves and eye-shades had rushed from telephone to tape machine, insulting and betraying one another in surroundings of unredeemed squalor'. There are surprisingly few personal narratives which detail the reality. The most difficult task in structuring this book has been to prevent it from lapsing into a narrative of British politics and international events between 1986 and 1995. This is not its purpose. My period as an editor embraced an extraordinary succession of dramas at home and abroad: the collapse of apartheid, the end of the Cold War, Irish terrorism, the fall of Thatcher, the Tory civil war over Europe, the break-up of Yugoslavia, the Gulf War, the tribulations of Britain's Royal Family, together with all manner of natural and man-made disasters and tragedies. I have tried to describe how these developments impacted upon a national newspaper and its editor, even at the cost of some fragmentation and loss of chronology, rather than to create an historical narrative.

After I left the *Telegraph*, I went on to spend six years at the *Standard.* I have confined this book to the *Telegraph* phase. The saga of dragging a national institution into the twentieth century had a beginning, a middle and an end. I inherited the *Evening*

Standard as a going concern rather than as a chronic patient. Also, of course, the *Standard* experience was more recent. Alan Clark once told me that he liked to leave his diaries to mature for a few years before publication, like good wine. He also believed, I fancy, that it was prudent to allow a decent interval, to diminish the number of people who remembered enough of the events which he described to contradict his own version. Perhaps the same applies to me. I hope the seven years that have elapsed since I left the *Telegraph* count as a 'decent interval', and justify recounting some private conversations.

'History is not what happened, it is what you can remember,' wrote Sellar and Yeatman in *1066 And All That*. I did not keep a diary of the *Telegraph* years, but I have preserved all significant correspondence. I drafted contemporary notes of important meetings with politicians and other key figures, which form the basis for my quotations in these pages. If it sometimes seems that I am too reliant upon citing documents, I have done so because a verbatim record of what was written down at the time seems more convincing than a paraphrase composed ten or fifteen years later. Duff Hart-Davis's book *The House the Berrys Built* is an invaluable account of the family's rise and fall, which has reminded me of some important details. I have trespassed upon Conrad Black's good nature, to borrow the archive volumes of the *Telegraph* during my editorship. Both he and Andrew Knight have been gracious enough to give me permission to quote from our correspondence. I have reread every issue of the paper for which I was responsible. I learned a lot I had missed, and studied some hair-raising editorials my colleagues slipped into the leader column while I was away on holidays.

Four friends – Don Berry, Christopher Bland, Roy Jenkins, Ferdinand Mount – have read my draft manuscript. I am warmly grateful for their comments, most of which I have acted upon. It seems legitimate to tell the story at this distance from events, but it is hard to strike a balance between recording what happened, together with some of the things people said, and avoiding gratuitous embarrassments. One yardstick for a book of this kind is whether it can pass the Woodrow Wyatt decency test. When he was alive, Woodrow and I found each other unsympathetic: 'I do not like Max Hastings. I think he was beastly to Petronella. He is so absorbed by the impression he is making.' Posthumous publication of the old scoundrel's diaries occasioned his critics much satisfaction. The volumes confirm that Woodrow's shameless cultivation of any fount of power or hospitality was matched by relentless disloyalty and condescension ('Conrad Black is boring. He is limited. He has read some history books, which he understands somewhat, but I don't think he has really got a grip on the policy the paper ought to have'). A book of the kind I have written would be unreadable if it was not – well, fairly indiscreet. Since a few politicians have made me blush by quoting some of my own sillier remarks in their memoirs and diaries, it seems not unfair to get a little of my own back. But I have tried to do better than the awful Woodrow, in sparing innocent bystanders.

My deepest gratitude goes to my family, who endured for so long the tensions and traumas inseparable from living with an editor; to my former personal assistant at the *Evening Standard,* Annabelle Fisher, without whom I could never have written this book; to Rachel Lawrence, who was my PA at the *Telegraph* and fulfils the same invaluable role for me today; to Garland, Griffin and the inimitable Matt for allowing me to reproduce their cartoons; and to my old editorial colleagues, who made the *Telegraph*'s transformation possible. It is impossible to name them all, but I must mention Don Berry, Neil Collins, Jeremy Deedes, Trevor Grove, Andrew Hutchinson, George Jones, Charles Moore, Nigel Wade, Veronica Wadley and, unforgettably, my predecessor in office and Fleet Street's longest-serving star reporter – W. F. Deedes. Their support and friendship contributed mightily to the joy of being Editor of *The Daily Telegraph.*

MAX HASTINGS
Hungerford, March 2002

1

WILD CARD

IN OCTOBER 1985 I WAS thirty-nine years old, living deep in
the Northamptonshire countryside surrounded by chickens, dogs,
sheep, horses and children. I wrote a weekly piece for *The Sunday
Times*, which I had joined a few months earlier at the invitation
of Andrew Neil. I visited the paper's offices in Gray's Inn Road
every fortnight or so to gossip and collect my expenses. Occasionally I went abroad on assignments. That autumn, for instance, I
contributed a 4,000-word portrait of Reagan's America, for which
I travelled from coast to coast. I made occasional television
documentaries – I had just presented *Cold Comfort Farm*, a fifty-
minute film for ITV about the crisis which I believed was coming
to Britain's countryside. I earned most of my living from books –
I was researching a study of the Korean War, which involved a lot
of work in Asia and the US.

On Tuesday 1 October, I took the train from Market Har-
borough to London for lunch with a man I had scarcely met, the
Editor of *The Economist*, Andrew Knight. He had invited me to
join him at Brooks's, the St James's club we both belonged to. He
said he wanted to 'get to know me better'. Andrew was affable,
charming, impeccably controlled. His cleverness was not in doubt,
nor was his success in building *The Economist*'s circulation during
eleven years in the editor's chair. A man of striking pale, ascetic
good looks, he appeared exactly the Ampleforth head boy he
once was. He had long ago shed any evidence of his family roots
in New Zealand, and now glided effortlessly between meetings,
conferences and dinner tables in Europe and America. Andrew

could have been mistaken for a youthful ambassador or Whitehall permanent secretary. He was a brilliant networker who made it his business to know everybody who was anybody. For some years, he had been a member of the Steering Committee for the biennial Bilderberg Conferences, where the good and the great rub egos.

Andrew was a decisively urban figure. I did not often venture to Hampstead where he and his formidable wife Sabiha entertained, and thus our paths had never crossed socially. He was now forty-five, yet I felt a much wider gap than a few years between us. I had been taught to believe that the first duty of a journalist is to cause trouble. Politically I called myself a Conservative, but I had seldom contrived to remain on easy terms with ministers. Andrew looked every inch a natural ruler.

At Brooks's, I enjoyed the opportunity to study his bedside manner. He acquired an almost oriental look when his eyes narrowed as he smiled. His meticulous courtesy also held a touch of the East. He had always possessed in the highest degree the ability to make the mighty feel safe in his hands, comfortable that he was on their side. We gossiped about the newspaper business; the travails of the *Daily Express*; Rupert Murdoch's interminable struggle with the print unions. We drank coffee in the Great Subscription Room, looking out on St James's Street, my legs stretched on the sill of the huge Georgian window. We began to talk about the poor old *Daily Telegraph* – no definite article in the masthead, at that time. The paper was struggling. In recent months its difficulties had spilled onto the front pages of its rivals. Its sale was still vast – more than three times that of *The Times* – but circulation was in free fall. Financial troubles were afflicting its owners, the Berry family, who had recently been obliged to sell a minority stake to a Canadian businessman, Conrad Black. I knew some of the younger Berrys well. I told Andrew I had often urged Nicky, a country neighbour, that unless his father Lord Hartwell, then seventy-four, brought in a tough outside chief executive and gave him a free hand, they would lose the business. I even suggested a name – Christopher Bland, another friend. Christopher had just rescued an ailing printing company, Sir Joseph Causton & Sons. He had sold out after making the beginnings of a fortune. He was looking for a new challenge. He was perfectly suited to manage the sort of draconian action needed to save the *Telegraph*. Nicky grinned puckishly: 'Nothing will change while my father is alive,' he said. I responded: 'Have you got that long?' He shrugged. He possessed the fey charm of all the Berry family, together with its reluctance to face unpleasant realities. We both knew there was no chance that his father would change the manner in which the *Telegraph* was run.

In the window of Brooks's, I told Andrew that I thought the *Telegraph* franchise remained a wonderful asset, if the paper was completely overhauled and upturned, and younger people brought in to run it. It was a great opportunity for somebody. 'Why don't you do it yourself?' said Andrew with a grin.

'I'd love to,' I said, 'but I can't think of anyone the Berrys would be less likely to want. I'm a one-nation Tory. I wouldn't get on for five minutes with their resident dinosaurs. And Michael Hartwell would never let me or anyone else make the changes that are needed.' We talked some more about the problems. I said I thought that one of the commonest mistakes among journalists was to suppose that the normal laws of economics did not apply to newspapers. Most reporters looked upon the titles for which they worked as mutual societies, run for the benefit of the staff. Yet surely the same financial and industrial disciplines should apply to a newspaper business as to any widget-maker. Whether Fleet Street would recognize this before disaster overtook several companies seemed a nice question. All our working lives in the trade, my generation of journalists had known only decline and decay – obsolete technology, weak management, the tyranny of the unions. Printers were being paid far more than most writers. For almost all of us, commitment to the craft of reporting was matched by weary cynicism about the world in which we practised it. I was grateful to have become semi-detached, to have forged a life dominated by books, in which I did not have to face the day-to-day horrors of Fleet Street's decline. We agreed that the industry was running out of time. I thanked Andrew for lunch, and we parted in the hall. I went home to Northamptonshire to pack a bag for my American assignment.

For two months I did not give another thought to that meeting with *The Economist*'s editor. Then, one December morning, I picked up the papers and read that Conrad Black had bought a majority stake in the *Daily Telegraph*, and wrested control from the Berry family. He had appointed Andrew Knight to become the company's chief executive. In an instant, lunch at Brooks's fell into place. I said to my wife Tricia across the kitchen table: 'I have a hunch that I'm about to be asked to edit the *Daily Telegraph*.' She said: 'I can't believe you're that lucky. Is there anything you don't get? Surely they wouldn't give a job like that to somebody like you?'

Most of my colleagues in the business would have said the same. The resident chorus at El Vino's, the 'Stab in the Back', the Kings and Keys or any other Fleet Street watering hole would have voted me the least plausible candidate to run the *Telegraph*. For years I had been a loner, and not a very popular one. My only executive experience was gained during a few months as editor of the *Evening Standard*'s Londoner's Diary back in the 1970s – oh yes, and some years running a pheasant shoot. The only man who had ever before seemed to think that I might edit something was the *Standard*'s managing director, Bert Hardy. One afternoon in the early 1980s, Bert took me to see Lord Matthews, proprietor of the *Express* group, which then owned the *Standard*. A desultory conversation ensued. Matthews suggested that I might become editor of the *Sunday Express*. The existing incumbent, John Junor, could be elevated to editor-in-chief. I can't say that for a moment I took any of this seriously. I asked who would be the lucky person to sell the arrangement to the ferocious Junor. 'Oh, old John'll be all right if we give him another Roller,' said Matthews dismissively. Most people who met the *Express* chairman emerged thinking that they had taken a wrong turning and gatecrashed the office of an

East End casino manager. I made my excuses and left. The only outsider to whom I ever mentioned that conversation was my old boss Charles Wintour, who had himself run the *Standard* for almost twenty years. I don't even want to be an editor, I told him. I'm making a good living as a writer. I would be much worse off shackled to an office desk. 'The expenses are pretty good,' Charles said wryly, before we turned to talk about other things. That moment of Fleet Street low comedy in 'Fingers' Matthews' office was soon forgotten, with no regrets.

But now, the prize was the *Daily Telegraph*, a national institution. I knew that I wanted it passionately. Almost all editors are chosen from the ranks of serving executives, men and women who have proved themselves over years in the daily grind of commissioning writers, appointing staff, laying out pages. I had done none of these things. My qualifications for editorship stemmed solely from success as a writer, together with a little celebrity gained during the Falklands War three years earlier; and now also, presumably, from Andrew Knight's instinct that I could do it. I felt a surge of exhilaration and mischief, thinking of the shock that would run through Fleet Street if it was known that I was in the running. Most people, if they succeed in crossing a certain threshold in life, get the things they want badly enough. The richest men are not the cleverest, they are those who most urgently want to be rich. In journalism, competing on assignments all over the world, the successful reporter is the one with the most manic yearning to get the scoop. Sitting at my desk in Northamptonshire, mind racing, I asked myself what I could do to bring closer this wonderful coup. There is sometimes a lot to be said for forcing the pace. Yet I had no immediate excuse to telephone Andrew Knight. Did I misread the signals from that lunch, as I now understood them? Were there other runners in the race? It was hard to get back to work on the Korean War, or to keep silence among friends with whom I yearned to weigh the odds. But it would be too humiliating to talk, and to see my balloon pricked.

Events now took a hand. The phone rang. It was Don Berry, Assistant Editor Features at *The Sunday Times*. 'We want you to do a big piece on the *Telegraph* goings-on,' he said. 'About 3,000 words?' I thought furiously. There was no plausible reason to say no. And here was a perfect chance to try the pitch. I put in a call to Andrew Knight. As soon as we had exchanged hellos, he said: 'I was about to get in touch with you.' Yes, I was right. The chance was there. What a stake, and what a tricky hand now to play with the *Sunday Times* piece. I told him about my commission. He laughed and said: 'Well, you'd better go ahead and write it. When you've done that, we should meet.' He told me whom I should talk to, for details of the extraordinary story which the *ST* headlined five days later 'THE FALL OF THE HOUSE OF BERRY'.

The *Daily Telegraph* was founded in 1855, and by 1877 had become a big success, 'the paper of the man on the knifeboard of the omnibus', with a cover price of twopence – less than half that of its rivals – and a sale of 250,000 copies. It was the *Telegraph*'s correspondent George Augustus Sala who received the legendary instruction: 'Please write a leader on Billingsgate and the price of fish and start for St Petersburg this evening'. The paper languished, however, in the face of competition from Northcliffe's *Daily Mail* and *Times*. By the time Sir William Berry took it over in 1928, sales had fallen to 84,000. In the years that followed Lord Camrose, as Berry became, made the *Telegraph* one of the success stories of the age. He had already achieved a formidable commercial reputation – in 1922 he and his two brothers controlled some fifty-seven companies worth £55 million in the money of the day. Now he halved the cover price of his new acquisition to a penny, and over the next twenty-six years created a great bourgeois title. Snobs called it 'the footman's paper', because of its shamelessly prurient reporting of scandal, above all divorce court evidence. But the *Telegraph* also made its reputation as the paper which recorded everything. It employed a huge foreign staff. Its coverage of parliament, sport and business was rivalled only by specialist titles. By the time of Camrose's death in 1954, his newspaper was selling a million copies a day. The proprietor, son of a Welsh estate agent, had become a vastly rich man. Few grudged him his fortune, built upon brilliant creative as well as commercial instincts.

On Camrose's death his elder son Seymour inherited the title, but it was the younger brother who took the principal role in running the company. A quiet, shy, dedicated man, Michael Berry lived for the newspaper. He worked until all hours in the panelled splendour of the fifth floor of the *Telegraph* building in Fleet Street, driving himself to and from work in a little brown Mini, often lingering in his office deep into Saturday afternoons. For some years, the paper's circulation continued to climb. Michael Berry's greatest personal achievement was the launch of the *Sunday Telegraph* in 1961.

His wife was the daughter of F. E. Smith, the first Lord Birkenhead. The formidable Lady Pamela Berry entertained lavishly – her election-night parties at the Savoy were famous. She took a close personal interest in all that went on at the papers. She might not possess her husband's eye for editorial minutiae, but she cherished her favourites and heated coals for her enemies. While Michael Berry – who became Lord Hartwell in 1968 – seemed scarcely to bother about what he ate or where his suits came from, Lady Pam spent for three. It was a running joke at the *Telegraph* that the paper's lavishly staffed Paris office on the Rue Castiglione was maintained chiefly to service Lady Pamela's Continental visits. Her death in 1982 robbed Lord Hartwell of a driving force in his life. Always a retiring man, he became a tragically lonely one. Afterwards, some old *Telegraph* hands suggested that if Lady Pam had lived, the family empire would not have collapsed. This seems implausible. For all her wit and vitality, there is no evidence that she possessed commercial instincts. She basked in confidence founded on the paper's huge circulation, together with the family's riches, which supported their lifestyle. A junior member of the prolific Berry clan once worked out that by the 1980s, some thirty-one families were living off the wealth created by the first Lord Camrose, and none of them was keeping house in a suburban semi. But there is no evidence that Pamela Hartwell, any more than her husband, understood the malign power of the worm that was eating deep into the *Telegraph* titles.

The paper's brand of whalebone-corseted Conservatism seemed well past its time. It remained the last serious press supporter of Ulster Unionism, of the apartheid regime in South Africa. Its old readers were dying. They were not being replaced. A new middle-class generation found little with which to sympathize in the '*Torygraph*'. The paper was being produced by an extraordinarily elderly staff. Michael Hartwell disliked change in the people around him as much as in the world outside – the average age of the Arts Department's critics was seventy-two. There was still a fund of high professionalism on the *Telegraph*'s editorial floors, but arteries were hardening fast. Both *The Times* and *The Guardian* had overtaken the *Telegraph* in the key area of classified advertising. More serious even than this, the company's management was conducted in a fashion the brothers Cheeryble would have found quaint a century and a half earlier. Accounting was rudimentary. Book-keeping was still done on paper, in longhand. The Finance Director in 1985 was a man of seventy-two. A recent company secretary had stayed at his post until he was over eighty. Number-crunching was almost unheard of. Yet in the last years of Berry control, the family still seemed not to grasp the gravity of its own plight.

The avarice of the print unions at the *Telegraph* was no more nor less outrageous than everywhere else in Fleet Street. The printers rejected the introduction of new technology which had been in use for a decade and more elsewhere in the world. 'World-beating spectacle! Come and see it for yourself!' declaimed a managing director of the period with infinite bitterness. 'Medieval printing just as Caxton used to do it!' The unions and their extortionate piecework rates restricted paper sizes. Printers received regular payment for non-existent work. Many men held down full-time jobs elsewhere in the London economy while appearing every week on newspaper payrolls. Any threat to the unions' control of production was met by industrial action, to which daily newspapers are uniquely vulnerable. Even a title with the *Telegraph*'s huge circulation – 1.3 million in 1985, falling fast but still dwarfing that of every other broadsheet – could no longer make profits in such catastrophic commercial conditions.

Against this background, Lord Hartwell made a remarkable decision. He visited America, inspected modern printing works, and committed his family company to a huge and costly programme of replanting. In Manchester and at a greenfield site on the Isle of Dogs outside London, construction started on new buildings and presses which would cost £105 million. Hartwell also agreed an extraordinarily generous deal with his workforce, whereby some 2,000 men would accept redundancy, at a cost of £38 million. The most notable aspect, however, was that the company's grand plans were undertaken without a plausible idea of how they were to be paid for. The *Telegraph* possessed no significant assets save its newspapers. As its cash-flow difficulties grew, a major crisis threatened.

In May 1985, NM Rothschild as bankers and Cazenove as brokers set about raising £80 million in loans to bankroll the *Telegraph* replanting. Three banks would put up the money, on condition that £30 million of new shares were issued. Lord Hartwell accepted the necessity to pay for his new printing presses by selling a 40 per cent stake in his family empire. The *Telegraph* board seemed almost insouciant about the proposal, confident that a blue-chip British household name would have no trouble finding eager investors. It came as a brutal shock, therefore, when response to the share offer in the City proved cool. Nobody trusted the company's numbers. Pundits observed that an enormous amount would need to go right, to justify the *Telegraph* prospectus. Had the figures been put forward by any other house, they would have been condemned as recklessly irresponsible. Given the Berrys' unimpeachable honesty, however, it was plain that their fantasy forecasts stemmed from naivety and incompetence. After weeks of uncertainty, 26 per cent of the 40 per cent of shares on offer had been placed. A further 14 per cent – £10 million worth – remained unsold. There would have been a rush of buyers for a chance to take over the *Daily Telegraph*. But few people cared to become minority shareholders in a company run by very old men who had lost their grip.

It was at this point that Andrew Knight, an extremely interested bystander, telephoned his old acquaintance from Bilderberg, the forty-one-year-old Canadian businessman Conrad Black. Andrew had done his time at *The Economist*. He was eager for a move, which might make his fortune. He saw in the *Daily Telegraph* a glittering opportunity. He knew that Black, an ambitious man of self-consciously intellectual inclinations who had already made some millions from a chain of small newspapers across North America, was keen to gain control of a big title in the US or Britain. Few opportunities occurred. Now, Andrew told Black that a minority stake in the *Telegraph* was available, which could lead to bigger things. The Canadian was immediately interested. He called another British friend and contemporary, Rupert Hambro, whom he had first met as a student in Toronto years before. The banker was at home in the Berkshire countryside for the weekend. Black asked him to arrange a meeting with Hartwell. Three days later, on 28 May, Hambro flew to New York on Concorde with the *Telegraph* chairman and his sixty-nine-year-old managing director, H. M. Stephen, for a rendezvous implausibly arranged at a hotel beside Kennedy Airport. Hartwell seems to have liked Black, whose right-wing politics did not bother him. The Canadian put forward a barrage of questions, mostly about the print unions. After four hours of talks, the British delegation flew home. A deal had been agreed on the spot by the *Telegraph*'s travel-weary old men. Black got his stock, along with the right to appoint two directors. In the subsequent restructuring, Rupert Hambro and Fleet Street veteran Frank Rogers, Chairman of EMAP, joined the board as Black's nominees, along with Hartwell's sons Nicholas and Adrian as those of the Berrys. 'Good man, Conrad Ritblat,' muttered Lord Hartwell to a disconcerted

Telegraph staffer. It quickly became apparent that his new partner's name was not the only aspect of this deal about which the chairman's understanding was flawed.

Beyond the purchase price, a key element of the deal between Black and Hartwell stunned the newspaper and financial worlds when it was revealed: Conrad Black had been granted an option to buy any further stock which came on the market. Black insisted upon this clause as a reasonable protection against Hartwell selling control to some unwelcome new partner. I later asked one of the men responsible for handling the share issue why his firm had not warned Hartwell of the devastating implications of what he was doing. 'Our job was to place the issue, not to advise the Berry family,' he answered. 'It was up to the Berrys to take their own steps to safeguard the family interest.' Cazenove and Rothschild undoubtedly discharged their fiduciary responsibilities to the *Telegraph*, but some members of the Berry family retained lasting bitterness about their advisers' failure to protect the elderly chairman from his own imprudence.

Characteristically, Hartwell never consulted his children – nor, so far as we know, anybody else – before signing the deal. Conrad Black's option to buy formed the basis of Nicky Berry's anger about what he regarded as the theft of the family heritage, and of his lasting enmity towards Black. 'I don't criticize the man for being what he is – a predator,' said Nicky in a rare moment of moderation. 'I just notice.' His father's behaviour is only comprehensible, of course, on the basis that Michael Hartwell was convinced that having secured £80 million in outside funding, the *Telegraph* would never again need to raise cash beyond the reach of the family's wealth. Those of us who are not rich are obliged to know where we stand financially. I have always believed that Lord Hartwell was handicapped by lacking any sense of the limits of his own resources. All his life, he had been able to take it for granted that the Berrys could afford to pay for whatever they wanted – houses, yachts, ad hoc subsidies to their own newspapers. Hartwell could not conceive a situation in which he might overreach himself beyond recovery. Yet this, of course, was what he had done. In a signed article, Hartwell told *Telegraph* readers he was confident that the paper was now on the road to recovery. He appealed for their patience with its collapsing typography and printing until the new plant came on stream. Yet even the front-page trailer for this piece proclaimed groggily: 'I believe we have taken the right steps to give our newspaper a godo [sic] future'.

Within six months of the initial deal with Black, the *Telegraph* found itself confronted with another financial crisis. The company had got its sums disastrously wrong. A new audit committee headed by the merchant banker David Montagu found gaping holes in the *Telegraph* books which had gone unnoticed by the bankers and brokers who studied them for months before the share issue. 'What passed for a system of financial control was in reality just a series of inspired guesses,' Montagu told me. He was scornful about what passed for a company management: 'Hopeless, geriatric, and like small boys being brought one after another into the headmaster's study.' Not only were the profit forecasts discredited, the *Telegraph* was surging into the red. Instead of making a profit of £5 million for 1985, as it had anticipated, the company faced a loss of over £6 million, which would soon grow to £12 million. The costs of funding redundancies among the print workers had been seriously underestimated. The *Telegraph* could no longer pay its bills without an injection of new money. £20 million was needed immediately.

On two brief visits to Britain, Conrad Black forcefully expressed his views about the shortcomings of the company's management and financial projections. He had himself telephoned the *Telegraph*'s Classified Advertising Department, purporting to want to place a small ad. He experienced a farrago of incompetence, culminating with a suggestion from a small-ad sales girl that the paper might be able to find him a space in two or three weeks. Readers were disappearing at the rate of 10,000 a month. It was plain that the Berry family faced loss of control. Their authority was crumbling by the day. At one crisis meeting in the boardroom,

Hartwell suffered a seizure, and collapsed in his chair. Black's lawyer and chief negotiator Dan Colson watched appalled alongside David Montagu and other directors as the chairman's secretary helped him to revive, standing defiantly over the gasping old man as if she anticipated that the Black team would assault his prostrate figure. Indeed, the onlookers feared that they were watching Hartwell die, that he had suffered a terminal stroke. In reality, he recovered quickly, and lived for another fifteen years. But the grisly little melodrama intensified the sense of doom.

A cluster of prospective buyers for the newspapers was now gathering: Mohammed Fayed, Lord Hanson, United Newspapers. Nicky Berry held an anguished dinner at Boodle's with friends from the Australian Fairfax Group, to explore the possibility that the Fairfax family might play white knight. All this sort of straw-clutching was rendered void, however, by the simple reality of Conrad Black's shut-out option to buy any *Telegraph* stock which came onto the market. On 5 December 1985, a new deal was struck between Black and the Berrys. The Canadian would purchase a majority stake, appointing his own chief executive for the company, and assuming responsibility for control of the newspapers. The Berry family would become minority shareholders. Lord Hartwell would retain the title of Editor-in-Chief, but he was almost the only person to delude himself about its significance. The world knew that this was the end of the Berry dynasty as proprietors of great newspapers. 'Black the prospect,' the *Daily Telegraph's* editor Bill Deedes wrote in his diary. For a total investment of just £50 million, the Canadian had gained control of one of the jewels of the British newspaper industry – if it could be saved from the brink of financial, industrial and editorial disaster. 'I seem to have lost out,' said Hartwell, still bemused by his personal tragedy, to Deedes.

This was the story I wrote for *The Sunday Times* of 15 December 1985. Researching it was a bizarre experience. Lord Hartwell declined to see me, but his editor did so. This was the first time I had set foot in the marbled halls of the paper's building, a monument of crumbling magnificence in the centre of Fleet Street. By the lifts, I met an old colleague from the Falklands, Charles Laurence of the *Sunday Telegraph*. Charlie greeted me warmly but casually. As I ascended to the first floor, I reflected: what in God's name would the poor man have thought, if he knew that within weeks I might be running the *Daily*? I felt equally light-headed sitting in Bill Deedes's office, overlooking Fleet Street. Bill, a sprightly seventy-two, had been editor for almost twelve years. He had spent most of his life in the service of the Berrys, interspersed with periods moonlighting as an MP and even briefly as a Cabinet minister, responsible for the information policy of the Macmillan government in its dying days. His charm was legendary. So was his loyalty to the Berrys, though it had become as plain to Bill as to everyone else that the old regime was losing its grip. As we talked, I glanced curiously around the room, taking in the battered Victorian desk, the big, ugly table and panelled cupboards. Would these be my desk, my table, my cupboards in a few weeks? Was I going to start fighting the campaign of my life from this room?

When the *Sunday Times* piece appeared, its informed tone attracted comment. With Andrew Knight's blessing, all the principal players outside the Berry camp had briefed me. Reading the outcome in the paper, I wondered: would Black hold it against me that I had described him as a 'controversial right-winger with a reputation for fast talking', and quoted his aphorism that 'I may make mistakes but right now I can't think of any'? Yet when I wrote the story, I thought that I had better concentrate on doing the reporting job for which I was being paid, rather than worry about any putative future as an editor for the Canadian.

Through the days that followed, Fleet Street was gripped by the drama of the *Telegraph* and by fevered speculation about the paper's future – not least about a new editor. Andrew Knight rang. 'Good piece in *The Sunday Times*,' he said. 'Yes, I am serious about discussing the editorship of the *Telegraph* with you, though of course any appointment is subject to Conrad's approval. We should meet. As soon as possible after Christmas. What about the 30th? We'd better go somewhere we're unlikely to meet anyone from the business. Let's make it the Ritz.' The next ten days seemed very long. My yearning to get the job never faltered. My wife Tricia was deeply uneasy, however. If I became an editor, an extraordinary change of lifestyle from our familiar rural round would follow, and not one that she welcomed. One of my oldest friends, Tom Bower, came to stay with his wife Veronica just after Christmas. I told them I thought I would be offered the *Telegraph*. Tricia described her misgivings. The Bowers were visibly bewildered that anyone could hesitate. Tricia said to me: 'But you admit yourself that as an editor, you would be making a lot less money than you are now.' 'Yes, but this is one of those chances that come once in a lifetime.' I was earning around £160,000 a year out of books and newspapers, good money; but in order to maintain that level of income, I would need to produce not merely a book, but a bestseller, every couple of years until I dropped. The strain would be appalling. I did not think the financial sacrifice of becoming a newspaper executive would be very great. And anyway, what the hell? I felt committed to taking this wonderful job if it was offered to me.

The day before I lunched with Andrew, I sent him a long letter, setting out some of my own thoughts about the *Telegraph*. It is worth quoting, in the light of what came afterwards:

> One is starting with some notable strengths on which to build: a comprehensive News service that none of its rivals have matched, and which must be protected at all costs; strong and respected Sport and City coverage; better than average Books and Arts pages.
>
> It seems essential both to staff morale and reader confidence that in the early stages of the new regime, there are no dramatic wrenches, and reassurance and praise generously distributed. The objective must be to maintain existing loyalty, while attracting new and younger readers. The *Daily*

Telegraph should continue not only to present the case for capitalism, but to represent traditional moral values. There is no reason why this should be incompatible with presenting a more sceptical and challenging view of the world. The most conspicuous sign of the *Telegraph*'s senility in recent years has been its mindless attachment to certainties: the rectitude of the Metropolitan Police, the decency of white South Africans, the inevitability of confrontation with the Soviet Union. Among a younger generation of newspaper readers, whatever their political beliefs, the only certainty is their uncertainty about their own society and its future.

The Times . . . seeks to conduct a reasoned debate within its pages. Its leaders and features, like those of the *Economist*, honestly attempt to attack issues on their merits. This the *Telegraph* has never done, but must now do. The greatest single problem is to gather a new range of intellects around the Editor. Change . . . must begin with its features. There is a good case for moving Peter Simple, and making room on that page for two analytical features . . . Peterborough must be dragged out of the stone age. The Letters column must cease to be a playground for Disgusted of Cheltenham and become a genuine forum.

I would make no immediate or dramatic changes on the News and Foreign side . . . The paper badly needs one or two people who can write. It is striking how seldom any of the *Telegraph*'s journalists are quoted on the radio, or invited to appear on television. Star writers have never been encouraged, or even wanted, on the paper. However reliable much of the reporting, it is not a well-written newspaper. It needs more spark and brightness in its general tone. There is a desperate need for a political writer of real quality. At present, the *Telegraph*'s political coverage is lacklustre, to put it mildly.

The Women's pages are awful, entirely untalented and middle-aged in outlook. There is a serious problem there, not easy to resolve rapidly because there is a lot of space to be filled, and a lot of faces that need to be changed.

The *Telegraph*'s greatest asset, which must be preserved at all costs, is its digestibility. It presents a far less frightening face to the semi-literate reader than either *The Times* or *Guardian*. But a continuing commitment to stories of manageable length need not preclude running two or three solid, thoughtful reads a day, of a kind the paper absolutely lacks at present. There is no attempt to tackle big issues in a serious fashion: What is going on in our schools? What will Britain live off in the twenty-first century? What are children learning? There is scope for punchier and more provocative arts coverage, though I do not regard this as a priority.

On the executive side, I am very impressed by the quality of the *Sunday Times*'s current Assistant Editor Features, Don Berry. I think it would be a major coup to recruit him in the same capacity for the *Telegraph* ... I am not impressed by the paper's typefaces, though I am not sufficiently expert in this field myself to suggest which way they should go ...

I am in no position to play poker with you about my own interest in the paper, since I showed my hand at lunch in October, before I had any inkling that you would be dealing the cards. The prospects are tremendously exciting for getting the paper into the twentieth century.

This was the nearest I came to submitting a formal job application for the editorship. Andrew returned my letter, annotated in the fashion of a schoolmaster's marks upon an essay, which I learned to recognize as a habit of his. Happily for me, there was a long list of ticks against key paragraphs, though there were also scribbled comments in the margins. I had mentioned Hugo Young of *The Sunday Times* as a possible Political Editor. Andrew demurred – 'not right for the *Telegraph*' – and of course he was correct. He noted that a redesign was a major priority. He agreed about the importance of reasoned debate in the paper's pages, 'provided that its attitudes remain clear'.

We met in that most beautiful of London hotel dining rooms. The Ritz was almost empty in the post-Christmas lull. Andrew was dismayed to spot Maxwell Aitken, a scion of the former newspaper dynasty and grandson of old Lord Beaverbrook, sitting a few tables away. I said it was unlikely that Maxwell would register our presence together. We began by discussing my letter, about which he was encouragingly positive. We talked about some candidates for key roles. He suggested George Jones of *The Sunday Times* as Political Editor. We had to find a new City Editor to replace Andreas Whittam-Smith. Whittam-Smith had just quit the *Telegraph* along with two leader writers, Matthew Symons and Stephen Glover, nursing a plan to launch a new newspaper – *The Independent*. We considered several possible successors for Whittam-Smith, and agreed to start with Neil Collins of *The Sunday Times*, whom I had known slightly since he and I worked together at the *Evening Standard*. I said that I wanted to recruit Veronica Wadley from the *Mail on Sunday* as Woman's Editor – I had formed a great admiration for her sharp mind and incisive judgement. I would try hard to get Don Berry. Sooner or later, I also wanted Trevor Grove, another old *Standard* colleague, from *The Observer*, and Jeremy Deedes from *Today*.

Andrew reflected with characteristic frankness about my own limitations as a candidate for the job: 'You are not well liked in the business. Indeed, a lot of people dislike you very much. That could be a problem, especially when you will have to win the support of all sorts of established *Telegraph* people like Andrew Hutchinson, the Managing Editor, who's terrific and whom you will rely on heavily.' He ruminated for a moment. 'On the other hand, they will all need to go on making a living. Gordon Newton was a very successful editor of the *Financial Times*, even though everybody detested him. It could work.'

He told me that he was planning to make Peregrine Worsthorne, the veteran right-wing enfant terrible of *The Sunday Telegraph*, that paper's new editor: 'I think it could be fun, don't you?' At the age of sixty-two, Perry was at last to be granted the prize he had coveted for so long, and which Lord Hartwell always denied him. I was increasingly encouraged by the manner in which

Andrew was talking as if my appointment was going to happen. He would scarcely reveal so many secrets, unless I was to become part of the plot. We discussed some mundane problems of my own. I possessed a tiny flat in Notting Hill; but if I was to do this job, I would need a bigger one, which the company would have to fund. I still had months more work to do, finishing my book on the Korean War. 'You could put it aside for a while, couldn't you?' said Andrew.

'I know if I do that, it will never get finished. And anyway, like most authors, I desperately need to pay the tax on my last book.'

'We could lend you the money to pay the tax.'

'No – I've got to get this sorted. I know I can do it, if I work flat out.'

Then I asked: 'When do I get to meet Conrad?'

'Yes, we'd better do something about arranging that. You should fly incognito. Too many people might get a hint of what's in the wind if they know you're on a plane to Toronto. You'll like Conrad – he's a very remarkable man. And remember – it will be his decision about who is appointed to the editorships.'

The five weeks that followed, before I went at last to Toronto, were among the most difficult I have ever spent. I was working relentlessly on my book. I was thinking feverishly about the *Telegraph*, and what I would do with it, while Andrew laboured in his new office in Fleet Street to assemble a management team and somehow get a grip on the affairs of the vast, ailing pachyderm. I had to continue to write for *The Sunday Times* as if nothing was happening. The Westland crisis broke, precipitating the resignation of Michael Heseltine from Mrs Thatcher's Cabinet. I contributed a big piece on Heseltine for the paper, and wrote its editorial comment on Westland. Then, as the row escalated, I was commissioned to do an assessment of Leon Brittan's role following, his resignation, and a profile of Lord Armstrong, the Cabinet Secretary. 'The Westland affair', I wrote, 'has cost Mrs Thatcher's government a significant portion of the moral high ground in

British politics which it has commanded for the past seven years'.
I thought wryly: none of this is likely to make the Prime Minister's
day, if I become editor of the *Telegraph*.

And then, suddenly, the newspaper industry was plunged into
a new drama of its own. On 28 January 1986, I was among the
usual throng of some twenty *Sunday Times* executives and writers
attending the paper's weekly conference in Gray's Inn Road, held
by its editor Andrew Neil. Although Andrew had been responsible
for hiring me from the *Standard*, over recent months I had seen
little of him. I respected his abilities. He had always been courteous, but we were never likely to be soulmates. He seemed what his
fellow Scots call 'a braw laddie'. I saw a pathos in the loneliness
of this abrasive, awkward, driven, talented, somewhat uncouth
middle-aged bachelor, but I knew Andrew would have scorned my
sympathy. In many respects, I represented old Britain. He saw
himself as the embodiment of a new one.

The conference was proceeding routinely until Andrew suddenly dropped in a bombshell: 'This week, we shall be producing
the paper from Wapping.' There was a stunned silence. For almost
everyone in the room, this was the first intimation of impending
revolution. It was Rupert Murdoch's most brilliant achievement,
to prepare and equip in absolute secrecy a new state-of-the-art
plant in London's East End, to produce his newspapers with non-
union labour, and to break the tyranny of the old print workers.
Over recent days, there had been increasing speculation that
something big was afoot, that Wapping represented a dramatic
break with the past. Now, at last, the truth was out. A strangled
voice – was it that of Claire Tomalin, the Literary Editor? –
demanded: 'What happens if some people aren't willing to go?' A
significant number of journalists on Murdoch's papers flinched
from supporting the ruthless Australian in an assault on trades
unionism. Neil shrugged: 'Well, they'll just have to, won't they?'
The meeting broke up in consternation. The editorial departments
of Murdoch's papers were plunged into days of bitter argument
about the merits of supporting the Wapping revolution. A majority

immediately acceded. Had I remained at *The Sunday Times*, I would have gone to Wapping without a quaver. However great my distaste for Murdoch, any move to break the death-grip of the unions deserved support. A small minority of journalists, however, almost all on the *Sunday Times* staff, declined to move to the new plant, where for months to come the newspapers were produced in conditions of siege, protected by barbed wire and mounted police from the baying mob of union demonstrators outside.

The most prominent 'refusenik' was the *ST*'s Assistant Editor, Don Berry. Don was a slender, charming, understated Yorkshire-man, now forty-nine, with immense experience of the newspaper industry in Britain and America, a veteran of Harold Evans's regime at *The Sunday Times* in the 1970s. He knew everything worth knowing about editing, layout, typography and production. That he had not himself become an editor reflected a gentleness and modesty unusual among newspaper executives. The warmth of his smile masked a fierce commitment to the job, but Don recoiled from the most ruthless demands of our trade. He was a man of profound, unobtrusive integrity. Among the unacceptable faces of Fleet Street, he now concluded, was the Wapping putsch. So Don was out of a job, and looking for another. He had no inkling that I was in a position to offer him one. I had to play for time. He was bemused by my hints. Here was I, a mere *Sunday Times* writer, mysteriously urging him not to accept any other employment for a week or two, because something exciting might turn up. He said he was talking to *The Guardian*. 'Don't rush anything,' I begged. Andrew Knight said to me: 'Do we really want somebody here who has just refused to take part in a revolution to displace the print unions, when we may have to do exactly the same ourselves at the *Telegraph*?' I said I was confident that Don would not merely be an asset, he would be indispensable. The *Telegraph* possessed no design team or presentational skills of any kind. If I was to transform the paper, it would be vital to have at my side someone with the technical knowledge I lacked.

On the morning of 6 February, I flew to Toronto for an

afternoon appointment with Conrad Black. The booking was made by Andrew under another name, but no one noticed me anyway. It was one of the first Lord Beaverbrook's less agreeable customs, occasionally to invite his journalists to stay in Jamaica, without offering to pay the fare. Sadistically, a prospective guest was invited to gamble upon whether the great tycoon had summoned him as a preliminary to dismissal, or a proposal to edit the *Daily Express.* Either outcome was equally plausible. In my case, happily, the fare was taken care of. I checked into the King Edward Hotel, then walked around the corner to the elegant offices of Conrad's holding company, Hollinger. During a brief wait in his room, I studied the paintings, which reflected his passion for military and naval history. We were on common ground here. Conrad's heavy figure, clad in an ill-fitting double-breasted suit, steamed through the door not unlike a capital ship entering harbour. I pointed to the picture behind his desk: '*Warspite* attacking Narvik in April 1940?' I have no idea whether he was impressed, but it seemed to get our conversation off on the right foot. I told him that I made no bones about my passionate enthusiasm to take on the *Telegraph.* I was convinced I could resurrect the paper, and work well with Andrew. We talked about politics. I said I was a left-of-centre Tory. I recognized that my own views were some way off those of Conrad. 'Any newspaper that attempted to impose my convictions on its readership would be in danger of possessing a circulation of one,' he responded, in an encouraging moment of self-deprecation. We exchanged historical gossip for a few minutes. Conrad's mind was quick, but his portentous manner was that of a man much older than forty-one. He said that one of his overriding concerns was that no paper he owned should treat America with less than the respect it deserved: 'I have sometimes observed among the British, and among British newspapers, a mean-spiritedness, a bitchiness, a raw envy towards the United States which does your fellow-countrymen no service at all, Max.' Conrad wrote later, in characteristic vein: 'I have tried to revise the widely cherished caricature of America as inhabited by a gregarious but rather unsophisticated population of men with loud voices and jackets, trousers and hair too short, being too demonstrative at the Changing of the Guard.' I told him I had no problem with any of this. He said he noticed I had once written a book about the United States. Er, yes, I said. It was a very immature young journalist's effort, published when I was twenty-two. 'I'd like to see it some time,' he said. I regretted that it was out of print. In truth, I made a mental note to keep my American book out of Conrad's hands. It included disparaging, if not contemptuous remarks about American politics and culture which reflected the callowness of the author. (It was 1999 before Conrad's remarkable persistence secured him a copy of *The Fire This Time* from a second-hand bookseller. His comments after reading it make me doubtful whether I should have become editor of one of his newspapers, had he read it back in the beginning: 'In truth, Max, we must recognize the reality that you are a closet pinko beneath the skin!').

On this February afternoon in 1986, Conrad said finally: 'Well, Andrew believes that you are the right person to do the job for us at the *Telegraph*. I am happy to endorse his judgement.'

'I'll do everything I can to make sure you don't regret this, Conrad,' I said, with heartfelt warmth. As a parting gift, he presented me with his own massive literary effort, *Duplessis*, a biography of the French-Canadian politician. I gave him an inscribed copy of the favourite among my own books, *Bomber Command*. With a song in my heart, I almost skipped down the pavement to the King Edward. It was still only mid-afternoon. I checked out of the hotel and caught the evening flight back to London. I was to be an editor. The Editor. The Editor of the *Daily Telegraph*. As Tricia had said two months earlier, my luck was unbelievable. After years as a foreign correspondent, a television reporter, an author, suddenly I was being granted the opportunity to do one of the biggest jobs in British newspapers.

In London, there was another conversation with Andrew. The announcement of my appointment and that of Perry Worsthorne

would be made on Friday, 21 February. Thereafter, I would have
to move swiftly, to secure the loyalty of key people at the paper.
Andrew was concerned lest Andrew Neil should seek to hold
me to my contract at *The Sunday Times*, if only to defend the
Murdoch interest by making matters more difficult for a rival.
This could only be put to the test on 21 February. I would be
paid £75,000 a year – a lot less than I was making as a writer, but
the company would now be responsible for my overheads. Almost
as an afterthought, Andrew said: 'We're going to give you 300,000
share options in the company. I'd like you to go away with a nest
egg when you finish. This should give you a chance to make a bit
of capital.' My naivety may sound extraordinary, but in those days
I had no conception of what a share option was. For many months
I thought nothing about the value of this holding, which three
years later got me out of debt for the first time in my life. In this,
as in other respects, Andrew Knight in those days established a
strong hold on my loyalty. To be sure, he possessed vulnerabilities
of which something would emerge later. But he secured my
gratitude by presenting me with an opportunity no one else would
have contemplated.

Why did he do it? Why did he take the huge gamble of
making me, a 'wild man' in the eyes of Fleet Street, Editor of the
Daily Telegraph? He believed, I think, that the paper's fortunes
were in such desperate straits that only the boldest measures had a
chance of success. An unknown figure, from the ranks of established newspaper executives, would be unlikely to capture popular
imagination. The Falklands War less than four years earlier had
got me into *Who's Who*, onto *Any Questions?*, and given me a
standing among the middle-class public, the *Telegraph*'s public,
which might be valuable when we embarked upon our revolution.
We both knew that it would be a bumpy ride. 'Remember,' said
Andrew, 'the banks own even the desk you will be sitting at.' The
company was close to bankruptcy. I found myself wondering what
would happen if people simply refused to do what I told them. I
had never possessed the opportunity to give orders to anyone save

waiters and schoolboy cadets. I wondered if Andrew would offer any further advice or guidance, but he did not. He simply discussed the practicalities of dates and public statements, and left me to discover for myself how to run a newspaper.

I began to make discreet preparations. I invited Veronica Wadley to drive down to Northamptonshire for lunch. I told her what was coming, and asked her to become Woman's Editor. 'I won't do that, Max,' she answered, 'because I believe it's completely obsolete having such a title as Woman's Editor, and it's patronizing to call the pages "Woman's pages". But I will be Features Editor and I will do the Features pages.' Veronica was heavily pregnant with her first child, but she assured me that she would only need to take a few days off to have the baby in April, and so indeed it proved. This cool, clever, wonderfully focused and fiercely determined woman, then thirty-three, became one of my most trusted colleagues. Don Berry was at last let into the secret. I met him in a pub off Gray's Inn Road and told him what I wanted him for. After a few days of agonized debate – mostly, I think, about how far he could trust my assurances that the *Telegraph*'s rabid brand of Conservatism would no longer prevail under my editorship – he accepted.

I wrote to Andrew:

> It is a pleasure to be able to write with the uncertainties removed. I wanted to say how much I feel I owe you for your demonstration of faith in me. I shall do my utmost to justify it. Plainly, I shall lean heavily on you for advice in the early stages. I am sorry my father didn't live to see a third successive Hastings generation in an editor's chair. My grandfather edited the *Bystander* just before the First World War, my father the *Strand* magazine, and my mother *Harper's Bazaar*. If you were superstitious, you would be daunted to notice that all the above-named are now defunct.

The nervous strain was immense, in those days before 21 February. I never set foot in the beleaguered *Sunday Times* office at Fortress Wapping. Andrew Neil had more important matters on his mind than wondering about where I was. That Friday afternoon, I sat alone in my car parked in Chancery Lane, waiting on tenterhooks for the call from Andrew Knight in the *Telegraph* building, to confirm that Lord Hartwell and the board had been told of the new editors' appointments. At last, the car phone buzzed. 'Well, you're the Editor of the *Daily Telegraph*,' said Andrew laconically. I remembered *The Spike*, one of my favourite pieces of Fleet Street fiction, a novel about the 1950s *Daily Express* written by Peter Forster, an old Beaverbrook hack of the period. Its first words are those of a new editor, sitting down at his desk, and contemplating his newly won empire: '"And now it would all be different," he thought.'

And now it would all be different, I thought.

2

BAPTISM OF FIRE

MICHAEL HARTWELL exploded in frustration when Andrew Knight told him, a few minutes before the board meeting of 21 February, that he intended to appoint me and Peregrine Worsthorne editors of the two *Telegraph* titles. 'Surely if I'm still Editor-in-Chief, I control these appointments?' he demanded. 'Why didn't you tell me what you were doing?'

Andrew answered coolly: 'I didn't think you'd agree.'

At the meeting proper, Hartwell raised curiously little objection to my appointment, save to say that he did not know me. But he had plenty to say about Perry's. The former chairman had never forgiven his star columnist for once saying 'Fuck!' on television: 'He couldn't edit his school magazine, let alone a national newspaper. He's a brilliant writer but terrible with people. It would be a disaster. You're mad!' Hartwell's elder son, the mild, sweet-natured Adrian, astonished the other directors by disagreeing. He applauded Perry's appointment. Adrian said that while he would not vote against his father, he would abstain. There was no vote. The decision was carried by acclamation, as it was bound to be.

Darkness had fallen by the time a brief statement clattered out over the agency wires, telling the world about the new editors of the *Telegraph* titles. Andrew and I had agreed that I should not enter the Fleet Street building until Monday, to allow time for the dust to settle. For the next two weeks, Bill Deedes would continue in operational charge of the paper, to give me time to start on the huge task of meeting staff and planning changes. We were both deeply apprehensive that, in the face of such extraordinary events, the *Telegraph* would unravel. Key people would simply throw up their hands and leave in disgust though, as Andrew observed drily, 'I suspect most of them will stick around in the hope of getting a cheque.' The vital personality, he told me, was the Managing Editor, Andrew Hutchinson. Hutch was a long-serving veteran who knew everybody and everything. He would be the man upon whom I relied to get the paper out while I learned how this was done, who held the enormous staff together while I won their confidence – or not as the case might be. Hutch was the one man who, at all costs, I must get on side. I rang him that Friday, as soon as the board statement had gone out. I said that I would like to see him urgently. We arranged to meet in St James's, well away from curious eyes, at 6.30.

Andrew Hutchinson and I sat down before the fireplace in Brooks's library. I am uncertain which of us was more apprehensive, but he showed it less. A tall, white-haired, monkish-looking figure of fifty-two, he was the son of a well-known popular novelist of the 1930s, R. C. Hutchinson. A Wykehamist, Andrew had been forged by years as a subeditor and then as Night Editor, before attaining his present title on the recent retirement of a legendary éminence grise, Donald Eastwood. Hitherto, the paper had been managed under a unique Berry arrangement, whereby the News side was controlled by Eastwood, a man loathed and respected in equal measure, who reported directly to Michael Hartwell, while Bill Deedes was responsible exclusively for Comment and Features. In future, I explained to Andrew, the *Telegraph* would become an integrated operation like any other newspaper, under my control, answerable to Andrew Knight. The plan was that he should assume the title of Deputy Editor. Would he do it? Yes, he responded, to my overwhelming relief. All sorts of changes were needed, I said. I would be dependent on him to run the paper while I set about recruiting and planning. As I quickly learned, Andrew Hutch was a man of few words, most of those opaque. Like many old *Telegraph* types, he was formidably literate, with a taste for quotation and military metaphor, together with an exceptional capacity for alcohol. This had no visible effect save to give the eye of the sphinx a distant glaze. It would be foolish to suggest that Andrew applauded everything I did in the years which followed. But unlike many old hands, he understood that change, and drastic change, had to come if the paper was to survive its crisis. He remained with me through the next decade, latterly as Managing Editor again. I was always grateful for his counsel, his dry wit, his long experience of the mechanics of our business and of the *Daily Telegraph*.

Driving home through the darkness back up the M1 to Northamptonshire, I listened to the late news on Radio 4, with the announcement of my appointment. Andrew Knight rang me in the car, to say that Andrew Neil had at once agreed to release me from *The Sunday Times*. Neil could not have been more gracious, and wished me luck. The phone rang all weekend. Even old friends were amazed by the turn of events and, I suspect, privately sceptical. Over the years, I had accumulated at least my share of enemies, who were appalled. 'They tell me poor old Paul Smith had to lie down in a darkened room for two hours when he heard the news,' a colleague remarked with relish.

Acquaintances at the *Telegraph* rang to assure me of support, and in some cases to explain that they had been waiting years for the boss who would appreciate that they were born to become news/foreign/fashion/features editor. My children – who were twelve, eight and three respectively – scarcely grasped what it all meant. My wife Tricia was deeply apprehensive about a new life, after many years during which I had been either abroad on assignments, or at home writing books. It was a long time since I had spent more than a day a week in London.

Pottering about the wintry garden, I was thinking furiously. I had never been 'a *Telegraph* type'. I was too politically wayward to have been a plausible recruit for the paper, even if I had been willing to take the pay cut that would have been necessary to work for the Berrys. Most *Telegraph* writers eschewed the wilder ways of our trade. I had never forgotten the horrified look etched on the

face of Philip Evans, a *Telegraph* reporter in Belfast, one night at
the height of the 1969 riots. The rest of the press corps, drunk
on fear and whisky, unleashed the fire extinguishers in the horrible old Grand Central Hotel. Even through a haze of alcohol,
I perceived that Philip, the epitome of careful and responsible
reporting, was appalled that a *Telegraph* representative should even
be a spectator of such goings-on.

My own politics were well to the left of those of the paper.
I had always been a Conservative. Much as I admired Margaret
Thatcher's achievement as Prime Minister, however, I was already
critical of some aspects of her policies, above all neglect of the
underclass and the belief that all the difficulties of Britain's public
services, as well as utilities, could be addressed by privatizing them.
I was a passionate opponent of capital punishment, and of the
apartheid regime in South Africa. *Daily Telegraph* readers were
widely assumed to be hangers and floggers to a man. Hitherto, I
knew that I had led an incautious life, and had enjoyed doing so.
Henceforward, I believed I must be bold in my objectives for the
paper, but careful about means. There would be no overnight
transformation, to frighten staff and readers. We must change the
title by stealth, step by step over a period of months and years,
seeking to hold on to our loyalists, while we reached out for a
new audience. The paper represented the traditional voice of the
Conservative Party. I did not doubt that the *Telegraph* must always
be a Tory title, but it should now become an independent one,
supportive of the government in general but critical of its policies
in detail. The paper must also break away from its traditional
attitudes on such issues as race, opportunities for women, crime
and punishment.

I arrived in Fleet Street early on Monday morning, gazing up
at the great paper palace past which I had walked so often, that
was now to become the focus of my life. A procession of *Telegraph*
retainers greeted me with the ceremony to which they, if not
I, were so well accustomed. Uniformed commissionaires saluted.
Journalists and executives were deferential. My car was whisked

away to be parked. I sat down at the ugly old Victorian desk which Bill Deedes had occupied for the past twelve years, peered around at the dusty cupboards, the windows which looked down two floors upon Fleet Street teeming below, the neat stack of imposingly headed stationery which asserted that it came 'From The Editor'. How did one learn to be an editor? Would anybody do anything I said? The sensation was boundlessly exhilarating, yet as frightening as any battlefield. And I did not doubt that, for many months to come, the paper must be a battlefield, on which all manner of hard and unpopular things would have to be done. I felt an overwhelming sense of loneliness, here in this creaky, fusty, frankly dirty old building where I possessed some acquaintances, but no close friends or former colleagues. What I needed quickly were some allies, men and women who were my own appointments, committed to the purposes I wanted to fulfil.

All that morning, indeed all that week and the next, I sat through a relentless series of meetings with writers, executives and prospective recruits. To the good people – and the *Telegraph* possessed a core of superbly professional journalists – I was seeking to give reassurance, as their familiar world trembled on its foundations. The basis of the paper would not change, I told each of them. The *Telegraph* had built its success upon being the best News paper in Britain, and that was what it would continue to be. But there must be new layouts, designs, writers, features. It was going to be a tough ride, but an exciting one. I passionately want you, John (or Joan or Bill or Simon) to be part of it. I interviewed an alarming number of very old people, who were eager to be paid off but remained unable to leave until somebody agreed to give them a proper pension. Michael Hartwell in his later years could not bear to see a familiar face depart. One of the least attractive aspects of Berry paternalism was that the *Telegraph* possessed no proper pension scheme – retiring writers were dependent on the whim and benevolence of the proprietor, to grant them a competence in old age from his family trusts.

I heard a long procession of old men assert nervously that

'Michael always promised he would look after me.' The new regime was being asked to pick up a great many blank cheques drafted by the Berrys. Andrew Knight looked increasingly grim as I read him the roll-call of people who would have to go as soon as possible. The company was almost bankrupt, yet to begin dragging the titles out of the mire we must somehow find the cash to get rid of old faces – scores of them – and to recruit much younger replacements.

I interviewed most of the people I wanted to hire at Brooks's or over lunch at Green's in Duke Street, to avoid the embarrassment of having them seen in the building. Some I failed to catch – the brilliant foreign affairs writer Tim Garton Ash; my old friend and colleague the *Times* columnist Simon Jenkins; writer and novelist Jamie Buchan; *FT* political columnist Peter Riddell. Garton Ash, for instance, later said that he was put off by my assertion that I did not want to run pieces longer than a thousand words, because I believed that breadth and comprehensiveness, rather than length, were what mattered to *Telegraph* foreign coverage. I learned that there are few more irksome ways to waste an hour than wooing a man or woman who, one quickly senses, is only interested in acquiring a bargaining chip for extracting more money from an existing employer. One leaves the encounter as bruised as by sexual rejection. Some impressive talents, fortunately, accepted my blandishments. Kathryn Samuel agreed to be Fashion Editor. An old friend, the military historian John Keegan, had rung for a casual gossip before he even heard that I was going to the *Telegraph*. 'Can I come and be your Defence Correspondent?' he asked at once, on hearing the news. I was astonished. John seemed a fixture at Sandhurst, where he had taught for twenty-six years. Yet now, he said, he was eager for a change. I agreed enthusiastically. John expressed momentary hesitation about his own ability to adjust to the demands of daily newspapers. I responded with Dr Johnson's line, to the man who expressed 'some modest and virtuous doubts' about his fitness to work in a politician's office: 'Don't be afraid, Sir, you will soon make a very pretty rascal.' I rang Andrew Hutchinson and asked for the desk of the paper's existing military man, a retired general, to be cleared as swiftly as possible. It was a Berry custom with which I had no sympathy, to employ retired senior officers to write about the services. John's arrival was greeted with applause from even the most sceptical in the old *Telegraph* ranks of Tuscany. He is a sparkling personality, brimming with erudition and enthusiasms. Within a few weeks, though he was fifty-one and had done little journalism save book reviews, he proved himself a brilliant newspaper commentator. He fell in love with the *Daily Telegraph*.

I rang the fashionable cartoonist of the moment, Mark Boxer, to ask if he would switch his daily drawing from *The Guardian*. The *Telegraph* was short of wit and jokes. I went to see Mark in the Condé Nast building in Hanover Square, where he worked part-time. He was at his most feline. 'As it happens,' he said, 'I was about to ring you, because I've been asked to draw you for *The Observer* this week.' So he drew while we talked, the Boxer charm at its sharpest as he glanced up and down from his pad. I said: 'I haven't forgotten that we once met twenty years ago, when you interviewed me for a job on *The Sunday Times* mag.' Mark, then the magazine's editor, had received me curled up on his legs in a huge designer chair. He chatted charmingly for the ten minutes which he thought was owed to my mother's reputation, before turning me down. 'I remember the occasion well,' he now responded sweetly. 'You told a friend afterwards that you thought I spent too much time admiring myself in the mirror, and I suggested that you should try for something on that new theatre mag *Playbill*.' He added: 'I'll offer you one bit of advice now – don't be an editor like Rees-Mogg at *The Times*, who only really cared about the leaders, and disappeared off to Somerset in his big Daimler after lunch on Fridays.' I said that however my own editorship turned out, it was unlikely to resemble any aspect of William Rees-Mogg's. And indeed, I struggled manfully for the next sixteen years to sustain a convincing interest in Sport, the Bridge column, ballet reviews and all the other things a 'proper' editor should address. I was delighted when Mark at once accepted my offer to join the *Telegraph* – he continued for draw for us until his tragically early death, two years afterwards. He finished his caricature of me. I bounded downstairs to the car.

That first day, I lunched with Bill Deedes at his favourite restaurant, an Italian establishment in the Strand. Its name was the most imaginative thing about the place – Paradiso e Inferno. But in matters of the table, as in his insistence on travelling by bus rather than using the customary editor's chauffeur-driven car, Bill was a master of understatement. He had spent fifty-five years in the service of the *Telegraph* and *Morning Post*. He was deeply beloved within the paper and outside it, though some believed he could have done more to press upon Michael Hartwell an understanding of impending doom. It may be that Bill himself thought so too. In his recollection of our lunch in his memoirs, Bill described my demeanour as 'harassed but full of goodwill'. My first request was that he should continue to write for the paper, to which he acceded. I heard afterwards that a colleague asked why he did so. Bill answered: 'Well, old boy, since presumably I must accept some responsibility for the mess this company has got into, it seems to me that the least I can do is to stick around and try to help us get out of it.' For that, and for the unfailing joy of his company, I owed Bill an enormous amount. He was the only recruit I ever encountered who insisted upon accepting a smaller salary than that which I offered. We badly needed some continuity, to reassure both readers and staff. To this, W. F. Deedes's contribution was very great. I suspect that some of the changes I made, both political and editorial, dismayed Bill, yet he offered no hint of reproach. He simply embarked upon a new daily routine, turning up for the leader conference, writing whatever was asked of him, and making some excellent jokes, as if the grandeur of his editorship had never been. In between, he travelled the world, reporting for us with extraordinary skill from places that would have alarmed men and women half his age. I believe Bill is happier today as a columnist and star reporter than ever he was as an executive.

That Monday lunchtime in the Strand, I was chiefly impressed by the aplomb with which he met the shock of change at the paper. The fall of the house of Berry, his own abrupt retirement however welcome, would have rattled many younger men. Bill received it all as he might have done the news of an innings defeat in a test match – the sort of little setback that is inseparable from life's rich pageant. Perhaps part of the inheritance of that wartime generation – Bill won an MC with the Rifle Brigade – is that, after witnessing global catastrophe at close quarters, a mere change of ownership in Fleet Street recedes to its proper perspective. Over our spaghetti, Bill itemized problems at the paper in urgent need of address, and people in need of speedy dismissal. He shook that famous skull: 'I hope it is not a poisoned chalice you are taking on, dear boy,' he observed, in the sombre tones of a rural vicar lamenting an outbreak of delinquency among the choir.

After lunch, we returned to the Fleet Street building. One of my first embarrassments was the need to dispense with the services of a leader writer, Rod Junor, who had been little seen in the *Telegraph* office for months. My secretary returned from telephoning him in some dismay: 'He says he's too busy working on something to come and see you this week.' The Company Secretary was eventually obliged to give Mr Junor a formal demand to present himself the following Monday in my office.

Meanwhile, however, a colleague who knew my intentions dashed in with unwelcome tidings: 'John Junor is telling everybody he is going to write in his column on Sunday about how disgraceful your appointment is, and how badly Bill has been treated.' This was a poser. John Junor, *Sunday Express* editor and by common consent one of the most disagreeable men in Britain, could scupper everything. If he wrote in the threatened terms on Sunday and I sacked his son on Monday, the world would perceive cause and effect. Mercifully, Bill Deedes telephoned Junor senior and dissuaded him from writing. Master Junor departed from the *Telegraph* as scheduled. His father, never any friend of mine, became a sworn enemy.

A more serious crisis blew up in our City Office. The City Editor, Andreas Whittam-Smith, had departed for the embryo *Independent* some weeks before. His deputy, who had since been in charge, cherished hopes of being confirmed in the top job. I was warned, however, that amid the vacuum of command, a state of near-anarchy now existed within the City Office. I knew I must act decisively. I saw the deputy, and broke it to him that I had already asked Neil Collins to come to the paper as City Editor. I knew this would be a disappointment, I said, but I hoped he would continue to run the department loyally until Collins arrived. He seemed subdued, but acquiescent. Then I walked to the City Office, up the other side of Ludgate Hill. I spent fifteen minutes haranguing the entire twenty-five-strong staff about the need to pull together, support the paper at a difficult time, show some spine. I started to enjoy the sound of my own voice, and to think how well I was handling a difficult situation. I barked a confident invitation for questions. A subeditor said hesitantly: 'Can you tell us who's running the pages?'

'The Deputy City Editor is in charge, pending the announcement of a new appointment.'

'But didn't you know,' enquired a funereal voice, 'that the Deputy City Editor left the building twenty minutes ago and says he's never coming back?'

Figuratively, if not literally, I collapsed in a heap. I crept back to the Fleet Street building badly shaken. Somehow, the Deputy City Editor was induced to return, and the City Office was kept going until Neil Collins arrived to take over. In those first days, there were more than a few shocks of that kind. I felt very lonely. None of my own new men and women had arrived – they joined the staff in ones and twos over the months that followed, as their notice periods expired elsewhere. Most of the old *Telegraph* staff were politely wary. Some were overtly hostile and resentful, especially those who knew that radical change was imminent, such as the inhabitants of the Features and Women's departments. On my first day, I addressed all the Newsroom staff, amid the usual detritus of paperwork, coffee cups, desks and typewriters. I tried to boost their confidence, by talking of my huge respect for the *Telegraph* news tradition, describing how I wanted to build on the paper's heritage to make changes, rather than simply to wipe out the glories of the past. I left the Newsroom feeling that I had not done badly. Gossip disabused me. The old hands were not much impressed by my rhetoric. I made a mental note to be wary of mass meetings until I had learned to improve my eve-of-Agincourt technique. Nor was I much encouraged to hear some word of mouth from Fleet Street. Anthony Howard, Deputy Editor of *The Observer*, remarked to our cartoonist Nick Garland that when I had edited the Londoner's Diary, my staff 'absolutely loathed' me. Nick wrote in his own diary, 'I think of [Max Hastings] as intelligent, ambitious, crudely insensitive, self-centred and arrogant. It's an awful mixture. He's the kind of guy you can't write off and you can't like. You just have to lump him.'

Published comment on my appointment was more charitable. Charles Moore wrote generously in *The Spectator*, then owned by Algy Cluff: 'Max Hastings ... is an inspired choice, *Telegraph* man at his most wild, vigorous and amusing'. An *Observer* profile dwelt at some length on my rural enthusiasms, and recalled the old chestnut of Lord Camrose on his deathbed telling his children: 'My dears, before I depart this vale of tears I will leave you one piece of advice. If all of you wish to die as rich as me, never, never brighten up the *Daily Telegraph*.' The piece quoted my own declared intention to make the paper brighter and livelier: 'What on earth is that strange rumbling sound? Hell's bells, Max, it's Lord Camrose turning in his grave.' Michael Parkinson introduced me on *Desert Island Discs* as 'the wildest man ever to edit the *Daily Telegraph*'. The star of the *Clive James Show*, who liked my military history books, gave me a friendly fifteen minutes' worth of television time. A profile in *The Spectator* was written by my old friend and colleague Valerie Grove. She concluded that 'the only reason he never found a *Telegraph* home before was that they did not go in for star reporters; nor for direct-control, gimlet-eyed, personal-stamp editors in the Charles Wintour mould. But they have one now.'

In the first weeks of the new regime, the Berry family continued to believe that they could retain an active role in the management of the papers. One day, I was lunching socially with Lord Camrose amid the splendours of Hackwood, his Hampshire home. Joan Aly Khan, Seymour's companion for many years before becoming his wife, was talking enthusiastically about Conrad Black: 'There's something of the old Max Beaverbrook buccaneer about him, isn't there?' She said how much she liked Conrad. She and Seymour thought they could forge a good working relationship. Camrose's brother, Lord Hartwell, retained his old title as Editor-in-Chief, and his office in the Fleet Street building. For several months he maintained his familiar working routine, reading all copy destined for the papers, and dispatching notes to executives, commenting upon aspects of editorial policy. His old employees were, for the most part, content to sustain this charade. For me, the situation was more difficult and embarrassing. Several long memoranda came down from Hartwell, discussing the changes I was making in the paper. He sought to arrange that I should attend regular meetings in his eyrie on the fifth floor of the Fleet Street building, amid the panelling, marbled fireplaces and discreet liveried servants of a Thirties country house. During the first few weeks, some desultory encounters took place. On my side, they were deeply uncomfortable. On issue after issue, I could not accept Hartwell's views. I answered the sad, bitter old man evasively for as long as I could. Andrew Knight urged me to persist with the meetings, merely to delay a showdown. By midsummer, however, I perceived no choice save to tell the Editor-in-Chief directly that I could answer for what I was doing only to Andrew, as Chief Executive. Hartwell's anger was muted, but no less fierce for that. Andrew relieved me of the obligation to make regular calls on him. But to my infinite sadness I received a letter from Hartwell's younger son, my old friend Nicky Berry. Nicky was far more discomposed by Conrad Black's takeover of the family company than his elder brother Adrian, who remained the *Telegraph*'s Science Correspondent. When we spoke on the telephone after my appointment, Nicky had shown dismay that I should have accepted office under the usurper, as he regarded Conrad. Now, he wrote a controlled but cold letter, suggesting that I owed it to his father to see him and hear his comments about the paper at least once a week. I answered temperately, but sadly, that I could not serve two masters. I was doing my utmost to rescue the *Telegraph* alongside Andrew Knight. Nicky wrote me one more letter, suggesting that I should perceive my own relationship with his father as that of a Prime Minister with a constitutional monarch. The casting of both roles seemed wildly unrealistic. Nicky never spoke to me again. The Berrys were reluctantly compelled to recognize that their influence upon the direction of the great newspapers their family had created was at an end.

From the first day, the range of problems that fell on my desk seemed extraordinary. There was a letter from the Serjeant-At-Arms at the House of Commons, enquiring what steps I proposed to take to prevent the repetition of an incident in the Lobby the previous week, in which the two alternating *Telegraph* parliamentary Sketch writers, deadly rivals, had fallen to fisticuffs in a dispute over whose turn it was to possess the paper's Gallery ticket. I desperately needed a room in the building in which to entertain staff and visitors for lunch, to get to know people and discuss the paper's direction, yet the Berrys were still denying us access to the dining room in their fifth-floor sanctum. The printing presses in the depths of the building were operating erratically in extreme old age. Their state-of-the-art replacements, the cost of which had broken the old regime, were under construction in the new Docklands plant, but remained months from completion. Our Fleet Street office, the exterior of which presented such an imposing face to the world, was a crumbling rabbit warren within.

Despite all those glittering commissionaires, there was no effective security to prevent passers-by from roaming the corridors. One morning, I arrived at 6 a.m. to find a tramp asleep outside my office, comfortably blanketed in swathes of insulating material he had ripped from a switchgear cupboard. He protested vociferously against eviction, asserting that he had been dossing there for months without interference.

Dashing between meetings across London from breakfast until far into the evening, I had to part with my first driver after a fortnight. A charming old man who had served the *Telegraph* for years, his nerves and my pace were ill-matched. My second driver lasted little longer. One evening I told him that I would be working late at the office, and suggested he should go home, leaving me the car keys. 'Can't do that,' he said irritably. 'I've got my own arrangements tonight, and I need the car.'

Momentarily stunned, I enquired whose car he thought it was. Our difference of opinion on this point proved irreconcilable. In despair, I turned to the one institution I was sure would not fail me, the Ex-Services Employment Bureau. I interviewed a succession of retiring soldiers. Though I was not short of enemies, it seemed extravagant to recruit an SAS veteran who had passed the army's personal bodyguarding and anti-terrorist driving course. I finally settled on Sergeant Bill Anderson, twenty-two years in the Scots Guards and Military Police, a quiet-spoken, infinitely obliging Scotsman as tall as me (the source of much mirth to the world) and a year younger. Bill proved the perfect chauffeur, a tower of strength who went everywhere with me and my family and dogs from that day forth, and remained beside me in bad times and good for more than fifteen years.

Another marvellous support was Ettie Duncan, the Features secretary, who moved into my office when Bill Deedes' personal assistant decided to retire. Ettie was a weighty Scotswoman with a heart of gold, the daughter of a Hebridean ferry captain and wife of a minister of the Church. I never asked how old she was, but later realized that she must have been well north of sixty at the time I came. Ettie was devotedly loyal, flourished on office drama – of which, Heaven knows, there was no shortage – and remained my counsellor and favourite aunt until she retired eight years later. I loved to hear the sound of those rich Scots cadences lilting down the telephone or reporting sardonically on the latest office crisis. She was an indifferent typist, and the serious secretarial work fell upon my personal assistant, for the first year Josie Heard and thereafter Rachel Lawrence. But it was Ettie who took the strain on days when I felt like bursting into tears about missing one of the children's school carol services, was savaged in *Private Eye*, or faced the necessity of sacking yet another of the paper's old retainers.

On 10 March, I became fully responsible for the running of the paper. My office was starkly lit by neon, and intolerably hot and stuffy even before summer came. I was traditionalist enough to keep the cramped old desk, but I installed a PC on a big modern table in the opposite corner. The roar of traffic below filtered even through closed windows. I did not care. The view onto Fleet Street was my heritage. Newspapers had been in my family's blood for three generations. Three of my grandparents and both my parents were writers. None ever knew the thrill I had been granted. Sheer exuberance did much to keep me going through those first weeks, when the strain sometimes seemed overwhelming. I was confronted with the additional self-imposed burden of finishing my book. Most days, I arrived in the office soon after 5 a.m., and worked with feverish address on the Korean War for a couple of hours before turning to the affairs of the *Daily Telegraph*. I often wrote another few hundred words of the book in the evenings, after I finished editing. Somehow, the manuscript crept towards a conclusion.

Andrew Hutchinson and the Night Editor, David Ruddock, managed the News pages with minimal participation from me. I was focused upon recruiting new staff, planning the future, and supervising the Comment and Features pages. As the weeks went by, my loneliness eased as the first senior executives who were my own appointments arrived to join. Jeremy Deedes, forty-three-year-old son of Bill and an old friend and colleague, came from the ailing *Today* as Editorial Director – in effect, my chief administrator. An experienced manager as well as journalist, Jeremy possessed all the discretion I knew that I lacked. George Jones left *The Sunday Times* to become Political Editor, an appointment which greatly enhanced the credibility of our paper. George's mild manner and apparent diffidence masked a sharp mind and excellent judgement. He was not in the business of pleasing Prime Ministers. He knew Westminster inside out, and simply reported politics without fear or favour. This was what I wanted, but would lead to a good deal of trouble before we were much older, from Tory ministers accustomed to privileged treatment from the *Telegraph*. More of that later.

Veronica Wadley, heavily pregnant, was beginning the task of creating modern Features pages for a modern readership, but she could not take hands-on charge of the big changes until after her own delivery day (an embittered *Telegraph* matron demanded of her: 'And just when are *you* planning to abandon your baby?'). *Telegraph* women were to be dragged out of their ghetto. Features would in future address a unisex audience. Trevor Grove, with whom I had worked at the *Standard* almost twenty years earlier, became our leader page editor a few months after my arrival. Trevor, a touch older than me at forty-one, was an immensely experienced newspaper and magazine executive of catholic tastes, who knew a lot of people and lived an energetic London social life. I appointed a big, tough, burly thirty-six-year-old New Zealander, Nigel Wade, who had served as *Telegraph* correspondent in Moscow, Washington and Peking, to become Foreign Editor. And, to my huge relief, the marvellous Don Berry – 'Uncle Don' as I always knew him – arrived to undertake the visual transformation of the paper.

We recognized this as a very big job. The old *Telegraph* was not so much a badly designed newspaper, as a paper which prided itself on having no design at all. A huge amount of information

was packed into the twenty-eight or thirty-six pages which were all
that union greed and limited press capacity enabled the Berrys to
print – indeed, we were still running a good many twenty-eight-
page papers as late as 1987. But there was no sense of direction or
focus about the manner in which material was presented. Stories
of all shapes and sizes were poured piecemeal into the forms.
Departments suited themselves about typefaces and headings.
Pictures were grudgingly accorded whatever space news allowed.
Half-tone photographs anyway reproduced so atrociously on the
tired old presses that picture-editing scarcely seemed to matter.
There was no logic about the manner in which the paper was
assembled, and no labelling or signposting of material. Because of
the company's perilous financial position, the management allowed
pages 2 and 3, vital news space, to be dominated by huge display
advertisements which made proper projection of stories almost
impossible. Likewise, we could not get rid of the two horribly old-
fashioned little ads which appeared each day alongside the front-
page masthead, the 'ears', because they brought in a precious
£200,000 a year.

Gardening Calendar, of all things, popped up in the middle
of our sixth news page on Saturday. Classified advertising was
strewn in blocks through the book, and ran from the back page for-
wards. While every normal newspaper recognized the importance
of making the most of its early flagship pages, 4 and 5 in the
Telegraph were regularly given over to concert advertising. The
women's and fashion pages seemed more appropriate for *The Lady*.
The gossip column, 'London Day By Day by Peterborough', was
time-warped in the early 1950s, full of stories about the Speaker
of the Commons finding his flies undone, or a witch doctor in
Sudan who had held up famine-relief supplies for a fortnight. I
wondered how we should ever get around to changing all these
things. Old *Telegraph* hands declared proudly that it was the
serendipity of the paper, the randomness of its arrangement, that
won readers. We thought otherwise. Veronica Wadley remarked
one morning that packaging and design had become critical to

every kind of merchandizing in modern life: newspapers could not afford to suppose themselves exceptions. Don Berry said: 'A lot of people now look at newspapers, rather than read them.' It was upon these premises that we set about transforming the *Telegraph* over the next two years. It was no good for old hands to insist that we tampered at our peril, that we should remember our newspaper still possessed almost three times the circulation of *The Times*. *Telegraph* readers were dying off at a terrifying rate, and not being replaced by new ones. Our new marketing team used a slightly different analogy: old readers were disappearing rapidly down the plughole. We could save the paper only if the tap discharged a strong stream of new readers. Right now, it was running dry. Jocular suggestions were made, that the paper might best salvage its circulation by offering massed injections of monkey glands, to prolong the lives of its dying customers. We gained some leeway from the fact that *The Times*, traditionally our most important rival, was at that stage a poor paper; but the *Daily Mail* was pulling in thousands of the young middle-market readers we needed, if the *Telegraph* was still to exist a decade thence. We had to create a formula which continued to satisfy our loyalists, while attracting a new generation.

As Don Berry began the visual makeover of the paper, he was somewhat shocked by the paucity of resources. At *The Sunday Times*, which Harold Evans had made the quintessential modern newspaper, departments were equipped with every technical facility. At the *Telegraph*, there was no resident designer, no graphic artist – only a couple of spare hands on the Picture Desk capable of drawing quaint little maps of the world's trouble spots, of a kind familiar to nineteenth-century newspaper readers. Over time, we hired designers and built a superb seven-strong Graphics Department. But in those early months, Don was ploughing a lonely furrow.

My own experience was somewhat the other way around. As a foreign correspondent and an author of books, for many years I had grown accustomed to working by myself, with only the aid of an occasional part-time secretary, researcher or translator. At the *Telegraph*, one of the earliest joys I discovered was that of working with a team. Many of its members were people whom I not only respected and liked, but also grew to love. Each day, I found myself rejoicing in the experience of meeting in the office men and women, almost all in their late thirties or early forties, with whom I shared excitements and agonies, and also a lot of laughter. When I left the paper almost ten years later, most of the senior executives with whom I set out on that extraordinary journey in 1986 were still with me. I knew that I could have accomplished nothing without them.

And, of course, there was Andrew Knight. I visited his fourth-floor office most mornings, to discuss ongoing dramas and long-term strategy. He would grin a welcome through those crinkled eyes, looking up sombrely from his sheaves of numbers, so many of them painted red. Andrew favoured the conventional office garb of an English businessman, the effect mildly impaired by a weakness for shirts with frayed collars, his pale features furnished with gold-rimmed glasses suspended rather fussily on a cord. At first sight, it was unlikely that he and I should have worked comfortably together. He was the archetypal head boy addressing a member of the upper fifth. Andrew's de haut en bas style was not to everybody's taste, and indeed not always to mine. He was an unembarrassed namedropper, and had acquired ample ordnance for this purpose over years of networking around the world: 'Going to Paris? Why don't you see Giscard?' 'You've *never met* the Prince of Wales?' – this with an eyebrow lifted in gentle surprise at such a lacuna in one's social education – 'I'll take you round there one evening' (though I must confess that he never did). I had spent twenty years as a journalist learning to treat the representatives of wealth and power with respect but without deference. Andrew cherished an inherent regard for the possessors of riches, nicely graduated in accordance with scale. Conrad Black featured at about a median point. Rupert Murdoch stood near the top, up there with the Agnellis and Fords.

To achieve the symmetry Andrew found indispensable for the comfortable conduct of life, he sought to ensure that executive decisions should be acknowledged not merely as inescapable, but as desirable, even ideal. He devised creative arguments to perfume the most brutal economic necessities: 'But readers *like* big ads'; 'the pages look *better* with a narrower web width'; 'the "ears" are part of the personality of the front page'. I sometimes teased him about this. If Andrew had been chief executive of the White Star line, sitting in a lifeboat watching the *Titanic* plunge beneath the Atlantic, he would have asserted that aesthetically, the ship looked much better at that angle. Yet as a boss, and especially in those early days, my respect for him was very great. He was quick, sympathetic, shrewd, and in most of the things that mattered, supportive. Here was he, who had been running a successful organization for years, facing the challenge of rescuing an almost bankrupt company. He told me that at one desperate financial moment early in 1986, he came within an ace of agreeing to sell our new Docklands printing plant, to raise cash. He finally flinched from doing so, merely because West Ferry Printers represented the *Telegraph*'s only tangible stake in the future. Day after day we sat in his office, discussing sackings, disappointments in the market place, editorial policy. He was sometimes critical, occasionally patronizing. One of Andrew's habits, when anyone disagreed with his own verdict, was to knit his brows and recite the argument once more. 'If you listen properly this time,' ran the unspoken message, 'you will appreciate that I am right.' Sometimes, he was not. I resisted not a few of his editorial suggestions, such as that of creating a double-column news summary and index on the front page. Yet his confidence, high intelligence and grip were the rocks upon which the revival of the *Daily Telegraph* was founded. At this period, Conrad's attention remained overwhelmingly focused on the other side of the Atlantic. Even those of us at the heart of the paper saw little of him for the first year of his reign. Andrew Knight was clearly understood to be Conrad's viceroy, with plenary powers, though Conrad's lawyer Dan Colson kept a close watch on financial and contractual issues. Andrew picked a remarkably successful management team at the outset: Frank Rogers as Deputy Chairman, Stephen Grabiner from Coopers & Lybrand to become Marketing Director before he was thirty; Joe Cooke as a management consultant to handle the vast task of reconciling the print unions to radical change; Len Sanderson as Advertising Director. When we arrived, the management of the paper was moribund. Vital information about costs, revenue and circulation was either non-existent, or had been wilfully distorted to conceal the truth from Lord Hartwell. Somehow, out of all this, a modern management structure was created and led by Andrew towards brilliant, remarkably rapid success.

It was at my own darkest moments that his serenity and assurance meant most. One morning, I stumbled up the stairs into his office and said: 'Garland's going.' I had felt sure of the loyalty of Nick Garland, the *Telegraph*'s cartoonist. I had won Nick a big pay rise, after years in which he worked for a pittance under the Berrys. It was a bitter blow to my confidence, as well as to the paper, when Nick walked into my office and announced that he was leaving to join the team putting together *The Independent*. Not only were we to suffer the loss of a well-regarded artist – and cartoonists are very hard to find in Britain – the '*Indie*' thereby gained a big boost to its credibility.

I knew that Nick was going because he did not like my regime. In the diary of those months which he afterwards published, he vividly chronicled the gloom of old *Telegraph* stalwarts, the fevered discussion of how long I might last – or deserved to. I had one protracted conversation with Garland soon after he arrived, which encouraged him, and temporarily dislocated his long-running negotiation with the *Indie*'s founders. But his journal revealed how depressed and neglected he felt in the weeks that followed, because I seemed to have little time for him or others. Leisurely chit-chat had been one of the joys of the old dispensation. He experienced a stab of disgust one day as he entered my office and was invited to 'take a pew'. After I read his narrative, I never used

that unfortunate phrase again. Garland and other old *Telegraph*
contributors expressed scorn about what they perceived as my
'hurried decisions, snap judgements and a fundamental and fatal
absence of any guiding plan'.

At that time, indeed, so intense were the pressure and sense of
urgency, there was little chance of spending more than half an
hour apiece with any one of the 300 people desperate for personal
attention. I was striving to get a grip on a big and unwieldy
organization, juggling a dozen balls. My own tensions and fears
were apparent to those around me. It is also true that I was less
than frank to the old guard about where I hoped to take the *Daily
Telegraph*. I knew how distant was my intended destination from
any which they would find acceptable.

When I told Andrew of Garland's going, he merely glanced up
from his mound of paper and smiled: 'Don't worry,' he said,
'you'll find another cartoonist.' He was not quite right – though
we recruited brilliant pocket cartoonists, we never found a convincing replacement to do our big drawings, until Garland rejoined
the paper five years later. But at that moment, when my own
confidence had fallen so low, it was Andrew's support which
enabled me to walk back downstairs and carry on. He helped me
to learn the lesson that no one is indispensable, so that I would
later view with relative equanimity the staff comings and goings
which take place in any organization.

It would be wrong to create the impression that everything
about the *Telegraph* was fatally flawed when Conrad assumed
control. We inherited from the Berrys what was still the greatest
News paper in Britain. It was the knowledge of its residual
strengths which made me so confident that it could be resurrected.
Many of our reporters and specialists had become long in the
tooth, but their reputation for thoroughness, professionalism,
accuracy was second to none, in an age when our rivals were
increasingly cavalier about the handling of information, indeed
about attempting any honest assessment of whether what they
published was likely to be true. The *Telegraph*'s stalwarts were

formidable people. Reporters such as R. Barry O'Brien, Guy Rais, David Fletcher, Maurice Weaver were little known to the public, but immensely respected in the industry. No title could match the range and thoroughness of our Sports coverage, even if its layout and presentation were as awful as those of the rest of the paper. Above all, the *Telegraph* possessed a strong foreign staff. By the mid-1980s, most British newspapers had drastically reduced their international coverage. The *Telegraph*, however, retained a chain of bureaux and 'stringers' matched only by that of the *Financial Times*. We treated foreign news, even from the most obscure corners of the world, with high seriousness. Of the sixteen stories on the *Telegraph*'s front page the day after I was appointed, I counted six foreign ones. Even on a day when the paper was exceptionally tight, there were twenty-four reports and 'shorts' on the foreign pages.

Ian Ball, the famously debonair, chain-smoking Australian who had run the New York bureau for years, filed thousands of words a day, each one impeccably crafted. Ian flew to London a few days after I was appointed. He overwhelmed me with ideas which he had been developing for years, about how to transform the paper's layout and typography. He was in love with one face in particular. For many months afterwards, we never mentioned Ian's name in the office without mumbling the rueful aside: 'Modern Bodoni'. I was sensitive to the fact that he knew far more about the technicalities of newspapers than I did – and to the knowledge that Andrew had seriously considered appointing him as editor before offering the job to me. In the end, both men had agreed that Ian, in his fifties, was a decade too old and had lived in America too long to take the chair of a British newspaper. He remained a peerless New York correspondent until his retirement in the early 1990s.

Nigel Wade and I made early changes elsewhere in the foreign bureaux. We switched some of our American staff, and made Ian Brodie Chief Washington Correspondent. Our Moscow office was vacant. I persuaded that fey, clever journalist Xan Smiley to take the job, after protracted negotiations about how we could afford to house him and a young family in conditions he thought acceptable. 'As far as I am able to discern, Max,' Conrad growled at a moment when he found himself passing through London and privy to our expensive discussions, 'Mr Smiley appears to believe that he would be most appropriately accommodated in the Winter Palace.'

Eager to reduce the age of our staff, I was trawling universities in search of young recruits for the Peterborough column and almost anywhere else on the paper that I could place them. I plucked Robert Hardman from Cambridge, Quentin Letts from Trinity College, Dublin. I sent an impressively mature twenty-two-year-old named Jeremy Gavron to Nairobi. It seemed unacceptable that a paper which purported to cover the world should have no representative anywhere in black Africa, and my own experience persuaded me that youth should be no barrier to a foreign posting. Jeremy produced some memorable reporting over the next three years, above all when the young British tourist Julie Ward was murdered in a game park in 1988. We had no correspondent in Tokyo, simply because the city was thought too expensive. I believed that we could not call ourselves a serious international newspaper without a representative covering the affairs of the second largest economy in the world. With Andrew Knight's support, we identified a fluent Japanese speaker and sent him to Japan despite the horrific cost.

Yet, in my early weeks as editor, it was on the foreign side that I made my first conspicuous mistake. Through the early days of April 1986, tensions between Libya and the United States were rising. The Foreign Desk demanded: Do we send our own man to Tripoli, just as other major papers and TV networks were sending? No, I said. Mindful that we were spending big money on all manner of new features and new recruits, I wanted to save cash on the margin wherever I could. The chances were that Libyan tensions would slacken, as they had so often done before. I also thought – though I did not acknowledge this to the Foreign Desk

– that we possessed no descriptive writer, no 'wordsmith', of the right calibre. There were plenty of solid, reliable, veteran *Telegraph* reporters who would attend the press conferences and provide us with files carrying a Tripoli dateline. But we had no colour writer, of the kind I was determined to recruit, who would bring to dry paragraphs that touch of stardust which – in my eyes, anyway – was needed to make big air fares worthwhile. Thus we did not send a man, and thus the *Telegraph* was unrepresented in Libya on 14 April, when the Americans bombed. Our front-page lead story – the 'splash' – had to be written from the Washington Bureau. Next morning I met reproachful faces around the office, and of course gleeful ones among my critics in the Newsroom. At the morning conference post-mortem on the day's paper, I felt obliged to avow: 'The most serious error has been made by me.' *UK Press Gazette*, the trade weekly, ran a story headed 'HASTINGS MAKES FIRST MISTAKE'.

However energetically we were paddling underwater, through the spring of 1986 a casual reader of the *Daily Telegraph* saw little in the paper to suggest that change was taking place. Many of the front page headlines were as doggedly dull, as determinedly uninviting, as ever: 'PRICE FALL BOOST FOR BUDGET', 'FRANCE GOES RIGHT IN TIGHT POLL', 'ELECTRICITY PRICE RISE CUT BY 3pc'. A leader was headed 'TIN OF WORMS', and addressed the doings of that celebrated body, the Tin Council. Old staffers, sniffing the wind to detect which way I was going, passed withering comment when I was heard to remark in the Newsroom that we must get more pictures of young people into the paper. Yet it seemed incontrovertibly true that pages dominated by pictures of the old – and above all, of men – conveyed to readers a sense of the paper's decrepitude. Peter Simple, beloved columnist of the old Right and a source of embarrassment to everybody else, daily denounced the Channel Tunnel and the possibility of reform in South Africa. The main story on the front page seldom occupied more than two thin columns, around which eighteen or nineteen stories and a mean little picture were crammed in. Showbusiness, which by the millennium would increasingly preoccupy even the allegedly serious British press, scarcely got a look in. The Academy Awards rated just 300 words in the *Telegraph* of 24 March 1986. The paper 'splashed' most days on political stories, frequently arcane, which highlighted its familiar role as house magazine of the Conservative Party.

We made our first substantial design change, appropriately enough, on April Fools' Day. I contributed a 1,000-word article, explaining to our readers what we were doing. The centre pages were wholly reshaped and redesigned, to provide space for a big leader-page article alongside the editorials, with Letters underneath. The facing page – 'op-ed' as the trade calls it – became a showcase for big news features, under the inspired stewardship of Nigel Horne, with the Peterborough gossip column underneath. Our first, not untypical op-ed page included a profile of the new Chairman of Nuclear Fuels, a file from Ian Ball on the American advertising business, and a law piece on the Crown Prosecution Service. Op-ed started life carrying five pieces a day, too many, and settled down to three. We still had to live with two advertisements on the centre spread, which severely cramped our style, but the new arrangement provided an incomparably better showcase for our best reporters and writers than they had ever known. The leader page was to be our sole forum of comment, though there was a daily slot for a column at the foot of BMDs – the Births, Marriages and Deaths page – which followed in the new make-up.

This gave us far less commentary space than *The Times* or *The Guardian*, yet it was not an accidental arrangement. I believed that the key to the *Telegraph*'s huge readership was not merely its streak of populism and vulgarity, but the fact that it was the paper which gave readers more hard news than any other. I made a reasoned decision to keep it that way – to seek to present news better, to modernize, to deploy new and brighter writers – but to ring-fence punditry within the leader page and the modest opinion columns further back in the book.

Our Letters column was much tighter than those of other

broadsheets. For the time being, I was also untroubled by that constraint. The general quality of *Telegraph* readers' letters was poor, indeed embarrassingly so. Many of those who dispatch letters for publication to newspapers are not entirely sane, and this seemed especially true of our correspondents. The *Telegraph* post-bag was dominated by readers complaining about falling standards of service / lack of respect among the young / criminal justice / the presumptuous ambition of black men to govern themselves, or a combination of all these issues. Under a new Letters Editor, we began to solicit and even pay for contributions from more interesting correspondents. The overall standard remained low. We made no impact on the standing of the *Times* as the chosen forum of debate for intelligent correspondents. In these circumstances, I believed that to yield more precious space to Letters would merely serve to highlight the gulf between the new readership to which we aspired, and the old readership we were stuck with. Time enough to carry more Letters, when we could find better correspondents. Today, *Telegraph* Letters get much more space than they did in my day. I am amazed that so many veterans of the Crimea, together with their prejudices, survive to dominate the columns.

Through the rest of 1986 and into 1987, the paper's new design continued to evolve. We put the definite article back into the masthead, to make ourselves once more *The Daily Telegraph*. After a long, hard fight the horrible little advertising 'ears' were dropped. We gave Weather, so important to our readers, a fixed slot on the back page, and introduced a Specialists' page to showcase their work. On a typical day, there were pieces on Medicine, Motoring, Engineering, Agriculture, the Law, and Heraldry. Obituaries gained a permanent home: one of the worst vices of the old paper was that its furniture shifted whimsically from day to day. Births, Marriages and Deaths were now consolidated on a single page under a proper heading. Our City pages were redesigned. The rejuvenation of Sport began. The Arts and Features pages were dramatically improved, and looked as if they might belong to a modern newspaper. Signposting and labelling, to introduce clarity and logic, were Don Berry's key objectives.

Although the *Telegraph* possessed an editorial staff of some 300 people, it was astonishing how short of talent we found ourselves in key areas. When the Soviet Chernobyl nuclear plant exploded on 28 April, our 'splash' had to be written by one of the Diplomatic staff. We possessed no specialist capable of providing proper scientific analysis of the disaster. I never slept easy in my bed until, a few months later, we hired the omniscient Dr Roger Highfield as Technology Correspondent. Christine Doyle joined us to write about Health, which Veronica Wadley had identified as a vital new area for attention. I was horrified to discover that no major obituary pages had been prepared for the eventuality of the Queen Mother's death. I commissioned Philip Ziegler to write a big piece – he became one of our principal royal writers – and diverted Don Berry to put together an eight-page section as a matter of urgency. A decade later Don found himself doing the same job at my request for the *Evening Standard*. We were retired from both titles before either supplement was needed.

I trawled old colleagues on the foreign corresponding circuit in search of a star 'wordsmith', and eventually hired Trevor Fishlock, who was soon joined by my fellow Falklands veteran Robert Fox. We recruited a design specialist from the *Financial Times*. We were hunting hard for a new generation of photographers. It would be naive to pretend that the process of removing old stagers enhanced my popularity. One day, a detective inspector from Vine Street turned up in my office. He enquired whether I recognized a certain name. I looked blank. Then my visitor told his tale, and all became clear. I had sacked a writer whose spouse, the police now believed, was bombarding me and other prominent figures with hate mail and death threats. Ettie Duncan revealed that for weeks, the office had been receiving parcels of excrement addressed to me, though she had ensured they were never delivered. The policeman said that they would be raiding the house of the suspect next day. My heart sank. I envisaged a sensational court case, gleeful publicity in rival titles about how my cruelty had driven a victim over the edge of sanity. In the event, to my immense relief, somehow our trade failed to notice this bizarre and lurid story. The suspect's house was found extravagantly furnished with guns and sheaves of hate mail. Charges and a conviction for firearms offences followed, without a word about the case appearing in print. The abusive letters and deliveries of excrement stopped. This was a somewhat extravagant example of the passions coursing through the *Telegraph* office in 1986.

One morning, I asked Nigel Wade how morale stood in the Newsroom. He answered with characteristic bluntness: 'Among the good people, it's pretty good. Among the not-so-good people, it's pretty low. They're all wondering which of them you're going to chop next.' It was hard not to succumb to moments of self-pity. Didn't all these people realize the pressure on me? Didn't they understand that I was a novice editor who was having to learn from scratch? Wouldn't they forgive a few mistakes? Couldn't they see that it must take time to restore the paper's fabric, after decades of decay? But I knew that the answer to such questions is always 'no'. Most of mankind is capable of making itself only marginally interested in the fate of an organization. What matters is his or her own personal livelihood, mortgage, family. For our staff, these things now seemed to hinge upon the whims of a tall, noisy interloper who bore little resemblance to Superman. Very early in my life as editor I vowed to stop feeling sorry for myself, whether about staff defections or troubles with Andrew Knight, tensions with the leader writers or wildly mendacious stories in *Private Eye*. In moments of anguish, doubt and self-indulgence, I confided in Jeremy Deedes alone. Years later, I was pleased to discover how little even close colleagues such as Don Berry ever knew about – for instance – the political struggles between management and editorial. Perhaps I was less indiscreet than I feared. It is one of the vital responsibilities of any editor to shield his staff from knowledge of pressures from above.

But if I tried to banish self-pity, very soon also I told myself that I would never again feel embarrassed about my salary, chauffeur, expenses, perks. Like everyone who has ever run anything, I felt alone in taking the strain. Especially in those dark and perilous early days, all of us at the top of the *Telegraph* were earning every penny of our money. It was impossible to apologize to old staffers or to the outside world for what we were doing. They thought the manner of the sackings and job switches was brutal. Bill Deedes wrote generously in his memoirs that he thought I might have done well in the war, but added a droll rider that casualties among those under my command would have been heavy. Some of the old guard said scornfully that I was merely serving as hatchet man, at the whim of Andrew Knight. Years later, encountering Richard Chartres as Bishop of London, I said: 'I don't think we've met.' The Bishop corrected me: 'Oh yes, we have – back in 1986, when you sacked me as Religious Affairs Correspondent of *The Daily Telegraph*!'

David Ruddock, the Night Editor, observed not without prescience to Andrew Hutchinson: 'Max will find it far harder sacking people when he starts having to get rid of his own appointments.' But all our senior executives recognized that we were engaged in a race with the clock. We could not afford to show extravagant sensitivity, to hold back to the pace of the slower ships in the convoy. We had to bring change, reform, purpose and new vitality to the *Telegraph* titles as fast as we dared. Our purpose was always to give the readers 'change by stealth', to eschew a noisy 'big bang'. But the company was still haemorrhaging money – we lost £21 million in the last nine months of 1986. The paper's sale continued to decline, at the rate of more than 5,000 a month. Circulation had fallen from a high of over 1.4 million in 1980 (then, admittedly, artificially boosted by the temporary closure of *The Times*) to 1.17 million early in 1986. *The Times* had come back from a low point sale of 290,000 in 1981 to 475,000 five years later. It takes a long, long time for the public to notice change in any newspaper, to switch familiar buying habits. By autumn, as we all knew, Andreas Whittam-Smith and his group would be ready to launch *The Independent*, a paper explicitly targeted at the *Telegraph* audience. The very reason Andreas and his colleagues had been able to raise money for this bold new venture was that the City, like most of Fleet Street, perceived our paper to be on its knees. The *Indie*'s investors were confident that a new title aimed at a new generation of middle-class, middle-brow readers weary of *Torygraph* politics could move in for the kill. It was widely believed in the British newspaper industry that the *Telegraph* could be driven out of business altogether, once it became exposed to a three-way squeeze between *The Times*, the *Daily Mail* and the new *Indie*. I said many times to sour and almost mutinous old hands in our office: 'I don't set the standards we've got to achieve. Our competitors do it.' In 1986, we seemed to have a perilously long way to go, in a very short time.

3

POLITICS AND POLICY

ON SUNDAY 9 MARCH, a fortnight after my appointment was announced, Margaret Thatcher invited me to lunch at Chequers. She and her Press Secretary, Bernard Ingham, assiduously culti-vated the editors of Tory papers, and indeed conferred knight-hoods on six – William Rees-Mogg of *The Times*, Nicholas Lloyd of the *Daily Express*, John Junor of the *Sunday Express*, David English of the *Daily Mail*, Geoffrey Owen of the *Financial Times* and Peregrine Worsthorne of *The Sunday Telegraph* – as well as honouring a bevy of sympathetic broadcasters. My arrival at the *Telegraph* was greeted with some dismay in Downing Street. For generations, the Conservative Party had been able to place absolute reliance upon the paper's support. Bill Deedes was a family friend of the Thatchers, and a golfing companion of Denis. Carol, the Thatchers' daughter, was employed in the *Telegraph* Features Department.

I had met the Prime Minister occasionally, when I was on political assignments. She once rebuked me for suggesting in the *Evening Standard* after the Falklands War that we should seek a rapprochement with Argentina: 'You, of all people, Mr Hastings, should understand why that is impossible.' I had written my share of leader-page articles, but I had never been a political journalist at Westminster. I was a warm admirer of Mrs Thatcher's achieve-ment in transforming the British industrial and economic land-scape since 1979, but I was among those increasingly sceptical about her style of leadership. I had never been comfortable with the Tory Right. Thatcher's indifference to the fate of public services and of the underclass dismayed me profoundly. In a word, I was a 'wet'. I believed that Britain's future must lie with Europe, because we had no other credible destiny. I had no intention of deliberately rocking the Telegraph boat at the outset by opposing Mrs Thatcher's governance. On political matters, as on other things, I wanted to bring gradual change. But the first job of any journalist, any editor, is to report and comment upon events as circumstances demand. Obviously The Daily Telegraph would maintain an important working relationship with the Conservative Party. I have always been inclined to give any institution the benefit of the doubt, because I believe that my trade's instincts are too brutally iconoclastic. But I did not think it was part of our editorial duty to assist the Conservative government or its ministers, unless we sincerely believed they were right on the issue in question. Paul Johnson once observed witheringly: 'Max Hastings doesn't have political ideas. He has bits of ideas.' He was correct, in the sense that I did not bring to journalism a fully shaped creed embracing all points of doctrine, such as Perry Worsthorne or Charles Moore possessed. More than anything else, what politicians of all parties seek from newspaper editors is predictability. This is, of course, the enemy of good journalism. I never sought to be a controversialist merely for the sake of it, but I was imbued with the belief that a good writer, a good newspaper, is surprising. Against this background, it was unremarkable that Downing Street felt alarmed by my appointment to the Telegraph. I doubt whether Mrs Thatcher was much looking forward to her meeting with me that Sunday at Chequers.

Our relationship could scarcely have got off to a less auspicious start. My driver did not work at weekends. I was obliged to get the Telegraph to arrange a hire car to take Tricia and me to the Chilterns from Northamptonshire. The driver got lost finding our house. We set off very late. He had taken no steps to explore a route to Chequers. We circled the area for half an hour before finding the gates of the Prime Minister's lair. I was due at 11.30. We eventually reached the house at 12.40, to find Mrs Thatcher on the steps to greet us. My nerves were in shreds. I despise unpunctuality in myself or others. On that point if nothing else, our hostess seemed in warm agreement with her guest. Mrs Thatcher, Bernard Ingham and I sat down to a frosty and attenuated tête-à-tête. Much of this focused upon the ongoing crisis surrounding the survival of Land Rover, that British icon then threatened with sale to the Americans. When ill at ease, I am prone to blurt foolish remarks. I made one on that occasion, about the damage that a Land Rover sale would do to confidence in the government among rural Tory voters. 'Unfortunately, Mr Hastings,' replied the Prime Minister acidly, 'your friends in the Shires do not seem willing to buy British vehicles in sufficient numbers to preserve the British motor industry's independence.' Round one decisively to Mrs Thatcher. We lunched with a dozen or so assorted guests of impeccable Tory loyalist credentials, and departed chastened. In my letter of thanks, I wrote: 'Neither Conrad Black nor Andrew Knight have given me any political directive ... but there will be no wavering of support either for yourself as the only credible leader of the Conservative Party at the next election, or for the Conservatives as the only party fit to govern. I have no doubt that we shall irritate you rather more often than in the past, but I intend to be properly modest about leading the paper in any political direction until I am much better informed and more closely in touch than I am today.' All of which was sincere.

In the first weeks of my editorship, the government can have found little in our leader columns to cause ministers concern. Familiar *Telegraph* writers continued to generate familiar *Telegraph* sentiments. Every afternoon at 3.30, the leader writers assembled in my office, to discuss the editorials for the following day's paper. Bill Deedes was there, apparently untroubled by his change of role, without pretension, happy to turn his pen to whatever circumstances demanded. With his instinctive distaste for confrontation, some of Bill's utterances for the paper could be construed to mean whatever best suited the reader. A hundred times I have heard him murmur gently: 'I think we might sound a cautionary note there . . .'

Charles Moore, once a *Telegraph* leader writer himself, loved to tell a story of Bill, as Editor, remarking with unwonted firmness at the leader conference on the day after an intruder broke into the Queen's bedroom, that he thought Willie Whitelaw, as Home Secretary, really would have to carry the can. At that moment, on cue, Willie himself came on the phone, wringing his hands down the wire and pleading with his old friend W. F. Deedes for sympathy and understanding. 'Of course, old boy, of course . . . do understand . . . not your fault at all,' said the Editor soothingly. He was indeed Dear Bill. Yet, if he chose often to be circumspect in print, his views on all matters pertaining to politics, the Conservative Party, the monarchy and public affairs were unfailingly to the point. I have never regretted a moment spent listening to Bill on any subject, before committing our newspaper or sitting down at a keyboard myself. He was, and remains, a wise old bird, whose company gave me as much pleasure as his counsel continued to profit the *Daily Telegraph*.

Jock Bruce-Gardyne, who wrote our economics leaders, was a sharp, abrasive former Treasury minister in his late fifties, whose political career had been fatally handicapped by an inability to stop himself saying – or worse, committing to paper – whatever came into his head. Having lost a couple of Commons seats, he had much trouble finding another. At last, in 1979, he was adopted as Tory candidate for Knutsford. One of his friends rang another to pass on the good news:

'Have you heard? Marvellous, isn't it? Jock's absolutely safe now.'

'Stop, stop. How big's the majority?'

'Over 10,000.'

'*Not enough for Jock!!*'

Sure enough, in April 1982, at the height of Falklands jingomania, the beak-featured Member for Knutsford was rash enough to write a letter which was mischievously leaked to the papers, asserting that he thought the whole Task Force adventure a lot of nonsense. When Jock's seat was subsumed into two new constituencies, neither would accept him as its Tory candidate. That was the end of his Commons career, though he continued to bicycle regularly down to the Lords of an afternoon, and was an uncommonly witty as well as acerbic contributor to our leader conference. Jock was a no-nonsense Thatcherite. Without mercy even for his own follies, he arrived in the office one Monday morning without a couple of fingers, having carelessly inserted them in a lawnmower: 'Don't say it!' he roared. 'Don't give me sympathy! It's all my own bloody fault.'

Edward Pearce and Godfrey Barker, our Commons Sketchwriters, also attended leader conferences, as did John Keegan. There was an occasional welcome appearance from Ferdinand Mount. Ferdy wrote an elegant weekly political column, which we now promoted with far more space and projection. I was strongly influenced by Ferdy's views on almost everything. He seemed to represent the most civilized strand of thoughtful Conservatism. A former head of Mrs Thatcher's Downing Street Policy Unit, he admired the Prime Minister, but acknowledged her shortcomings. When the government acted foolishly, for example in proposing to replace the domestic rating system with a poll tax, he said so. Above all, he adopted a pragmatic and generally benign attitude to Europe. Again and again in his column, Ferdy chastised Mrs Thatcher for hectoring our European partners. He urged a change of language and style, if not of policy, by Britain towards Brussels. When Conrad met Ferdy for the first time, the Chairman observed ponderously as he shook his contributor's hand: 'I disagree profoundly with every word of your column this morning – but I will defend to the death your right to say it.'

My most serious difficulty in dealing with the leader group stemmed from the presence of T. E. Utley. Peter, as he was universally known, had been a central figure at the *Telegraph* for many years, a passionate advocate of Thatcherism before Thatcher was heard of, a high Tory guru whose writings influenced party thinking for a generation. Now sixty-five, his intellectual and literary gifts were never in doubt. His blindness affected his office life only insofar as a succession of pretty and devoted girls accompanied him wherever he went to show the way, and to mop up his smouldering cigarettes in advance of a conflagration. From the outset, Peter and I treated each other with an exaggerated courtesy designed to defer acknowledgement, for a while at least, of the fact that we were political irreconcilables. I felt obliged to say that in future I would write the paper's Northern Ireland leaders, rather than him. Peter was a devoted apologist for the Protestant cause, and indeed had once stood as a Unionist parliamentary candidate. I had been a bitter critic of Unionist doings for over fifteen years, since my days as a reporter in Ulster. Utley retained his signed column, however, and observed one August day in 1986: 'In Ulster we are confronted with a challenge to the authority of the state to which we have not the guts to respond, either by efficiently suppressing violence or by devising a statesmanlike and honourable manner of transferring our responsibilities to the only other people [the Protestants of Ulster] who might be capable of bearing them.' He concluded by urging the reintroduction of internment for terrorist suspects, a policy I had always thought political madness, save in the implausible case that it could operate in both Northern Ireland and the Irish Republic. Utley's column caused me special grief when he turned his pen to South African affairs. He was an unembarrassed advocate of the white minority regime which still ruled the country in 1986. He wrote with open contempt of demands for a 'liberating process' towards black majority rule, which he predicted would provoke 'the dissolution of the Union into anarchy, barbarism and poverty'. He confided to his girl assistant, who passed the remark around the office, that he feared I was not a gentleman. I had no idea how to behave. He was right in supposing that I believed the business of newspapers should be directed by players rather than gentlemen. The latter had made an almighty mess of the *Daily Telegraph*. I have often thought newspapers would be best of all run by women, irrespective of whether they chance to be ladies. Utley was too formidable a Conservative intellectual force for me to think of dispensing with him immediately. My own position was too precarious. But his continuing presence troubled me, because the paper seemed unlikely to attract the sort of new young readers we must win to survive, as long as Utley was preaching the doctrines of Victorian Conservatism on our centre pages. I heaved a sigh of relief when, a year or so after my arrival, he departed to write obituaries for *The Times*.

The daily leader conference, which in the past sometimes extended to an hour or more, now seldom lasted more than twenty-five minutes. This partly reflected my own impatient habits, and became the object of some teasing and also of more serious criticism, that I was not treating leaders with the gravity they deserved. This was not so. From start to finish, I wrote many of them myself, on what seemed the most important issues of the day. This also enabled us to dispense with the services of several old stagers who supposed that drafting a couple of Editorials a week justified a salary. But I have always doubted whether more than 10 per cent of any newspaper's readership look at its Editorial columns. It may be argued that this 10 per cent includes some of the most important people in the country. But in 1986, faced with huge problems in turning around the *Telegraph*, I did not believe our leaders would influence the outcome nearly as much as many other things – above all the quality and presentation of news and features.

In those first months, I did not want Editorials to cause any major shocks in Conservative circles before I was ready for them. Most were still being written by the familiar old hands. I felt no embarrassment about trimming our sails according to my perception of what our readership would stand, until they grew used to the new dispensation. Yet I could scarcely run an Editorial on a vital issue which was wholly at odds with my private convictions. In the spring of 1986, like it or not, I found myself faced with my first serious policy dilemma. 'Events, always events, dear boy' crowd in on newspaper editors quite as often as Harold Macmillan complained that they do upon Prime Ministers, in our case happily with less import for society.

Throughout the escalating confrontation between Libya and the United States, we expressed doubts about whether a direct American strike against Colonel Gaddafy, the Libyan dictator, was sensible. John Keegan wrote a leader-page article declaring that US missile and bomb attacks were not the answer to rogue states. On 14 April, the very day American bombers at last struck against Tripoli, some of them flying from bases in Britain, we ran a leader arguing against military action. Next morning, we devoted the paper's entire centre spread to the Libyan bombing, examining its legality, the motives for Thatcher's support for President Reagan, and the domestic response in America. Most unusually, the leader conference group was unanimous in agreeing that the attack had been a mistake. Our opinion column next day was headed 'A bad decision'. I wrote: 'Colonel Gaddafy of Libya is mad and bad. If not dangerous to the Western Powers, he is at least a chronic source of mischief to their citizens. [The American bombing] seems to presume a degree of rationality in Tripoli about cause and effect, which is palpably lacking. It is difficult not to contrast the restrained reaction of Mrs Thatcher's Government two years ago, when WPC Yvonne Fletcher was murdered by Colonel Gaddafy's servants in St James's Square, with its acquiescence yesterday in the use of F111s from British bases.'

We urged Western resolution in the face of likely terrorist reprisals, but our course was set: we believed the government had been wrong to agree to British participation. In particular, in leaders over the days and weeks that followed, we argued that the Prime Minister had acted for the wrong reasons. Heavy leaking from Downing Street indicated that the government possessed its own reservations about the efficacy of bombing Tripoli, but that Mrs Thatcher had believed there was a paramount need to show support for the Americans at a critical moment, especially after their aid to Britain in the South Atlantic war four years earlier. The *Telegraph* said that British participation would have been far more convincing if the government showed wholehearted support for the mission, rather than muttering about 'debts of honour for the Falklands'.

Ferdy Mount denounced the raids in his column. If Britain had taken part in one act of retaliation for Libyan terrorism, he said, how in logic could we not commit ourselves to more of the same, if there were more Libyan attacks in the West? Opinion polls showed Thatcher's popularity plunging in the wake of the crisis. There were approving nods at Westminster for President Mitterrand's alleged response to America's request for French participation: 'I might help you to destroy Gaddafy. I will not assist you in merely annoying him.' Even Peter Utley was unimpressed by Western policy on Libya. In a column full of praise for Mrs Thatcher, he nonetheless suggested that too many ill-considered decisions were coming out of Downing Street, and that it was bad for Britain to appear to have been dragged unwillingly into providing support for the raids: 'This admirable and almost indispensable lady does not reflect enough.'

The *Telegraph*'s criticism of the Libyan bombing caused shock and dismay at Tory Westminster. We compounded our original sin by launching a broadside against that foremost of Mrs Thatcher's henchmen Mr Norman Tebbit, who had denounced the BBC's coverage of the Libyan attack as unpatriotic. We ran a 3,000-word analysis of the BBC's coverage and of Tebbit's criticism, concluding that the minister was quite out of court.

Downing Street was furious. If this was the first earnest of my editorship, it was felt, then prospects for the relationship between the paper and the government were bleak indeed. At a *Telegraph* board meeting the former Tory Solicitor-General Lord Rawlinson, now an independent director, voiced fierce criticism of what the paper had done, and described the chagrin he had heard expressed at his local Tory association. If we went on like this, he suggested, we would soon have no readers left. Michael Hartwell responded, with admirable detachment, 'in principle a board should not seek to give instructions to an editor'.

Conrad Black was especially dismayed by the paper's stance. Although himself a Canadian, among the great enthusiasms of his life were the United States and the Reagan Presidency. One of his strongest criticisms of the British people, and especially of the British intelligentsia, was that its principals sought to belittle and patronize America. I was always sensitive to the fact that, while I enjoyed considerable latitude in many areas, the paper must tread warily in its treatment of the United States. At dinner with me one night, the Chairman sharply contrasted his admiration for Perry Worsthorne's *Sunday Telegraph* leader, supporting the bombing, with his dismay about my own 'pusillanimity' – one of Conrad's favourite terms of disapprobation.

Yet not for the last time, at the *Telegraph* board meeting – and at this stage, I was not myself a member of the board – Conrad declined to censure me. He was most concerned, he said, 'that the editor should not feel undue pressure from me on every individual point of editorial policy, though obviously if there were frequent variances of view, the position would have to be assessed'. In the years ahead, relations between myself and Conrad on political issues were sometimes sensitive, periodically stormy. It must have been especially hard for him when the Libyan controversy broke. I had been in charge of *The Daily Telegraph* for only a few weeks. Whatever good things my regime might attain still lay in the future. My first visible achievement as Conrad's Editor was publicly to embarrass him. By chance, he had booked a table at the somewhat inappropriately named Relai des Amis, to enable me to introduce him to some of our political contributors across the dinner table. We found ourselves meeting shortly after he returned from lunch at Chequers with the Prime Minister. Expecting to be congratulated upon saving the *Daily Telegraph*, instead he had found himself lambasted by Mrs Thatcher for the paper's coverage of the bombing. Our dinner table at the Relai was liberally coated with frost.

In the midst of the furore, Andrew Knight penned me a long memo. He wrote from the perspective of a former *Economist* editor as well as the company's Chief Executive. His words bear quoting at length, because they offer some interesting reflections about the responsibilities of editors and proprietors:

> It is often said (Michael Hartwell is one who says) that great reporters and columnists rarely make great editors. Reason: reporters and professional debaters have their being in the immediate rights and wrongs of what they see. An editor's function, by contrast, is to know and manage the long-run position of his newspaper. This frequently means holding things steady through collective hysteria or a fashionable lurch. It can be very lonely: in my time I can remember horrid weeks of isolation over Angola, as an early disbeliever in [President] Carter; in the first Reagan election; over the Falklands and Grenada . . . on all of which I can now feel quite smugly comfortable that I was right not to give in to first wave of lemmings declaring that the world should jump over the precipice in an orgy of despairing condemnation.
>
> An editor (and a newspaper) has to have a few anchors. When the gale pulls, his first instinct (unlike the reporter or columnist, whose very living depends on immediate discussion of the vivid issues seemingly at stake) should be to strengthen the lines holding him to his anchors.
>
> Is his newspaper's long-run interest and belief in:
>
> – Tory government?
>
> – sustaining the fundamental aspects of the Thatcher revolution?
>
> – NATO?
>
> If 'yes', then obviously the newspaper should not give good beliefs a bad name by supporting idiocy. But every Tom, Dick, [Robert] Fisk and sometimes [Simon] Jenkins is ready at the drop of a funeral to proclaim that this and that action is 'pure idiocy' – that is their job. An editor's job is:

1. To doubt, almost by nature, the enthusiasms of his pundits when they talk that way or
2. to give at least the benefit of the doubt to the upholders of his anchor beliefs when they are under attack: eg above

– Tory government, Thatcher revolution, NATO. If the editor is in doubt, then he should give himself time to think by a) rallying solidly to the cause of his anchor beliefs on the first day, giving himself the chance of second thoughts later, or b) waffling a bit to give himself time to think . . . until more is known.

In a way I think *The Times* [which supported Thatcher on Libya] did better than us last week. They waited till Friday, and only then came up with a memorable leader which . . . marked the first turn of the intellectual tide.

I confess that I recalled John O'Sullivan's amused and ironical remark to us . . . that the *Times* and *Telegraph* seemed to be changing sides, with the *Times* now becoming the natural thinking paper of the intellectual right.

. . . Perhaps that is the key phrase for an editor: steadiness of purpose.

Andrew went on to argue the detailed case for Reagan's action against Libya. He made the point that Reagan's military operations against small targets such as Grenada and Libya achieved a deterrent effect out of all proportion to their military significance, even though it might be irrational to leave unscathed major sponsors of international terrorism such as East Germany and Syria. He concluded: 'The *Telegraph* needs to fashion a strategic view of its domestic priorities, its attitude to local deterrence and the projection of power. Columnists can enjoy the privilege of picking through this menu *à la carte*, picking here, choosing there. If its readers are to keep their bearings and their familiarity with it, a newspaper cannot.'

The memorandum was characteristic of Andrew: cool, rational, well argued. I never resented such notes – of which there were more than a few over the years – because I was conscious of how much I had to learn as an editor, and also of how large a personal stake Andrew possessed in my success or failure. On the point of substance: years later I was discussing the Libyan bombing with Professor Sir Michael Howard, an old and admired friend. 'It worked,' he said. 'It worked. Even though I was against it at the time, afterwards it became plain that the bombing had deterred Gaddafy from high-profile terrorism.' Thus, with hindsight, Andrew could call upon powerful support for the view he took at the time. Yet even on the long view, I found myself in rare disagreement with Michael Howard, as with Andrew. Gaddafy shipped more than twice the weight of arms to the IRA after the Tripoli bombing that he had sent before. There is little doubt that Libya had a large hand in the Pan Am Lockerbie bombing, which took place nearly three years after Tripoli was attacked. Libya became less publicly assertive in its sponsorship of terrorism after the 1986 bombing. But I remain doubtful both about the operation's efficacy and about British participation.

Entwined in the debate about the *Telegraph*'s handling of the specific issue, there was also, of course, another matter: whether the paper bore a responsibility to back the Tory government anyway, right or wrong. On this, I did not hesitate. If the *Telegraph* under my editorship was merely to continue to act as the voice of Conservative Central Office, then I could not achieve the objectives for which Conrad and Andrew had employed me. I believed that many of the sentiments Andrew expressed in his memo were valid only if a newspaper was to be perceived as an arm of the executive, which in my view it was not. *The Daily Telegraph* must always be a Conservative newspaper, but I wanted it to become a sceptical, independent voice.

Because I wore pinstripe suits, belonged to clubs, lived a traditional Conservative rural lifestyle, and shared many Tory views, more than a few Tories supposed me far more right-wing than I have ever been. Their disillusionment was correspondingly great during my first year or two at the *Telegraph*, when I showed my hand progressively on the issues of the day, as these emerged onto the front pages. It would have been naive to expect that the Right would sacrifice its traditional dominance of the *Telegraph* without a struggle. Paul Johnson was among the first to express scorn for my political conduct of the paper, writing in *The Spectator*. He was soon in strident company. I knew that plenty of Tory voices were expressing to Conrad and Andrew their private disdain for what I was doing. Anthony Howard, a sardonically detached observer, remarked to Nick Garland that he did not expect me to last much past Christmas: 'He based this view on Max's poor showing so far, and on what he thinks about the hard-headedness of Black and Knight.'

The chorus of criticism rose dramatically in volume during the course of the summer, as the issue of South Africa began to make headlines once more. For a good many years, the *Telegraph* had been one of the last important media bastions of support in the West for the white Nationalist apartheid regime. *Telegraph* writers had always been welcome in Pretoria, even when work permits were almost unobtainable for journalists from less favourably disposed titles. Soon after I became Editor, I was invited to lunch at the Savoy by the South African Embassy in London, and duly presented myself to meet the Ambassador and two of his aides.

After the conventional courtesies, he enquired in the inimitable nasal tones of the Cape: 'And when did you last visit our great country, Mr Hastings?'

'He had not been well briefed, I reflected.

'1977.'

'Oh dear, oh dear, Mr Hastings. Why so long?'

'You expelled me. It was just after your Justice Minister Jimmy Kruger announced that Steve Biko's murder left him cold, and got a chorus of laughs by saying "I, too, shall be sorry when I die." I wrote a piece about Mr Kruger which your people didn't like. They have refused every application I have since made for a work permit.'

The South African delegation reeled. After a silence, the

Ambassador made a brave attempt at recovery: 'Oh well, of course
there will be no problem in the future about anything of that
kind.' We parted civilly enough, but it was plainly a shock for the
embassy to discover that the *Telegraph* had fallen into the hands
of a journalist committed to black majority rule. On 13 June, I
wrote my first leader about South Africa, in the wake of President
Botha's Declaration of a State of Emergency. It seemed a good
moment to set out my stall: 'A black majority will ultimately
prevail and govern there. The question . . . is not whether but
when.' Next day, I wrote: 'The world is closing in on South Africa
. . . What Mr Botha has declared is not a state of emergency, but
a state of siege. The curtain has gone up for the last act, of
uncertain duration.' Nick Garland recorded that the old *Telegraph*
leader writers agreed among themselves that this was the worst
editorial the paper had ever carried. I believed then, as I do now,
that this was merely because they so profoundly disagreed with it.
Andrew Knight was also highly critical, however, and described it
to Charles Moore at a dinner party as 'pathetic . . . just not good
enough'. A week later, I wrote another leader on South Africa,
saying: 'The State of Emergency is perceived by the world as a
desperate measure to shore up the crumbling edifice of white
supremacy. As such it is indefensible, and it is essential that the
British government should be seen to condemn it . . . It seems
historically inevitable that white minority government in South
Africa will pass within our lifetimes. It will be a misfortune for the
Conservative Party as well as for Britain, if we are perceived to be
resisting the tide of fate.' Jo Grimond, the former Liberal leader,
wrote a leader-page article for us under the heading: 'Only
South Africa threatens South Africa'. Peter Simple in his column
continued to denounce the forces of change, but the thrust of
the paper's coverage was unmistakable, and deeply shocking to the
Right. Lord Hartwell sent me a note on 20 June:

> Your leader on South Africa this morning seemed to me to
> go much further than we have ever gone before and to be a

little over the top. What it seems to be advocating is an early commitment to one man one vote, with its corollary, if the rest of Africa is to be taken as a pattern, of a unitary black one party state ... I do not think it is logical to assume that there will be a black government there within the next twenty years ... Even Helen Suzman has gone no further than a proposal for a federal government. Please do not think I am trying to urge you to do something you do not want to do. I do not claim to be an expert on South Africa, and I have never been there. The above, therefore, is merely for your consideration.

In my answer on 23 June, I suggested that any excess in one political direction by *The Daily Telegraph* was more than counterbalanced by Perry Worsthorne's enthusiastic expressions of support for President Botha and his apartheid regime in the *Sunday*. Perry wrote, in direct riposte to my own editorial: 'Such deterministic views about the tides of history, etc., are almost always bunk ... [The Afrikaners] will almost certainly prove invincible at any rate for the foreseeable future.' This ideological crossing of swords between Perry and me did not go unnoticed elsewhere in Fleet Street. I made a deadpan comment, in answer to an enquiry from the *Standard*'s Londoner's Diary: 'Perry Worsthorne and I have somewhat different views on South Africa. Since both newspapers have editorial freedom, both are free to express it.' To Lord Hartwell, I wrote: 'I admit that I do feel very strongly about South Africa, as do most of my generation. I think it is very difficult to take an entirely detached moral or political view of any society so fundamentally founded upon injustice of the most grievous kind.' Andrew Knight seized the occasion of a subsequent leader, suggesting a more tolerant attitude towards the use of cannabis, to write on 16 July:

At a time when we have tested the traditional loyalty of our readers by attacking Thatcher in her loneliest hour over Libya, and lunged a bit over South Africa, we now contemplate

legalisation of cannabis . . . However discussable these are as
notions in liberal Princeton or metropolitan London drawing
rooms, they simply are not what our yeoman readers look to
the *Telegraph* for. Our retired colonels will abandon it in
droves if we do not put down anchors in a seabed of clear,
firm attitudes well and openly argued. Every month now, we
give readers a shock, a further uncertainty to doubt us . . .

I answered Andrew:

I am not . . . averse to stirring controversy on our leader page
. . . We need more provocative journalism on the page, not
less . . . I am not displaying casualness about what goes in
the leader column when I say that the future of the paper
in the next few critical months will depend far more on
what we can make of the general shape of our pages than
on the content of the leaders. I am astonished how very
little correspondence our leaders provoke, either positive or
negative.

I think their importance is much greater in influencing
perceptions of ourselves at Westminster than in selling the
paper . . . It is interesting that the market research suggests
that so many readers buy us in spite of our politics, not
because of them. These thoughts in no way signal reluctance
from me to receive your strictures . . . You have all the
experience I lack. I try not to make same mistake twice. But
I believe we are making progress, and I really think the
number of things going wrong is outweighed by the number
going right.

The general tone of our leaders about domestic politics
remained respectful of Mrs Thatcher's leadership, and supportive
of many aspects of government policy. Yet we could scarcely
ignore the mounting unease in both the Conservative Party and
the country about the authoritarian manner of her governance.
John Biffen, the Leader of the Commons, found himself in hot

water when he suggested that his leader should 'promote a more caring image'. We commented on 13 May:

> There is a need for a change of tone. Mrs Thatcher's taste for 'presidential politics', her tendency to preach, and her false belief that the British electorate likes its prime minister always to seem 'a great international statesman' – all this should be corrected, or at least modified. But she and her Cabinet cannot, without absurdity and humiliation, abandon the very themes of their existence – the need for sound money and for turning back the frontiers of state economic control and expanding private choice. Mr Biffen's counsel is worth attention, but why should it not have been given in private? Possibly, of course, because it would not have been listened to. In that case, Mrs Thatcher has another lesson to learn.

The Prime Minister came to lunch at the paper one day in the autumn. It was not an auspicious occasion. The serried ranks of the Fleet Street building's commissionaires had been deployed to greet her, and to keep a lift in readiness to waft her to the fifth-floor dining room. I met the Prime Minister and Bernard Ingham on the pavement, led them to the lift, pressed the button – and plunged promptly to the basement, where the doors opened to reveal a crowd of curious and dishevelled printers. If this confirmed our guest's perception of my incompetence in practical matters, the conversation at lunch did not improve matters. It remained frosty and strained. Bill Deedes, Jock Bruce-Gardyne, together with Perry Worsthorne and Bruce Anderson from *The Sunday Telegraph*, were present. It was Bruce, oddly enough, though later regarded as a diehard Thatcher loyalist, who on this occasion battered his heroine with a succession of provocative questions, which did nothing to ease the atmosphere. I heard later that she had expressed bitter displeasure about the lunch to Bernard Ingham in the car back to Downing Street. 'You noticed the sinister thing?' she enquired darkly. 'Bill Deedes never said a word.'

If relations between the *Telegraph* and Downing Street were now strained, a further development sufficed to render them permanently glacial. All summer, we were dispensing with a steady stream of staff for whom new heads of department could see no role in the paper we were creating. William Rees-Mogg once wrote magisterially about my stewardship of the *Telegraph*, criticizing me as 'a sacking editor'. This, he argued, mitigated against the maintenance of stability and harmony among staff. I could not accept Rees-Mogg's stricture, which seemed merely to reflect his view that the sole business of an editor is intellectual, and that little heed is necessary to the less exalted aspects of newspaper management. If the *Telegraph* was to survive, never mind prosper, we had to shake off a great deadweight of staff who were contributing nothing, and who were filling posts badly needed for new talent. Conrad once declared approvingly before an audience that 'Max is good at drowning kittens.' This may not have enhanced my popularity, but helps to explain my longevity in office.

Early in the autumn of 1986, Veronica Wadley gave me a list of people in her department whom she believed must go. One of these was Carol Thatcher, not least because it seemed conspicuously unfair to make others redundant while she remained. I handled personally most of the awkward interviews about staff departures. Summoning Carol one morning, I told her that we thought it would be difficult to find a role for her in the new Features Department. I suggested that she should start looking around for another job. 'Take your time,' I said easily. 'It is obviously in everybody's best interests to do this discreetly and amicably.' I sat back in my chair, comfortably conscious of a sticky conversation well managed. I was disabused.

'That may be in your interests, but it's not in mine,' said Carol briskly. 'If you want to get rid of me, you'd better just sack me, the way you have done to lots of other people.'

'But surely,' I spluttered, 'it's not a good idea to have this all over the front pages.'

'That's your problem, not mine. All I've ever wanted is to be treated like everybody else. That's why I work in England and my brother doesn't. You want to get rid of me – you'll just have to pay me some money to go away.'

Nonplussed, for I was genuinely unable to perceive any advantage to Downing Street, any more than to ourselves, in adopting Carol's uncompromising solution, I parted from her to consult colleagues, lawyers and Andrew Knight. He was dismayed, and inclined to temporize. But matters had gone too far for that. We saw no choice save to make the Prime Minister's daughter redundant. I was naive enough to cherish some hopes that her departure might pass unnoticed. Carol loudly vented her dismay to her friends. A spate of headlines in the gossip columns followed. *The Mirror*'s cartoonist Griffin published a drawing of the foaming Prime Minister shouting down the telephone at me.

'What do you mean by sacking my daughter. We're trying to get the unemployment figures DOWN!'

Griffin's cartoon for the *Daily Mirror* when Carol Thatcher left *The Telegraph*. In reality, the Prime Minister never rang me, but the tone is right.

Mrs Thatcher was furious about the *Telegraph*'s treatment of her daughter, which she perceived as a calculated insult to herself. I told Conrad that I had hoped she might perceive my decision as Thatcherism in practice. 'Far from that, Max,' he replied bleakly, 'she sees it as Hastingsism in action, and she likes no part of it!' For some days, I trembled for my chair amid the fevered publicity, and the unconcealed wrath of Downing Street.

A couple of years later, when Jock Bruce-Gardyne was fatally ill, I gave him what both of us knew was a farewell lunch, tête-à-tête at Brooks's. Jock, who I don't think had ever much liked me, was characteristically blunt. 'I'll tell you the moment at which I thought you'd gone mad,' he said, fixing me with his glittering eyes, 'when you sacked Carol Thatcher. You can't go around sacking Prime Ministers' daughters. I'll add this: if it had been Mark you ditched, you wouldn't still be editor of *The Daily Telegraph* today!'

Whether or not Jock was right, Carol Thatcher's departure was a turning point. Her mother never spoke to me again while she was Prime Minister, though oddly enough she began to send me Christmas cards after her retirement, when the *Telegraph* became critical of her successor. In most respects, exile to outer darkness made my job easier. Had I been subject to regular grillings at Downing Street, as was the lot of some of my Fleet Street peers, I might have found it more difficult to retain the paper's independence of judgement. As it was, from that moment I knew that I could expect no favours or even civilities from the Prime Minister. I ceased to think much about whether the paper was generating storms or sunshine in Downing Street. Charles Moore observed at lunch one day that editors of major Conservative newspapers had become accustomed to receiving knighthoods, but somehow it seemed unlikely that I would be getting one from Mrs Thatcher (Bill Deedes described Harold Macmillan's attitude to handing out baubles to those who needed sweetening as 'giving him a little something to wear under his white tie').

In the paper's Features pages, we were pushing women's rights and women's issues in a fashion the *Telegraph* had never contemplated before. My own enthusiasm in this area was reinforced by a growing belief that woman newspaper writers and executives are more professional, hard-working, loyal, rational and disciplined than many of their male counterparts. Editorially, we attacked the government's plans to privatize the water industry. We opposed the ban on the voices of IRA members being publicly broadcast. We campaigned strongly against Mrs Thatcher's War Crimes Act and Broadcasting Act, which threw open ITV's franchises to a crude cash auction. I criticized the Prime Minister's failure to protect the underclass, in a full-length leader:

> It is a serious weakness of this government that its rhetoric fails to address a problem which disturbs even some of its strongest supporters – the institutionalising of an underclass which seems destined to play no part in the real triumphs of the Thatcherite revolution. Losers there must be, in a society which has restored winning to its proper place as a social virtue. The protection of those losers is also a virtue, however.

Facing our leader was an entire op-ed page devoted to an examination of winners and losers from the government's welfare shake-up, and an analysis of the difficulties this created for the underclass.

Given Conrad Black's passionate personal admiration for Mrs Thatcher, and looking back on the exchanges above, it is remarkable that I survived my first two or three years as Editor of *The Daily Telegraph*. Late in the summer of 1987, Andrew wrote me another 2,000-word memorandum on the nature of editorship, in which he argued that I should appoint a political deputy, or at least a senior leader writer, as soon as possible, to 'maintain the coherence of policy' on the paper. I was unwilling to do this, though I did not say so. I believed such an appointment would be a fatal blow to my own authority. Through most of the years ahead, the *Telegraph* provided a platform for all manner of voices, including some very right-wing ones. There was a rotating cast of bright young political aspirants at the leader conference – Simon Heffer, Daniel Johnson, Oliver Letwin, Michael Trend, and later Richard Ehrman, Dean Godson, Paul Goodman. Most became more or less openly frustrated by the paper's 'wet' tone, and several departed in consequence. I admired the literary gifts of our young Tory turks, but was dismayed by the reluctance some displayed to acquire a store of personal experience before settling down to a lifetime of armchair – or House of Commons – punditry.

I originally hired Simon Heffer as an expert on health matters, at the urging of Peter Utley. It was quickly clear that Simon was a superb natural journalist. He was clever, well read, and wrote with speed and fluency. I was initially somewhat bemused that he had chosen to cast himself at the age of twenty-five as an old Tory sage of sixty. Red-haired, portly, invariably clad in double-breasted suit and old college tie, he had created a persona which seemed to be modelled upon a 1920s Dornford Yates caricature of an English gentleman. Enoch Powell was his idol. I was alarmed when he mentioned with approval in an article Sir William Joynson-Hicks, perhaps the most reactionary Home Secretary of the twentieth century. I urged Simon to travel, to see the world, to discover what happened to real people in terrible circumstances, as in South Africa. On one occasion, I proposed dispatching him to Afghanistan for a few weeks with the mujahedin, an assignment I would have sacrificed three fingers for when I was his age. He temporized for a few days, then told me that Afghanistan was not remotely his sort of thing, that Afghan food would have a disastrous effect on his insides. I once cajoled him into spending a few weeks in Washington, but he later refused a permanent American posting. I have always felt that Simon's talents would have yielded him greater rewards, had he been willing to test prejudice, an armoury of implacably held opinions, against some contact with the humbler realities of human affairs.

Yet though I sought to limit the influence of the Right on the paper to signed pieces, I never held the view that I could expect editorial freedom to be an absolute. Andrew in one of his notes to me listed the constraints as: 1) the tolerance of the readership, 2) the need to maintain the broad confidence of the board and 3) of Conrad. 'An editor who is a player at the top table, a participant to an extent in national debate, policy and conduct . . . will lose his authority over a period,' Andrew wrote, 'if he relies on expressing the common denominator of a broad church among staff or, indeed, if he gives any impression that he is acting reluctantly for somebody else (e.g. Conrad or me). He has to determine his own conduct given the undoubted freedoms which he has, and the undoubted limits to that freedom.'

Although I could sometimes have used a few more words of praise from Andrew and Conrad, and a touch less criticism, all this seemed perfectly reasonable. Editors of a few newspapers such as *The Sunday Times* under Lord Thomson's enlightened owner- ship, or the titles of the aforementioned Rothermeres, have pos- sessed genuine independence. Whatever protestations other titles make about editorial freedom, this is seldom wholly unconstrained. *The Washington Post*'s editors, for instance, were expected for many years to defer to the views of the paper's publisher, the legendary Kay Graham, who frequently attended editorial confer- ences. Most British newspapers are owned by businessmen who expect their titles to reflect their own views strategically, if not on a day-to-day basis. I am a professed free-marketeer. I never felt embarrassed about tempering my own opinions when I believed that it was in the wider interest of *The Daily Telegraph* to do so. I believed that such a paper as ours should maintain a bias in favour of the status quo. But I took a much bolder view than Andrew about what our readers would swallow. I was convinced that we must create a newspaper for a readership of the future, not for survivors of the past.

Retired colonels were a dwindling breed. When the House of Commons held one of its periodic votes on capital punishment,

I wrote in a leader that 'hanging in a modern society is quite unacceptable'. Though four members of the Cabinet and fifteen other ministers voted to restore the rope, there was no great outcry from readers about our declared view. I believed that many, probably most *Telegraph* readers understood that we were living in a new world (no matter whether or not they welcomed it) in which hanging, apartheid and overt contempt for johnny foreigner were no longer acceptable to any reasonable person, save a handful of ageing *Telegraph* columnists in the Peter Simple mould. As for the proprietor, I have always thought it absurd for anyone to pretend that the owner of newspapers is not entitled to a measure of deference from those whom he employs to write for them and run them, including his editors. Since Conrad was the principal shareholder in the paper, it would have appeared discourteous to trample gratuitously on his most cherished convictions. The issue became more difficult, however, if a strongly held belief of mine came into collision with one of his own. When Conrad first expressed vigorous dissent from a position we had expressed in a leader, I urged him to write a letter for publication. It seemed perfectly proper that he should have a platform in his own newspaper to express his views, and far more honest that he should do so openly in the Letters column, rather than by privately urging changes in our leaders. The Chairman's published letters (sometimes of remarkable length) prompted some mockery of the paper from rival titles, but I am confident this was the right way to ensure that the proprietor maintained a voice. I am relieved to have relinquished my *Telegraph* chair before I had to make decisions about the editorial acceptability of publishing Lady Black's formidably fluent and fantastically long articles about Israel, which have become such a feature of the *Telegraph* in recent times.

It did no harm to my professional relationship with Conrad that socially I enjoyed his company and he seemed also to enjoy mine. Lunches and dinners with the Chairman sometimes stretched on for hours. I could be certain of provoking him by asserting my own conviction that before the coming of Hitler, no dictator had wrought greater misery upon Europe than Napoleon; and at least today Germans readily admit that Hitler was a mistake, while the French idolize their home-grown tyrant. Faced with such provocation, Conrad's response was good for a couple of hours.

When we dined, I had to plead for my bed at eleven or twelve. He was lonely when he came to Britain at that period. He had not yet become the social lion of later years. Beneath the bombastic exterior, there was a streak of insecurity and vulnerability that I warmed to. Conrad can be extremely witty. No man can make himself more agreeable. His intellect is formidable, and he possesses an endearing glint of self-knowledge about his own pomposity. Demonstrations of his extraordinary memory for the minutiae of history, catalogues of Presidents' and Prime Ministers' terms through history and suchlike, are delivered with a hint of conscious self-parody, or at least they were in those days. Conrad sometimes failed to appreciate the nuances of a British broadsheet newspaper – for instance, he supposed that it was as necessary for a leader-page article to reflect the editorial views of that title as for the leaders to do so – but he possessed an eagle eye for solecisms. Here is a typical Conrad missive, from September 1986:

Dear Max,

    . . . I agree with most of the points you made [in a letter of mine to CB], and particularly that a good and well-motivated team is taking shape. I am not so convinced that our readers easily distinguish between opinions in leaders and those which are published in the spaces next to the leaders, unless the latter are very carefully presented. It is certainly desirable for us to live down our stuffy and overly partisan image which is now at some variance with the facts, but I am fearful that without very careful management, we could alienate the bedrock of our support – which has been extraordinarily solid and loyal – without impressing those whom we wish to attract. One does not have to agree with everything Paul Johnson says, to feel that firmer daily political coordination than you or any editor overseeing a whole newspaper can possibly supply is necessary on the leader and op-ed spread.

I have two minor comments on detail in last week's editions.

It was somewhat irritating to read in Godfrey Barker's review of the play Eleanor that Franklin D Roosevelt died in Mrs Rutherfurd's house. Every informed person in the world knows that he died in his own house at Warm Springs, Georgia, although Mrs Rutherfurd and a number of his own people were present when his cerebral haemorrhage occurred.

Similarly, in Saturday's account of the present NATO exercises off Norway, it was annoying to read that the battleship *Iowa* was, next to the *Nimitz*, the largest ship in the US Navy. There are 14 other aircraft carriers in service that are much larger vessels.

These are small points, but you should discourage our writers from making unnecessary and un-researched assertions that are in fact untrue. I realise that you have other matters to deal with, but I would have been remiss if I had not at least indicated again how closely I am following your progress.

With Best Wishes,

I might have replied to Conrad that it is the nature of newspapers, and the extraordinary speed at which they are produced, that even the greatest titles have to live with a daily roll-call of errors far more alarming than those which he noticed. As it was, I confined myself to telling the writers responsible for the pieces which caught Conrad's eye that their sins had not gone unnoticed.

Conrad's mention of Paul Johnson irked me. While I admired Paul as an historian, I regarded his political views as extravagant. He exercised considerable influence, however, in the right-wing social circles which Conrad frequented in London. Andrew Knight wrote Paul several long notes, copied to me, explaining his hopes for the papers, and implicitly seeking the *Spectator* columnist's acquiescence. I thought this correspondence a waste of ink, if not a rash admission of vulnerability, in dealing with a man as intemperate as Paul. At Andrew's behest I did, however, unwillingly go to lunch with him a couple of times. These meetings were strained, because Paul was visibly struggling with his rage about the grotesquerie, as he saw it, of my masquerade as a newspaper editor. On various occasions, harsh words were spoken by Paul, to which I responded in kind. Yet when we met after one bad-tempered exchange, to my surprise he began with a barked apology: 'I shouldn't have spoken to you as I did last time we met.'

'Oh come on, Paul, we both behaved pretty badly.'

'Yes, yes, but I am the older man, so it was for me to behave better.'

One never knew from one day to the next what to expect from that spectacularly choleric figure. Passing him at a party of an evening, I asked cheerfully: 'Are we on speakers at the moment, or not, Paul?' The great sage gnashed his teeth – the only occasion outside the pages of P. G. Wodehouse that I have known this feat physically accomplished – and snarled: 'No, we are not. You are a swine and a guttersnipe of the lowest sort. And what's more, if you weren't a coward as well, you'd hit me for saying that!' I could never bring myself either to hate Paul, or to fear him. For all his literary gifts, absolute lack of judgement rendered him finally ridiculous. But it was irritating to know that others in our building took his views seriously. I wrote to Conrad, 'violent Conservatism of Paul's variety is not a commercial proposition, but a commercial liability . . . Our brand of Conservatism *must* be forward looking.' We occasionally invited Paul to contribute to the paper, and some of his pieces were well done, but he was never any friend of my editorship.

Most important to my survival at the *Telegraph*, I think, was the simple fact that on many issues, I was not in disagreement with Conrad or Andrew. Europe had not yet attained the primacy in Conservative debate which it would assume in the 1990s. On Cold War matters – and remember that in the mid-1980s there was little hint of the dramatic thaw to come – on the economy and most domestic policy questions, I was every inch a 'sound' Tory. I supported control of immigration, low taxation, private enterprise, the right of management to manage, strong defence, family values insofar as these could be reconciled with irresistible changes in society, warm beer, teasing the French and foxhunting. Above all, at that period few people even on the left of the Conservative party perceived much temptation to defect elsewhere. Certainly, I did not. The Opposition led by Neil Kinnock remained committed to unilateral nuclear disarmament, Clause 4 nationalization and old Labour's bleakly familiar economic policies of tax and spend. In June 1987, Kinnock was proclaiming his undiminished commitment to 'a major extension of public ownership and control'. His party seemed wholly unfit to govern Britain. Week after week, we carried editorials heaping scorn and derision on Labour's principles and performance. Composing these was among the least demanding tasks that fell to my lot.

The *Telegraph* constantly reiterated that the Conservatives under Margaret Thatcher were the only credible rulers of the country. We argued that they still had much to do to complete the 'Thatcher revolution'. We were increasingly critical of the government's failure to address the huge problems of the public services, and of its folly in placing unlimited faith in the ability of privatization to solve all problems. These were details, however. In the pages above, much has been said about issues on which there were tensions between myself, Andrew and Conrad. There were also many days, however, on which old *Telegraph* readers found themselves reading leaders that could as well have been written under the old regime. This was no embarrassment. I was not in the business of promoting change for change's sake, nor of seeking to ruffle feathers gratuitously. Indeed, at that period of chronic turbulence for the paper, I was grateful for each day when there seemed no necessity to engage in combat with the government, our own management or readers. We had enough to do, on our own doorstep.

4

GLEAM OF LIGHT

FEAR OF FAILURE hung heavy over me – and, I think, over Andrew also with the banks' cold eyes upon us – throughout our first years at the *Telegraph*. Yet it would be wrong to convey the impression that it was thus a gloomy time. There was the constant exhilaration of helming a great newspaper; the companionship of colleagues whom I loved and admired; and plenty of laughter. The only editor I had worked closely with and admired was Charles Wintour of the *Evening Standard*. Inevitably, perhaps, I modelled my own management style on his, notably by distributing a daily stream of memos (which became known, with varying degrees of enthusiasm, as 'Maxograms') to every corner of the building, offering praise or blame. My purpose, of course, was to convey the impression that no good or bad deed passed unnoticed by the Editor's eagle eye, though I fear that a certain scepticism persisted about whether I read Sports pages properly. I also believed that an editor should inspire fear as well as respect. I wanted anyone rebuked by me to know that he or she had been in a fight. The cost of success in this direction was a widespread belief that *Private Eye* had been right to nickname me 'Hitler', not merely for alliterative reasons. I doubt, however, if a successful manager in any walk of life succeeds by pursuing any other principles.

My working day started and finished earlier than that of most editors, because that was the way I liked to do it. Once I finished my Korean War book and the dawn patrol which this had demanded, I normally rose at 7 a.m., and was driven to the office from my company flat in Notting Hill by Bill Anderson. In the car, I studied the morning papers, making notes. Half a lifetime in this business has persuaded me to believe most stories if they appear in the *Financial Times* or *International Herald Tribune*, and thereafter to recognize a diminishing scale of credibility which bottoms out with the *Express* and *Daily Star*. I aimed to be at my desk by eight. Ettie, who worked the early shift, was already bustling about opening mail and making tea in an otherwise deserted office. She was often rolling her eyes and clucking over the first lunatic of the morning. Deranged people telephone and write to newspapers in large numbers, imposing considerable strain on the people who must take their calls or answer their interminable screeds. Overworked News Desks have a regrettable tendency to dismiss angry readers brusquely. Editors' secretaries are expected to be more decorous. Those who suppose racism an extinct phenomenon would be rapidly disabused by listening to the diatribes against blacks, Jews, socialists, the yellow peril and suchlike to which the secretaries of newspaper editors are routinely subjected. After a few unfortunate experiences, I myself never picked up an outside call in the office, for fear of encountering a foaming reader. For some reason, the closer to dawn the caller came on the line, the more persistent he or she was likely to prove. Ettie was seldom able to clear the line in less than fifteen minutes. Her patience and sympathy were marvellous to behold. I could only hear her end of the conversation, but this enabled me to guess what was going on at the other: 'Yes. Yes. Yes. I agree. It's awful. It's shocking. It shouldn't be allowed. Yes. Yes. I'm so sorry that Mr Hastings is tied up just now. Do you think it would be helpful to write a letter? Yes. I'll see he gets it. I'm sure he'll understand. Yes. Yes. Absolutely. Thank you.' Phew.

With my tea, Ettie brought the morning budget of office gossip. There was more clucking and headshaking: 'What are we going to do about that Michael?' – all names have been changed here, for obvious reasons – 'You'll never bring him round to what you're trying to do, and he's an awful Mr Gloom to have about the place' . . . 'You know Diana's having a walk-out with Peter the

News sub?' . . . 'Do you really want to go to that dinner at the Belgian Embassy on the 18th? You know you'll only be sorry when the time comes.' I seldom took any personal or professional decision without consulting Ettie.

After those opening exchanges, I had a precious hour or so in which to think undisturbed, or to consult with Jeremy Deedes. When could we get rid of that subeditor who was no good? How should I respond to a note from Andrew Knight about staffing? Where could we find a new woman feature writer with a detailed knowledge of technology, chess and men's fashion? There were usually a couple of long notes to be drafted. I might have to compose a letter for Conrad or simply an aide-memoire to myself about priorities. Executives in any field are often forgiven for making bad decisions, but never for indecision. I admire the Duke of Wellington's adage, when asked late in life to what he attributed his success: 'I always did the business of the day on the day.' My chronic impatience sometimes irritated colleagues. There was much teasing, and some genuine dismay, about the manner in which the Editor's foot started to twitch restlessly if a visitor had failed to make his point within say, five minutes. Critics deplored the brevity of my attention span. Yet rapid thought and consequent action, as well as serendipity, are essential ingredients of success in any media organization. Each night when I quit the office, I sought to leave behind an empty desk.

I never posted a note on anything important without first showing it to the Editorial Director. If Jeeves had gone to Eton and embarked upon a career in journalism, he might have turned into Jeremy. Urbane, sympathetic, witty, discreet, shrewd, he was arguably the key figure in enabling me to accomplish the transformation of *The Daily Telegraph* without impaling myself on my own misjudgements. If a crisis with Management was looming, again and again he found means of deflecting confrontation by patient mediation. My wife referred to him as my nanny, on the basis that I seemed incapable of taking a decision without him. I told a *Financial Times* interviewer that Jeremy would be my

preferred choice of companion on a desert island. Many times I
plunged into his office at 8 a.m. exclaiming 'Crisis, Baldrick,
crisis!' I would emerge twenty minutes later confident that we
could find a way out of whatever drama threatened. Andrew
Knight applauded Jeremy as a steadying influence on me. 'We
really owe you a great debt for bringing him into the company,' he said one day. I have always believed that the Royal
Family might have spared themselves some of their worst tribulations had they employed Jeremy as their chief executive. I
suggested such a course to Buckingham Palace on more than one
occasion. Happily for me, but not for the Palace, the idea was
never pursued.

By the autumn of 1986, Andrew Knight and Conrad's lawyer,
Dan Colson, had made one vital decision: the *Telegraph* must quit
its Fleet Street offices. Not only would the cost of modernizing
and cabling the old building for new technology be prohibitive;
if we departed, it would become much easier to leave behind
thousands of staff the company must shed to survive. Our new
management possessed a critical advantage: Rupert Murdoch's
victory over the print unions and their riotous picket lines at
Wapping had opened the way for the transformation of working
practices throughout the industry in the years that followed. No
other newspaper company faced comparable union resistance over
the introduction of new technology. There were negotiations,
there were rows and tensions, to which our company was prey as
much as any. But when the showdown came, the *Telegraph* and
other titles could begin to operate new plant at vastly reduced
cost, without long and expensive battles.

Our own staff hoped desperately that we could find a new
building in central London. I took senior executives to visit a
couple of likely sites, the Adelphi building behind the Strand and
Sea Containers House on the river opposite Blackfriars. Our hopes
were lifted, then dashed when the deals fell through – we were
gazumped at Sea Containers by Customs & Excise, so poor
were we and so rich the Civil Service (Andrew Knight protested

in Whitehall, and was told by a minister: 'Everybody in government is much too frightened of C&E to deny them anything'). It became increasingly clear that the cash incentives on offer to a struggling company for a move to the vast new office developments in Docklands were irresistible. By the spring of 1987, we found ourselves committed to a small six-floor building still under construction, on the waterside at South Quay Plaza. The compensation was that with exile from central London came the big leap into new technology, on-screen journalism, which represented liberation for every journalist from generations of tyranny by the printers. Everyone from Bill Deedes downwards quickly adjusted to working on our new Atex computer keyboard system. Henceforward, 'direct inputting' from screen into page make-ups ended centuries of printer power, and ensured that the published spelling mistakes of journalists became entirely our own fault.

At 9.30 in my office, I held the morning editorial meeting. I began with a few comments on that day's paper, then heads of department recited their diary lists. A key weakness of the old *Telegraph* was lack of coordination. Where every other title had always held conferences, at the *Telegraph* such exchanges of information were unfamiliar. This state of affairs contributed to the sameness of the newspaper. Each morning, its pages looked much like those of the day before. There was no imaginative guiding hand focusing resources, space and presentation on selected News highlights, signalling to readers that some events mattered more than others.

We had to make the paper if not fashionable, then talked-about. Veronica Wadley said: 'We must write more about the kind of people we want to read us.' The *Telegraph* had never lost the respect of the media as a great News paper, first read of the morning for the industry's magpies – and we are all, of course, professional magpies. But it did not offer surprise, electricity, excitement. These were the qualities I was striving to inject. Don Berry began to hold seminars for subs and make-up men, patiently talking them through the principles of modern layout. Over the first year, we achieved a dramatic improvement in our handling of big stories and disasters, urging the back bench, which controlled production, to throw out everything in the early pages to make way for big news when it came. Our new team's first big test of reporting public disaster came with the sinking of the *Herald of Free Enterprise* with the loss of 200 lives, at Zeebrugge on 6 March 1987. Our coverage was a great improvement on anything the old *Telegraph* might have contrived, but it could not match say, *Sunday Times* presentation. By the time of the Piper Alpha oil rig disaster in July 1988, however, we had made a quantum leap forward. The *Telegraph* had never used 'poster' front pages, but we did so on the morning of 13 December, with a huge picture of the dreadful Clapham rail crash which killed 33 people. The story was supported by graphics, explaining what had happened, which were at last worthy of a modern newspaper. Our coverage of the Lockerbie tragedy, which killed 270 people on the night of 21 December 1988, was exemplary, above all for its imaginative picture-editing – traditionally one of our weakest areas. I felt a surge of pride in our pages, and how far we – and above all Don Berry – had brought the paper. Terrible human tragedies test any title to the utmost, because readers' expectations are so high, and judgements of taste are often so difficult. At last, the quality of our reporting was matched by the design and layout of pages. There was a coherence in our handling of the story, which we needed to extend to every aspect of the paper's operations.

Many of the news items listed at the morning conference came to nothing by nightfall, because court cases were postponed, Features pieces failed to measure up or were overtaken by events, morning political rows ebbed into insignificance by afternoon. But it is essential for every editorial team to start somewhere. At conference, I highlighted a couple of items on the News list, suggesting writers or proposing treatments or background Features. Then we canvassed each specialist in turn. The Arts Editor told us what plays and galleries were to be reviewed. The Peterborough

Editor mentioned a couple of likely squibs. Sport gave us pointers on the most promising matches or races. Most of the departmental schedules were rehearsed without comment from me, but they gave everybody a picture of where we were starting from. I expected that meeting to be over in twenty-five minutes.

After the News conference, there was a procession of executives to see. Nigel Wade, the Foreign Editor, might want to discuss whether we should send a reporter to an earthquake in Turkey or to a revolution in the Caribbean. Veronica Wadley would brief me on a possible recruit she wanted me to interview. Andrew Hutchinson reported on the latest round of the argument between the Editorial and Advertising departments, endemic to every newspaper every day, about the number, size and shape of display advertisements on key pages. Editors want the fewest and smallest possible ads; but since our wages must be paid, we are obliged grudgingly to concede advertisers space for their wares. In good times economically, there is plenty of advertising to support generous news space. In recessions, as advertising falls so does pagination. Sometimes the shrinkage is alarming, and thus the need for pressure upon management to subsidize news pages becomes intense and constant.

Jeremy Deedes might come in with our lawyers, to discuss an actual or potential risk of litigation. Most legal threats to newspapers are swiftly disposed of, by an apology and/or the payment of a modest sum of money. The noisiest legal threats almost invariably come from high-profile crooks, the Maxwells and Archers. These cases demand delicate balancing of a newspaper's principled position, against the huge costs of a trial going wrong. In the 1990s, *The Guardian* won great admiration in our industry by persevering with its defence against Jonathan Aitken's libel writ, which would have cost the paper disastrous sums but for a breakthrough at the eleventh hour. All Fleet Street trembled a year or two ago, when the *Daily Mail* had to pay close to a million pounds, after losing an extraordinary case brought by the chairman of a football club, Spurs, about a Sports article which seemed to most of us to represent routine fair comment. The unexpected cases are always the ones which go horribly wrong.

Some of the biggest rows in my years as an editor related, oddly enough, to our Obituaries page. One of the most talented recruits we captured in 1986 was Hugh Montgomery-Massingberd as Obituaries Editor. Hugh's appointment, suggested to me by Ferdy Mount, transformed the *Daily Telegraph*'s Obituary column from a musty backwater of the paper into the most brilliant feature of its kind in the business. Hugh possessed a fervent devotion to his craft, and to telling all. His frankness sometimes caused dismay among relatives of the dead. When poor, mad Lord Rayleigh died, Hugh spared no detail of his eccentricities, and provoked a barrage of furious letters from members of the Strutt family, copied to my home lest I should escape them at the office. 'Cruel ... tasteless ... disgraceful' were among the milder adjectives. 'But everything we said was true!' expostulated Hugh when I called him in.

I drew the line, however, when the dowager Duchess of Buccleuch was known to be close to death. Hugh enquired eagerly: 'Can we say in the Obituary that she was generally known as Midnight Moll?' No, I said firmly. I also seem to remember a row about whether we could report the circumstances of the death of a businessman who had the misfortune to expire while energeti- cally engaged with a girlfriend in a bedroom at the Dorchester. A half-truth was circulated by his family, to the effect that he had died at a sybaritic dinner in the hotel. This prompted a letter to the grieving widow from a friend, who suggested that it must be a comfort for her to know that the old boy had pegged out while doing what he enjoyed most.

Here are some characteristic Massingberd nuggets from 1987: 'Captain Ronald Blacklock, who has died aged 97, was a pioneer submariner and one of the few people still able to recall enjoying the friendship of the Tsar of Russia...' And again: 'Colonel Charles Clark, who has died aged 99, had a remarkable record in the 1914–18 war, and on one memorable occasion set about the organisation of a fox hunt at the front. Encouraged by the presence of a former Master of the Wexford Hounds, Clark and some companions of the South Irish Horse acquired a scruffy fox, whose stamina they built up with a liberal diet of fowl. Unfortunately, before the chase could begin the fox was claimed by a member of another regiment, who proved he had brought the beast to France as a pet, and that it had escaped'. Another Hugh gem was inspired by the death of the Marquess of Huntly, who a few years earlier had married a nurse more than forty years younger than himself. The piece was headed: 'I'm cock of the North,' and recorded that the Marquess defended his engagement by saying: 'I'm a very fit man, I walk my dog every day. I don't have to wear spectacles. I still have my own teeth. Why should I marry some dried-up old bag?'

Hugh's researches were prodigious, and his accuracy was seldom called into question. Within two years of his arrival, his allocated space in the paper had grown to three full columns on most days. But his department somehow attracted trouble. Our most unfortunate Obituary fiasco was no fault of the writers, but merely of a hideous computer error. The Atex system entangled the lives of two prominent peers, one of whom had suffered a series of domestic tragedies. We published a tribute which enraged both families, and caused us in atonement to pay substantial sums of money to each.

Almost every day, there was a potential new recruit to see, some bright young man or woman relatively newly come out of university, who sought a career in the media. I have often heard Bill Deedes lament it as a flaw in our society that so many of the country's ablest young men and women nowadays want to work in our trade, rather than in the public service: 'There is nothing so embarrassing, dear boy, as to watch a not very clever minister being dismembered on television by a visibly much brighter interviewer. We need more brains in government, not in our business.'

In principle, I agreed with Bill, but it is an intoxicating

sensation for any modern media employer to be able to draw upon such a pool of talent. My interviewing and hiring techniques, like those of most editors and most newspapers, were whimsical. I asked what the interviewee imagined himself (herself) doing in a perfect world five years hence. A young Cambridge don, Niall Ferguson, for instance, confidently asserted: 'I want to be the A. J. P. Taylor de nos jours.' One consequence of this aspiration was that we had to dissuade Niall from supposing that it was necessary to mention Bismarck in every leader page he contributed for us. Having heard about a young man or woman's ambition to become (almost invariably) either a foreign correspondent or a political columnist, I asked what newspapers they admired and why. What did they think were the weaknesses of *The Daily Telegraph*? How impressed were they by the recent performance of the Prime Minister? What did they read for pleasure? What movies had they enjoyed? Beyond showing evidence of a lively personality, almost invariably the most important criterion was that a candidate could produce evidence, from university or afterwards, of a real commitment to our business (though a degree in Media Studies usually proves a fatal barrier to employment in the media). Editors look for a passion, a sense of vocation in a would-be recruit, which far transcends mere job-hunting. An uncommonly feisty girl demanded to know whether I thought journalism a gentleman's profession. Absolutely not, I said, it is a trade for cads and bounders. Thus satisfied that she would fit in, she took the job – and prospered.

Most of our new recruits already possessed some journalistic experience. Those who did not, but who seemed to show potential, were given a few weeks' trial either as leader writers, or on Peterborough. Even those who came to us for brief stints during university vacations were always paid. If that seems unremarkable, it may be noted that many television companies now invite young aspirants to work for nothing for months on end, before deciding whether they are worth paying. This seems shamelessly exploitative.

Among my sorties into the recruitment of stars, I tried to persuade Bernard Levin to transfer his column from *The Times* to us, and over lunch offered him a handsome salary. Dear Bernard explained, however, that the only inducement of any interest would be the purchase of a flat. That was a bridge too far. Jilly Cooper also resisted my advances. Her letter caused the almost unshockable Ettie to purse her lips in deep disapproval: 'Dear Max, I won't waste your time on lunch, much as I should love it, because I do hate prick teasers, don't you?'

A generation ago, an editor recruiting for a broadsheet newspaper might have seen some young hopefuls from 'red top' tabloid newspapers. No longer. After a few years working at the bottom of the British newspaper market, most 'red top' journalists are, ipso facto, unfit to work for a broadsheet. All newspapers make factual errors, misjudgements of taste. But a partition now divides British newspapers. On one side of it are those titles which make some honest attempt to tell the truth in what they publish. They swiftly correct errors in print, even without the threat of legal sanctions. On the other side are those which traffic unashamedly in fantasy. The fantasists are presumably happy in their work; but it is impossible to imagine them as reporters on *The Daily Telegraph* or *The Guardian*. This view does not represent snobbery, as 'red top' journalists would assert. It reflects a cultural chasm, which no amount of cant can bridge. British newspapers employ some of the best and worst journalists in the world. 'Red top' and broadsheet reporters no more belong to the same trade, or are pursuing the same objectives, than do abortionists and obstetricians.

In the early days after my elevation, I encountered some embarrassments in dealing with requests from old friends for jobs, or at least for space. Some showed bitterness that now, when I found myself in a position to commission their work, I did not do so. I told friends truthfully that, while I often drew the attention of department heads to possible talent, if the line executives strongly disagreed, I seldom overruled them on a final decision about whom to hire or what to commission. I don't think I ever convinced the disappointed suppliants, but that was the way it was.

From time to time all day, reporters put their heads round the Editor's door, to press their cases either for an exciting assignment (I had done more than my share of this kind of soliciting in my days as a correspondent), a change of job, or to discuss a story they want to pursue. One morning, my visitor was John Miller, a long-serving *Telegraph* foreign correspondent. He had recently been working in Moscow, he said, and had picked up an amazing yarn from a KGB source. The man alleged that British intelligence had been running a mole at high level within Moscow's intelligence service, who was on the brink of exposure. With the Soviet wolves snapping at his heels, in the nick of time the British Secret Intelligence Service smuggled him out of Russia to safety. This sounded an extraordinary tale, on a par with the Hitler Diaries or 'I found Martin Bormann.' I was frankly disbelieving. A high degree of scepticism, especially about spy stories, is indispensable to any broadsheet editor – witness the ghastly embarrassments that befall the credulous.

At the root of my disbelief on this occasion was the nature of the source. If the story was true, and highly embarrassing to the KGB, why should a KGB officer have leaked it? In an uncertain world, I felt confident that it was not the job of *The Daily Telegraph* to run any story that suited the KGB. I asked Miller whether he could make any checks at the British end. He said he had been hoping that I had an SIS contact I could call. I did not. I feared making the paper look absurd if the story was a KGB plant. Remember: the Cold War was still pretty cold in 1986. Whatever my limitations as a Conservative ideologue, I was deeply committed to a belief in 'our side' against 'theirs' in the confrontation between the West and the Soviet Union. I told Miller he had better forget the story, unless he himself could confirm it independently. Sorely disappointed, he left my room and, soon afterwards, the paper. A year or more later, the revelations of Colonel Oleg Gordievsky's defection – he was smuggled out of

Russia by SIS – were splashed over every newspaper, the biggest British intelligence coup for years. Miller had got onto a huge story. As his editor, I had failed him.

Sometimes, it was not for want of trying that we missed a scoop. One evening in the spring of 1987, I took a telephone call from the businessman Sir Jack Lyons. He proved to be in an emotional mood, indeed audibly frightened.

'I want to talk to you about this story you're running about me.'

'What story?'

'The story your people are doing. You should know that if this comes out, it could bring down the government. Thatcher would be finished. The Tories could say goodbye to any chance of winning another election.'

'I'm still at a loss, Sir Jack. What story are we talking about? Could you explain?'

There was a pause, then: 'I'm not saying any more, in case you don't know about it – but you should be warned – you'll do for this government if you print it.'

After I put down the telephone, we spent hours scouring the files, quizzing our City journalists, trying to work out what Lyons could be talking about. Nobody acknowledged awareness of any story related to him. A few weeks later, of course, Lyons was charged alongside Guinness Chairman Ernest Saunders for his part in the huge Distillers takeover scam. I cannot say we felt much sympathy. Saunders shared with Mohammed Fayed of Harrods a disagreeable conviction that he could browbeat newspapers into giving his affairs more sympathetic treatment, by threatening a withdrawal of advertising unless the paper adopted a more sympathetic attitude to his commercial antics.

In the early years of the new *Telegraph*, senior executives spent a formidable amount of time attending meetings with advertising agencies who were soliciting our business, and with market researchers eager to tell us what we were doing wrong. Newspapers are regarded by agencies as nightmare clients, because journalists invariably believe they can create better ads than the copywriters. Our sessions with agencies produced hours of verbiage and precious few credible advertising ideas. We heard a lot about the *Telegraph*'s problem with its 'badge'. The key to most successful products is that young and successful people should want to be known to use or carry them. Nobody young and successful, it seemed, wanted to be seen dead reading the *Telegraph* – or, more accurately, reading the paper was perceived as a signal that the grave was drawing nigh. It was less embarrassing to be spotted deep in *Playboy*. The *Torygraph* was associated with aged grandparents and suburban bank managers. We gained one useful prize from our first ad agency – a reader's game named Passport, offering holiday prizes and shamelessly echoing a *Times* game named Portfolio. The newspaper industry has nowadays learned to be wary about the cost of these forays, which attract thousands of eager games-players who buy a paper for a few weeks, then move on again, from title to title as promotions come and go. But Passport shored up our flagging circulation at a bad time. In the years that followed, expensive TV ad campaigns such as our 'Hitchhikers' Guide to the Galaxy' helped on the margin at least, and showed that there was still life at the *Telegraph*.

Market researchers produced huge reports on our readers' supposed tastes and wishes, which seemed partly statements of the obvious, and partly nonsense. Readers have no rational idea about what they do or do not want in their newspapers – by proxy they employ editors to decide for them. In the beginning, we listened respectfully to the researchers' briefings, and spent hours discussing their conclusions among ourselves. As we gained confidence, however, we understood that it was our job, on the editorial floors, to analyse and satisfy our market, rather than to surrender the problem to expensive researchers. In a memorandum to senior executives, I set out my own analysis of what the paper was, and should aim to be:

> *The Daily Telegraph* is a middlebrow newspaper. While the *Times*, *Independent* and *Guardian* are competitors, we must

never make the mistake of imagining that we are trying to be like them. Our readership operates at a slightly lower intellectual level. A cynic might suggest that the *Telegraph* is for people who think they want a serious newspaper, but really don't. There is a lot of room for making our news coverage more intelligent, but if we overdo this we shall drive readers to the *Daily Mail* ... We must make our pages brighter, better-written and more intelligent, while keeping them accessible.

The *DT* is also 'nice'. Our readers regard the press in general with distaste, and even if they read the *Mail* or *News of the World*, they feel secretly rather ashamed of doing so. We are trying to ensure they never feel ashamed of themselves for reading the *DT*. We wouldn't do – for instance – Penny Junor's book on Prince Charles. One of our most important inheritances from the Berrys is that – page 3 not excepted – this is an honourable newspaper. The *Times* will probably never recover from the memory of the Hitler Diaries fiasco.

One area in which we are achieving real success is coverage of the countryside. It is a fundamental weakness of British newspapers, that they are overwhelmingly written by and for an urban and suburban constituency. Yet even many of those who don't live in the country wish they did, and we do well to show we can identify with them. The essential provincialism of the *Telegraph* has always been one of its charms and virtues. Most of our readers do not merely not want to be metropolitan sophisticates – they dislike such creatures.

Don Berry brilliantly expressed a fundamental thought about the paper the other day: he said that other titles are in the business of telling people each morning that the world is a quite different place from what it was yesterday. The *DT* is much more in the business of reassurance, of providing confirmation each morning for our readers that their world is looking pretty safe and stable. This can make it all the more effective and create all the more impact, on the rare occasions when we tell them that something important and different has happened. We are not a strident campaigning newspaper – our business each day is to seek to give our readers the fullest possible information about what is happening in the world, and to suggest what it might mean.

We should move in a very cautious and measured way towards new developments. [Our new section] is a big success because we spent much advance discussion and preparation on it. Whatever is our next move, we should feel our way towards it with equal care and caution. Above all, we must get the core product right. We still have a long way to go before our News operation is the way I want it to be.

I have urged Andrew Knight and Conrad that the *Sunday Telegraph* is the right platform from which to promote intellectual right-wing conservatism, not the *Daily*. I have argued for our own more liberal line not on principled grounds, but on those of our commercial interests.

I was still concerned that in Conrad's enthusiasm for his wonderful media property, he was too eager to take a 'hands-on' role, especially in political matters, and also in discussing the merits and deficiencies of named writers. George Jones warned me early in 1987 of a growing belief at Westminster that pressure on the *Telegraph* from the government was having some effect; that if Downing Street kept pushing, they might not get me removed, but they could achieve my containment. I wrote to Andrew: 'If the idea gets around that a writer for *The Daily Telegraph* requires some sort of Conservative loyalty test, then we would be in very serious trouble indeed.' I never ventured to commission work from Conrad's special bête noire Christopher Hitchens, though I much admired his dispatches from the United States, where he lived. But a long roll-call of other left-of-centre contributors, from John Mortimer and Peter Kellner to David Owen and Roy Jenkins, appeared in our pages without much proprietorial protest. We even found frequent leader-page slots for Thatcher's most famous critic, Michael Heseltine. It seemed a bridge too far, openly to espouse Michael's cause in the Editorial column. But I gave him all the space I could, ignoring renewed rumblings from Downing Street.

Within the office, I developed an early affection for our young Marketing Director, Stephen Grabiner. Quick, sharp, funny and above all cheerful, it was a pleasure to see Stephen's grinning features poking round the door, a sheaf of papers invariably clutched under his arm. Somebody once described him as 'the sort of kid who at school was always shooting his hand up in class and saying, "Please, sir! Please, sir! I know the answer!"' An insatiable gossip, Grabiner gave me a useful steer on what was happening above us on the management floor, often long before I heard it officially. Though he was a newcomer to the newspaper industry, his views were always worth listening to, even if we did not always act upon them. Above all, he was an optimist. We needed every optimist we had.

Among many criticisms of my regime made by staff from the old *Telegraph*, one was that I adopted too consensual a style of management, and was too readily influenced by the views of colleagues, Andrew Knight, Stephen Grabiner or others. Yet I argued that this was how it should and must be. I believed in consultation and delegation (though I also believed that one should never announce a decision on anything at the end of a consultative meeting). I hope I was never ashamed to admit ignorance, nor to change my mind in the face of argument from Don, Veronica, Andrew Knight or others. I sought to make plain to heads of department what were our objectives, and then left them to get on with achieving them. Old stagers who proved chronically resistant to change were ruthlessly replaced. Especially in the early years, of course, there were plenty of open or closet dissidents, who strongly opposed what we were doing. But I tried to make all our senior team feel that they were at the heart of decision-making, that they shared with me the opportunity to lead the escape from the old *Telegraph* world.

I moved the leader conference from mid-afternoon to late

morning. By noon, we had a good sense of what we should be commenting upon. This was not popular with leader writers who liked to earn their pay merely by popping into the office for a couple of hours after lunch, but it suited me. I tried to have leaders organized before I got into the car for the City or the West End.

Lunch was a critical phase of my working day, not only because I like food. Some editors are accomplished hands-on orchestrators of every page in their papers until far into the night, but they spurn socializing with those they write about. They believe this should be left to their reporters. I believed that generating ideas was the most important contribution I could make, not least because I lacked the technical skills of Don Berry. Newspaper ideas come from two sources – reading other titles, and meeting people. Almost every day while I was an editor, I lunched with politicians, businessmen or writers. In the early days in Fleet Street, when at last we were granted grudging access to the Berry dining room, I introduced a regular series of lunches for twelve or fifteen people from each department in turn, getting to know staff.

When I led a group from the Newsroom into the first of these, the reporters were a trifle awed by the very notion of being allowed access to the Berrys' fifth-floor shrine. As a flunkey opened the dining room door, the humble hacks paused, gaping. There, laid before us, was a great mahogany table set for a banquet: glittering with silver, crystal, four glasses beside each place. Only the stuffed boar's head with an apple in its mouth was missing. This was the only style of entertaining with which our white-gloved butler, the charming Roger, was conversant. As the peasants swept forward, we felt as if we were storming the Winter Palace. A final fantasy touch was provided by the clatter of a lawnmower as we ate. A trim rectangle of greensward lay outside on the big balcony, overlooking the office windows of Lords Camrose and Hartwell.

For future occasions of the kind, I made more modest catering arrangements, despite Roger's pained expression when I told him that one wine would be enough. We entertained a succession of prominent figures on the Fifth Floor as long as we remained in Fleet Street, giving varying degrees of pleasure to hosts or guests. Roy Hattersley came, and consumed one of the heaviest meals seen in those parts for many a season, down to the last grape. Terry Waite sat brimming with confidence in his own powers of negotiation, on the eve of his latest – and disastrously ill-fated – negotiation with the hostage-takers of Beirut. Enoch Powell proved very spiky. He refused to be drawn on any conversational topic. At last, in despair, I sought to encourage his views on an issue just beginning to hit the headlines – Aids. He turned his glittering ancient mariner's eye upon me without enthusiasm. 'Mr Editor,' he inveighed, in those extraordinary nasal tones, 'Mr Editor: when one has attained the age of seventy-nine, the prospect of death from a sexually transmitted disease appears *remarkably* remote!' I retired crushed.

Most days, I lunched with politicians or businessmen at a restaurant in the West End, usually Wilton's or Green's in St James's, which possess useful private partitioned tables. Whatever the mutual suspicions between journalists and MPs, we cannot live without each other. Like most editors, I loved those privileged encounters with members of the government who seldom passed a couple of hours in company without yielding at least one studied indiscretion. In those days some were men I already knew pretty well – Kenneth Baker, William Waldegrave, Norman Lamont, Michael Howard (though before we were finished, political differences sharply divided me from the last two). Other ministers were at least acquaintances – Geoffrey Howe, Douglas Hurd, Nigel Lawson. It was to William Waldegrave that I owed one of our early scoops. A highly publicized new book on Cold War espionage suggested that Lord Rothschild, legendary Whitehall eminence and a former head of the Downing Street think-tank, had been a traitor, passing information to Russia. William, a close friend of Rothschild, rang me one morning in December 1986 to ask if I would see his lordship, and publish his denial. Of course I said that I would do so, and hastened to a rendezvous at Rothschilds bank in the city, where Victor had an office. He expressed his anguish forcefully. On 4 December, we 'splashed' our front page on the story of the bizarre missive on our Letters page:

From Lord Rothschild GBE, GM, SDE, FRS

Dear Editor and Readers,

Since at least 1980 up to the present time, there have been innuendoes in the press to the effect that I am 'the fifth man', in other words a Soviet Agent. The Director-General of MI5 has to state publicly that it has unequivocal, repeat unequivocal evidence that I am not, and never have been, a Soviet agent. If the 'regulations' prevent him making such a statement, which in the present climate I doubt, let him do so through his legal adviser or through any other recognisably authoritative source. I am constrained by the Official Secrets Act, but I write this letter lest it be thought that silence would be an indication of anything other than complete innocence.

Yours Truly

Mrs Thatcher eventually made a tepid statement in the Commons, to the effect that there was no evidence Rothschild was a Soviet informer. The *Telegraph* basked in the widespread publicity the story brought us, but I resisted congratulations from colleagues, on the grounds that we had done nothing very clever to get it. Any scoop deserving of plaudits is the fruit not of luck, but of painstaking investigation.

Douglas Hurd gradually became my closest friend and connection in government. He was extraordinarily frank in his successive roles as Home Secretary and Foreign Secretary. I found his briefings invaluable, and we spent many evenings hunched over the corner table at Wilton's. Douglas never seemed a good politician. His instinct for public sentiment was imperfect, to say the least. He was, however, a natural governor, imbued with the traditions of English public service. Even when the Thatcher administration found itself sinking deeper and deeper into diffi-

Marc's cartoon for our front page when the Rothschild letter
appeared in the paper.

culties, Douglas's outward serenity remained unruffled. He
believed that the business of the Queen's government must be
carried on.

One morning I found myself hopelessly stuck in traffic on my
way to lunch with the Chancellor. Thinking Nigel Lawson's time
rather more valuable than my own, I abandoned the car, took the
tube to St James's, and sprinted across the park towards Jermyn
Street – those were days when I could still make a show of
sprinting. An outraged passer-by's voice pursued me as I crossed
the bridge over the lake: 'Editors of *The Daily Telegraph* should
not be *seen* to *run!*' I have never been good at doing dignity. I was
still panting through the first course of the enormous lunch in
which Nigel indulged (there must be something about Chancel-
lors' appetites – Ken Clarke was another occupant of the office
who never missed his pudding). Where some ministers flattered
editors, the Chancellor's courtesy could not mask his amazement

that so callow a figure as myself had by some reckless misdeal of fate been elevated to the chair of the *Telegraph*. Encounters with Lawson left me floundering like a member of the Lower Fourth who has been mistakenly promoted to an Upper Sixth maths set for the afternoon. It was reassuring to be told by his Cabinet colleagues that Nigel made them feel much the same.

Not many ministers aspire to Lawson's remarkable confidence and ebullience. A few holders of office use power eagerly and vigorously. Many more, I came to perceive, spend their years in government preoccupied only with clinging to office, living exemplars of what Malcolm Muggeridge called 'the atrocious banalities and buffooneries of power'. They live and work in a permanent fever of apprehension about losing their official car and those wonderful red boxes. I was drinking one day with a newly promoted member of the Cabinet, whom I did not know well. He astonished me by enquiring tentatively, head cocked sideways in the fashion of a novice gundog eager to please: 'How am I doing?' Asking a journalist a question like that seemed an unpromising start for a man with ambitions to become Chancellor, and it was not surprising that he failed to reach his goal.

Soon after I became Editor, I lunched one day with Sir John Harvey-Jones, who had just stepped down as Chairman of ICI. He asked:

'How long do you plan on doing this job?'

'Five years, maybe.'

'Then what?'

'Oh, I'll go back to writing books, living in the country, doing a bit of TV.'

'You'll find you miss all this.'

'What, the chauffeur, the secretaries, the staff?'

'No, not that. You'll miss *knowing*. When I was Chairman of ICI, anybody from the Prime Minister and the Prince of Wales downwards would take my calls. Nowadays, it doesn't matter how much money one's got or how nice a life – I don't *know* things in the same way.'

At the time, I did not fully grasp what Harvey-Jones was getting at. Within a few years, however, I understood it very well. There is an intoxication about access, about being told from the very top what is going on (even if the proffered version of events is wilfully or involuntarily deceitful), that makes almost all men and women who experience its charms reluctant to resign them. It was the addictive lure of 'knowing' which did more than anything else to persuade me to continue editing newspapers for at least a decade longer than I first intended.

Until I learned better, I sometimes took groups of colleagues to lunch at the offices of big companies. I hope our hosts profited more from these encounters than we did. In my early innocence, I assumed that we were bound to discover something of interest from an hour or two with top business executives. In reality, we seldom did so. More often than not, we sat through a ritual exchange of courtesies and gossip, for which none of those round the table should have been able to spare the time. Sometimes even the fare was a disappointment. The Chairman of ICI, Sir Denys Henderson, invited us to a board lunch. On arrival, asked what we wanted to drink, I suggested a glass of wine. For the first six months of editorship, I never drank at lunchtime, but thereafter I decided that I preferred the consequences of having a drink to those of not doing so. ICI's butler gravely invited me to choose between mineral water and fruit juice.

'I don't want either, thank you very much – I'd like a glass of wine.'

'I fear, sir, that we do not serve alcohol in this building.'

'I don't mind a bit if you feel obliged to keep your own staff away from the bottle, but I want a drink!'

'There is no drink, sir.'

At this point Denys Henderson himself became embroiled, and explained awkwardly that the staff had voted some time earlier for a regime of abstinence. I said crossly: 'But we are not your staff. We are your guests. And we want a drink!' I was being wantonly mischievous, but it seemed a bit steep for us to have to sit through ninety minutes of propaganda on behalf of ICI, which was then considerably embattled, without the consolation of claret. The occasion ended, as it began, with several inches of ice on the table.

*

BACK IN MY OFFICE after lunch there were letters to sign, copy to read, leaders to scan, a quick check to be made of the agency wires to see what was going on in the world. It is physically impossible for any broadsheet editor to read every word that goes into his paper before publication. Whatever crises are brewing, it is essential to keep a close eye on the leaders, the leader-page article, the gossip column, the key news stories. An editor must set the framework, create a clear image in the minds of his staff about what he wants the newspaper to be, but thereafter he is dependent upon others to transform the vision into reality.

All editors ride hobby horses, which become known to every subeditor, or should do so. I banned the use of clichés which irritated me: 'death toll', 'limousine', 'luxury home'. The word 'hero' is recklessly abused by journalists, and appeared in the *Telegraph* only with my explicit permission. When a quoted figure is said to be 'insisting' on a given point, it means that the reporter does not believe a word of it. Thus, surely, 'insist' should only be used when incredulity seems justified. Conversely, it is always possible to avoid lapsing into gullibility by using the words 'he claims' in front of a quote.

'Mistress' nowadays sounds absurdly prurient. I lamented carelessness about titles – calling Mary, Lady Smith 'Lady Mary Smith', for instance – not out of deference to a dying aristocracy, but because getting these details wrong marginally weakened our authority in the eyes of educated readers. I inveighed against split infinitives, and imposed a ban on the use of interrogatives in headlines – a precept taught by Don Berry – unless the question posed was answered in the text.

I shared with Andrew Knight a belief that the publication of corrections and apologies strengthened, rather than diminished, the credibility of the newspaper. Some titles will go to fantastic lengths to avoid admitting in print that they are wrong. It is often genuinely difficult to determine whether a reader's complaint reflects merely a difference of opinion (in which case he or she is invited to write a letter for publication) or an error of substance. In the latter case, I always demanded that we should publish a correction, labelled as such. These, and various other prejudices of mine, became well known in the Newsroom. So, too, I learned long after my departure, did some of my savage strictures upon members of staff, expressed in notes to the Night Editor. After he had gone home, the subs rifled his desk to discover against whom my spleen was at that moment directed.

Every editor depends above all upon the judgement of his Night Editor, the man who controls the 'back bench'. This is a row of desks strategically situated in the midst of the Newsroom between the News and Picture Desks, from which the key operational figures run the editions, and direct the work of the subeditors. The Night Editor remains at his post until at least 1 a.m. David Ruddock, who had succeeded Andrew Hutchinson in the role a few months before my arrival, was a superb conductor of the Newsroom orchestra. A cheerful man of great charm, like many long-serving newspaper executives who have worked for decades through the hours when most of us are asleep, David with his thinning hair looked more than his forty-seven years. He was fluent, quick, clever, witty and not in the least afraid to argue vehemently with my judgements.

He was also a skilful office politician, who never troubled to disguise his scepticism about many of the innovations Don and I were seeking to introduce, indeed about the whole concept of designing and packaging copy. He raised to an art form a technique I often employed myself with our management, that of assenting gracefully to a proposal, then doing nothing towards implementing it. He was steeped in the old *Telegraph* culture of giving readers News without frills or ribbon. He and his colleagues sometimes seemed to take a perverse joy in the grey slabs of print they offered readers, defying them to hunt out gems buried in the morass. David was proud of the *Telegraph*'s heritage as a paper full of delicious vulgarities *The Times* traditionally spurned. Page 3, in particular, was our showcase for all manner of fantastic sexual excesses, justified for the prurient as court reporting. The *Telegraph* conveyed the impression that it printed these dreadful tales only from its painful duty as a newspaper of record. Take the Page 3 headings on a typical summer's day in 1986: 'RAPIST "POSSESSED BY DEVIL"'; '"CRAZY" GUNMAN RETURNED TO CRIME A WEEK AFTER PAROLE'; 'KILTED DOCTOR CLEARED OF DRINK CHARGE'; 'WIFE ACCUSED OF BURGLING HOME GETS DAMAGES'; 'LORDS TOPLESS STRIP MODEL WALKS FREE'; 'MERCY RELEASE FRAUDS-TER DIES'. And one day in December: 'KNIFED WIFE SAYS "I MARRIED A MURDERER"'; '"I WAS RAPED AS A CHILD TOO", MOTHER TELLS HUSHED COURT'; 'PRIEST "KILLS OFF SANTA".' On such foundations, Lord Camrose might have said, are great newspaper fortunes made. Melancholy old *Telegraph* subs com-plained that reform of the divorce laws to exclude the sort of hair-raising evidence which so enlivened the Argyll case in the early 1960s had taken the heart out of page 3. But David and his team remained justly proud of the populism of their news selection. He declared with relish: '*The Times* gives readers a "splash" about what they ought to want to read. We give them a "splash" about what they really want to.'

Part of David Ruddock's creed, which caused us much grief, was his insistence that 'the day starts at four o'clock'. He himself arrived to begin his twelve-hour stint soon after 1 p.m. He took gleeful pride in tearing up many of the outline schemes devised by Don Berry and others during the morning. He began to address his own agenda at teatime. There was no more brilliant master of the art of reshaping the paper at short notice when a big story broke. The trouble with starting on page layouts at teatime, however, is that it becomes far more difficult to craft their design, to play the tricks with graphics and styling which can contribute so much to their appearance. Don gently suggested to David that while pages obviously had to remain flexible, it was absurd to pretend that advance scheming of pages, together with more sophisticated design and layout, were inherently pernicious.

Whatever the virtues of the old *Telegraph* News pages, they were scarcely unimprovable. Picture caption-writing, for instance, was appalling. I shuddered at such horrors as: 'The Prince of Wales sharing a joke with Mr. Norman Tebbit' and a shot of a lion with a South African beauty queen captioned 'In marked contrast to the violence and unrest in the black townships around Johannesburg, there is a restful air of tranquillity not far away at the Malula safari lodge'. The price of getting seventeen news stories on page 2, fourteen on page 3, nine on page 4, eight on page 5, twenty-four on page 6, and eleven on the back (as we did on a typical day in 1986) was that every page looked alike. David Ruddock remained a valued member of our top team, who did a lot to preserve the best values of the old *Telegraph* in the new. But it was hard work through the late 1980s, fighting the Night Editor every inch of the way to make the changes upon which I was determined. The tensions between David, Don and me persisted until 1992, when I gave Don overall charge of the Newsroom with a brief to enforce better News presentation, and above all picture use. David decided to depart for *The Times*.

There was a wide range of issues the old paper had never troubled to report at all, Consumer Affairs and the Environment prominent among them. These seemed increasingly important. We became the second newspaper in Fleet Street, after *The Guardian*, to appoint an Environment Correspondent, Charles Clover, and we gave him a lot of space. Charles soon began to win prizes. Veronica Wadley dramatically increased the attention we devoted to Health and human interest stories, and transformed our Fashion coverage. We began to use big pictures boldly. We hired Imran Khan as a Sports columnist. Norman Stone started to contribute regularly on Eastern Europe, where the first stirrings of huge change were discernible. Getting Norman to produce his copy to length and on time required extremely heavy maintenance work on the erratic pundit by Trevor Grove and Don even before lunch, never mind afterwards, but the results were generally worth it.

I was bent on removing tired old lags from the Newsroom, where they had been gathering moss for years, but I understood the splendidly byzantine cautionary note entered by Andrew Hutchinson: 'Is it your ultimate intention,' he enquired innocently one morning, cigarette held poised aloft between the first and second fingers of his right hand, his eyes fixed on the ceiling, 'that the paper should be staffed entirely by Renaissance Man?' What Andrew meant, of course, was that even as I was seeking to crowd the *Telegraph* with clever young graduates and sparkling metropolitan women, we must retain experienced reporters who would cover fires, by-elections, train crashes and all manner of other vital matters which my young turks were neither willing nor competent to address.

From 5 p.m. onwards, at every daily newspaper there is a visible quickening of pace. Desks fill, as writers who have been out on assignment through the day come back to read cuttings, make check calls and deliver copy. Through our first years, the clatter of typewriters was being progressively supplanted by the almost inaudible patter of computer keyboards, but the sense of urgency never faltered. One significant consequence of new technology is that there are fewer career alcoholics in newspaper offices, simply because drunks cannot readily handle high technology. I managed to shed our heaviest elbow workers over the years, and I do not think they were a great loss.

Save for a brief stint as Editor of the *Standard*'s Londoner's Diary, I had never handled other journalists' raw copy. The experience was a revelation. I possessed no conception of how many professional writers submit work to newspapers in a condition which requires hours of patient rewriting to render it publishable. It is an odd phenomenon, that even in an age when some of the brightest graduates of Oxbridge queue for jobs in the media, and even when they have gained some years' experience of the journalist's trade, so many 'writers' – even stars in the eyes of the public – cannot themselves create publishable prose. The *Telegraph*'s corps of subeditors was a source of justified pride to the paper. They possessed exceptional skills in their field, turning raw copy into usable stories – and they needed to.

I sometimes found myself sitting at a keyboard, seething with exasperation that I had to rework words submitted by men or women who were being highly paid for their contributions, to render them fit to appear. I once paid a handsome fee to a celebrated historian to produce two big pieces for us to mark some historic anniversary. When his articles arrived, I retired home in despair to spend two days editing the words myself. Then I had to pass the torch to Don Berry, who spent another two days on the pages before their final appearance. A few weeks later, I met the author at a party. He said loftily: 'I thought those pieces of mine came out rather well, didn't you?' I stifled an expletive. The author seemed quite unembarrassed by the gulf between the words he had submitted and those which we published. He appeared to regard the transformation of his tortured prose as part of a service to be expected from us.

Recriminations about drafts submitted by leader writers were seldom appropriate, because no one else could be expected to anticipate the personal spin I sought to set upon the editorials which I edited. Not infrequently, I changed our morning plans and wrote a new leader myself early in the evening. Whatever my other shortcomings as a journalist, I could write and rewrite very swiftly, composing a leader in twenty minutes if necessary. Despite Andrew Knight's belief in the merits of holding back before making judgements on major events, I thought his view that of a weekly journalist. In a daily paper, readers are entitled to expect some editorial comment on their breakfast tables next morning if there has been a major news development the previous afternoon or evening. Leaders in most newspapers reflect at least some element of team discussion, even if the editor writes or rewrites them himself. Thus, I never troubled to clip my own contributions into the volume in which every journalist files signed pieces. I was surprised when Charles Douglas-Home's *Times* leaders were published as a book after his death. Whatever the merits of my own efforts in this field, I cannot say that, as an editor, I would care to be remembered posthumously for contributions to any newspaper's leader columns.

Bill Deedes used to keep open house in his office for Tory MPs to look in for an evening drink. I maintained this custom for a few months in Fleet Street, but by nightfall I felt impatient to escape. I preferred to meet people in clubs or West End bars. Later, there were dinners to attend, and sometimes to host. I discovered the ineffable dreariness of diplomatic bunfights. I seldom attended big, formal affairs at Guildhall or the Mansion House. The dinners that were valuable were those where one could have good conversation with chosen neighbours, especially politicians. I was often stumped by finding myself in company with luminaries of film or theatre, who can be hard going for anyone outside their own trade. I spent an evening next to Jerry Hall. We failed to find any topic on which our minds might meet. Next day, when I told a mutual friend about the experience, he shook his head impatiently: 'You wasted a great opportunity. You should have got her onto sex. It's her favourite subject, and she really knows what she's talking about.' To add insult to boredom, the *Independent* gossip column reported next day that I had caused trouble at the dinner by smoking between courses. In truth, it was Ms Hall who had done the smoking, not me. Experience convinces me that gossip column stories in all newspapers are seldom less than 10 per cent, rarely more than 50 per cent accurate on any occasion. The same might be said of all stories in *Private Eye*.

In the first two years of my editorship, we replaced three-quarters of the *Telegraph*'s heads of department, introduced a string of new younger writers, and paid off scores of the old guard. The Features pages were transformed. We had made a start on

News. The leader page carried a far wider range of opinion, presented in the manner of a modern newspaper. Whatever the limitations of our leaders, the paper's attitudes no longer appeared to be pursuing readers into undertakers' waiting rooms. The Arts pages under Miriam Gross's inspired editorship were to become models of their kind. Neil Collins made his pages compulsory reading in the City. George Jones's political reporting was unmatched. Nicholas Shakespeare became an outstanding Literary Editor. Our Education coverage was transformed when I recruited my old friend and colleague John Clare to become Education Editor, a field in which he has become recognized as the media's doyen.

On the Features side, a rival editor remarked to me one day that in his opinion, Trevor Grove, Veronica Wadley and Don Berry together constituted the strongest senior team in the business. Trevor was responsible for introducing one of our most splendid recruits, an absurdly young tyro cartoonist named Matthew Pritchett, son of our humorous columnist Oliver Pritchett, and grandson of V. S. Pritchett. Matt's pocket cartoons began in May 1988. He was just twenty-three, and attained almost instant stardom.

Our greatest success, perhaps, was that we identified Saturday as the key to the financial revival of the company. At that stage, the only newspaper which exploited Saturday's full commercial potential was the *Financial Times*. Since it did not publish on Sundays, the *FT* sought to offer on Saturdays most of the features Sunday newspapers provide. Trevor Grove, more than anyone, deserves credit for convincing Andrew Knight that we could outflank *The Sunday Times* by producing a powerful weekend package on Saturday. The first edition of our new Weekend section, sixteen pages of leisure, arts and travel, which soon swelled to twenty-four, to thirty-six and even forty, was published with the paper on 24 February 1987. Writers such as John Mortimer (who travelled the world for us), Bill Deedes (on his armoury of garden machines), Martyn Harris (on pubs), Christopher Fildes (on owning losing racehorses), John Keegan (on the anniversary of Waterloo) created wonderful 'fronts'. I often contributed myself on rural or military matters, and took a keen interest in book serializations, as well as reviewing for the Literary pages. As a lifelong admirer of Patrick Leigh-Fermor, I was thrilled when we persuaded him to return to his old prewar stamping ground in Romania, to contribute two brilliant 'fronts' on his experience. Weekend proved an immediate, dramatic success. It paved the way for a major breakthrough in our sales and revenues on Saturdays, with a colour magazine (transferred from the Sunday), and later Arts & Books, Children's Telegraph and Motoring.

Trevor continued to supervise Weekend, even after an executive editor was appointed. We agreed that the section should major heavily on rural affairs, a policy on which my personal enthusiasm was reinforced by commercial conviction. David Profumo wrote on fishing, Celia Haddon on pets. I indulged myself by offering occasional shooting pieces, and the great Willy Poole contributed a hugely popular column from Northumberland. I had met Willy for the first time some years earlier, when I went hunting for a day with the West Percy, the wild and woolly pack of which he was Master. A Falstaffian figure with a keen appetite for pleasure of all kinds, he had lived in cheerful genteel poverty since leaving Eton, to sustain his single-minded devotion to the chase. In his young days as a Master of Hounds, he once told me, he was obliged to rely for his own rations upon the same knackers as his animals. I had never read Willy's column in *Horse & Hound.* My heart sank when he first asked if he might try a few pieces on me. It is generally a source of embarrassment for any editor when a friend enquires coyly whether you might cast an eye over some amateur jottings. In Willy's case, however, Trevor and I only needed to read his first couple of essays to know that we had a star in the making. It was always fun thinking of ideas for Willy. I would tell Weekend's editor – for instance – that I wanted to see a 'front' by R. W. F. Poole on shrimping in Morecambé Bay, dominated by a picture of our correspondent's enormous bottom, viewed bending

'Apparently Max Hastings was the first editor into Docklands'

One of Matt's private jokes for me.

to the sea in pursuit of his quarry. The outcome did not disappoint. One always knew with Willy that, if we got the idea right, he would deliver brilliantly. He became one of those rare contributors, of which every title needs a few, for whom readers buy the paper. Weekend as a whole remains one of my proudest contributions to *The Daily Telegraph*. In the years that followed, the Saturday edition became overwhelmingly the greatest contributor to our revenues.

After two years of losses, by 1987 the company was at last producing modest profits – £800,000 against losses of £15 million the previous year. There was the promise of much better things to come, fulfilled by a profit of £29 million in 1988, £40 million the year after. Andrew Knight, with the advice of management consultant Joe Cooke, had accomplished an extraordinarily peaceful transformation of the *Telegraph*'s staffing, making redundant more than 2,000 production workers without a day's loss of publication through industrial action. We recognized that this was achieved on the floodtide unleashed by Murdoch at Wapping, but it seemed a miracle to all of us at the time. The will of the unions to resist modernization, implacable through several generations, had collapsed. We now had the makings of a modern newspaper, in new buildings with state-of-the-art technology. The dramatic reduction of our costs, together with the introduction of disciplined management practices, had transformed the company's accounts with remarkable speed. The editorial revitalization of the titles made it possible to raise cover price and advertising rates, while stemming the circulation loss. There remained a long way to go, but we knew, and the rest of the industry was beginning to acknowledge, that the resurrection of *The Daily Telegraph* was gaining momentum.

*

UNLESS THERE WAS a big story breaking, I believed that David Ruddock, Andrew Hutchinson, Don Berry and Nigel Wade best handled the production of the paper into the evening without much tinkering from me. When I went home, they faxed the principal pages there. I seldom asked for major changes when I saw the first edition, and David Ruddock's feathers could be heard ruffling down the telephone if I did so. Yet in the early days, I could not resist occasionally returning to the office in Fleet Street after dinner, for the sheer thrill of descending to the stygian depths of our building, and watching the presses thundering into the night. This was part of the high romance of my job, holding cheerfully shouted exchanges with printers over the roar of machinery, then ascending into the chilly darkness to watch the vans loaded with newspapers, *my* newspapers, accelerating away towards the ends of the country. Our first year, when we were operating in the old plant, was landmarked with nerve-racking technical breakdowns, and consequent renewed injections of fears about our sale, revenue and survival. Yet there was a romance about running a newspaper at the heart of Fleet Street which was never again achieved in the later days, when our printing plant at West Ferry Road lay a mile from the editorial offices. The divorce of printing from editorial did wonders for our balance sheet, but for ever severed the link with the old business of hot metal and Linotype composition, which my generation of journalists had grown up with.

I tried never to go to bed later than 11 or 11.30 p.m., but sometimes dinners dragged on interminably into the night. On the evenings when I did not need to turn out for a formal gathering, more often than not I simply collected a hamburger from McDonald's in the Strand, on the way home from the office in deep darkness. Whatever problems I faced at that time, exhaustion ensured that insomnia was not among them.

5

COVERING THE WORLD

IT WOULD BE FOOLISH to pretend that the move to Docklands which began in April 1987 was welcome to our editorial staff. Many people resented the exile from central London that was forced upon them, along with the greater cost and difficulty of travelling to work. I worried that it also became incomparably harder for them to meet people – the vital stimulus for any kind of journalism. At South Quay, at last we had a newspaper with a modern floor plan. But something important was lost throughout the industry, amid the Fleet Street diaspora which took place between the late 1980s and mid-1990s. *The Guardian*, together with the *Daily Mail* and *Evening Standard* in Kensington, are left, much envied, as the only titles with central London offices. Many young journalists now spend their entire working lives chained to their screens, far from contact with the outside world.

It was a pleasure at last to work in a clean, brightly light modern building after the squalor of our old Fleet Street head-quarters. I won a small personal battle with Andrew Knight, who wanted every office in the new premises to have glass partitions. I insisted that my own should have solid walls, not only to conceal from colleagues the moments when I was watching tennis on television, but also to preserve privacy for delicate conversations. It did not seem helpful for morale that passers-by should be able to watch some hapless reporter sobbing over personal problems to the Editor. A welcome consequence of our move was that we left behind the *Telegraph*'s Fleet Street watering hole, the Kings and Keys, focus of relentless dissent and reactionary muttering about the good old days. You could get a drink in Docklands in the late 1980s, but only at the price of administrative difficulties which taxed all but the most dogged imbibers.

In those days, communication with the metropolis hinged upon the precarious link provided by the new Docklands Light Railway. Its chronic technical problems, and our reporting of them, caused grief both to its passengers and its manufacturers. Early one morning, I took a call from Arnold Weinstock, then Chairman of GEC.

'What are you trying to do our great company?' he enquired furiously. 'Your newspaper this morning is saying terrible things about us!'

'Well, Arnold, the problem is that you built the Docklands trains, and they aren't working very well.'

'Nonsense! Nonsense! When did you ever hear of a project at the cutting edge of technology which did not have a few teething troubles?'

'Yes, well, our technically minded staff say the DLR does not represent any great advance on the principles of Stephenson's *Rocket*.'

'Rubbish! And why do you exaggerate these little things so much? Are you trying to destroy one of this country's great exporters?'

'As it happens, Arnold, if I lean out of my window right now I can actually see the broken-down GEC train on which sixty of our staff have this very morning been stuck for forty minutes, and that's the second time in a week.'

After ten minutes on the telephone with the great Lord Weinstock, I could readily understand how Arnold had cowed the Ministry of Defence into buying torpedoes that ran amok. I ended our conversation feeling that the DLR's troubles were somehow my fault, rather than GEC's.

To ease the problem of travel, we decided to exploit the river. The company bought two twenty-seat launches, christened the *Max* and the *Perry*, on which staff could travel daily to and from

Charing Cross. In principle, this was delightful. On a fine summer's day, I loved to sit on the open stern in the sunshine as we cruised to lunch amid the finest views in London. I even survived the embarrassment of seeing one of my guests conspicuously light up a joint on board, though I lived in fear for weeks that *Private Eye* would get to hear about it. Except in the worst traffic, however, the boats proved to take as long as any taxi on the journey to civilization – and in those days, of course, there was no Underground connection. The river craft were also too fragile to cope with the alarming currents and debris of the lower Thames. We often found ourselves drifting in midstream while the doughty old watermen who crewed the boats struggled to restart an engine or plug a gash in the hull. The *Max* and the *Perry* were eventually made redundant. I was grateful, for symbolic reasons, that they escaped foundering with all hands.

The biggest boost to our morale in 1987 came from something that did not happen, rather than something which did. When *The Independent* launched in October 1986, it was widely predicted that the *Telegraph* would lose 200,000, even perhaps 300,000, sale to the wunderkind. As it was, the new paper's impact upon us proved astonishingly small, indeed much less significant than upon the *Times* and *Guardian*. The *Indie* was beautifully designed, serious, worthy, thoughtful – and just a trifle dull. It came as a great relief for us to discover that its politics were set firmly left of centre, and certainly to the left of the *Telegraph*'s existing or potential readership. The night before the new title was launched, I sent Andreas Whittam-Smith and his team a magnum of champagne. Next day, after we had all read their first edition, I sent the paper a wreath. At the time, my purpose was to boost the precarious morale of my own staff, by showing that we were not afraid of a new competitor. Afterwards, I saw that I had made a tasteless gesture. I should make amends now, by acknowledging that for three journalists to create a new title from scratch was an achievement beyond anything of ours.

In the first months after *The Independent*'s arrival, as its

1. In the beginning: arriving at the *Daily Telegraph* building in Fleet Street, when the struggle began to save the paper. I was deeply apprehensive about whether I could do the job – and so was everyone else.

2. My predecessor as Editor, Fleet Street's longest-serving star reporter: Bill Deedes in characteristic pose for a Weekend 'front'.

3. Relations with Margaret Thatcher got off to a stormy start, and grew worse. At the top of this picture of the Prime Minister in the West Country during the 1983 election campaign, a reporter may be glimpsed taking notes for the *Evening Standard*. Mrs Thatcher's bodyguard, with moustache, is looking suspicious even before I reached the *Daily Telegraph*.

4. Andrew Knight, Chief Executive of the *Telegraph* from 1986 and architect of the company's resurrection, picked me to do a job no one else would have considered me for. His abrupt departure in 1989 provoked a bitter row with Conrad Black.

5. Michael Hartwell, whose financial misjudgements cost the Berry family control of the *Telegraph*. Conrad Black gained a majority shareholding in the December 1985. Though Lord Hartwell for a time retained the title of Editor-in-Chief, his authority was gone.

6. The Queen visits our newsroom in Docklands in 1988. Left to right:
Night Editor David Ruddock; a mildly dishevelled Andrew Knight;
lady-in-waiting; HM with Conrad behind her, alongside his first wife Joanna.

7. The RAF always believed that the *Telegraph* neglected them.
In a rash moment, the Chief of Air Staff decided I would be more
RAF-conscious if I flew in a Tornado. By the time we landed,
both the cockpit and I looked rather less happy.

8. Barbara and Conrad Black pursued by their Editor-in-Chief at the
Telegraph summer party, Stowe, 1991.

Favourite colleagues
(*anti-clockwise from top left*):

9. Don Berry – the peerless
'Uncle Don',

10. Trevor Grove,

11. Veronica Wadley,

12. Nigel Wade,

13. Boris Johnson,

14. Neil Collins,

15. Charles Moore

16. Editorial Director, Jeremy Deedes – the 'nanny' who saved me from so many of my own misjudgements.

17. The one and only Matt, who started pocket cartooning for us at the age of twenty-three in 1988, and doesn't look much older today.

circulation rose steadily – aided by that brilliant advertising slogan 'It is – are you?', of which we were so envious – we studied our own sales nervously. We were still suffering decline. But the great haemorrhage of past years had been stemmed. When senior management executives sometimes asked us why we could not do this or that 'like the *Indie*', we enquired gently whether they would like the two titles to swap circulations. At last, thank Heaven, our Manchester plant and the first new presses in London were producing copies of the *Telegraph* which reproduced words and – more important – pictures to a vastly higher standard than the old monsters in Fleet Street. By the summer of 1987, *The Independent*'s sale had reached something approaching 350,000 copies. At its zenith, it topped 400,000, before beginning a steep descent to its present level, around 220,000. Our own circulation in mid-1987 was 1,150,000.

*

THE LATE 1980s AND EARLY 1990s marked a period of extraordinary importance in international events. There has seldom been a time when the world's media found ourselves so preoccupied with foreign coverage. The *Daily Telegraph* had always possessed a powerful foreign machine. We reshaped and strengthened this in our first years. The paper was exceptionally well equipped to report the succession of dramas which now began to unfold. A seismic change was taking place in the Soviet Union. 'There is absolutely no doubt,' Xan Smiley wrote on our leader page in May 1988, 'that something exciting, indeed in Soviet terms very peculiar, even dangerous, is happening in the Kremlin ... The West should not expect too much of Mr Gorbachev too fast ... He cannot admit that *glasnost* may result in a fading of the ideology on which the Soviet state is still officially based.' Xan contributed immensely to the quality of our coverage of the collapse of the Soviet Union and the fading of the Cold War. He filed hundreds of thousands of words to us, and we published almost all of them. Day after day, we found ourselves devoting the

DOES YOUR
EDITOR KNOW
WHERE YOU ARE?

Our Foreign Editor, Nigel Wade, produced a *Telegraph*
handbook for embryo foreign correspondents, for which
this was a characteristic Matt illustration.

paper's entire centre spread to analysis and comment upon the
latest developments in Moscow. It is difficult to remember, a mere
fifteen years later, just how vast is the gulf between where the
Soviet Union stood then, and where Russia is today.

Elsewhere in the world, some *Telegraph* readers were no doubt
surprised to read a leader in their newspaper arguing that 'Gibraltar
should be left in no doubt that the British Government considers
the Rock's long-term future to lie in a closer relationship with
Spain, rather than as an isolated relic of Empire on the tip of the
Iberian peninsula'. I wrote a signed leader-page article on the 1987
anniversary of the Falklands War, urging that 'sooner or later, we
are bound to negotiate with the Argentines about the future of the
islands. This is not a betrayal of those who died in 1982, but a
recognition of reality.'

At the core of Don Berry's view of our business was his
mantra, by which I was profoundly influenced: 'Tell readers the

facts before you comment on them.' One of the most serious vices of modern British newspapers is that comment has largely displaced the presentation of hard news. Readers are often invited to digest the views of editorialists and columnists on a given issue or government decision, before they have seen any proper exposition of what has taken place, or what is being proposed. Ian Jack, himself a former editor, wrote vividly in *The Granta Book of Reportage* a few years ago: 'Britain has developed a singular sort of media culture which places a high premium on excitement, controversy and sentimentality, in which information takes second place to the opinions it arouses.' Likewise *Observer* columnist Nick Cohen: 'Look at the inability of your local paper to tell you what has happened at the council or in court, and of your national paper to tell you what a politician actually said in a speech, as opposed to what other people think of what he said.'

This was the beartrap which Don Berry did much to help us avoid. Under his guidance, we first presented the facts, often at exhaustive length, then commented. He was passionately committed to the maintenance, indeed extension, of our position as a newspaper of record. For instance, when the Irish Attorney-General published a sixteen-page document setting out his reasons for declining to extradite an IRA suspect, it was Don who persuaded me that we should publish the entire judgement in our News pages, allowing readers to make their own assessment, before turning to our leader, highly critical of the Irish government. We began to highlight social issues such as unemployment, the plight of northern cities, the shortcomings of our education system. One day, we devoted the entire op-ed page to profiling a single street of twenty houses on the north bank of the Ware, where almost every inhabitant was out of work. And above all, we sought never to allow political comment to infiltrate the News pages. One of the saddest trends in broadsheet newspapers today is that many front-page headlines do not announce news, they merely advertise an editor's partisan view, above all when the issue is Europe.

It was scarcely surprising that some of our international coverage provoked outbreaks of friction with Andrew and Conrad. In the summer of 1987, the Reagan Administration was rocked by revelations of the so-called Iran–Contra scandal, in which US Marine Colonel Oliver North was found to have been acting as a broker in covert deals to use cash generated from illegal arms sales to Iran, to fund the right-wing Contra guerrillas in Nicaragua. We said in a leader in July that 'the President has diminished his own administration, and his country, by doing deals with terrorists when he protested that such machinations were beneath him.' I had just held a summer party for the *Telegraph* staff at Cowdray Park, at which we issued T-shirts proclaiming on the front: 'REAL MEN READ THE TELEGRAPH', and on the back 'WIMPS WALLOW IN THE INDEPENDENT'. Andrew sent me an anguished hand-written memo after the Iran–Contra leader:

> How can you justify your T-shirt? Our leader on Oliver North is pure *Grauniad/Independent* . . . The issues are far more interesting – starting with the impossibility of conduct-ing a foreign policy under US rules – and the sight of North tweaking Congress's tail is far more humorous than we have allowed. Law v. reality – a classic American dilemma. Oh dear! Couldn't you have checked in here before you wrote? Do eschew instant leaders, particularly if they follow the *NY Times*. Above all, we show a prejudice and impatience with things American in such blimpish liberalism of just the kind our proprietor justifiably deplores, incidentally – I await the telephone call when he gets out of bed.

I answered Andrew:

> I don't think the fact that North was able to conduct a private foreign policy in the least comic . . . the freedom of operation granted to North, by default or otherwise, is deeply disturbing. If Brits were revealed as behaving in the same way, we should be withering. I am always mindful of Con-

rad's known views about the US . . . But . . . *The Guardian* is
not always wrong.

Our correspondence on this issue continued at some length.
Andrew concluded the last round with the warning:

> Conrad is in London for several weeks in the summer. He,
> too, will participate. You must relate to him, not wish it were
> otherwise. He is far cleverer than me, and you, and his
> judgement on the US and the Iran–Contra hearings [which
> Conrad regarded with scorn] has been nearly 100% right,
> while ours has been far less nearly so. He does not regard
> the *DT* as 'a splendid toy' [a phrase I had used]. Like me,
> he takes its leader line deeply seriously . . . good though many
> of our leaders are, they are frankly not our best or most
> consistent point . . . There is an attitude, but not a mind, at
> work.

I sometimes found myself reminding Andrew and our Chairman of an essential point about our treatment of US affairs:
The Daily Telegraph was British. Its role was to provide our own
national perspective upon events across the Atlantic, not to express
that of Washington Republicans: 'It may be our misfortune not to
be American, Conrad, but that's the way it is.' I shared his respect
for the United States, its extraordinary power and achievement.
But I did not consider it my job to use the paper to proselytize on
behalf of American foreign policy. This was a debate which
recurred frequently during our decade together. I have never seen
anything inherently wrong with foreign ownership of British
media. Difficulties must arise, however, if a proprietor with a
foreign perspective (and Conrad was sometimes a trifle hypocritical, in attacking British small-mindedness towards the United
States, while loudly expressing disdain for aspects of our own
society, such as its grotesque shortage of television channels) seeks
to impose this on his titles.

For every British newspaper, of course, reporting of and
comment upon the United States is by far the most important

element of foreign coverage. America is the world's only super-power. Its doings impact profoundly upon us all. Moreover, even in an age when our own nation has become perversely more insular in its preoccupations, despite the vast increase of inter-national holidaymaking, the British public's appetite for reading about transatlantic life, culture, eccentricities and extravagances remains voracious. *The Telegraph* maintained staff correspondents in New York and Los Angeles chiefly to satisfy the latter require-ment, while a two-man bureau in Washington addressed the former. A constant procession of special writers crossed the Atlan-tic to reinforce our residents, especially for magazine assignments.

The five- or six-hour time difference between London and the East Coast renders coverage of the US chronically stressful as well as exciting for any media organization. So much news is breaking across the water just as first editions are closing here. America is incomparably the most media-friendly society on earth, as I had learned for myself during two years there as a young reporter in the late 1960s. But there are great frustrations for a modern British journalist based in Washington. When I became an editor, I resolved to improve the *Telegraph*'s lacklustre American coverage. Yet as I studied the problems, an underlying truth became apparent: not since Henry Brandon of *The Sunday Times* was a personal friend of the Kennedys in the 1960s has a British correspondent possessed an important inside track at the heart of power in Washington. This reflects no lack of diligence on the part of the British press corps in the US, merely the fact that British journalists rank below American regional newspapers in Washington's media food chain. It is extraordinary that intelligent and sophisticated British people, up to and including Tony Blair, continue to delude themselves through successive generations about our influence in Washington. Americans treat British visitors with courtesy and generosity. But the British, like all other foreigners, are locked out of the decision-making network. Only Margaret Thatcher, for a time, successfully breached this conven-tion. During one of my own trips to Washington the British

Ambassador, Antony Acland, observed that it was one of his more painful duties to enlighten visiting British ministers that they would not be wanted on *Good Morning America*; that Barbara Walters would not be interviewing them. Thatcher was the only British visitor who could routinely gain access to prime-time US television. I learned a few home truths in this department myself, when seeking access to people on Capitol Hill. By staying at the British Embassy when it was occupied by one of our rare ambassadors with clout, such as Robin Renwick, it was possible to gain important entrées. But one day when I had arranged to call upon the Editor of *The New York Times*, I suffered the embarrassment of waiting for forty-five minutes in the editorial office, being assured by a secretary that Mr Frankel would be back from lunch any minute, before I quit in frustration.

For a resident British correspondent, the wisest course is to recognize that if one cannot enjoy direct contact with the people at the top of a US administration, the best option is to create relationships with those who do have access. This provides vital insights at one remove. During the Reagan years, and initially at Conrad's suggestion, the *Telegraph* built an important relationship with the columnist George F. Will, a close friend of the White House and especially of the First Lady. George contributed regularly to our pages, and I found him an invaluable sounding board when we met. Any honest reporter or media organization should acknowledge, however, that British coverage of the US is founded overwhelmingly upon diligent study of its media output, rather than upon privileged sources. It would be necessary to go back a very long way indeed, to identify the last occasion on which a British journalist broke a genuine American scoop. None of this is very surprising, but it is a reality which some people in our trade are reluctant to acknowledge.

Second only to the US, the Middle East is a constant preoccupation of every serious British newspaper. Today, Conrad Black is perceived as a passionate, even extravagant advocate of Israel, and of the draconian policies of the Israeli government towards the

Palestinians. Looking back, I am grateful that when I was Editor, though Conrad periodically criticized our line on the Middle East, he did not seek to interfere with our coverage. In October 1988, for instance, we ran a big piece by our excellent Middle East Correspondent Patrick Bishop, about the Palestinian intifada. It was headed: 'WILL ISRAEL POSTPONE HER RENDEZVOUS WITH REALITY?'

> The fact of the matter is that Israelis have been insufficiently frightened by the uprising. They are not yet ready to jump at radical solutions. A year ago, the conventional wisdom was that Israel's occupation of the Territories could continue for another 20 years without any serious threat to the State. Today, having been driven underground by the intifada, that perception is emerging once more. The uprising is expensive and inconvenient. It has drawn the unwelcome attention of the outside world to Israel's backyard. But in terms of lost Israeli lives, the cost has been negligible. In short, Israel is learning to live with the intifada. Until some event more traumatic than the daily riots and shooting incidents forces an elemental change in Israeli attitudes, there seems little chance of the internal machinery of the country producing a solution to the Palestinian problem.

I have quoted Bishop's dispatch because it seems interesting to reflect upon how little has changed in the fourteen years since it was written. In the same fashion, I would not find much cause today to alter an editorial we ran at the same period: 'Continuing Israel occupation of the West Bank and Gaza, bordering on their annexation, merely prolongs the country's internal insecurity. Israel's Foreign Minister, Mr Shimon Peres, is acting in his country's best interests in prodding his government towards an international conference on the future of the West Bank; at such a conference, the intransigence of Israel's Arab neighbours ... might, or might not, be exposed. As it is, Israel is losing the argument by default and petty repression.' This remained the constant theme of our Middle East leaders between 1986 and 1995. 'I think it is justifiable to suggest that we should be ruder about the PLO,' I wrote in answer to a remonstrance from Conrad on this issue, 'but I would be most reluctant to see us become more indulgent towards the Israeli government. [Premier Yitzhak] Shamir's policy is plainly directed towards integrating the West Bank within the frontiers of Israel, and many of his supporters, from my personal knowledge, would greatly like to see the Arab community in the West Bank sooner or later disappear from the borders of Israel.'

*

ON 7 MARCH 1988, the paper found itself in serious disagreement with the British government. I was again in the hot seat. At lunchtime on the previous day in Gibraltar, an SAS team had shot and killed three IRA terrorists, including a woman. They had been reconnoitring the Rock for a bomb attack on the band and guard of the Royal Anglian Regiment, which had just arrived from a posting in Ulster. Our Irish Correspondent, Anton La Guardia, described the shootings on our front page as 'an important victory for the security services in their intelligence war against the IRA'. 145lb of Semtex explosive was later found in an underground car park in Marbella.

By chance, that afternoon I was entertaining two senior army officers in my office at South Quay. I asked them: 'Does anybody think it was absolutely necessary to shoot dead all three of these people?' Neither of my guests argued that it was. I have always opposed any hint of a shoot-to-kill policy, either by security forces in Ireland against terrorists, or by armed police against criminal suspects on the British mainland. It is obviously reasonable to open fire, if there is an immediate and inescapable threat to public safety. But it is striking how many men shot in wars are wounded, rather than killed, while few suspects survive being hit by SAS or police bullets. It seems a measure of a civilized society to seek to ensure that, even in the bloodiest and dirtiest conflict, the forces of democracy do not stoop to the depths of terrorists. Lawrence Durrell vividly argued in his classic account of the 1950s EOKA war in Cyprus, *Bitter Lemons*, that excessive reaction merely serves the terrorist cause. His book has strongly influenced my perception of how counter-terrorist operations should be conducted. One of the key purposes of all insurgency campaigns is to provoke the security forces to respond extravagantly, and thus to win new supporters for the insurgents' cause among the population at large. Since this thesis is widely accepted by anti-terrorist experts around the world, it seems unwise for governments to pursue policies which conform to the purposes of society's enemies. Terrorist movements have very occasionally been defeated by the absolutely ruthless employment of force, on a scale inconceivable in a democracy; but they have never been beaten by the moderately ruthless employment of force. Intelligence, diplomatic and political means, employed hand in hand, are the essentials of success in counter-terrorism.

I accepted that the Gibraltar SAS team sincerely believed the IRA to be carrying a remote-control detonation device. But I felt deeply uncomfortable about the convincing eyewitness evidence that men from Hereford administered a coup de grâce to at least one suspect, standing over him as he lay on the ground. The pathologist who subsequently gave evidence to the Gibraltar inquest said there was evidence to show that, in the case of one of the dead men at least, four shots had been fired into him from above, when he was already prostrate. I argued then, and believe today, that if even one wounded terrorist had survived, there would have been no reasonable grounds for dissent about what was done. As it was, I recoiled from the ruthlessness of the SAS operation, and from the government's overt triumphalism about it afterwards.

Our leader on Tuesday 8 March 1988, which I wrote myself, was headed: 'EXPLANATION NEEDED'. I criticized George Robertson, the Opposition Defence Spokesman, for so readily applauding the killings. The 'neutralizing' of three terrorists was indeed a victory. There was no doubt of the malevolent intentions of the Irish group on the Rock. Few British people could be expected to mourn the deaths of terrorists. But the authorities had important questions to answer:

> It is an essential part of any successful anti-terrorist policy, to maintain the principles of civilized restraint, which are essential to a democratic society. A failure to do so argues that terrorism is succeeding in one of its principal aims, the brutalization of the society under attack. Unless the government wishes Britain's enemies to enjoy a propaganda bonanza, it should explain why it was necessary to shoot all three terrorists, rather than to apprehend them with the considerable force of SAS and police deployed in the locality. There is no requirement for this, or any other civilized state, to allow known terrorists to fire the first shot against members of the security forces or the public. But at a time when relations between Britain and Ireland are already under strain, it seems politically prudent to give ill-wishers no further grounds to suggest that the authorities operate a 'shoot to kill' policy.

Andrew Knight was deeply dismayed by what I wrote. 'Since the Libyan affair, I have not been so sad or worried at heart about an incident . . . Several people including two out-of-favour Tory MPs came up to express shock to me yesterday . . . about the timing and the hurry into "public moralising".' He quoted former *Express* editor Robert Edwards saying to him, 'Surely no newspaper should ever stand on the sidelines of an intense security forces situation and ask questions in that manner until it is absolutely sure.' I answered: 'I entirely agree that the saloon bar wisdom up and down the land will be that these people deserved to die, and good riddance. But I am surprised that you, who so often rightly plead for greater intellectual rigour, should endorse saloon bar wisdom. If we start to chase our readers' perceived saloon bar views in the leader column, we shall quickly be in difficulties on hanging, South Africa and suchlike.' Andrew had spoken approvingly of Perry Worsthorne's *Sunday* leader, applauding Gibraltar. I said I thought that the *Sunday Telegraph* editorial reflected Perry in his most repugnant Genghis Khan mode.

Few of our readers, and few people at Westminster or in the media, showed much sympathy with our squeamishness about the Gibraltar killings. But the government's handling of the case continued to seem clumsy, or worse. The Foreign Secretary, Geoffrey Howe, announced repeated postponements of the inquest into the terrorists' deaths. There was heavy official lobbying against witnesses on the Rock who professed to have seen the shootings, and who painted an ugly picture. We argued that the government behaved deplorably by seeking to pressure the Independent Broadcasting Authority to ban a Thames Television film about the incident. It cannot be said that we won our campaign to persuade the body politic to adopt a more sceptical view about what had been done on the Rock. Public sentiment ran too strongly against us. But that winter, when I was given the Editor of the Year prize at the annual Granada *What The Papers Say* Awards, I was pleased that our coverage of the Gibraltar shootings was highlighted in the citation.

Paul Johnson observed witheringly in his *Spectator* column that matters had come to a pretty pass, when *The Daily Telegraph* was given prizes for producing nonsense which gratified left-wing television companies. To some people who perceived me – rightly – as a warm admirer of the British army, it seemed bewildering that I had taken such a strong line about Gibraltar. In my own eyes, however, there was no paradox or contradiction. My admiration for the army, and for that matter for the SAS, was undiminished by the shootings. But I shall always believe the episode represents a blemish on Britain's military record almost as serious as that created by Bloody Sunday in Derry in 1972.

The chief consequence of our criticism of Gibraltar was to confirm the view of Mrs Thatcher and her government, that *The Daily Telegraph* must be considered an enemy, indeed an

unpatriotic one, despite our continuing support for a wide range
of Tory policies. In the Prime Minister's eyes, it was never enough
to provide partial endorsements. A man, a woman, a newspaper
was either 'one of us', or not. We were now ranked among the
outcasts.

*

FOR AT LEAST my first three years at the *Telegraph*, Conrad's
and Andrew's dismay about the paper's editorial policies seesawed
with respect for our perceived achievements in managing and
changing the paper. Towards the end of 1988, Andrew wrote me
one of his long memoranda, summarizing what he saw as my chief
weakness:

> There are two kinds of Editor. There is Ben Bradlee who, in
> the American way, delegates total intellectual authority over
> the 'editorial page' . . . Or there is William Rees-Mogg, whose
> mind was his own instrument, and whose moral authority
> derived from his personal intellectual control over the leader
> page, not from much else.
>
> You are the first sort of editor, not the Rees-Mogg kind.
>
> You are not an intellectual.
>
> Your mind is a highly reactive one, your instincts are
> journalistic, and, to this extent, unstructured. Your deeply
> moral and loyal view of politics is governed by attitudes and
> personality rather than by argument. This constraint leads to
> an opinion record that often features good leaders, but is
> episodic and unconvincing as a whole.
>
> If I may be melodramatic, you will prove to be a great
> editor only if you make *The Daily Telegraph* the leading organ
> of original and well-argued Conservative thought.

I have always been a sceptic about how far editorial positions
adopted by newspapers influence political outcomes. The media
possesses great power in setting the agenda, highlighting issues.
Happily for democracy, few voters obey the instructions of news-

paper editors or proprietors about which way to cast their votes. I
would be slow to suggest, therefore, that the *Telegraph*'s criticisms
of the Tory government in the late 1980s achieved any decisive
impact on its fortunes, not least because the overwhelming
majority of our readers were Conservatives, and unlikely to change
sides. Also, of course, while in this book I have highlighted some
issues on which we dissented from Mrs Thatcher and her policies,
there were many days when the *Telegraph* continued to express
warm support both for government decisions and for the Prime
Minister's personal leadership. Our criticisms may have helped,
however, to convince the public, as well as Westminster and Fleet
Street, that the *Telegraph* was becoming a new kind of newspaper.
My own credibility as an editor was probably not diminished by
gossip about the unhappiness of Andrew and Conrad – not to
mention that of the Conservative lunatic fringe – about the paper's
policies. I spent many hours pondering how far I could safely go
with both our proprietor and our readership. Not a few *Telegraph*
leaders wilfully prevaricated, to avoid a showdown with either or
both of the above constituencies. Douglas Hurd chided me one
day that an editorial I had written on European policy was 'a
camel'. This was just. I was not infrequently seeking to point the
paper in one direction, while attempting to avoid an explosion in
our rear. Looking back over *Telegraph* editorials through the years,
plenty of inconsistencies and outright changes of course can be
observed. But all newspapers, even the best, are guilty of this. So,
too, are governments.

*

SINCE AT LEAST the 1960s, coverage of international affairs had
been in steady decline in the British press. At the end of the
1980s, however, we suddenly found ourselves in an era in which
the *Telegraph*'s strengths in this area could find full play. To give
an idea of the breadth, as well as the depth of our coverage, I will
risk a yawn from readers outside our business by itemizing the
stories in our four Foreign pages on a typical day in April 1988.

Robert Whymant filed 400 words from Tokyo about its Stock Exchange. There was a brief report of a Japanese dispute with Washington on fishing rights; a light piece on Japanese government demands that their workers should take more holidays. Our Rome 'stringer' reported on a priest who was being questioned after a police drugs raid. Frank Taylor in Los Angeles filed on a new initiative to curb drug abuse. Our Air Correspondent reported that the Soviet Union was developing a cruise missile. More than thirty-seven tons of rice bugs had been collected in just two provinces of Vietnam. Associated Press in Tokyo said that the Soviet Union was expanding its military build-up in the Far East. Our Scandinavian correspondent said Moscow might scrap visa requirements for foreign tourists. We carried a page-long report on changing attitudes to smoking around the world. On our third page, Jeremy Gavron filed from Nairobi on the Ethiopian famine. There were 200 words from Cameroon on a local political crisis, and a brief dispatch on an isolated Aboriginal tribe in Australia offering its lifestyle to white tourists. Patrick Bishop in Nablus reported on a Jewish settler stoned to death by an Arab mob. George Jones filed 400 words from Ankara on Mrs Thatcher's first official visit to Turkey. David Graves had 200 words about the Chinese authorities' refusal of entry to an expedition hunting the Abominable Snowman. There was a picture story about a psychiatric patient shot by police marksmen in Pennsylvania. The Panamanian government had issued an arrest warrant for two exiles. Ian Ball sent a 1,000-word update on the US election, and 100 words on a ceasefire in Nicaragua. A 'short' reported on nine potholers trapped for four days in a cave in northern Spain. There was a single paragraph on a demonstration against pollution by 10,000 inhabitants of a town in the Urals. European distillers were demanding that Korea lifted import restrictions on Scotch whisky before the Olympics. A kidnapped Dutch businessman had been found alive in Amsterdam. And a 250-word report suggested that Romania was getting tough with its Hungarian minority.

Now, if all that sounds a mouthful, it is the best way of illustrating the scope of *Telegraph* international coverage in the late 1980s. I once commissioned a word count of BBC Television's *Nine O'Clock News*. Including the utterances of presenters, reporters and interviewees, many of which merely described the pictures on screen, the total was around 5,000 in a thirty-minute broadcast. This compared with 75,000 words contained in an average edition of *The Daily Telegraph*. Regardless of whether television is in the hands of competent practitioners or otherwise, irrespective of the undoubted emotional impact of moving images, the medium is simply incapable of delivering more than a small fraction of the information provided by a tabloid newspaper, never mind a broadsheet.

Yet it is worth emphasizing the price that must be paid for modern design, in diminishing the volume of information a newspaper can provide: contemporary layout is bright and clean; ugly corners are tidied; readers can enjoy big pictures and lots of white space between words. But David Ruddock and other *Telegraph* hands resisted our design changes in the 1980s, precisely because the new look reduced the number of stories the paper could fit in. Today, a step further on, *The Daily Telegraph* is a more handsome paper than it was in my day – but at the cost of a further reduction in story numbers, and loss of many of those precious 'shorts' – the little stories that maintained the *Telegraph*'s reputation as a paper of record. I have made a random comparison between our story counts on a single day in November 1987, and those on the same date in 2001. The front page carried eight stories in 2001 against seventeen in 1987; page 2 had five against sixteen; page 3 ran three stories against ten in 1987; page 4, five stories against sixteen. This shortfall is somewhat, but nothing like fully, compensated by increased pagination. On a randomly selected day in February 2002, the *Telegraph*'s three world news pages carried a total of just fourteen stories. These statistics may be of interest only to professional journalists. But they help to explain an important reality of our business. The triumph of the packagers, the design kings, has imposed a cost, especially on the margins of foreign coverage.

*

As THE 1980s drew to a close, we knew that we were watching history being made both in South Africa and in the Soviet Union. Xan Smiley wrote from Moscow in his valedictory despatch of August 1989, wrapping up three years of brilliant reporting of the unfolding story:

> Even if Gorbachev falls tomorrow, he must be marked down in history as a very great man. Monumental and irreversible changes – so far chiefly psychological, but none the less momentous for that – have already occurred. For the first time in nearly 70 years the Russians have scented freedom. My bet is that somehow or other, within 20 years, and perhaps after a bout or two of repression, a drastically reduced Soviet empire will indeed have acquired some sort of parliamentary democracy. Gorbachev may have fallen off the wagon on the way. But it was he who got it rolling, and it cannot now be stopped in its tracks, even if the Conservatives, the generals and the KGB were to throw Gorbachev aside tomorrow.

From Poland, Germany, Czechoslovakia, Hungary, Romania our reporters, most of them very young, were sending every day stories of events we had never thought to see in our lifetimes, as communist Eastern Europe crumbled, and the Soviet Union staggered in its death throes. East Germans, especially young ones, were pouring out of their country through Hungary and Czechoslovakia in their battered Trabants. The Czech Prime Minister was demanding that Soviet troops withdraw from his country. German reunification was plainly inevitable. We sent Norman Stone eastwards, to file a series of big reports on the collapse of communism. 'The Iron Curtain is not cracked, but shattered into a thousand pieces,' he wrote on 24 November 1989. 'A new chapter in

Europe's history has begun.' Mrs Thatcher's bitter resistance to much of what was happening, especially in Germany, raised new doubts about her fitness to govern. We said: 'A year hence, the Tory Party will either have shaped a consensus on Europe, or it will have become fatally divided.' George Walden, the Tory MP for Buckingham who was now one of our leader writers, argued that the approaching end of the Cold War made it even more important for us to engage with the EC.* 'The less involved we appear to be in the building of a new Europe, the less inclined the Americans will be to heed our pleas that they should stay and help to defend it. The time for diverting rumination about whether we are Europeans or Atlanticists has passed. Economically, militarily, and diplomatically for us the worst of all possible worlds will be an insular Britain and an Americanless Europe.'

I warmly endorsed George's sentiments. As Thatcher railed against German reunification, we ran a full-length leader in January 1990 entitled: 'Working with the grain of history'. We deplored continuing British resistance to reunification:

> Calls for caution and warnings about instability are clearly justified; but they do not add up to a policy. Britain's reaction should be three-fold. We should welcome, loudly and without reservation, the advent of a Germany that can decide its own future democratically. We should do everything to reassure Mr Gorbachev, by encouraging the Americans to stay in Europe (now as much in his interests as in ours). Finally, we should look for ways to give substance to the Germans' own manifest hope that eventual reunification will take place within the framework of a dynamic EC.

I hope that I never underestimated the immense difficulties of making the European Community an effective entity. I have never been attracted to the vision of a federal Europe. I share the regret

* Throughout this book, for consistency and simplicity I have referred to the European Community, though latterly it became the European Union.

of the Eurosceptics that Europe has sought to advance so rapidly. In particular, I have always wished that Monetary Union had been delayed by at least a decade, until economic convergence had come much closer to reality than it achieved by the end of the twentieth century. But I differed deeply from the Eurosceptics, who supposed that an isolated Britain could stand permanently aloof from Europe, or – more eccentric still – forge an alternative relationship with the United States. If this made me a cautious pro-European, less enthusiastic than (among my friends) Roy Jenkins, Michael Heseltine, Kenneth Clarke, it also made me an implacable foe of the jingos, inside and outside Mrs Thatcher's government, who believed there was a historic refuge for this country enfolded in the Union flag. The Eurosceptics' big lie is that Europe is a failure. By any measure of history, it must be judged an extraordinary success, of which we should be proud to be part. Even in 1990, the notion that a reunification of Germany, for instance, did not provide cause for celebration among all supporters of democracy seemed perverse, if not pernicious.

Even as the great East European drama was still unfolding, events in southern Africa were moving with extraordinary speed. When Frederik de Klerk was elected President of South Africa in March 1989, few observers anticipated for a moment what his term would bring. Our very bright young Cape Town correspondent Stephen Robinson wrote that the nation's new leader stood on the centre right of the National Party: 'Mr de Klerk is no more enamoured at the prospect of black majority rule than his predecessor.' Yet on 2 February 1990, de Klerk dramatically lifted the thirty-year ban on the African National Congress, and invited its leaders to join him in negotiations towards a constitution which granted the vote to the country's black majority. We carried his historic speech in full, 3,000 words of it. Its message was so remarkable, so radical, that at first we scarcely believed it. We welcomed the President's words, but commented cautiously: 'There is still no guarantee that the repressive, exclusive party which has ruled South Africa for the past 42 years will make way for an inclusive, multi-racial democracy.' In those faraway days, we had not yet learned to believe in miracles. Just a week later, Nelson Mandela was freed from captivity. We quickly learned to join with the rest of the world in admiration for President de Klerk: 'Comparisons with Mr Gorbachev are not fanciful. Both men's attempts to bring radical changes to their societies deserve our admiration and support.' Afterwards, of course, Nelson Mandela became justly recognized as one of the heroes of the twentieth century. But I have always believed that de Klerk, whom I met several times, has received less lasting regard than he deserves, for his courage and imagination in making possible the relatively peaceful transition to black majority rule. We forget what giant steps he took, amid the bitter hostility of many of his own people.

W. F. Deedes played a key part in our coverage of South Africa, as of many other foreign stories. As he neared eighty, Bill continued to travel indefatigably. His reporting seemed to improve with age, like great claret. In addition to his gifts as a descriptive writer, his despatches reflected that rarest of all qualities in journalism, wisdom. In parallel with his work for the *Telegraph*, he also began to accept assignments for an international aid charity, and to campaign for an international ban on the use of landmines, the human cost of which he chronicled in war zones across the world. A colleague once asked Bill why he was wearing himself out on his charity work, at an age when most people find that a bridge evening provides as much stress as they need. 'When you are as close to giving an account of yourself to your Maker as I am, old boy,' he is alleged to have responded, in a line which enchanted his colleagues, 'you want to have a trifle more on the credit side of the ledger than sixty years of newspaper journalism!'

The 1989 Christmas revolution which overthrew President Ceausescu of Romania marked yet another extraordinary international landmark. Under the heading 'HAS THERE EVER BEEN A YEAR LIKE IT?', Norman Stone assessed for us the huge upheavals in Eastern Europe. It was only on 28 December, six days after the initial big explosion of violence on the streets of Bucharest, that our own correspondent Trevor Fishlock's first despatch was 'splashed' on the front page – before that, like most titles, we were dependent on agencies and 'stringers'. There is nothing more frustrating than to find a huge story developing, and to lack reporters on the ground. But, unlike my mistaken decision over Libya back in 1986, the difficulties of reporting Romania reflected the sort of problems all media organizations experience, in getting reporters across closed frontiers at short notice, especially when a holiday season closes embassies and visa offices.

It became our task as journalists, in the months that followed, to report upon changes in the world we had known all our lives which were so profound that they altered every perspective, almost entirely for the better. The events of that period did much to reinforce my own conviction that, contrary to the general tenor adopted by my trade, most things in life turn out slightly better than we fear. Which of our generation would have dared to predict, even twenty years ago, that we should see within our lifetimes an end of the Cold War, the collapse of the Soviet Empire, and a relatively peaceful transition to black majority rule in South Africa? Much of the business of newspapers is to purvey tales of disappointment, failure, tragedy. How intoxicating it was, that for a season we found ourselves bearers of historic and happy tidings on two of the greatest issues that faced the world in the second half of the twentieth century.

6

KNIGHT'S MOVE

ONE MORNING IN FEBRUARY 1989, I was languishing at home in Northamptonshire with flu, when at short notice Andrew Knight arrived to pay me a visit. I assumed, rightly, that it was not concern about my health which had prompted him to drive ninety miles up the M1. He came with a dramatic proposal. *The Sunday Telegraph* was faltering. Its fortunes and circulation had languished since its colour magazine was transferred to the Saturday paper. Sale was down from over 700,000 copies in 1987 to around 650,000 two years later. Andrew perceived two issues. First, amid intense general pressure on costs, the management was eager to reduce apparent duplication of staff between the *Daily* and *Sunday*, and to look for economies by using resources across both titles. Second, there was a problem of editorship. Peregrine Worsthorne had gathered around himself a personal following of talented right-wing eccentrics, intensely loyal to Perry and to Margaret Thatcher, headed by Frank Johnson and Bruce Anderson. Their pages attracted widespread controversy and comment, not least because Perry enthused with unembarrassed elegance about Conservative causes most people thought lost years ago, such as capital punishment and white domination of South Africa. Conrad felt much more comfortable with the *Sunday*'s editorials and political features than with those which we ran in the *Daily*. Our management believed that Perry's absorption in politics and writing his own weekly column caused him to take less interest than was healthy in the boring appurtenances of the paper such as

Features, Sport and City, which also exercised some influence upon whether people read it.

Andrew's vision – and he brought with him to Guilsborough a complex organizational chart to explain how it would be implemented – was that for all operational purposes the *Daily* and *Sunday* should be merged under my overall control. However, Perry would be left in editorial charge of the *Sunday*'s political pages, his private *bantustan* as I thought of it, though this was not a term which would have commended itself to him. He and his group on the Comment pages would continue to report direct to Andrew. Looking back, the idea of a merged newspaper was itself rash enough. The division of responsibility made it grotesque. Because I knew that Andrew himself was under intense pressure from Conrad, backed by a bevy of management consultants, to achieve dramatic cost savings, I was reluctant to reject the plan out of hand. With hindsight, I should have done so. But on 24 February I sent Andrew a note, copied to Conrad, pointing out some of the pitfalls:

> . . . Newspaper readers want a different package on a Sunday. It is not feasible to replicate the *DT* . . . To achieve a readable, saleable package on a Sunday, it is essential to have a different set of minds working on it . . . I am most concerned that even if a paper 5-day shift pattern is created for senior key people, in reality they will be asked to direct a juggernaut that never halts . . . I am concerned lest the Management (and Conrad) suppose that integration promises a certain, or even probable improvement in *ST* circulation . . . There will be undoubted cost savings from such a merger, but it would be naïve to expect major staff reductions. No one can work a seven-day week.
>
> I believe we should all be asking ourselves whether dismay about the *Sunday* operation has not been created chiefly by unhappiness about lack of administrative direction in non-political subjects at the top. Cannot this problem be tackled by putting everything on the *Sunday* except maybe the

political stuff in the hands of a really first-class Features man or woman? Why should it be necessary to endure all the odium of closing down a title (and let us not beat about the bush about the reality of this) to give readers a better-balanced *Sunday* package?

Shorn of circumlocutions, of course, I was arguing that the merger proposal represented a risky and byzantine alternative to the more direct course of changing editors. Yet I knew how fierce was the struggle on the management floor about cost-cutting. Some of those who advised Conrad possessed no understanding of or sympathy with journalism. I concluded the memorandum:

> my own hesitations stem from the belief that, while the laws of commerce should be applied almost totally to a newspaper company, there are moments when there is a case for measuring and moderating their effect. The prestige value to Conrad and to the company of having a second title, demonstrably politically independent, is considerable. If we embark on a 7-day operation, we are taking a major leap in the dark, of whose benefits I am unsure. Before the rattling train gets too far down the track (and public knowledge of the existence of this debate has already had a deeply corrosive effect on *ST* morale) I think we should all think long and hard.

The merger went ahead anyway, in an atmosphere of intense unease on *The Daily Telegraph*'s editorial floors, and of bitterness and rancour on the *Sunday* one. The strain on Features, especially, was immense, as Veronica Wadley laboured to produce pages for the seven-day operation, as well as launching a Sunday review section. Some good journalists such as Donald McIntyre and David Blundy at once quit the *Sunday* in disgust. After a phase when Perry's Deputy Editor, Ian Watson, ran the news side of Worsthorne's lost empire, Trevor Grove moved across from his role as Assistant Editor of the *Daily* to edit the *ST* – except for its Comment pages. Perry and his little team – 'Worsthorne College', as Conrad jovially referred to them – fortified their bunker for a last stand. We entered a period of intense unhappiness for all involved, which only ended in 1991 with Perry's departure, and the confirmation of Trevor Grove as Editor with traditional responsibilities for the whole of the *Sunday* as a separate entity. The merged structure was always clumsy. The Comment section's defiant refusal to coordinate with Trevor, or sometimes even to disclose what features they were planning to run the following week, ensured that tensions grew and mistrust festered. Perry's team never concealed their bitterness towards Trevor, me, and above all Andrew Knight. The merged paper looked what it was – a pantomime horse. The front and back legs were pulling in opposite directions. The merger was the biggest strategic mistake the company made in my time. It inflicted severe damage upon respect for our regime within the newspaper industry.

And even as we were struggling to make the merger work, in the summer of 1989 a new and related internal crisis arose. The management enlisted the services of an ambitious subeditor and a management consultant to conduct a time-and-motion study of the editorial floors. One afternoon early in July, Jeremy Deedes and I were invited to hear these two men present their report to Conrad, Andrew, Stephen Grabiner and other management figures in a room at a West End hotel. The authors of the document professed to have uncovered chronically inefficient and extravagant working practices. They concluded that the distribution of labour among reporters and subeditors was wasteful, and badly managed. It was suggested that subediting operations could be carried out centrally, by a new combined grouping of subs who owed no departmental loyalty to News, Features or other specialist divisions. By imposing this structure, it should be possible to run the *Daily* and *Sunday Telegraph* with at least 25 per cent fewer editorial staff. At the close of the presentation, I was told that it was the management's intention to implement its findings forthwith. The atmosphere as we parted was highly charged. Conrad and the management were obviously expecting a fight.

But over the past three and half years, I had learned something about curbing my natural impatience, and about the merits of prevarication. I commented cautiously that this was a very serious matter, which would need careful study. I wanted to go away with the editorial team, discuss it at length, and then meet again. Jeremy and I adjourned to the bar of Brooks's, where we said nothing to each other until we were on the right side of a large drink. Then I asked: 'Do I resign now, or later?' I was in a state of shock. Even Jeremy's usual urbanity was visibly fractured. It seemed insulting that two men, one of negligible achievement in journalism and the other with no knowledge of the business at all, should have been invited by the management to produce a report which revealed an absolute lack of understanding of how a serious newspaper works. Perhaps the greatest strength of *The Daily Telegraph* lay in its corps of literate, intelligent subeditors, who processed copy to a standard no other title in Britain could match. The new plan called for an overall reduction in editorial staffs across the two titles from 442 to 335. I was wholly supportive of the management's determination to end the subs' four-day working week, a Spanish practice long overdue for the scrap heap. I was happy to remove some people who were either no good, or who worked in areas that were overstaffed. But a cull on the scale the management proposed would destroy my credibility as Editor in the eyes of the staff, and strike a devastating blow at the quality of the newspapers. Jeremy said: 'It's obvious they are serious about this. We'd better go and talk equally seriously about how we should respond.'

I went home that weekend deeply miserable, believing there was a realistic prospect I would have to resign as Editor. For the only time in my years at the *Telegraph*, I took the expensive precaution of consulting lawyers about my contractual position, in the event that I was forced to go. Then we began a long, painful process of discussion with heads of department about the management's proposals. If possible, the senior executives were more dismayed than I was. Trevor Grove commented: 'This is intended to produce a saving of some £5 million by introducing longer working hours for ¾ of the staff, redundancy for ¼, and the break-up of self-motivated, closely-knit cells to produce larger, impersonal units under non-hands-on executives (the very opposite of theories current throughout modern industry). This is a recipe for sullenness, disloyalty, and possible disruption. It would place in jeopardy much of what we have achieved since 1986.' Nigel Wade, the Foreign Editor, wrote contemptuously: 'What can one say about a plan that would fire a quarter of the staff . . . ignore the advice of all journalists, however senior; treat all journalists as if they are interchangeable and infinitely replaceable? Why is this insane course being proposed?'

But all of us recognized that the struggle to avert disaster must be conducted on the basis of logic and negotiation, rather than of mere rhetoric. Painstakingly, department by department, we set about considering what savings and reorganization were attainable, without affecting the quality of the titles. We had no difficulty in compiling a list of some thirty journalists who could be made redundant without any loss – most, indeed, were people I was happy to part with. But the knowledge that management was promoting far more draconian measures strained the atmosphere within our building in a fashion I never experienced before or afterwards at the *Telegraph*. It became difficult to conduct daily business amicably. At one point early in August, I lost patience with Andrew Knight when he asked me to sit down with the authors of the time-and-motion study, and to debate details of their ideas. I wrote to the Chief Executive, saying that I was happy to discuss the issues with him or Conrad at any time, but not with mere stooges: 'Together with the rest of Editorial, I have done my utmost to produce sensible answers to some extraordinarily silly questions, but I find it remarkable that you should expect me to negotiate about editorial staffing with [the authors of the T&M study].'

It was a wretched period. In his autobiography, Conrad declares that the T&M study 'became a flashpoint for virtual civil war between Max and Joe Cooke' – 'Andrew . . . having ignominiously abdicated ... *The Daily Telegraph* was like a great ship knifing through the water satisfactorily, her rudder fixed amidship because no consensus for a course correction could be found among the fiercely factionalized and quarrelling flag officers who milled around in shambles on the bridge.' Conscious that we were in danger of losing our grip on the newspapers, Conrad now involved himself more directly with the company's management than at any time since his arrival. Though he was determined to demonstrate his toughness, he also seemed susceptible to patient, reasoned argument. I believed that we were fighting a battle we had to win, to preserve everything we had been doing since 1986, and indeed to save *The Daily Telegraph* from becoming a mere money-making machine. I suspect that word filtered through to Conrad that I was seriously considering my own position. No grown-up executive threatens to resign. Either he stays or he leaves. It is foolish to bluster. But it did no harm for the management to recognize that much of what was being proposed was unacceptable to me.

The crisis was defused in an unexpected fashion. From the moment the merger of the *Daily* and *Sunday* was first proposed in February, Andrew Knight found himself in an increasingly unhappy personal position. He had grown accustomed to the respect of both editorial and management. Since 1986, he had exercised a high degree of autonomy in directing the company. As 1989 advanced, he found himself assailed by management and losing the regard of the journalists. Senior editorial staff believed, and showed they believed, that Andrew had let them down by acquiescing in proposals for arbitrary mass redundancies. The merger of titles was perceived as his brainchild. Meanwhile, some of Conrad's personal advisers were growing sceptical of Andrew's performance as Chief Executive. They believed that he was insufficiently ruthless in pursuing the company's bottom line. Yet, as company profits rose, the value of *Telegraph* stock had soared, even though it could only be traded privately. All those who had been granted options back in 1986 at a price of 50p a share, including me and twenty or so senior executives, were able to cash these three years later at a price of £3.26. For the first time in my own life, I found myself clear of personal debt, a heady sensation. Andrew's 5 per cent of the *Telegraph* now yielded him a profit of over £14 million. I believed that he had earned it, insofar as anyone can earn £14 million. The turnaround of the company's fortunes was overwhelmingly his achievement, however much others subsequently sought to rewrite history. He had personally identified and appointed most of the winning team.

But others on the management floor were resentful. Conrad was plainly irked that he, the great deal-maker, had conceded to Andrew terms better than he thought any paid hand deserved. Some years later, when Conrad rejected a request of my own for a rise, I remarked mischievously on the large pay-hike he and Dan Colson had recently accorded themselves. 'Ah, Max, but Dan and I are capitalists, while you are a seeker after truth. Would you seriously wish to make yourself a contender for the Andrew Knight Award for Corporate Greed?' Even long afterwards, his former Chief Executive's huge capital gain still rankled with Conrad. The *Telegraph*'s Chairman has always asserted that Knight's role in setting up the original scheme to buy into the Berrys' company was far less pivotal than Andrew claimed. Be that as it may, the two men had visibly fallen out of love.

On 19 September 1989, Andrew Knight's resignation as Chief Executive was announced. Subsequent events provoked a seismic row between him and Conrad. Andrew told the world, amid widespread disbelief, that he was off to enjoy his newly gained fortune, and to contemplate his garden. Three months after he left our building, however, on 1 January 1990, it was announced that he was to become Chairman of Rupert Murdoch's News International, our deadly rival. Andrew had never concealed his enthusiasm for Murdoch. It was impossible not to admire the Australian tycoon's dramatic contribution to the modernization of the British newspaper industry. But editorially, I was among those who believed that Murdoch's style of journalism had made us all poorer. Murdoch's contempt for institutions, especially British ones, together with his disdain for personal privacy or dignity, sooner or later tarnished every title he owned. What a sorry thing *The Times* became, and remains, under his suzerainty!

Andrew often rebuked me for expressing hostility to Murdoch journalism. He maintained a warm personal relationship with Rupert, which he never sought to conceal. On one preposterous occasion, the American evangelist Billy Graham was visiting London. Andrew organized a joint lunch at the Stafford Hotel for Graham, with a *Telegraph* team and a group from News International, led by Rupert in person. I flinched from attendance, and sought to excuse myself. Andrew insisted. I turned up with bad grace, and annoyed Murdoch at the outset by declining to notice the outstretched hand of Kelvin Mackenzie, Editor of *The Sun*, which had just committed some new crime against human dignity. Murdoch, as always when I have encountered him, cut a curiously joyless figure. He appeared to have no life beyond his business, no cultural or aesthetic interests. He conveyed no sense of pleasure in anything beyond the deal of the moment. That he is a kind of genius, few can doubt. No newspaperman of the twentieth century displayed a more brilliant understanding of popular taste. But Murdoch will leave this planet having added precious little to the store of decency, culture, humanity that sustains civilized societies.

It seemed baffling that the News International boss should have signed up for such a grotesque affair as the Billy Graham lunch. Whatever the merits of journalism, I have always thought it implausible to associate the doings of our trade with the Christian ethic. The mismatch makes most Fleet Street funeral eulogies and memorial services seem blasphemous affairs. Yet perhaps Rupert Murdoch, like Lord Beaverbrook in his old age, had decided to make some belated stab at amends for his earthly crimes, in advance of the prospect of divine retribution. I sat munching my smoked salmon at the Stafford, recalling Malcolm Muggeridge's peerless satirical essay on Lord Beaverbrook's view of Christ: 'His was essentially a success story. From humble origins (though, as the son of God, he might have been considered to have exalted connections) he achieved a position of astounding power and influence. The Crucifixion was a setback, certainly, but the Resurrection more than compensated for it . . . his astounding career, from carpenter's son to an accepted position on God's right hand, exemplified Lord Beaverbrook's favourite proposition, that dazzling opportunities await whoever has the shrewdness, energy and perspicacity to see and seize them. Not even the sky was the limit.'

God help us, did Rupert's ambitions, likewise, now extend to the celestial? I suggested to Billy Graham across the table at lunch that the spectacle of such a group as ours gathered under one roof invited a divine thunderbolt to strike the Stafford. It was a serve into the net. Graham seemed more than happy to bless Rupert, Andrew, or anyone else present who would provide a decent plug in our newspapers for his next mass meeting. Nobody seemed to find anything incongruous about the occasion, which might have jarred the sensibilities of Lord Copper himself. It was rumoured that Murdoch himself was dallying with Christianity at the time, though it would have required an assiduous student of his titles to discern any indication of an interest in the hereafter. I went away from lunch embarrassed that a man as intelligent as Andrew could have contrived an occasion so steeped in absurdity.

In the *Telegraph* offices, we began to speculate about the Chief Executive's future, first, when his share options matured, and second, when he invited Murdoch to lunch on the old Hebridean steamer which was permanently moored alongside South Quay as the *Telegraph* staff restaurant. Conrad had begun to spend more time in London. He and Dan Colson, his key adviser, were playing an increasingly active part in management decisions. The Chairman was showing burgeoning confidence, even exuberance. He was the focus of intense social curiosity, feted at dinner tables and boardroom lunches. Not surprisingly, he enjoyed the sensation. Andrew once said to me: 'You must always remember that in America, Conrad does not rank as a very rich man. But

in Britain, now, with the *Telegraph* he is becoming a big player.'
Senior executives felt increasingly conscious that Andrew was being
marginalized; having achieved his ambition of making a fortune,
he felt restless; given his links with Murdoch and, indeed, his
fascination for the man, News International was where he seemed
likely to go. Editorial executives were thus much less startled than
Conrad by the announcement that Andrew was joining our key
rival.

The day after Knight's appointment at NI was announced,
Conrad wrote, and widely circulated, a scorching letter to him. 'It
seems to be a universal view, among people whose friendship we
both value in Britain, Canada and the United States,' observed
our Chairman in one of his more temperate passages, 'that your
prolonged (if sporadic) courtship with our principal competitor
while continuing as the ostensible Chief Executive of *The Daily
Telegraph*, leading to a consummation just 80 days after retiring
(awkwardly) as a director of ours, and with your pockets loaded
with a net £14 million of free *Telegraph* stocks, raises substantial
ethical questions . . .'

The Chairman's letter, handwritten from Palm Beach, provoked a lengthy reply from Andrew, disputing most of Conrad's
charges. This was also widely circulated. A further bombardment
from both trenches ensued. Then and later, Andrew sought to
gain the endorsement of former *Telegraph* colleagues for his actions
– an odd revelation of vulnerability, but not an uncharacteristic
one. There is a good line in one of Anthony Powell's novels: 'The
disagreeable aspect of so many people is not so much their doing
unpleasant things, as wanting to justify them.' I was at some pains
to tell Andrew that I had no personal quarrel with him. Indeed, I
owed him a lifelong debt for giving me a job no one else would
have considered me for. His quarrel was with Conrad. But it was
a bridge too far, to hope that I or other colleagues would feel
moved to applaud his actions, as he seemed to wish, and as indeed
he sought in lengthy correspondence over the years that followed.
The commercial struggle between the *Telegraph* and *Times* was

bitter and costly. Neither then or later did Rupert Murdoch conceal his determination to use his vast resources to break us. He told David English that, in his opinion, in twenty years' time there would be only three British national titles which counted: *The Times*, *The Sun*, and the *Daily Mail*. It was a bitter pill for us to see our old boss, alongside whom we had battled against NI for so long, ensconced at the summit of power in Wapping.

Andrew was not immediately replaced as Chief Executive. Joe Cooke, formerly our management consultant and now elevated to Managing Director, took over some of Andrew's administrative responsibilities. Conrad and Dan Colson exercised overall supervision. Happily, the Chairman abandoned a short-lived notion that he himself should become Chief Executive. I became a member of the board, and was later given the title of Editor-in-Chief of the *Daily* and *Sunday*. It was conceded by the management that the editorial merger was a failure. We began painfully unpicking the mess. In one of Conrad's scornful notes to Andrew, he said: 'Max Hastings has asked me to commend to you the merits of combining the *Times* and *Sunday Times*.' The rest of Fleet Street learned the lesson. Only the *Independent*, in the face of desperate financial necessity, later attempted a similar union of its daily and Sunday staffs. Mergers of technical resources often make sense. But the demands of Sunday journalism are so specialized that it is unrealistic to suppose that the same creative staff can work through seven days.

When Trevor Grove assumed full responsibility for the *Sunday* title, Charles Moore moved from editing the *Spectator* to become my deputy, and to write a political column for the *Daily*. Charles and I were poles apart politically, but I readily accepted Conrad's view that he should be given the opportunity to gain experience as a newspaper executive with an eye to the future. Charles is a superbly gifted writer, and the most delightful of colleagues. In the years that followed, while we had plenty of political differences of opinion, he never allowed these to get in the way of working loyally for me, though I missed Trevor's grasp of Features commissioning and of some technical aspects of running a news-paper. I was always irked when I felt that Conrad undervalued the skills of our non-political executives, and was too eager that I should crowd the staff with ideologues. I told him many times that if we recruited the sort of stable of right-wing polemicists Paul Johnson would welcome, we would set back the commercial fortunes of *The Daily Telegraph* by a generation. I also remarked delicately upon the fate of Perry Worsthorne's *Sunday Telegraph*. Conrad was not slow to take the point.

A trifling postscript to the Andrew Knight saga: six months after his departure, we ran a leader-page article by Michael Grade, Chief Executive of Channel 4, in which he attacked Murdoch's grip on British satellite broadcasting. Andrew, in his new role as Murdoch's apologist, wrote to me suggesting that he should contribute a riposte on our leader page: 'It would doubtless be much read, and would be regarded as responsible editing on your part,' he observed splendidly. I had no hesitation in accepting Andrew's offer. I wrote to Conrad telling him what I was doing, saying I thought that this would be perceived as a good joke in the industry. So it was, but I would not have cared to push my luck with Murdoch by demanding reciprocal space for myself on the leader page of *The Times*.

By some mysterious but benign process, Andrew's departure cleared the air after the bitter quarrels of 1989. In many ways unjustly, he became a sin-eater for the embattled factions in the *Telegraph* building. A few weeks after he left, some anonymous members of the staff sent a round robin to Conrad, setting out in great detail, and with considerable penetration, their view of what had happened to the company and the poor state of editorial morale, along with personal assessments of each senior manage-ment executive. Their spleen focused upon Andrew. They criti-cized several senior personalities shrewdly. My own 'school report' was a curate's egg. The authors wrote: 'While Hastings is notori-ously difficult to work with, he is highly professional and has been a vital force in repositioning the paper. Hastings brings out the best in people around him, and has attracted good journalists who are not afraid of a challenge. His arrogance is frightfully boring at times, but unlike Knight he is at least taken seriously.' I found this qualified vote of confidence encouraging, though the letter went on to express sympathy and admiration for Jeremy Deedes who 'has the difficult task of trying to deal with the unpredictable Hastings and the nonsense of [the management consultants'] ideas . . . He is one of the few people who understands journalists.' The letter observed that Perry Worsthorne possessed a more agreeable personality than my own, but suggested that Perry should have shown the conviction to resign when most of his empire was taken from him. We puzzled for weeks, and in vain, over the likely authorship of this well-informed document. I suspect that the Chairman was quite uninfluenced by it, for good or ill.

Yet I was encouraged that, in the wake of Andrew's departure, Conrad was at pains to assert his confidence in me: 'You and I, Max, must stick together as closely as David and Jonathan. We must bind ourselves with hoops of steel.' The five-day working week was imposed on the editorial staff with my strong support, the pill sweetened by substantial pay rises. We suffered one night of industrial action – led by some chronic grumblers from the old regime who perceived this, rightly, as their last stand – when most of the journalists downed tools. But senior executives were able to produce a newspaper, and next day the strikers returned to work. I accepted full responsibility for making thirty-three journalists redundant, and interviewed most of them myself, always a miserable task. I had to break the news by telephone to one reporter who was enjoying a prize fellowship in Washington at the time, for which we had warmly recommended her. The fact that we were able to weather these upheavals with relative ease owed a lot to the fact that the entire staff knew how far-reaching had been the original proposals we resisted. The authors of the T&M study left the company, amid much rejoicing. Once again, I recognized a personal debt to Jeremy Deedes. He had steered me, and all of us, through a ghastly period with incomparable tact and discretion.

But for his counsel, there were many days when I should have been tempted to throw in the towel, to walk out of the door. Along with Trevor, Veronica Wadley and Nigel Wade, Jeremy reminded me that to quit would be a betrayal of the paper, and of the staff. After the events of those months, the bond between our little executive team was closer than ever. Now, thank God, we could get back to thinking about our newspapers and what we should put in them.

7

THE FALL OF THATCHER

BEFORE I BECAME AN EDITOR, and even for some while after I did so, I harboured delusions that one could run a newspaper on the same basis that a good journalist writes a column: with prejudices, but without commitment to any grouping. In reality, however, few editors and few newspapers can wholly detach themselves from a responsibility to some interest, political or economic. *The Daily Telegraph* was the dominant newspaper of the Conservative Party's politicians and rank-and-file. I was often willing to express views which ran counter to our old readers' supposed prejudices. I had already done so on South Africa, Northern Ireland, capital punishment, Gibraltar, the Libyan bombings and other matters. But on the broad issue of who ruled, it seemed right that a Conservative paper should maintain a prejudice in favour of the status quo.

Through the late 1980s, we faithfully reported the mounting difficulties of the Thatcher government. We ran many leaders critical of government policies, and for that matter of Mrs Thatcher's increasingly unstable personal behaviour. But we remained supportive of her position as Prime Minister, even when privately I and most of my colleagues believed that she had lost her way, and would not find it again. Some critics argued that this was not courageous journalism. I said that it was the price an institution such as *The Daily Telegraph* must pay for its position vis-à-vis its Conservative readership. Though we sometimes adopted positions directly contrary to those espoused by Conrad, Andrew Knight and the Tory Right, not infrequently our editorials compromised in accordance with my own instinctive caution, not theirs. In particular, I have never thought it is the business of newspapers to campaign to depose Prime Ministers, as distinct from commenting, adversely if necessary, on their performance.

The scale of Mrs Thatcher's election victory in June 1987 reflected the unelectability of the Labour Party, rather than the popularity of the Prime Minister, even within her own party. Labour's policies, above all the continuing commitment to unilateral nuclear disarmament, held little appeal for any voter in the middle ground. I wrote for the leader page on election day: 'If the British people reject the Conservatives today, the implications would far transcend any mere change of political power. The nation would be declaring its preference for a relentless return to economic decline and a political preoccupation with the distribution rather than the creation of wealth . . . Mrs Thatcher is unlikely to become a figure beloved of the British people. She is too uncomfortable for that. But she seems immensely worthy of respect, not merely for what she has done for Britain, for what she may do yet.' Given the manifesto on which Labour fought, Neil Kinnock was thought to have done well to poll ahead of the Liberal–SDP Alliance.

Yet even in the immediate aftermath of the 1987 Election, there was ample evidence of trouble brewing for the government. George Jones wrote on 25 June about 'growing Tory unease over plans to replace domestic rates by a Community Charge', with Michael Heseltine, Stephen Dorrell, John Biffen and Sir George Young among the opposing forces. We gave Young a prominent platform, to highlight the objections. Nicholas Ridley and Michael Howard, the responsible ministers, expressed their determination to implement the Poll Tax. Howard wrote confidently on our leader page in July 1987 that 'the administrative problems of running a community charge have been much exaggerated'. Following his earlier untroubled enthusiasms for the Financial Services Act and water privatization, my faith in his political judgement never recovered, even before he embarked upon his disastrous tenure as Home Secretary. We said in a leader on 10 July that poll tax was likely to become 'the most vexatious political issue before this parliament ... Is this really how the government wants to allocate the foremost impetus for its efforts in the year or two to come? ... There is good cause to reflect on that, before plunging headlong into these treacherous waters.' At one of our leader conferences, Jock Bruce-Gardyne observed dismissively, and presciently, that in order to get a poll tax onto the statute book the government would have to allow so many reliefs and exemptions that the whole thing would become meaningless.

Some of us were increasingly troubled by the absence of concern in the government's policies and rhetoric for the underclass – this, at a time when there were well over three million unemployed. We were consistently critical of the government's failure to address public services. Privatization could not be regarded as a universal panacea. Privatizing state monopolies without also creating competition was a grave error, as we believed to be the case with the British Airports Authority, and later with the water industry. 'The state sector will always remain. And its revival is of the utmost importance,' we wrote on 1 August. 'This administration is seen as furtive, even contemptuous, in its attitude to public services.' That month, we ran a series of big articles by the likes of George Walden and Michael Heseltine, on the public services Thatcherism had failed – education, transport and the Civil Service prominent amongst them. Richard Hope, the railway expert, declared that while privatizing the system was in principle a good idea, it would be disastrous to do so by separating operations and track. This had been tried unsuccessfully on the Stockton to Darlington line in 1825, and had wisely never been repeated.

In a signed article, I argued that the government's appetite for anti-libertarian measures reflected the yearning of the Tory middle class to undo the perceived excesses of the 1960s:

Mrs Thatcher remains *par excellence* the mirror of the middle-class majority. Her own instinctive social and moral reactions – to broadcasters, criminals, the Gibraltar shooting, the Arts establishment, murderers and pornographers, pro-Europeans and educationalists – are their own. She says what they think. They believe she thinks what they say . . . This administration extends ever-wider the parameters of nannyism . . . I myself share many of the majority's prejudices, its determination to turn society away from a preoccupation with minority rights, in the direction of middle-class values. But I also fear the excesses and curbs of the nanny state. Random breath-testing seems . . . a disturbing step over the line . . . In our enthusiasm to reverse the huge moral and social misjudgements of the 1960s and 1970s, we should beware of creating a new edifice of restriction and surveillance, out of all proportion to the problems it seeks to confront.

Ferdy Mount was among those constantly irked by the style of the government's handling of Europe. There was 'something grudging and tepid in most of our public dealings with our nearest neighbours', he wrote in June 1988. We would never be a serious player in the world until we became more serious players in Europe.

Generally, should we not try a little harder and be more positive in our approach? Should we not give just as high a priority to teaching modern languages as to the sciences? Should not the Royal Family be encouraged to see fractionally less of the Commonwealth and rather more of the Continent than Sir Harold Acton's lovely villa outside Florence? What is required is a kind of restrained self-restraint in our dealings, an unwillingness to revive old sores and pay off old scores – in short, the kind of tact and trust we now take for granted in our dealings with the Soviet Union. Is that too much to ask?

Although in 1988 few people were predicting Thatcher's imminent demise, speculation about the succession had begun. George Jones mentioned John Major's name as a rising young hopeful. Bruce Anderson suggested on our leader page that the party might turn to Geoffrey Howe 'for his unshakeable calm', while Michael Heseltine and Kenneth Baker looked strong candidates, alongside Malcolm Rifkind and Chris Patten. 'But the current favourite for a mid-90s succession is John Major. When the tipsters started mentioning his name, he was amused; more recently, he has become positively embarrassed. He has no enemies and, apparently, no weaknesses.'

Though the economy was prospering, there were mounting fears that the Chancellor's credit boom was out of hand. The pound was under serious pressure. The tensions between Mrs Thatcher and her Chancellor about his policy of causing sterling to shadow the Deutschmark were the focus of growing adverse comment. Mrs Thatcher launched her formidable broadside against Europe at Bruges on 21 September 1988, arguing the case for Europe to be 'a family of nations which looks outward rather than inward'. It was Ferdy Mount, again, who in my eyes expressed the sanest criticism of her attitude to Europe in his *Telegraph* column, after another storm of Eurosceptic rhetoric at the Tory Conference in October: 'The point is . . . that "Europe" cannot be pumped up into a single major issue. It is a series of diverse questions which deserve calm attention, not least because British public opinion has, I think, moved on from the old black-and-white, Beaverbrook versus Brussels stereotype and expects business to be done in a sensible fashion . . . Is it really such a good idea to teach a whole new generation that life inside the Community is one long hectic squabble, while relations with the USSR, as with the USA, usually run smooth as silk? Is there not a danger that in the long run, this rhetorical imbalance (or double standard) may make us less well-equipped to defend our own best interests?'

Today, almost fifteen years later, Mrs Thatcher is sometimes perceived as having possessed absolute dominance of British politics during her years of power. Yet the period of her undisputed command was far shorter than her premiership. In the early 1980s, she was struggling to achieve mastery. For perhaps four or five years, between the Falklands victory in 1982 and the 1987 General Election, she indeed occupied an extraordinarily strong position. But thereafter, dissensions in her government and mounting public dislike of her personality eroded her power rapidly. She was at odds about Europe with Geoffrey Howe, her Foreign Secretary, and with Nigel Lawson, her Chancellor. The poll tax grew in unpopularity, even as it came closer to implementation. Industrial disputes, above all in the transport system, reflected bitter residual resistance from the unions. Inflation was mounting. By 1989, it was evident that Mr Lawson had allowed his boom to run out of control. House prices were falling, while inflation stood at 13 per cent. The IRA maintained a steady tempo of terrorism, both in Northern Ireland and on the mainland. Neil Kinnock was leading a march to reform of the Labour Party, above all by gaining repudiation of unilateral nuclear disarmament at the 1989 Conference. The state of public services, and the government's apparent indifference to them, was causing growing public dismay. Meanwhile the East–West confrontation, which had enabled Thatcher to display her virtues to such effect, was receding in significance. For decades, defence of the West had been an obvious vital national interest, on which the Conservative Party gained votes at the expense of Labour. By 1989, it was no longer plausible to suppose that defence would be a major issue at the next British general election. One of the key Tory props, an important rationale for the Thatcher premiership, was gone. If now, also, her government's competence in managing the economy was the focus of increasing doubt, then how was the Tory Party to hold on to power?

The Daily Telegraph's relationship with Downing Street had been fractured back in 1986, and was never mended. Oddly enough, even Perry Worsthorne was frequently persona non grata with the Prime Minister for his bouts of Sunday criticism. One day in May 1989, Andrew Knight told me how distressing Conrad found it that neither of his editors was welcome at the residence of his idol. I sent a note to both men about the situation:

I believe the present state of relations with Downing Street reflects poorly upon the attitude of the Prime Minister and those around her, rather than upon us. It was Bill Deedes who remarked when we were discussing some spat that 'we have to accept that nothing less than a posture of slavish devotion is acceptable'. All regular readers of the DT know that, for every critical editorial or feature we carry, we run three or four that are strongly supportive. Yet George Jones reported an explosion from Downing Street following our editorial critical of the government's handling of the Father Ryan affair, which we said was guaranteed to ensure the Irish response it received [Mrs Thatcher had publicly denounced Dublin for lack of sympathy in an extradition case]. I did not regret what we said, and do not regret it now. But Bernard [Ingham] told George to tell us that she regarded our comment as 'disgracefully unpatriotic'.

The issues that have obviously caused her greatest rage are, in order: the departure of Carol; Libya; Gibraltar. It is reasonable to ask that she should consider our behaviour on each of these issues against the background of our general support. But she herself has several times been reported as saying: 'We do not want the support of *The Daily Telegraph* sometimes. We want loyalty that we can rely upon.' Only the *Daily Mail*, *Sun*, and *Times* provide this in adequate quantities to satisfy her.

I see no way out of the impasse. I hope I am not flattering our position when I say that I think our well-established posture of broad support and reasoned criticism enjoys a substantial measure of respect, not least among Cabinet

ministers, everywhere except from the far right. I believe our
role is honourable, and commercially and politically sound.

Because Conrad Black later came to be perceived as a tren-
chant spokesman for the Right, he has received less credit than
he deserves for resisting pressure from the Thatcher camp in the
increasingly fraught last years of her premiership. Though we
often held conversations in which he made plain his own sorrow
about relations between the paper and Downing Street, he
maintained his support through successive crises in which his
right-wing friends – the Aspinalls, Goldsmiths, Paul Johnsons and
Thatcher's personal entourage – would have feted him for sacking
me.

That spring of 1989, our relations with Downing Street grew
so bad that when Mrs Thatcher announced that she was to visit
South Africa, we were told that, while the *Times* and *Sun* were
sending correspondents, there would be no place in her party for
a *Telegraph* writer. This was so plainly absurd that I made a call to
Charles Powell in Thatcher's private office. I enquired, in not very
heavily coded terms, whether Downing Street wanted to escalate
our differences to open conflict. Powell took the point. A *Telegraph*
man travelled with the Prime Minister's party. But it was a
measure of how petty and vengeful she was becoming, as the
shades began to close in on her, that such an issue should have
arisen.

In July 1989 Thatcher staged the most far-reaching Cabinet
reshuffle of her premiership, which was widely perceived as
a symptom of the government's malaise. Geoffrey Howe was
pushed sideways to become Deputy Prime Minister, in order to
make way for his replacement as Foreign Secretary by John Major,
a move that caused widespread amazement, because Major possessed no experience of foreign affairs. Douglas Hurd, who had
been widely tipped for dismissal because Thatcher found him
unsympathetic, kept his job as Home Secretary. He wrote me a
note on 24 July:

Dear Max,

Well! I suppose Prime Ministers feel they must *surprise*. No point in having all that power if you use it as all the pundits have predicted.

I am content to survive.

Yours Ever

Soon afterwards, of course, Major moved on to become Chancellor, and Hurd became Foreign Secretary. Much as I loved him, I was dismayed by the fashion in which Douglas, like most of the Cabinet, allowed himself to be bullied by the Prime Minister. One evening, we were talking about memoirs. The then Home Secretary said: 'I don't think I shall write any, but I would like to write a book about what it was like serving under Thatcher.'

'Well, you'll have some explaining to do,' I replied. 'How could you have accepted responsibility for at least two pieces of legislation she insisted upon, the Broadcasting Act and the War Crimes Act, which you knew in your heart were indefensible? Why can't you all stand up to her?'

Douglas laughed, a shade uncomfortably. 'It's very hard to explain unless you know what it's like to be there.'

The resignation of Nigel Lawson as Chancellor on 26 October 1989 inflicted another devastating shock on the government. *The Sun* ('Goodbye and good riddance') and the *Daily Mail* ('his policies were bankrupt') applauded his departure. Most commentators, however, blamed Mrs Thatcher for the collision with Lawson. *The Economist* was fiercely critical. The *Financial Times* said this was 'the beginning of the end' for the Prime Minister . . . The questions that remain concern not [Lawson], but the government . . . A government of people committed to a set of coherent, radical and timely ideas . . . has now become a government committed to the Prime Minister herself.'

The *Telegraph* said: 'Leadership, in which she excels, must not degenerate into dominance, intolerance and a simple refusal to work with those she has appointed to serve her.' We wrote of

Lawson that 'he deserves to be remembered by his party and the country for his years of triumph, rather than for the manner of his eclipse'. Yet, though it was widely recognized that Mrs Thatcher's personal position was now precarious, it remained hard to paint a convincing scenario for her fall. No plausible successor, even including Michael Heseltine, seemed likely to expose himself to the charge of dividing the Conservative Party by standing against her in an election for the leadership. Only recognition by Thatcher herself that her position had become untenable seemed likely to create a vacancy. That still seemed implausible.

We expressed dismay when the Prime Minister declared her intention to continue in office through two more elections – which would have taken her into her seventies. By November, polls showed Labour leading the Tories by 10 points. Anthony King wrote on our leader page that for the first time since Mrs Thatcher came to power in 1979, the Tories faced a serious and credible threat from the Opposition. When the obscure and eccentric backbencher Sir Anthony Meyer offered himself as a stalking horse challenger to Thatcher in the December leadership election, no serious commentator suggested that Tory MPs should vote for him. Yet on the day, Meyer polled 33 votes to Thatcher's 314, with 24 spoilt papers and 3 abstentions. Given that the challenger was a political featherweight, subsequent attention focused upon the fact that 60 Tories had failed to support their Prime Minister. It was 'a miserable, stunted sort of outcome to a footling and foolish contest', wrote Ferdy Mount. 'No one comes out of it much better off, except Mr Neil Kinnock.' Our leader suggested that Thatcher still had a chance to rebuild her fortunes, but we made plain our misgivings about her rhetoric on Europe: 'Even those who support her attitude on points of substance, and are wary of the European federalists, believe her general demeanour on European issues threatens to marginalise Britain at a time of great upheaval and historic developments.' We carried a leader-page article by Michael Heseltine, arguing that we must 'move with the force of our destiny towards Europe'.

Looking back at this period, as Mrs Thatcher's government tottered and we entered the last turbulent year of her premiership, I am struck by how modest a part Conrad sought to play in the unfolding drama. Later, after Thatcher's departure, he became much more engaged. His enthusiasm to take a role on the stage in the struggle against European integration both personally, and through his newspapers, became increasingly pronounced. But in the winter of 1989, though we lunched together occasionally and discussed the government's plight, there seemed no important ground separating us. I wrote to the Chairman in November, acknowledging that, if the Prime Minister fell, I would expect to consult closely with him about which candidate for the succession the *Daily Telegraph* should support. But, I said, 'it is fruitless to speculate about who is best suited to succeed Mrs Thatcher until we see when, and under what circumstances, she goes.'

By now, studying the march of the Thatcher government towards disaster had become one of my chief preoccupations as an editor. In the last weeks of 1989 I lunched with Douglas Hurd, Kenneth Baker, David Waddington, Norman St John Stevas and John Patten, and this issue was invariably a focus of our conversations. As the Prime Minister became more embattled, so she also became more alarmingly strident. Her visceral, futile resistance to German reunification did more than any other single act to harden my private doubts – and those of more important people – about her fitness to continue in office. She seemed to wish to continue to combat, to confront, to dispute even as the rest of the world was ready to rejoice in the détente between East and West. Her vision of affairs seemed increasingly remote from that of the British people, and from rationality. As tensions rose between Downing Street and Bonn, and we attacked in the paper her Canutish resistance to great events which she possessed no power to influence, some Tories began openly to denounce the *Telegraph*'s 'treachery'. We continued to believe that Neil Kinnock's Labour Party did not deserve to form the government of the country, but it seemed impossible for any thinking Conservative to suppose that Mrs Thatcher's administration any longer merited unqualified support.

Having become increasingly sceptical about the government's social policies, we were especially dismayed by the introduction of the so-called 'Care in the Community' scheme for the mentally handicapped, which required the closure of many old-fashioned mental institutions – without the smallest credible provision to replace them. The folly of some government measures only becomes plain long after they have been introduced, but Care in the Community seemed pernicious from the outset. 'There is a satisfying political ring about the phrase . . . ,' we wrote,

> it contrasts with institutional care, and a vision of unsuitable Victorian buildings. It implies that we are a community to which care of the elderly and handicapped is safely entrusted. Yet . . . the development of our community care services has been slower than the government had hoped . . . if it is to flourish, it will require more than co-operative local authorities and voluntary organisations. It will call for a response from the whole community. This has not hitherto been conspicuous. Bluntly, we are ill-educated in the care of our neighbours.

Thirteen years later, nothing has changed. 'Care in the Community' remains one of the most shameful blunders in Britain's social policies over the past generation. If it formed one of the lesser failures of the Thatcher government, it was nonetheless a grievous one.

Perhaps the most significant political change at the paper in 1990 was brought about by the fact that Sarah Hogg became our Economics Editor. I had known Sarah quite well for many years. I first met her amid a Hampshire country house party at the age of sixteen, where I was deeply embarrassed by my inability to play kick-the-can. I admired her formidable intellect. She had been one of the founders of *The Independent*, but at lunch with me one day in October 1989, she said she felt ready for a change of scene.

Without hesitation, I offered her a job at the *Telegraph*. I was delighted when she accepted. In Neil Collins and Christopher Fildes, we possessed superb lead City commentators. But since the fatal illness of Jock Bruce-Gardyne, we could no longer call upon any educated economic intelligence among the leader writers.

I embarked on a professional honeymoon with Sarah from the day she came, founded upon my admiration for her brains, wit and loyalty. She wrote a weekly column as well as the economic leaders, and was perceived as a big catch for us. She was personally close to the new Chancellor, John Major, who relied heavily on her counsel. And, of course, their friendship added a lot to the authority of her journalism. She was a committed European. She believed Britain should enter the European Exchange Rate Mechanism as soon as possible. In this, her views diverged from those of Neil and Christopher, then as now resolute opponents of fixed exchange rates. I have never been troubled by pluralism, divisions of opinion between writers on any given newspaper. Intelligent readers reach their own judgements about which of a given title's pundits they wish to follow. But it was widely remarked, both at South Quay and Westminster, that on the ERM *The Daily Telegraph*'s leaders now expressed views about as remote as it was possible to get from those of our City team. In one of Sarah's first big editorials for us, on 19 January 1990, she asserted that the government's economic policy lacked the anchor either of monetary guidelines or of clear exchange rate targets. She opposed tax cuts, but suggested that interest rates must be raised to check consumer spending. Neil Collins's City Comment, by contrast, argued that even if a rate hike was needed to curb consumption, the impact on business of such a move would be disastrous. Neil predicted grave economic storms ahead, whatever the government did.

Our divisions with Downing Street continued to widen. On 8 February, Bernard Ingham delivered a scornful speech to the Commons Press Gallery, denouncing the media's treatment of the government. I wrote in a leader:

Like most politicians' press officers, it is Mr Ingham's role to act as purveyor of half-truths to the nation's journalists, but it is the business of the journalists to seek out the missing 50% ... The Press Secretary's delusions about the right of government to be believed on its own terms has fostered the conviction at Downing Street that enemies are everywhere, and hostile conspiracies are constantly afoot to undo the Prime Minister. If one of the criticisms of the Prime Minister in recent years is that she has allowed herself to become increasingly isolated, Mr Ingham is one of those trusted servants who have allowed her to become so. The most appropriate response by the parliamentary press gallery to his harsh strictures on Wednesday would be the gift of a large looking glass.

George Jones told me at lunch in February that he thought Thatcher would be lucky to survive the year. He said as much in the paper, a week or two later. I was astonished when Bill Deedes, whose own loyalty to the Prime Minister was never in question, took the same view at a leader conference. No one at the *Telegraph* doubted that the government was in deep trouble. Downing Street, meanwhile, was growing increasingly alarmed about our coverage. On 28 March that splendid professional mischief-maker, the Labour MP Tam Dalyell, put down an Early Day Motion, highlighting an alleged abuse of responsibility by civil servants, in the persons of Bernard Ingham and Charles Powell. He suggested that

> the non-party role of civil servants is further undermined by the participation of Charles Powell, one of the Prime Minis-ter's private secretaries, at a recent Curzon Aspinall Club lunch with Sir James Goldsmith, the honourable member for Plymouth, Sutton [Alan Clark] and Conrad Black ... held for the specific purpose of putting pressure on Mr Black to show greater support for the leader of the Conservative Party in the columns of his newspaper; welcomes the refusal of Mr

Black to succumb to the blandishments of two well-known Conservatives and a senior Whitehall official; and calls on that civil servant to take the only honourable course, retire from public service, and apply for more appropriate employment with Conservative Central Office.

We were baffled by this fragment of gossip Dalyell had picked up, having heard nothing about any such incident from Conrad or anyone else. It was not until Alan Clark's diaries were published that we learned the truth, or at least Alan's version of it. On the evening of Saturday 3 March, it seems, Clark, Powell and Sir James Goldsmith attended a dinner with Conrad at Aspinall's London house, in Clark's words 'to see to what extent he was amenable to being leant on, in the gentlest manner of course, to steer Max Hastings away from plugging Heseltine so much. The answer, it soon became clear was – not at all.' Good for Conrad – though he still denies that he was importuned in this way. In the case of three of the other four diners present, it was hard to imagine a group more devoid of political judgement, though they were all men whom he liked. To this day, I cannot imagine what Charles Powell, nominally a civil servant, thought he was doing playing such a game in such company. But the story gave us an indication of the mounting panic among Thatcher's supporters and associates.

After dining with Douglas Hurd one night towards the end of March, I reported in a note to Conrad that the Foreign Secretary

found it increasingly difficult to catch the Prime Minister on a day when she could reasonably be described as engaged, and in close touch with reality. She continues to act in a series of lurches and impulses, as with her interview with *Der Speigel* the other day, in which she (in Douglas's view; recklessly) undid all his recent efforts to rebuild broken fences with the Germans. He said she showed herself on good form on Sunday at the Chequers meeting with East European specialists, but her general behaviour is 'erratic' – not a ringing endorsement at this moment, when steadiness is all.

That said, Douglas shares my view that she will survive if she keeps her nerve . . . He simply cannot see the mechanics of the process by which she might be overthrown, and is confident that if Heseltine stands against her in the autumn (which he thinks he will not), he will be beat.

This was still the problem for all of us: to anticipate the political process for Thatcher's fall. To Conrad, I described the atmosphere in the Tory Party as 'something between fevered and hysterical'. I told him that some ministers envisaged a situation by the autumn in which conspirators dangled before the Prime Minister a candidate for the succession less distasteful to her than Michael Heseltine, to induce her to go. Though I changed my view a few months later, and grew to believe that Heseltine deserved the leadership, that spring I was still wavering about whether he could do the job. I feared that Douglas might not prove an election-winner. Who else was there to believe in?

Spring brought no remission from bad news for Thatcher's party. The Mid-Staffordshire by-election turned a Conservative majority of almost 15,000 into a Labour one of 9,449. We ran a half-hearted leader suggesting that, now the poll tax was law, we had better make the best of it. But the country thought differently. Popular hostility towards the tax was turning into real anger. Thatcher's personal poll rating had become the lowest ever recorded. We painted a huge graphic ladder down the length of our front page, depicting the Prime Minister's diminished standing against that of her predecessors in office.

Michael Heseltine was now being openly canvassed as Thatcher's most plausible successor, though Ferdy Mount cautioned in his column in March 1990 that he was not convinced such a change would be for the better. He was fearful that a Heseltine administration would prove soft on the hard choices: 'The trajectory . . . is easy to visualise. The rocket takes off in fine style, the burst of coloured stars draw gasps from the onlookers. Then the stick falls to earth, clattering through the bare branches. Marvellous while it lasts, but for how long?' Most of us continued to believe that, if Heseltine stood against Thatcher, he would be beaten, and that therefore he would not act.

*

YET EVEN IN THAT tumultuous year for British politics, it would be misleading to create an impression that for a newspaper, or its editor, the plight of the government remained permanently at the centre of our stage. We discussed politics two or three times a week at the leader conference, for up to half an hour at a time. But the usual kaleidoscope of issues at home and abroad dominated front pages in rotation. 1990 was an extraordinary historic period. Even while the fate of Thatcher persisted as a running theme, huge events were unfolding elsewhere. The collapse of the Soviet system, and its implications for Europe, absorbed space, energy and attention every day. In South Africa, white domination was drawing to a close, amid a fierce debate about whether international sanctions should be ended. The argument about the EC's advance towards monetary union entwined with British politics – Nicholas Ridley's assertion in a famous *Spectator* interview with Dominic Lawson that 'this is all a German racket designed to take over the whole of Europe, it has to be stopped' cost him his seat in the Cabinet, and shook the government once more. But the economic arguments about ERM and EMS were being debated in parallel with the political ones throughout 1990. The Iraqi invasion of Kuwait in August triggered a crisis, and a war, which became our chief preoccupations for months, and of which I shall say more later. BSE – mad cow disease – emerged first as a mere concern, then as a threat, and finally as an ongoing crisis.

It had taken four years for the *Telegraph* to transform itself into a modern newspaper, but now we had a shape, a design, a structure and a staff that we felt proud of. Following Xan Smiley's transfer to Washington, we posted two first-class young Russian-speaking correspondents to Moscow, John Kampner and Marcus Warren, who described the dramas of the Gorbachev presidency. Another very young but uncommonly mature reporter, Alec Russell, was reporting the fall of the East European regimes.

Continuing the remodelling of the paper, in February 1990 we moved Sport onto the back page, a long-overdue reform, and introduced a separate weekly Sports Section on Mondays, to exploit our dominance of the field. This was an immediate success, which helped to shore up our flagging sale at the beginning of the week. Saturday's circulation was rising steadily, with the aid of a growing string of heavyweight supplements, all generating big advertising revenue. Rival titles were struggling to match the *Telegraph*'s Saturday package, but we were perceived to be leading the pack.

Lest I seem to pretend that all innovations were successful, it is easy to recall some failures. We went through five Picture Editors in my first three years. We tried constantly, and in vain, to match Ray Snoddy's coverage of the media for the *Financial Times*. A decade earlier, the humorous writer Michael Green had contributed a fictional eighteenth-century memoir to Way of the World about a brutish rural reprobate. I invited Green to revive Squire Haggard's Journal as a weekly feature. I loved it, but everybody else on the staff cringed. The column was eventually dropped. I strove to persuade Frank Johnson to become our theatre critic, a role in which I believe he would have flourished. Frank, however, responded tartly: 'I might do it if I only had to see the good plays,' and turned me down.

Frank, of course, was the man who had created for *The Times* in the 1970s a parliamentary sketch of genius, which other broadsheets and other writers had been striving to emulate ever since. Matthew Parris and Simon Hoggart alone achieved comparable success, in *The Times* and *The Guardian* respectively. I made intermittent efforts to revive the *Telegraph*'s Sketch. Yet each of our writers, however talented a journalist, succumbed more or less quickly to a temptation to exploit the slot as a political column. Again and again I begged Sketch writers to remember that their role was to report what happened in the House, not to editorialize about it, but I never succeeded in making the feature work, and finally abolished it. Part of the problem was that the proceedings of Parliament seemed of diminishing importance, even to politicians. We changed the focus of our Parliament and Politics page to general political reporting. The televising of Parliament made old-fashioned coverage of the Chamber seem redundant. Today, I look back blushing at a notable editorial folly – the *Telegraph*'s opposition to admitting cameras to the Commons. How wrong we were.

Much as I liked our Marketing Director Stephen Grabiner, I found myself constantly resisting proposals which, shorn of his own verbiage, amounted to taking the paper downmarket. There was even a serious debate about turning the *Telegraph* into a tabloid, on the grounds that this was the preferred shape for younger readers. In Editorial, we were convinced such a course would lead us into a headlong confrontation with the *Daily Mail*, which we would lose. I continued to recite my personal mantra, that our role was to produce a 'popular quality newspaper'. We also saw off a determined, sustained campaign by the management to induce us to abandon the *Telegraph*'s traditional Gothic masthead, in favour of a more modern, trendy design 'like the *Indie*'s'. Don Berry spent weeks producing hundreds of alternatives. Finally, I sent a long note to the management, summarizing the arguments against change, whatever the advertising agencies were telling us:

> A change of masthead will *not* be perceived as a sign of confident strategic development, but as a symptom of loss of confidence, even panic . . . If we change the masthead and get it wrong, there is no going back. We are in the position of a jury in a capital case . . . if we get it wrong, it is not an innocent man who will hang, but ourselves.

Surprisingly Charles Moore, conservative in other things, was the only senior executive who favoured change. In the end, we made modest stylistic changes to our existing masthead, and left it at that. We also rejected, after much consideration, the notion of making the *Telegraph* a two-section paper every day, following the path adopted by *The Guardian*. I believed that our readers preferred to receive their news and features in a single manageable package on commuting days.

I contributed to one serious error of technical judgement, however. Back in 1987 when we were making printing plant plans, Andrew Knight had asked my opinion about editorial colour. I said that it seemed low on our priorities. I did not believe colour pictures would contribute significantly to increasing the sale of *The Daily Telegraph*. Thus far, I was probably right. Where I was wrong, however, was in failing to appreciate that a new generation of readers expected their world to be in colour, and took this for granted. Colour photographs might not induce them to buy a newspaper, but the absence of colour increasingly proclaimed that we were an old title. By 1990, we were moving into colour, but we were lagging behind our rivals. We were running colour advertising. We had published the *Telegraph*'s first front-page colour photo of – Heaven help us – the Duchess of York and her baby. Our black-and-white picture reproduction was much improved. But we were still years from possessing facilities to use regular colour photographs on our editorial pages, and my own lack of urgency back in 1987 was part of the reason for the delay. It would be 1995 before we could honestly call ourselves a colour newspaper.

*

ON 1 SEPTEMBER 1990, I sent a new note to Conrad about the Tory leadership situation. Kenneth Baker, who had been widely discussed as a possible successor to Thatcher, was out of contention, I said. Michael Heseltine's position also looked weak:

The three names upon whom discussion now focuses are Hurd, Major, [Chris] Patten. If Thatcher was run over by a bus tomorrow, I guess that Hurd would succeed ... I have always much liked and admired him. I share doubts whether he is sufficiently populist a figure to be a strong election winner ... Major is still the first choice of most younger Thatcherite ministers like Francis Maude. It may well prove that, if Thatcher goes on for two or three years, Major's age advantage over Hurd will tell, and he will emerge as favourite – but obviously, so much depends on his luck with the economy. I still have an open mind about Major. He has an unpretentious openness and charm that most of us find attractive. But there is also a certain lack of gravitas ...

When I wrote those lines, the notion that Michael Heseltine might launch a leadership challenge to Thatcher less than three months later would have seemed fanciful. It was acknowledged conventional wisdom that the Tory Party would never reward disloyalty to its leader by granting the succession to a traitor, an assassin. It was plain that Thatcher's authority was draining away, but not that her fate was sealed. Like others, I underrated the speed with which Thatcher's own Cabinet colleagues were losing confidence. There was a mounting climate of fear, especially among Tory MPs in vulnerable constituencies, that the party faced certain defeat at the next general election under her leadership.

Beyond personalities, political debate was increasingly dominated by the prospect that our partners in the European Community were bent on going ahead with monetary union. 'We would find it pleasant if monetary union would somehow evaporate from the agenda,' I wrote in a leader on 4 July,

but this will not happen. We are already committed, if later than the others, to joining the Exchange Rate Mechanism of the monetary system ... That is why the government is right to take EMU seriously, and to involve itself constructively in

intensive discussions with our partners. But, given the unpre-
cedented implications of political and monetary union for
the livelihoods and the constitututional birthright of everyone in Britain, Mrs Thatcher is also right to stand out for
an unhurried advance into extensively mined and uncharted
territory.

Through the autumn, Sarah Hogg wrote a series of leaders and
signed pieces, arguing strongly that the time had come for Britain
to enter the ERM. Her private advice to that effect made a
powerful impact on the Chancellor of the Exchequer. On Friday,
5 October 1990, John Major announced that Britain would join
the ERM the following Monday, and cut interest rates by 1 per
cent to 14 per cent. Share prices soared, the pound shot up.
We said in a leader that 'this long-delayed decision deserves our
support' – a view shared by almost all serious British newspapers.
Our City Editor argued, however, that it was a mistake to cut
interest rates as we joined. There were fears that the Treasury
regarded ERM membership as a panacea for deep-rooted economic
problems: 'Mr Major can expect to pay dearly for his standing
ovation yesterday. Intoxicated by his vision of lower inflation and
falling interest rates, the burghers of Britain really believe that
having done penance for the excesses of the past, they can at last
look forward to better times. They cannot.'
    Yet even as Britain made a gesture to draw closer to our
partners, the personal hostility and stridency of the Prime Minister
towards Europe intensified. At the EC Summit in Rome on 28
October, she denounced proposals for a European central bank
and said: 'We should block things which are not in Britain's
interests. Of course we shall.' The Deputy Prime Minister,
Geoffrey Howe, now expressed open dismay about the manner
in which Mrs Thatcher was conducting affairs. We echoed his
sentiments, in a leader after Rome: 'Mrs Thatcher should beware
of being seen single-handedly to wreck the programme of European integration on which the others have agreed. If, as she states,

Britain is determined to remain a full member of the Community, it must be seen making a creative contribution to its development.'

Howe quit the government on 1 November. Almost two weeks later, the leader writers sat together in my office, watching him deliver his devastating attack on Mrs Thatcher, in his resignation speech to the House of Commons. Bill Deedes murmured as Howe finished: 'That is the sort of speech which brings down Prime Ministers.' The next day, 14 November, Michael Heseltine appeared on the steps of his house to announce a challenge to Mrs Thatcher's leadership of the Conservative Party. Though Heseltine's prospects of victory seemed uncertain, to all save her devoted acolytes it was increasingly implausible that Mrs Thatcher could keep her job. As well as liking Douglas Hurd, I admired him as a governor. I was much more doubtful about his political instincts. I had come to believe that John Major lacked the weight to become an effective Prime Minister. Michael Heseltine seemed by far the most likely candidate to revive the fortunes of the Conservative Party. Conrad, however, not merely disliked Heseltine as the scourge of Margaret Thatcher, but loathed all that he believed Michael stood for. There was not the smallest possibility that Conrad would consent to any newspaper which he owned endorsing Heseltine for the Tory succession, even if Thatcher was beaten in the first round of voting.

I acted in accordance with that analysis. On 12 November, a week before the first ballot, we held a leader writers' lunch in the dining room at South Quay, to discuss the forthcoming contest. To my sorrow, Ferdy Mount had decided to give up his weekly column – he became editor of the *Times Literary Supplement*. Charles Moore, an equally elegant polemicist, had just succeeded him. Charles's views were much less close to mine than those of Ferdy, but whatever our political differences, our personal relationship was always cordial. Charles is an old-fashioned gentleman.

That Monday lunch, we spent little time debating Michael Heseltine's claims. I was perhaps the only figure at the table who thought Michael suited to become Prime Minister. All of us, however, with the possible exception of Charles Moore, agreed that Thatcher's position was extremely perilous. It was taken for granted that the *Telegraph* would support her in the first ballot, and indeed for as long as she remained a candidate. Thereafter, I made no secret of my preference for Douglas Hurd against John Major. Most of the others endorsed that view. The most surprising intervention came from Sarah Hogg. Sarah knew Major intimately, in a way none of the rest of us did. Now, she said succinctly: 'He's not ready for it. He might make a jolly good Prime Minister one of these days – but not now. I don't think he has the physical or mental toughness and resilience to do the job.' Coming from Sarah, this was a pretty damning verdict. We broke up, having agreed that the paper would support Douglas Hurd for the leadership if Thatcher was beaten. I told Conrad of our delibera- tions. I said we believed Hurd was the man best able to beat Heseltine in a run-off, if matters came to that. The Chairman did not demur.

On the evening of 13 November, I had dinner with Douglas Hurd at the inevitable corner table in Wilton's. It was an intense conversation. Loyal as ever, Douglas asserted that he did not regard Thatcher's fall as by any means inevitable. Yes, yes, I said. But let's assume for the purposes of this conversation that she is beaten: 'We will back you if you stand, but you've got to come out fighting. You've got to move quickly, and look as if you really mean business.' From the outset, my fear was that Douglas would approach a battle for the Tory Party leadership with the instinctive temperance and equanimity which he brought to much else in his life. It would be fatal to his chances if it seemed uncertain whether he wanted the job. Now, he acknowledged to me that he would stand if Thatcher was beaten. He intimated as much publicly to the media later that week, on Friday the 16th. But I left that dinner full of doubt whether Douglas's heart was in it, whether he wanted the job with the single-minded passion which can alone deliver the glittering prizes.

One morning in that last week of the contest, I paid a

melancholy visit to Michael Heseltine at his campaign office in Victoria Street. I said frankly that we could not back him. He did not disguise his disappointment: 'Would it do any good if I see Conrad myself?' he asked, ever optimistic about the power of his own personality.

'By all means do it,' I said, 'but I don't think it will change anything.'

'At the very least, I hope you won't be hostile.'

'We'll give you all the space we can.'

I climbed back into the car feeling less than pleased with myself. For all my moments of scorn about Rupert Murdoch and his titles, Andrew Neil in *The Sunday Times* felt free to come out for Heseltine with guns blazing on 18 November, along with *The Mail on Sunday*. *The Observer* and *Independent on Sunday* declared for Douglas Hurd. The *Sunday Express* was the only significant title save the *Telegraphs* which continued to express support for Thatcher. With deep reluctance, I recognized that part of the price of editing the newspaper which was, above all others, a Tory institution, was that there were times when it must behave like one. The best I could do for Michael Heseltine was to carry a big interview with him, conducted by George Jones and Charles Moore, across a spread on the 19th, the day before the poll. I consoled myself by recalling a remark Heseltine himself had made to me years earlier: 'I never care what the leaders say, because nobody reads them. I just count the column inches of coverage.'

I dissuaded Conrad from writing a signed article in support of Thatcher on the eve of the poll: 'My own concern, at this stage of this delicate and bloody crisis,' I said in a note to him,

> is that I can see no advantage for you in sticking your own neck out so far . . . No British (or Canadian!) proprietor in recent times has exposed himself this far above the parapet on a domestic political issue . . . I believe that the gratitude you can expect from the Thatcher camp for adopting such a trenchant political position will be outweighed by the unease

you will cause among other Tories, including some of the Cabinet, who are always deeply suspicious of newspapers treading upon them too heavily at a moment like this.

Conrad was eventually content that Charles Moore wrote an impassioned defence of Thatcher for the leader page on 20 November. Our front-page 'splash' that day declared: 'VOTERS' CHOICE IS HESELTINE, SAYS GALLUP'. More than 20 per cent of the electorate would consider switching back to the Tories if the party changed leaders in favour of 'Tarzan', said the findings of our own poll.

The leader writers sat together in my office watching television, as the first ballot result came through early in the evening of Tuesday 20 November. The figures were announced: Thatcher 204, Heseltine 152, with 16 abstentions. 168 Tory MPs no longer supported their leader. We sat stunned for a moment. Bill Deedes looked grave. George Walden shrugged: 'Well, that's about it for her.' Others nodded. Six of the seven of us agreed, with varying degrees of conviction, that Mrs Thatcher's credibility as Prime Minister was destroyed. 'If she's smart, she'll stand down now,' I said. Charles Moore, ever loyal to Thatcher, passionately dissented: 'No, no – she's got to go on. She must go on. She mustn't quit.' We argued the toss for a few minutes, then broke up. Conrad rang me, to discuss the result. I said it looked very bad indeed for Thatcher. 'But we're still supporting her, Max, aren't we?' said Conrad, with very little interrogative in his question.

The leader I wrote that evening bore scant resemblance to the piece I would have composed as a journalist writing under my own name, in my old life. This was one of those moments at which, whether I relished the role or not, *The Daily Telegraph* was too close to the eye of events, and its proprietor too fervent a supporter of Thatcher, for frankness to be acceptable. But if I could not say that Thatcher must go, I made it plain how hard it would be for her to stay. I said that she was no longer the most likely occupant of Downing Street, when the contest was over:

'It would be absurd to pretend that the situation in which Mrs Thatcher is now placed lends itself to easy answers.' This was the only occasion during my editorship when I discussed the wording of an editorial with Conrad before its publication.

On the morning of Thursday 22 November, our 'splash' said, 'THATCHER RESISTS CABINET CALLS FOR HER TO QUIT', alongside a *Daily Telegraph* Gallup poll which recorded overwhelming sentiment among voters that she should withdraw from the leadership contest. An hour after I arrived in my office, the Agency 'snap' burst onto the screens, electrifying us all: 'THATCHER QUITS'. Soon afterwards, John Major and Douglas Hurd announced their candidacies.

I held a long telephone conversation with Douglas at his home in Oxfordshire from my own kitchen at Guilsborough on Sunday morning, the 25th. I said that the more I heard about John Major, especially from Sarah Hogg, the more I doubted whether he possessed the qualities to run a government. I had been especially alarmed by a stab of revelation as I lay in bed the previous night, about Norman Lamont's role as Major's campaign manager. It was a sure bet that Norman's price for fulfilling the role would be the Chancellorship of the Exchequer. I had always enjoyed his company, witty and engaging. But he seemed at root a boulevard-ier rather than a statesman. The notion of Norman as Chancellor was almost risible. It would be the least convincing start to a Major government. I voiced all these fears to Douglas, who replied: 'I think you're wrong. I think John Major would be a very good Prime Minister.'

'For God's sake, Douglas,' I said in some exasperation, 'you're standing against him in a leadership fight and we are the major title backing your bid. You simply can't talk like that.' From that moment, I was sure Douglas had no chance of victory. All his decency, his moderation, his distaste for confrontational politics made him an unconvincing contestant in a struggle for the greatest political office in the land. But we were committed to Douglas, and we did our best for him. In the office the following day, I found Conrad under fire. His telephone was ringing constantly, he said, with calls from Mrs Thatcher's closest associates, demanding to know why we were not supporting John Major, her man. Sitting in his office on the floor above mine, we discussed the issue for some time. I focused on Major's limitations. Finally, I said: 'Why don't you talk direct to Sarah Hogg? She knows Major better than anyone outside his own family.' Sarah spent half an hour with Conrad. He respected her as much as I did. He was convinced by what she said, and I was suitably grateful to her. *The Daily Telegraph* continued to support Hurd. Personally, I then believed that Michael Heseltine had become the most likely victor. I underestimated the strength of support for John Major.

On the Saturday afternoon before the second ballot, I was shooting in Northamptonshire when I was summoned to take an urgent call on my car phone. It was a junior executive on *The Sunday Telegraph*. Audibly nervous, he said he thought I should know that Perry Worsthorne had written an unsigned leader, asserting that Michael Heseltine's personal life made him a wholly unsuitable person to become Prime Minister. Sitting in the midst of a ploughed field, I rang Perry and told him his piece was unacceptable on three counts: first, it was anonymously written as an editorial, and might therefore be construed as the paper's collective view; second, it contradicted his own column only three weeks earlier, in which he had passionately asserted the right of public men to have private lives; and third, it made unspecified allegations without a shred of evidence. Perry exploded. He asserted that the consideration of stopping Michael Heseltine from becoming Tory leader transcended any other. He denied my right to compel him to make any changes in the pages he controlled. After a prolonged altercation, I rang Conrad at home. I told him I thought it essential that, at the very least, Perry was compelled to put his own name to anything scurrilous. Conrad agreed. A heavily modified version of the piece appeared above Perry's initials. I would have preferred to see it dropped altogether; not because Michael or Anne Heseltine would have been bothered by

Perry's nonsense, but because it represented shoddy journalism. From that moment, I found it impossible to see how the Perry section of *The Sunday Telegraph* could continue as an autonomous subsidiary. Others agreed. It perished a few months later, after publishing one bitchy profile too many. Trevor Grove became Editor of the entire paper, to which his predecessor contributed a signed column. I have always admired Perry as a performer, but the very streak of recklessness which made him a good columnist also made him a poor editor. On this, I agreed with Michael Hartwell's verdict back in 1986, though I held my peace even with Andrew Knight and Conrad Black, until Perry finally over-reached himself.

In the run-up to the second leadership ballot, there was a series of foolish spats between the paper and John Major's camp. Even if we were not supporting Major, there was plainly a real prospect that he would become Prime Minister, given the passionate opposition to Heseltine among the old Thatcherites. I was keen to avoid a blood row with the Majorites. Now, they complained petulantly that their man had been denied leader-page space in the *Telegraph* to put his case. In reality, this reflected only a communications failure with the Major camp. I had asked Alan Clark to write 'the case for Major'. We could rely on Alan's prose, if not his judgement. I sometimes interviewed leading politicians myself, but on this occasion I asked Charles Moore to see Major, and to write a big piece. This was because I had heard that the prospective Tory leader did not care for me. My decision was apparently a mistake. The sensitive Major disliked Charles even more than he disliked me. I wrote to the candidate:

> I have heard extraordinary stories that some of your camp . . . believe there is snobbish social prejudice against you here.
>
> This is a bit thick, when Sarah and our leader column have warmly supported your Chancellorship. We are pluralistic enough not to try to muzzle Neil Collins and Chris Fildes, who have consistently opposed the ERM, but I am sure you

'There's a 10p fine every
time you say "It's the end
of an era".'

Matt's front-page cartoon on 23 November 1990.

would not expect me to deny them their voices . . . It is those
papers which strongly support you that have introduced the
class war element into this contest, by arguing . . . that an
Old Etonian is unelectable, and that your own background
gives you a clear advantage over Douglas.

It is absurd for such misunderstandings to exist between
us at this stage. You will receive our warm support as prime
minister. That does not mean uncritical support, nor that I
shall give our writers orders to toe a line. But you will need
the help of all Tories to pull the party together in time to
win a general election . . .

When the result of the second ballot was announced on the
evening of 27 November, Douglas Hurd had polled 56 votes
against Heseltine's 131 and Major's 185. John Major became the
new Prime Minister.

The following night, Tricia and I found ourselves fulfilling
a long-arranged engagement to dine at the home of Mark and
Arabella Lennox-Boyd. By a droll coincidence, among our fellow-
guests were both the Hurd and Major campaign managers, Chris

Patten and Norman Lamont. There was an atmosphere of exhilaration tempered by exhaustion. Chris Patten and I discussed
Douglas for a few minutes. 'I don't feel even a twinge of regret
about backing him,' said Chris. 'Just about everybody I respect in
the Cabinet did so.' I assented heartily. We agreed that Douglas's
heart had never been in it. Chris, of course, went on to become one
of John Major's closest advisers as well as party chairman. Norman
Lamont, though not a personal friend, was a long-standing friendly
acquaintance, not that much older than me. I still found it a strange
business, to see people whom one had known for years as mere
mortals, suddenly catapulted into the highest offices of state. I asked
Norman if he did not feel a spasm of unreality about hearing
himself described as Chancellor of the Exchequer, just as for many
months I had found it bizarre to be introduced as Editor of *The
Daily Telegraph*. Absolutely, said Norman, 'it will take time to get
used to the idea.' So it did for us all.

In the first days after John Major became Prime Minister,
Conrad was much exercised about our failure to back the winner.
He had endured the rebukes of Thatcher acolytes, who charged
him with failing to throw the weight of his titles behind The
Lady's anointed successor. Now, he found that the consequence
of following my counsel was that we had supported a loser. On
4 December, the day after a long and difficult conversation with
the Chairman on the issue, I sent him a memorandum:

> Any standing I have with you must rest partly on telling you
> what I think, for better or worse, rather than what you might
> wish to hear. Our credibility as a newspaper suffered more (if
> it suffered at all) from continuing to back Thatcher when
> it was obvious that she was finished – as I told you that she
> was, on that Tuesday night of the first ballot – than from
> backing Hurd for the leadership. I shall not now or in the
> months to come heed sirens like Woodrow Wyatt who argues
> (in *The Times* today) that the Tories made a huge mistake,
> and will live to regret dumping her.

At all levels in the country, and especially among Tories, I find overwhelming relief that she has gone . . . Obviously, her place in history is assured . . . But Mrs Thatcher had become the victim of her absolute dominance of British politics . . . Some of those who cry loudest about her going will do so simply because they have lost personal access or influence. Three or four months from now, when the Major government is riding out its own storms, there will be cant from the Right about the 'huge mistake' that was made in dropping her. This will not be shared in the country. I believe Major's links with the old regime will shrivel quite speedily, and that many of the old favourites will find themselves frozen out by spring.

Half the Cabinet – and the ablest half – supported Douglas Hurd's candidacy, and I myself continue to believe that he would have made a more substantial prime minister than Major. Major will have his honeymoon. But, come the spring, huge problems and strains await him. I do not believe our own course was disreputable or irresponsible, nor that it will be regarded as such by anyone who matters. I have a hunch that Major will prove less Thatcherite than Hurd would have been, in the end.

Sarah [Hogg] should prove an invaluable bridge builder between us and the Major government. It is of paramount importance that no one should have any inkling that Sarah also supported Hurd for the leadership . . . I shall be surprised if, come the New Year, we do not receive overtures from [Downing Street].

A few hours after I sent that note to Conrad, I was summoned out of a staff dinner at Brooks's to take a call from Sarah. John Major had asked her to become head of the Downing Street Policy Unit. The irony of the appointment was not lost on either of us. I was bitterly sorry to lose her from *The Daily Telegraph*, but obviously it was an opportunity she could not miss. I have waited until it no longer matters to either her or John Major to tell the story of her role in the *Telegraph*'s coverage of the 1990 leadership contest.

Neil Collins observed with a wrinkled nose, when *The Economist*'s editor Rupert Pennant-Rea was appointed Deputy Governor of the Bank of England, 'Don't they know that journalists can't *do* things?' Most journalists somewhere possess a secret craving to show that they can 'do things'. Now, Sarah had a wonderful opportunity. It always seemed a tribute to the discretion of our leader writers that none of the eight or nine others who had been around the lunch table at South Quay when Sarah expressed her scepticism about John Major as a candidate to become Prime Minister let on to the world, though it would have been a delicious crumb of gossip. Sarah became John Major's most trusted adviser, a key figure in his government. I sent the new Prime Minister a personal note of congratulation, to which he replied with his invariable courtesy. Two weeks later, Sarah persuaded to him to come to my annual Christmas drinks party at Brooks's, at which of course he proved the star of the show, encircled by admiring women. I gained a fresh glimpse of his sensitivity, however, when Sarah warned me that he had nearly ducked out of the party at the last minute, in fury towards some remark about him in the previous day's *Sunday Telegraph*. I was invited to breakfast at Downing Street a few days later with the two of them. The atmosphere was friendly and celebratory. All Major's charm was on display. But if the relationship between *The Daily Telegraph* and the new Prime Minister promised to be different from that with his predecessor, I harboured no delusions that it was going to prove easy.

George Walden, who remained Tory MP for Buckingham while he wrote leaders for us, said with a shrug: 'Well, that's it, then. Most people feel the Thatcher revolution has been very good and healthy and bracing for them, but they're grateful it's over. The British don't like change. They don't like being pushed. You have to keep your foot very hard on the pedal to keep things moving in this country. Now, we've voted for what the Party hopes will be a quiet life again.' The country, as well as the Conservatives, would be rapidly disillusioned about that.

8

SOCIAL DIVERSIONS

MOST PEOPLE ASSUME THAT the social life of a national news-paper editor compares favourably with that of the Congress of Vienna. In reality, each incumbent chooses a different path. Andrew Neil, late of *The Sunday Times*, has famously sustained into middle age a taste for nightclub life which would have alarmed and exhausted many of us even when we were thirty years younger. Most broadsheet editors, by contrast, live retiring domestic lives, disappearing every evening to suburban firesides in the manner of Evelyn Waugh's Mr Salter. Their names remain almost unknown to the public, however prominent their newspapers. Paul Dacre of the *Daily Mail*, the most successful editor of my generation, spends every leisure hour with his family and beloved garden, never broadcasts, seldom appears at parties, and shares with the star of *Wall Street* a belief that lunch is for wimps.

During the years I was at the *Telegraph*, my family remained almost entirely at home in Northamptonshire. I slept there four nights a week. I rarely went to dinner parties in London, though I sometimes spoke at events which might serve my own, a charity's, or the paper's interests. Delivering speeches is hard work – sometimes one wonders if hosts understand just how much labour is involved. It all seems worthwhile if an audience is sympathetic – and not, if not. One day in 1990, for instance, I was invited to address senior policemen at the annual ACPO conference in Preston. I talked about a subject close to my heart, the breakdown of the traditional relationship between the police and the middle class. I sat down to muted applause, to put the matter politely.

Chief constable after chief constable then stood up, to denounce my views. It was not true that public confidence in their forces was declining, they said crossly. It was monstrous to suggest that police evidence was less readily believed in courts. It was time people like me understood that sporting shooters in the country-side (for instance) caused a lot of trouble. The chief constables' protests were deeply depressing, because they highlighted the gulf between reality as the public knew it, and the delusions cherished by policemen. I often talk to service audiences, and seldom go home without being impressed anew by the quality of senior army people. It is dismaying to notice the contrast with police leader-ship, much of which is conspicuously inadequate. Most chief constables would not rise above the rank of sergeant major in the British army, and they display the warrant officer's limited perspective.

Under my editorship, *The Daily Telegraph* continued to sup-port the police – but we sought to acknowledge how deep in trouble they were. At the ACPO conference, one chief constable challenged me to cite my sources. I told him that among the most serious critics of police evidence were judges at the Old Bailey, with whom I had lunched the week before. Moreover, a member of the legal team which investigated the Guildford Four was a personal friend. He told me how shocked the lawyers were, to discover that the original notes of police interviews with the suspects had been left on file alongside the altered version which got the Guildford Four convicted. The only rational interpretation of the investigating officers' behaviour was that they assumed no one would be either surprised or troubled by discovering that they had wilfully distorted evidence. I did not cite this point to my audience at Preston, and I doubt whether it would have impressed those closed minds anyway.

I had shared the ACPO platform with John Birt, then Deputy Director-General of the BBC. 'As I listened to you,' he observed drily as we sat on the train back to London, 'I couldn't decide whether you were being very brave or very stupid.' He left me in little doubt which conclusion he finally reached. Yet I believed that the best reason to travel halfway up England for such an occasion as an ACPO conference was to offer frank opinions which no politician could express. As a citizen, never mind as an editor, I found it a depressing afternoon.

Soon after joining the *Telegraph*, I initiated an occasional series of lunches in major provincial cities for local business leaders. I took two or three of our senior executives, usually including the City Editor, to Newcastle, Bristol, Manchester, Belfast and suchlike. We invited our twenty-odd guests to ask anything they wanted about the paper, and to talk to us about economic and political conditions in their area. It was part of my vision of the *Telegraph* that we were the chosen paper of Britain's provincial middle classes. Most British journalists, and editors, pay too little attention to the regions. We learned a lot from our regional lunches, and they were a useful way of showing the flag for the *Telegraph*. I made sure the occasions were reported in our Court & Social column, not out of conceit, but because I wanted readers to know that we were getting out there, monitoring what was going on beyond the metropolitan hub.

Many national institutions invite editors to lunch perhaps once a year. Courtesy demands acceptance. I suffered some embarrassing encounters with successive Archbishops of Canterbury at Lambeth Palace – embarrassing, because our paper was so often recording the Church of England's follies and humiliations. It must have required a supreme exercise of Robert Runcie's and George Carey's Christian spirit to sit through meals with me. On the whole, everybody maintained the social niceties at these affairs. But I encountered growing tensions at meetings with senior Tories, because of the irreconcilable gap between their ambitions for *The Daily Telegraph* and mine. There was still a remarkable number of ministers who believed the paper had a duty to provide support to the Tory government of the day. One day in April 1991, I was invited to lunch by the Chief Whip, Alistair Goodlad, at his home in Lord North Street, round the corner from the Commons. I knew Alistair quite well socially, and so turned up in easy spirits. Though prone to public pomposity, he was the author of a peerless unpublished parody of Alan Clark's diaries ('on the way back from White's chatted up a girl outside St James's Piccadilly ... she made some pathetic excuse about the time of the month ... got home to Albany and rang Jane. Poor darling, she is so tired after cleaning out the moat all day'). The conviviality of our lunch did not long survive. The Chief Whip launched an irritable blast of invective about the *Telegraph*'s 'unhelpfulness' and 'disloyalty'. I felt like a subaltern being dressed down by the colonel for letting down the regiment – except I had to break it to Alistair that I was not under his command. I hope I gave as good as I got, urging him to wake up and realize that the cosy old *Torygraph* days were over. Not a lunch to be repeated in a hurry.

In the new era of glasnost surrounding the intelligence services, editors are invited from time to time to meet their directors. Few secrets are on offer – what matters is the chance to take the measure of the personalities at the top, some of whom are very impressive. I remember a jolly encounter with the bosses of GCHQ at Cheltenham. They were eager for guidance about how best they could make their public case for much larger resources, now that the Cold War had ended: 'It used to be so easy when we only had to listen one way. Now, we've got to listen to *everybody*!' I enjoyed meeting Stella Rimington, a notably cool customer, when she became Director of the Security Service, but received a rude shock when I ran into a friend who worked at Downing Street. I mentioned that I had just lunched with Rimington. My friend exclaimed: 'Oh God, I hope it's not like the last time you saw her. She included something you said in the weekly intelligence report, and the Prime Minister was *furious*.' I suppose that if one consorts with intelligence chiefs, one should not be surprised if they behave in character, but after that experience I never sought out Rimington again.

It is always a hard question, how any journalist – and especially an editor – interprets the rules of discretion governing private

meetings with politicians, tycoons, civil servants. The usual convention is that what they say is unattributable. Thus there would
be no point in such conversations taking place unless their fruits
were intended to inform future articles and editorials. But whatever is published should give no clue about the source. Beyond
this, however, if one achieves a close personal relationship, as I did
with Douglas Hurd, and later with Charles Guthrie as Chief of
the General Staff and Chief of the Defence Staff, one is offered
privileged information for background – strictly not for publication in the paper. I hope I never betrayed any of these tête-à-tête
confidences. But a journalist is a journalist, even if he or she is an
editor. It was impossible to resist printing some of the titbits one
heard at parties, and indeed not infrequently this was the inform-
ant's purpose in drawing one's attention to them. But, yes, once
or twice I found myself in trouble as a result. I am afraid that
while every journalist is capable of being discreet most of the time,
disclosure is so fundamental to our business that none of us can
keep our mouths shut all the year round. I once found myself
being lambasted down the telephone by an art dealer friend, who
was furious that our Art Critic had got wind of a deal he was
engaged upon. The story reached our front page. My friend lost
his deal, and believed that he had grounds for complaint, though
I had no hand in the leak: 'Discretion is the essence of my
business!' he wailed. 'I'm sorry, Charlie,' I responded. 'Indiscretion
is the essence of ours.'

   With the job of an editor came social treats which, like almost
every incumbent, I adored: Royal Box seats at Wimbledon,
entertaining at Ascot, evenings at Glyndebourne, the Chelsea
Flower Show Gala, and lots of Covent Garden and theatre
evenings. As one's social education progressed, however, it became
enlightening to realize how large a proportion of the clientele in
the Royal Enclosure or the Grand Tier at the Royal Opera House,
for instance, are the sort of people in whom the Serious Fraud
Squad takes a professional interest. Much that glisters is most
certainly not gold. Everyone who runs anything discovers that he

or she acquires a host of new 'friends'. There is nothing wrong with this, but it is essential to keep clear in one's mind the difference between these professional connections and one's real intimates. Only by doing so can one avoid an unhappy confrontation with reality when the job goes and the social leeches fall away overnight, along with many of the grand invitations.

At heart, I have always been more of a rural creature than a metropolitan one. My happiest off-duty hours are spent gardening. It is irksome forever to be described in print as 'shooting and fishing Max Hastings', when I spend far more time weeding than pursuing fish or fowl. But I managed to shoot thirty-odd days a season throughout my years at the *Telegraph*. By way of excuse, I could plead that I thus met a far wider range of people, especially country types, than most journalists encounter. I often came back from a shoot with a story or an idea. It was an encounter with Lincolnshire farmers, who expressed their acute concern about what manufacturers were putting into animal feeds, which caused me to ask our Agricultural Correspondent to write a big piece on the subject, some while before BSE hit the headlines. But of course, the principal reason I shot grouse and pheasants was that I liked to do it – and to write about it. I contributed a column to *The Field* through most of the years I was an editor.

My father was devoted to country sports. As a child, listening to his conversation, I assumed that he spent most of his time shooting on ducal estates or fishing in Norway. As I became older, however, I grew to understand that there was a significant element of romance about Father's reminiscences. In my forties at the *Telegraph*, I found myself living out in reality the sort of sporting life he had fantasized about. I liked to imagine him somewhere up there, looking benignly over my shoulder as I missed grouse or lost salmon. My staff – and probably most of our readers – regarded my lifestyle as eccentric. I was caricatured relentlessly in other newspapers, and I suppose I played up to the image, for the pleasure of teasing the politically correct. It seemed easy to justify rural passions at the *Telegraph*, with its large country readership.

And one of the nicest things about getting older is that one cares less what others think about one's personal choices – of pictures, books, friends, holidays, pastimes.

During one of the Tory Right's spasmodic campaigns to persuade Conrad to change editors, the Chairman declared one day – and I will borrow one of his own favourite adjectives – in a somewhat minatory fashion: 'Max, it has been represented to me that *The Daily Telegraph*'s interests would be well served, if you spent less of your time shooting and fishing.' I answered: 'Conrad, if you are not happy with the paper, you would be wrong to keep me here even if I was working seven days a week. But if you think the paper is being competently run, then surely it's up to me how I do it. Are you happy with the *Telegraph*?'

'Broadly, yes,' said Conrad, after a moment's pause for thought. Then he added: 'I accept your view.' He did not raise the issue again. My finest hour came when I persuaded the proprietor that the company should hold a shoot for its board members. Lords King and Swaythling, Rupert Hambro, Peter Buckley, Henry Keswick, Sir Evelyn de Rothschild and Sir Martin Jacomb warmly endorsed the proposal, and it became an annual fixture. Conrad even turned up for lunch.

Journalists can afford to adopt a more flexible code than politicians and civil servants about accepting hospitality, but it seems important for an editor to avoid the company of known crooks, arms dealers and so on. I never accepted a cup of tea, never mind a glass of Krug, from Lord Archer. I did not venture to anticipate that in reality Jeffrey would end up in prison, but I never doubted that he deserved to do so. In Archer's heyday, there were frequent opportunities to observe his energy and assiduity in wooing anyone who might promote his ambitions. One evening, descending the stairs after a Downing Street reception, my arm was seized by Jeffrey, on his way up: 'Max! I've just spent the weekend reading your book. It's simply *marvellous*.' I wrenched away my arm, and marched on downwards in stony silence. But Jeffrey had wrong-footed me. I was irked to feel that he had goaded me to behave boorishly. How does one deal with such a man? One day at the Tory Party Conference, he shouted down to the crowded lobby of the Grand Hotel from the top of the stairs, as if from Juliet's balcony: 'Max! Max! Are you coming to my party tonight?'

'Sorry, Jeffrey – I've got to get back to London.'

'Oh please – do come – *for Mary . . .*'

I was sometimes reproached by colleagues for priggishness in evading both Archer's and Jonathan Aitken's entertainments, on the grounds that it was my duty as a journalist to turn out. One would meet so many people one ought to talk to. But I never forgot Aitken's old schoolfellow Jeremy Deedes observing, long before his public fall from grace: 'You and I both know that Jonathan couldn't lie straight in bed.' My friend Christopher Bland, a former GLC councillor, once gave me a first-hand account of Archer's efforts to persuade him to join a syndicate of councillors for whom Jeffrey offered to handle expenses on commission. I also knew a good deal of detail about the various scandals in which Archer had been involved, even before Michael Crick's damning biography was published. The only moment at which I thought less than well of Douglas Hurd came when I asked him why he went to Archer's ghastly parties. He shrugged: 'Everybody else does.' I was touched, when the novelist at last disappeared into Belmarsh, that Bill Deedes wrote me a card: 'You were right all along about Archer, I fear.' I hasten to add that, on the big things, Bill was far more often right than me.

The only public relations man whose telephone calls I happily accepted was Alan Parker of Brunswick, not because I fish with him, but because he is clever, sophisticated, and realistic in his expectations. It would be hard to say the same about most of his rivals. Almost all PRs rush to first-name terms in correspondence, then advance some proposition which equates to starting to build a lifeboat on the upper deck as their client's ship sinks beneath their feet. Once when a big privatized utility found itself under media fire for the greed of its chairman and chief executive,

I received a call from its public relations man, inviting me to join the two men on the corporate plane to Cornwall for a blue-chip shooting weekend. Only very silly journalists rise to flies presented as crudely as that, or accept Mohammed Fayed's invitations to stay at the Paris Ritz. A colleague once saw Fayed gleefully produce from his desk drawer receipts for watches and other baubles purchased by a Sunday newspaper editor on the Fayed account during a colossal 'freebie' in Paris. There is always a ticket-collector at the head of the escalator.

One day I received a call from my wife Tricia in Northamptonshire, demanding irritably: 'What have you been buying now?'

'What do you mean?'

'There's a huge box in the hall, so big that we can hardly get through the front door.'

'You'd better open it and see what it is.' Long pause.

'It's an enormous hamper from Harrods, labelled "Happy Christmas from Mohammed Al Fayed". One of the children has looked it up in the Harrods catalogue. He says it costs £600.'

This was at the height of the ferocious public feud between Fayed and 'Tiny' Rowland. I treated Fayed's consignment as an unexploded bomb, and sent my driver post-haste to Northamptonshire to collect the hamper, and deliver its contents to Great Ormond Street Hospital. I wrote a letter to Fayed, copied to our Chief Executive, expressing regret that I couldn't accept his generous gesture. I mentioned the experience to Ian Watson, then *The Sunday Telegraph*'s Deputy Editor, who knew the Harrods boss of old. As a veteran hamper receiver, Ian growled cheerfully: 'All that palaver won't do you any good. Mohammed will just send you another one at the office.' I only met Fayed once, during his feud with Rowland, at much the same time that I had a one-off dinner with the Lonhro boss. Each man demanded to know why the *Telegraph* was not backing him. I told both that I was delighted to hear what they had to say, but that the paper preferred to stay in the safety of a slit trench. Fayed later claimed that I took against him because I was a snob. Oddly enough, at various times the same allegation was made against me in print by Robert Maxwell, Mary Archer and Dame Shirley Porter. A colleague observed briskly: 'Right charge. Wrong example.'

But avoiding high-profile rogues does not mean that journalists cannot enjoy hospitality. Most tycoons and politicians understand perfectly well that an editor cannot allow personal relationships to influence what his executives and writers do in the paper. For instance, I have often been entertained by Rocco Forte. I was embarrassed when, at the height of Forte group's difficulties, Neil Collins wrote a piece asserting that Rocco would never have become Chief Executive of the company if his name had not been Forte. Yet, just as I never raised with Neil the issue of my friendship with Rocco, so Rocco never mentioned Neil's piece to me, though I knew it had hurt him.

Rocco's sensible behaviour contrasted with that of the former Cabinet Secretary, Lord Armstrong, who stomped up to me at a party and barked, 'You should be ashamed of yourself – and of your newspaper!' following publication of an article critical of his disastrous chairmanship of the Victoria and Albert Museum. The wife of a former auction-house chairman attacked me at a bus stop for alleged persecution of her husband in print, after the 1990s' price-fixing scandal was exposed. I had to remind my inquisitor that her husband was a fugitive from American justice. I was suprised to receive a furious missive one day from Tom Boardman, a neighbour in Northamptonshire. Boardman was a somewhat moderate Industry Minister in the Heath government, who was fortunate enough after his retirement from politics to become Chairman of the National Westminster Bank. In July 1988, however, NatWest found itself deeply embarrassed by the scandal involving its subsidiary County NatWest. It was the considered view of all our experts (Collins, Fildes, Bruce-Gardyne), reflected in a leader, that 'Lord Boardman should surely accept responsibility . . . He declared this week that he saw no virtue in any ritual "falling on swords". Yet, despite sympathy for his own long and honourable career, in a scandal of this magnitude there must be a case for the man at the top to be seen to take the rap.' The following Sunday morning, I found a hand-delivered note from Boardman on my doorstep at home. 'What have I ever done to you and yours,' Tom demanded in outrage, 'to cause you to treat me as you have done this week in your newspaper?' I answered, of course, that our coverage simply reflected the views of our City writers. The NatWest Chairman eventually resigned with very bad grace, making plain that he believed the gesture should never have been required of him.

The Boardman case was no great embarrassment to me, because Tom was only a local acquaintance. Any editor would be insensitive, however, not to feel a stab of pain when personal friends are pilloried in the pages for which he is responsible. Like many others, I regard John Profumo as a secular saint, as well as an enchanting companion. Compare and contrast Jonathan Aitken's tawdry weekly parade of penitence and Christian spirit, with the absolute, unbroken dignity and silence of Jack Profumo. Every time the 1963 scandal that bears his name is revived – and it happens almost monthly – I feel grieved not only for Jack, but for my own part as a journalist in a trade that sometimes seems incapable of mercy. Likewise Sir Allan Green, formerly the Director of Public Prosecutions, is an old family friend whom I respect. On 4 October 1991, it was a miserable business to see our front page dominated – like that of every other title – by news of his resignation after a kerb-crawling incident. We could scarcely leave it out of the paper.

A woman acquaintance once importuned me on behalf of her nephew, a young peer who had been caught in a Sunday newspaper drugs 'sting'. Would we play down our coverage of the ensuing court case? She told me that her nephew was a decent young man, who did not deserve to be persecuted because, when short of money, he had been caught out by an especially nasty 'honey trap'. I sympathized with what she said, and despised the newspaper's action. But the court hearing began on what proved to be a slow news day. My deputy featured the story prominently.

I made no attempt to dissuade him. Next time I saw my woman acquaintance at a party, she strode forward and said simply: 'You bastard! You had to put it on the front page, didn't you.' I shrugged.

One cause for relief about no longer being an editor is that, over the years, it is remarkable how large an aggrieved acquaintance one builds up. In many cases, I was not even aware before publication of the pieces that upset people. One friend was bitterly dismayed when we gave prominent coverage to an industrial tribunal case involving one of his employees. The man in charge of the rattling train sometimes gets undeserved credit for writers' triumphs, but likewise takes the rap for any one of 300 journalists who cause grief. The only sensible policy for an editor is to let the normal news machinery of the paper take its course, unless something obviously unjust is being done. Unless an editor lives in social isolation – as some do – brutal brushes between personal friendship and headline stories are bound to occur.

*

OUT OF ALL SOCIAL OCCASIONS, of course, comes a stream of gossip and information, about how business and politics are being conducted at the highest level. One of the privileges of editorship is access, what John Harvey-Jones described to me back in 1987 as 'Knowing'. It is the one-to-one lunches and dinners, the confidences from politicians, which give editors a thrilling window into power. At the height of the Balkan crisis, I was touched to be invited to dine alone, at Douglas Hurd's home in Oxfordshire, with Warren Christopher, then US Secretary of State. John Major, during his premiership, was generous with invitations to Chequers. I attended one splendid affair with Boris Yeltsin, who came downstairs visibly drunk, and took an immediate dislike to his *placement*. He picked up his own table card, next door to that of Princess Alexandra, and deposited both the card and himself next to John Major, with whom he chattered amiably, if incoherently, all evening. Major described his own amusement, walking in the countryside around Chequers that afternoon with the Russian President, to find that most passers-by took no notice of the cavalcade of politicians trailed by security men. The only walker to address them said simply: 'Good afternoon, Prime Minister. Good afternoon, Mr President,' and strolled on with his dogs. All very British.

Among many reasons I liked Michael Heseltine was that I found him uncommonly frank, in office or out of it. In his days as Defence Secretary, we were once discussing a row involving a minister and a journalist who had allegedly misquoted the minister. I said I couldn't see how this could still happen, in the tape-recorder age. 'Nobody gets to interview me with a tape recorder,' said Michael drily. 'The last line of defence for a politician who says something he regrets is to deny that he said it.'

At lunch with him in the late 1980s when he was a back-bencher, I said how much I deplored the government's decision to maintain the Brigade of Gurkhas, because there would be no convincing role for them once Hong Kong was handed over in 1997: 'If you had still been Defence Secretary, you'd have axed them, wouldn't you?'

'No,' said Michael crisply.

'Why not?'

'Because the British public loves them, and I am a politician.'

I respected him for refusing to give me the answer I sought, when to do so would have cost him nothing. Contrary to the widespread perception of Michael, even among former colleagues, he has an unusual degree of self-knowledge. Though no one takes politics more seriously, he possesses an understanding that the play of human affairs is ultimately a comedy, that we all look equally ridiculous in the bath. This is rare among politicians of the first rank, though conspicuously shared by Kenneth Clarke. Once the barrier of Michael's shyness can be overcome – the weakness which did more than any other to prevent him from becoming Prime Minister, the fact that he was 'no good in the Commons tea room'

– he is the most sensitive and sympathetic, as well as witty companion.

I did my share of broadcasting, though most of the big political television programmes are transmitted at weekends. No power on earth would get me into a London studio on a Sunday except in a crisis. It is also tough to stay awake to appear on *Newsnight*, when this makes it unlikely that one can get to bed before midnight, and the day starts again before 7 a.m. I performed occasionally for *Today*, *PM*, *The World Tonight*, partly because radio makes fewer demands – one can simply talk down the office telephone – and partly because I enjoyed it. Radio is a much better medium for conveying information than television. Television suffers from a vast collective conceit, which is inflated by the desperation of so many people to appear on screen to peddle their wares, political or commercial. Unless one has a product to sell, however, only the star of a show gets much mileage out of it. For the rest of us, the bit-part players, it soon becomes demoralizing to turn up at Television Centre, say, at 7 a.m. to review the papers: one is rushed into make-up; processed through the system for a minute or two of air time in which precious little worthwhile can be said; then dispatched back into limbo with a brusque enquiry from some pimply youth (in abruptness and gaucheness closely resembling oneself twenty-five years earlier) whether one needs a taxi. As an author, I peddle myself shamelessly to any programme that will have me, because the need to sell books makes hookers of us all. But most editors, unless they are egomaniacs or their titles are directly involved in a news story or controversy, learn to recognize soundbite broadcasting as a waste of time. It is striking to notice how many professional television broadcasters develop a melancholy, even self-hatred, as they reach middle age. They become dismayed by the limitations of what they are trying to do. They have achieved vast fame, but the intelligent performers question whether they are engaged in an activity with the faintest semblance of intellectual dignity. I have often heard both Robin Day and

Jeremy Paxman say how much they would have preferred to become newspaper editors. They sounded as if they meant it.

I have seldom declined an invitation to appear on *Question Time*, though the programme became much less enjoyable after Robin Day's departure. The current emphasis on audience participation makes the programme more of a circus, less of a debate. Like most politicians and journalists, I gain much more pleasure from joining Jonathan Dimbleby on radio's *Any Questions?*. There is still a delightful sense of Fifties provincial England about it: the tense, studiedly matey meeting with Jonathan and the other panellists in a modest small-town hotel; the encounter with an eager, usually friendly and good-natured audience in some school or hall; the relentless strain of responding instantly to questions about which, contrary to popular myth, one is never briefed in advance. However often one has done the programme, there is a nervous excitement inseparable from live broadcasting which does not fade. I admire the best professional chairmen, Jonathan notable among them, because I know enough about their business to recognize how difficult the job is.

The politicians on the panel often bore for England, and ministers are prone to turn up clutching briefing notes. Shirley Porter arrived one day with sheaves of papers, determined to deliver her defence of the sale of Westminster's cemeteries. She insisted upon delivering her apologia on the air, even though no one in the audience had asked a question about it. The professional politicians tend, however, to score higher than other guests at repartee. Several times, I have found myself on an *Any Questions?* panel with Tony Benn. Having disagreed with him about almost everything all my life, I looked forward to these jousts – and I was always worsted. Benn's conceit is unprickable, his debating skills refined over half a century in the Commons. His sublime self-assurance invariably made nonsense of my clumsy thrusts, which reminded me of Saki's line about a cow trying to tease a gadfly.

All panellists dread the regular 'joke question'. In the early 1950s, a team which included my mother, Anne Scott-James, was asked who they would like to be, if not themselves. In that innocent era, my mother replied unhesitatingly: 'The Queen.' It is hard to imagine any sane person making the same choice nowadays, even for a tease. Once when I was doing the show, three of us struggled with leaden success to find something witty to say when asked what advice Prince William should give to his younger brother Prince Harry, who had been born that week. Finally, Jonathan Dimbleby turned to Tony Benn, who shrugged contemptuously: 'The question is frivolous. I have no opinion.' Only Benn could get away with it.

It is always the same story in the car on the way home after those shows. Exhausted in the darkness of a Friday night, I anguish over the string of ums and ers with which I have punctuated answers, and think of all the things I should have said on the air. Unless one is buoyed by the sublime complacency of a Benn or Norman St John Stevas, most panellists go through the same experience. I remain envious of performers who excel at *Any Questions?*.

An editor such as me does not become very famous, in the manner of a TV soap star, but he becomes a bit famous. That is to say, my face came to command a gleam of recognition in the sort of middle-class circles in which *The Daily Telegraph* was read. The insidious worm grew, of expectation that when one met somebody he or she would know who one was. I encountered an excellent corrective to this socially tiresome trait, one evening when I was posing proudly on our prize-winning garden at the Chelsea Flower Show Gala. Among the throng of celebrities inspecting Arabella Lennox-Boyd's design wizardry, I found myself chatting proprietorially to Susan Hampshire, an actress I have always admired. After a few minutes, however, she turned from the flowers to me and enquired tartly: 'I hope you don't mind my asking, but who exactly are you, and what does this garden have to do with you?' Very good for the soul.

One of the perils of serving for many years as a minister, a company chairman or an editor is that it becomes easy to forget that privileged access is granted to the holder of an office, rather than to an individual. When at last I abandoned editorship, I noticed wryly that in my final fortnight I had lunched or dined à deux with the Home Secretary, the Culture Secretary, the Leader of the Conservative Party, the Tory Chairman, the Commissioner of the Metropolitan Police, the Chief of the Defence Staff and the Director of SIS. I had spoken at one dinner at the National Gallery, another for our senior executives, and yet another for the British film industry, attended by the Prime Minister. Yet almost all the invitations of this kind over sixteen years were extended not to Max Hastings, but to the Editor of *The Daily Telegraph* or the *Evening Standard*. When I forsook the role, the wonderful window on power closed. Only very foolish former ministers, chairmen or editors expect matters to be otherwise.

9

THE GULF WAR

THE DAILY TELEGRAPH remained one of the last titles in Britain to treat defence seriously as an issue, partly because it was our job as a newspaper of record, and partly because we possessed a large readership which cared about military matters. In peace or war, John Keegan and Robert Fox covered the defence beat brilliantly for us. I also tried to keep my own lines open to friends in the services, visiting the Staff College and various army schools. The *Telegraph* was perceived by servicemen as a key platform for debate on defence. Thus we were often first port of call for Whitehall and would-be leakers from the services. We denounced John Major's idiotic introduction of 'classless' medals for servicemen. The paper consistently opposed allowing women to serve on ships and in the front line, not out of social conservatism, but because of pragmatic objections. Disgruntled naval officers briefed me privately about the unhappy experiences of ships on which women served. It always seemed naive for the Navy to pretend that it is possible to send large numbers of men and small numbers of women to serve in the cramped conditions inseparable from warship life without creating chronic sexual tensions. On land, Charles Guthrie expressed to me his passionate objection to women in the front line: 'You can't leave a woman behind on the battlefield.' This view we reflected in the paper, though it reinforced critical mutterings that the *Telegraph* had not changed its old ways as much as Hastings liked to pretend.

When Michael Portillo became Defence Secretary, he brought with him into office as Special Adviser his old friend David Hart.

David, a right-wing maverick who had at one time managed to get close to Thatcher ('She likes him because he upsets the civil servants,' said Ferdy Mount, then serving in Downing Street), frightened the life out of the service chiefs, and of Portillo's fellow Cabinet ministers. I used to know David well, and found him an entertaining fellow – but he seemed too erratic to fulfil a responsible role inside government. We did not, however, say much in the newspaper about the Defence Secretary's choice of special adviser, because I had learned everything I knew about David as a guest of his family. One day, I was astonished to receive a call from the Security Service.

'We are engaged in positive vetting of David Hart,' said the anonymous caller, 'and it has been suggested that you may be in possession of information which would be relevant to a decision about whether he should be granted security clearance.'

'I would be surprised if he was a Russian spy,' I said, and left it at that. It was a little dismaying to be fingered as a plausible nark for MI5. Hart got his security clearance, to the impotent fury of several senior members of the Cabinet. The discomfited ministers intervened energetically, however, when first Portillo sought to get his Special Adviser a knighthood, and then Malcolm Rifkind put him forward for a peerage. Outraged opposition from Cabinet colleagues quashed both proposals.

Throughout the later Tory years, there was a running current of bitterness about defence cuts. Everyone recognized that the end of the Cold War must bring a 'peace dividend' – reductions especially in armoured units which had been deployed to meet potential Soviet attack in Germany. But in the late 1980s and early 1990s, the Conservatives abandoned their traditional posture as the party of British defence, and cut back the armed forces savagely, simply to save money. Later, when Tony Blair became Prime Minister and Charles Guthrie as Chief of the Defence Staff was deeply concerned about the overstretch of British commitments around the world, Charles told me that he was reluctant to complain too much to the Labour government, since its Tory predecessor was chiefly responsible for the shortage of resources. He was right, of course.

In the early 1990s the leaders of the RAF, always sensitive to neglect, became almost obsessed with the belief that the *Telegraph* cared only for the army. They insistently demanded that John Keegan and I should spend more time with them. The two of us attended one or two uncomfortable lunches with a cluster of air marshals. The Chief of the Air Staff so often importuned me to visit a Tornado squadron that eventually I surrendered. I warned him, however, that past experience in war zones suggested that my stomach and fast jets did not get on well together. At last, there came a day when I was received with much ceremony at the Lincolnshire home of 617 Squadron. The crews spent a difficult morning, struggling to wrench my gangling 6 foot 5 inch frame into a G-suit, and thence into a cockpit. Rashly, they persuaded me to share a heavy lunch with them in the officers' mess before takeoff. I was then shoehorned into the aircraft by main force. Once airborne, I enjoyed our first ten minutes, above the flatlands of East Anglia. Thereafter, matters deteriorated rapidly as we began contour-chasing across the hills. I parted with lunch over Yorkshire, and with breakfast above a friend's house in Northumberland. I then slumped comatose in the rear cockpit while we air-to-air refuelled, dropped bombs and otherwise cavorted about the skies in a fashion unfamiliar to airline passengers. When we landed two hours later, both the cockpit and the passenger were sorry sights. I sent the unfortunate ground crew a couple of cases of beer as a token of apology for having to clear up the mess, and I didn't blame them for complaining to *Private Eye*.

Relations between the RAF and the other services are always sensitive. Since the air force was created, its leaders have suffered a morbid inferiority complex. Not all paranoiacs are wrong about having enemies – the army and Royal Navy look upon the RAF with limited respect and enthusiasm. One day during a serious inter-service row, I was having breakfast with a chief of staff, who inveighed fiercely against the airmen: 'You know the old saying,

Max – "Don't march on Moscow, don't get involved in the Balkans, and never trust the Royal Air Force"!'

'Come off it, Richard' – even all these years later, I have changed names here – 'you can't talk like that any more. You're supposed to be in charge of these people.'

'But it's true, isn't it!'

At a more exalted level, because *The Daily Telegraph* took defence seriously, ministers were correspondingly sensitive about what we wrote. One evening in 1993, for instance, our News Desk was preparing a 'splash' front-page story, declaring that the Chiefs of Staff were at loggerheads with the government about its proposals for future action in the Balkans. I was in my flat when I received a phone call from Marshal of the RAF Sir Peter Harding, then Chief of the Defence Staff.

'Max, I'm sorry to bother you at home, but I am extremely concerned to hear that you are planning to run a story tomorrow about an alleged row between the Chiefs and the government. This will do a lot of harm, if it goes in. I'm sure the last thing you want to do is cause trouble for the services. You really must drop it.'

'I'm sorry, Peter, but I can't help noticing that you haven't denied the story is true. I'm satisfied it's accurate and important. We're committed to running it.'

'You should realize that if you do, it will cause a lot of embarrassment for your friend Peter Inge. Everybody knows that you had lunch with him today.'

General Sir Peter Inge was Chief of the General Staff, head of the army, and a personal friend. I said to Harding: 'It would be outrageous if you blamed Peter. It has absolutely nothing to do with him. I am going to write you a personal letter, copied to the Defence Secretary, which I shall send round in the morning, promising that Inge had no part in any of this. Meanwhile, I'm afraid our story will run.'

Next day, I sent the letters to the CDS and to the Defence Secretary, Malcolm Rifkind. Peter Harding rang me, in emollient mood. 'I hope you didn't mind me calling you last night, but you know how it is.'

'Of course I do. Malcolm Rifkind was standing by your left ear, holding an enormous revolver.'

But I did worry about possible damage to Peter Inge's career. And I worried even more two days later, when the *News of the World* spread all over its front page the story of Peter Harding's dalliance with Bienvenida Buck, which caused him to resign. For some hours, I was on tenterhooks lest Peter Inge should be denied the succession to become Chief of the Defence Staff because of his alleged entanglement with me. However, to my enormous relief – and to his – Peter got the job, and as CDS continued to be a good friend to me and to the *Telegraph* in the years that followed.

*

FOR A NEWSPAPER such as *The Sunday Times*, scoops are its lifeblood. The success of any given Sunday newspaper editorship is measured by the number of exclusive stories it generates. *The Daily Telegraph* gets its scoops, sometimes on the front page and sometimes in the form of a steady flow of original reporting by specialist correspondents on inside pages. But the real business of the paper is to provide every day a vivid, comprehensive, reliable picture of the world's news. I never forgot how fortunate we were to possess tremendous resources to cover big breaking stories, of a kind few other titles could match. Above all, we had a top-class foreign staff, superbly orchestrated by our Foreign Editor, Nigel Wade. I could remember the days when newspapers were starved of cash. As a young reporter on the *Evening Standard*, it was a big issue whether the air fare to, say, Amman or Nairobi was affordable. At Conrad Black's *Telegraph*, despite frequent tensions with management about overheads, I seldom found myself inhibited by cash considerations about how we should cover a big story. Conrad took foreign news very seriously, and far more often expressed strong views about our coverage of America ('the headline on Ian Ball's story "US race riots flare in echo of 1960s" is grossly

misleading') or the Middle East ('I have read the editorial comment in the July 17th issue . . . and I thought it was too anti-
Israel and too pro-Palestine'). On more than one occasion when
our foreign budget was under strain, I successfully appealed to
Conrad for support. If it was sometimes exhausting to argue the
toss about, for instance, our comment on Israeli policy on the
West Bank (we maintained steady criticism of Israel's 'creeping
annexation'), the upside was that Conrad recognized the vital
importance to the paper of maintaining a high standard of
international coverage. Among our resident foreign correspondents, I especially admired the Middle East despatches of my old
Falklands colleague Patrick Bishop, whom I had brought to the
Telegraph and who was now based in Jerusalem. Witness a
prescient piece he wrote for us in September 1988, at the end of
the Iran–Iraq War:

> The West is now facing a victorious, confident Saddam
> Hussein with 50 battle-hardened divisions and a 16 million
> population, armed with scores to be settled and ambitions to
> be realised. Historically, Iraq has designs on neighbouring
> Kuwait . . . Above all, there is Saddam's hunger to be an Arab
> leader in the Nasser mould . . . One can expect with gloomy
> confidence that the name of Saddam Hussein will become
> depressingly familiar to westerners who currently have only
> the faintest idea of who and what he is.

It is worth telling the story of our handling of the Gulf War,
which broke out almost two years later, as a case-study of how a
newspaper like the *Telegraph* handles a big foreign crisis, whether
in Kuwait, the Balkans, the Middle East, or most recently in
Afghanistan.

Within twenty-four hours of Iraq's invasion of Kuwait on
2 August 1990, we were receiving files from Con Coughlin in
Dubai, Patrick Bishop in Cairo and Robert Fox in Ankara – all
staff correspondents – as well as from a long tail of 'stringers'
around the world. Wendy Holden soon joined the Baghdad press

corps, and Charles Laurence was sent to Amman. In addition, of course, all newspapers bolster their own correspondents' despatches with snippets from the files of the news agency correspondents – Reuters, Associated Press and Agence France Presse – which fulfil an essential function in filling the gaps. From the outset, every day we devoted three, four, sometimes five pages of the paper to the crisis. Nigel Wade was in operational charge of our correspondents on the ground, while Don Berry commissioned and laid out special features and pages. As ever, the Night Editor, David Ruddock, directed the make-up of the paper as a whole, with much more personal input than usual from me.

Editorially, we never wavered from urging the importance of a hardline Western response to Saddam's aggression. We recognized from the first day that it was essential to build a Middle Eastern coalition against Iraq, and not to allow the crisis to become a confrontation between Muslims and the West. We harboured no illusions about the difficulty of maintaining a solid front against Saddam in the Middle East. Patrick Bishop wrote from Oman a week after the invasion that 'while the rest of the world likens Saddam Hussein to Adolf Hitler, many Arabs prefer another figure from German history. They see the Iraqi leader as a modern day Bismarck, desiring to forge a powerful entity from a cluster of petty states.' It was also apparent from the outset, and reflected in our leader columns, that the Western stand against Iraq was rendered much more difficult because many Arab states discerned hypocrisy in the speed of America's implementation of UN Resolutions against Saddam, measured alongside its apparent indifference to those concerning Israel.

One of the greatest problems about making modern foreign policy is the short attention span of Western electorates, and especially of the American people. In the autumn of 1990, it was evident that it would take months to mobilize an effective armed response to Saddam. I was fearful that Western public support for war might wane during the long military build-up in Saudi Arabia which followed the Iraqi invasion. Our editorials emphasized the

importance of digging in for a protracted operation. 'It seems well
to think seriously now about our deepest convictions on the Gulf
issue, and for the West to steady itself for a long and difficult
diplomatic and military campaign,' said our leader on 11 August.
'For ourselves, we hold to the view that Western credibility is
irrevocably committed.'

As well as our news reporting, we were carrying commentaries
every day by either George Walden and Robert Harvey – both
Tory foreign affairs specialists – or by John Keegan. Rereading
these more than a decade later, I am impressed by how well the
judgements hold up. The Gulf War was John Keegan's finest hour
in journalism. From beginning to end, his military assessments for
the *Telegraph* were crisp, decisive, and entirely vindicated by
events. Many Western voices, and a substantial part of the British
media, expressed extravagant doubts about whether America was
militarily capable of leading a coalition to expel Saddam from
Kuwait. The memory of Vietnam, the legend of American military
incompetence, was very vivid. Keegan, by contrast, wrote on our
leader page that America's armed forces had been entirely rebuilt
over the past fifteen years. They were now led by an impressive
and highly capable command group, he said. He harboured no
doubts about US ability easily to defeat Saddam, given only the
time to deploy American might in the Saudi desert. He wrote a
big piece on 11 January outlining very accurately how the war
would evolve: there would be a fierce air battle to gain control of
the electronic spectrum, and to neutralize Iraq's air defences. This
would be the decisive encounter. Thereafter, when the Coalition's
ground assault was launched, 'it seems unlikely that even the Iraqi
elite could stand up to the firepower it would unleash'. Such a
view stood in sharp contrast to that of British liberal media critics,
some of whom seriously suggested in *The Guardian*, *The Independent* and elsewhere that Saddam's Republican Guard might see
off an American-led ground attack. Keegan was also prescient in
his observations about international forces. He suggested that
the Coalition being created to fight in the Gulf was the kind of

international army of which the world would see much more in the future. The era in which any single Western nation unilaterally engaged an enemy was probably over. In future conflicts, combined forces drawn from many countries were likely to be deployed.

By early in the new year of 1991, the *Telegraph* was deploying a formidable cast of reporters all over the region: Anton La Guardia in Tel Aviv; Robert Fox in Dhahran; Jim Muir, our 'stringer' in Nicosia; Patrick Bishop roaming the Saudi desert; Alec Russell in Turkey; Scott Peterson in Damascus; Ben Fenton in Bahrain. On our Gulf pages, we were also carrying regular files from Tim Witcher in Paris, Marcus Warren in Moscow, and Science Editor Roger Highfield. The cost of such operations for any newspaper is, of course, immense and unbudgeted. In addition to hotel and travel bills, satellite phone charges load the tariff heavily, even if mobiles give media organizations incomparably better communications with reporters in the field than they enjoyed in the days when I was a war correspondent. No one, least of all Conrad, grudged the expenditure, but as the crisis extended to five, six months, the bill ran into hundreds of thousands of pounds. That was before taking account of the cost of running extra pagination in the paper to make space for the coverage, unsupported by any additional advertising revenue – Britain was by now heading into recession.

For much of the war, the *Telegraph* writers most concerned with its coverage met regularly in my office to talk through policy. In contrast to bellicose voices elsewhere in the British media, we believed that the West would be unwise to march on Baghdad to depose Saddam. The Coalition's objectives should be restricted to the expulsion of Iraq from Kuwait, if possible through economic sanctions, but more likely by force. Very early, however, we identified a second essential war aim: 'The removal of Saddam's aggressive capabilities, above all in the field of nuclear and chemical weapons, is essential in order to justify the West's massive military and political commitment,' I wrote on 29 August. 'Any outcome of the Gulf conflict which does not achieve this will amount to failure – tragic failure.'

Our own assessments of the forces that would be needed to fight Saddam ran some way ahead of the British government's, and proved very accurate. When it was announced in September that Britain would be sending an armoured brigade to Saudi Arabia, I wrote a piece arguing that it was essential to dispatch a full division, because this was the smallest credible organic force that could fight as a national entity. Having written a book on the Korean War, I recalled the sorry plight of the first British brigades committed there in 1950, small units operating with much larger American formations. The British defeat on the Imjin in April 1951 could partly be attributed to the fact that when a British brigade commander told his American superior that his predicament was 'a bit sticky', the US general did not grasp that in British parlance, this meant disastrous.

Yet for all Mrs Thatcher's grandiose rhetoric in 1990, it proved extraordinarily difficult for her government to mobilize a British division for the Gulf. Her government had ruthlessly slashed the resources of Britain's conventional forces. Her budgetary squeeze had reduced the army to desperate straits. Long after she left the premiership, Mrs Thatcher continued to present herself as the Boadicea of European defence. Yet in truth, throughout her years in office her policy was ambivalent, if not hypocritical. She resolutely declined to conduct a Strategic Defence Review to match resources to commitments, because she feared the political embarrassment that would follow such a confrontation with reality. She spent a fortune, against the judgement of such far-sighted critics as Field Marshal Lord Carver, on the Trident missile programme (which, at a humbler level, I too opposed passionately) because she believed that only Trident could preserve Britain's season ticket at the nuclear summit table. The price of Trident was that Britain's conventional forces were stripped to the bone. Throughout the late 1980s, they endured chronic shortages of ammunition, fuel and training facilities. The government preserved an impressive paper array of British military formations, but denuded these of fighting credibility. In order to equip 1st Armoured Division for the Gulf, it proved necessary to strip Rhine Army of tanks and fighting vehicles, because so much of the armour displayed on Britain's order of battle was non-operational for lack of spares. The RAF's strike capability was critically handicapped by the limitations of the Tornado aircraft, and the shortage of precision-bombing equipment of the kind the Americans possessed in such plenty. There was an embarrassing chasm between British eagerness to play a leading role alongside the Americans, and our military capability to do so. The government was lucky to avoid a brutal showdown between its own rhetoric and reality in the Gulf.

*

ON A SUPERTANKER the size of the *Telegraph*, delegation is fundamental. The Editor customarily plays little part in the detailed layout of pages and writing of headings, other than to approve them. Don Berry had no peer in briefing reporters, laying out stories, writing headlines and pulling together the complex fragments into a coherent whole. David Ruddock, as Night Editor, possessed all the virtues of the old *Telegraph*, on which he had learned his trade – speed, literacy, integrity. But he also possessed its vices, which included a lack of interest in picture presentation, and a chronic contempt for display. The Gulf War gave Don his opportunity, and brought out the best in our new-model *Telegraph*. I played a much bigger part than usual in dictating News page content. Between us, we produced each day briefings on the conflict which were sometimes matched by our rivals, but never bettered. My own relationship with the Foreign Secretary was of great value in keeping me thoroughly informed, not on operational secrets, which Douglas would never have revealed, but on Coalition thinking. I wrote many of our leaders and a steady stream of signed commentaries.

Friends and colleagues often asked if I was yearning to be out there myself in the desert with 1st Armoured Division, like my old Falklands colleagues Fox and Bishop. The answer was an honest no. I loved my young days as a war correspondent, but I was now in my mid-forties. Life had moved on. The thrill of directing *The Daily Telegraph*'s coverage of great events was greater than any I could have gained from donning camouflage fatigues once again. Indeed, as Bob Fox discovered to his chagrin, the frustrations of bivouacking for weeks amid desert boredom, waiting for the Coalition to be committed to action, were intense. The 'pool' reporters officially accredited to units in the field filed a steady diet of 'colour' about what the experience was like for the troops. But Patrick Bishop and others were producing far more hard stories and information, roaming the Middle East under their own steam, with no official accreditation.

Because of my own military connections, it was widely assumed that I must enjoy warm personal relations with the Ministry of Defence. It was true that I had an easy relationship with Tom King, the Secretary of State, though we had been strongly critical of his recent cost-cutting White Paper, *Options For Change*. But in the build-up to war, I spent many hours squabbling down the telephone with MoD civil servants about the restrictions imposed on journalists operating with British forces. Before and during the Gulf War, correspondents in the field possessed nothing like the freedom of movement I had enjoyed almost a decade earlier in the Falklands. The Gulf became the most media-managed war in history – until Afghanistan a decade later, when official information became even scantier. I am among a minority of modern journalists on both sides of the Atlantic, who believe that when a nation is engaged in military operations, it is entitled both to impose censorship (if it can make this effective, which is very hard in the age of portable satellite communications) and to restrict journalists' movements. The sheer number of would-be war correspondents striving for admittance to modern battlefields makes it unthinkable to give them all free rein. That said, however, in 1991 the Pentagon and Ministry of

Defence used their powers ruthlessly and insensitively to control the media, assisted by the authoritarian nature of the ruling regime in Saudi Arabia, where the Coalition forces were deployed. While the Foreign Office performed at its best during the Gulf War, the Ministry of Defence was an unhappy place. The Chief of the Defence Staff was an airman, Sir David Craig, who suffered chronic difficulty imposing his personality on the machine. The ministerial team was rendered more colourful by the presence of Alan Clark, but this caused a permanent secretary to remark contemptuously to me: 'We've got only one minister here with any brains – and he's mad.' The same official observed about his Secretary of State: 'The trouble with Tom is that he believes all problems can be solved by getting everybody round the table and having a good chat over a glass of wine.'

I made one Gulf coverage decision which was widely criticized. When it became evident that war was imminent, to her chagrin I withdrew from Baghdad our correspondent Wendy Holden. This had nothing to do with fears for her safety – all war zone reporters expect to take their chances, and I have never lost a night's sleep worrying about the survival of our journalists on the ground anywhere in the world. No, it was because I believed that any journalist who stayed in Baghdad once hostilities began would merely become a tool of Saddam's propaganda machine. If Britain had not itself been a belligerent, I would have left Wendy in place. But if my own country was to fight Iraq, I found it repugnant to allow our reporters to be exploited by Saddam to tell the story he wanted. I knew that Wendy would have no freedom to go anywhere, or to assess situations for herself. She would be the prisoner of Iraqi censorship. I could see no role for her, save to trail along with official conducted tours of civilian carnage – collateral damage, as the generals call it. CNN was already being criticized for the extent to which its reporting was serving Saddam's interest, even though its men on the ground were highly experienced war reporters such as my old acquaintance from Vietnam, Peter Arnett.

Most of my senior executives believed at the time that I was wrong. Don Berry said: 'If we were at war with Germany and Hitler allowed you to keep a man in Berlin, it would have been your job to do so. It is up to us, back here, to put "health warnings" on copy, so that readers know the terms on which it is filed.' As soon as we began to hear John Simpson's unforgettable BBC voice reports as cruise missiles roamed the streets of Baghdad, I recognized that I had damaged the *Telegraph*'s interests by withdrawing Wendy. It was one of my worst operational decisions as an editor, which tarnished our pride in the paper's coverage of the story.

As tensions mounted during the approach to war, a minister friend rang me more than once, to ask if I could tell him what was going on: 'Unless one's a member of the War Cabinet, nobody tells us a thing.' This was an extreme example of a conspicuous phenomenon of Cabinet government. Ministers become absorbed in their own departmental affairs, and possess less knowledge of what is going on elsewhere in the Whitehall forest than the average political journalist. Under most Prime Ministers, there is next to no collective Cabinet discussion about broad government policy, a state of affairs which suits Downing Street very well. But it becomes frustrating for even the most acquiescent minister to see his own country on the brink of war, and to find that he is expected simply to get on with running Health, Transport or Education until the Prime Minister deigns to tell the Cabinet which side has won.

In some respects, wars bring out the worst in newspapers. Opportunities for pages of exuberant graphics, demonstrating how air and ground technology will pulverize the enemy, make us all prone to extravagance. Some of the scathing comment from critics about the media's 'toys for boys' approach to conflict seems justified. In the days before the Gulf War, there was almost gleeful speculation in some titles about the prospect of Saddam's capital being razed by cruise missiles. I wrote on 8 January: 'For all the loose talk in the West about the prospect of Allied air forces "flattening Baghdad", nothing of the sort will take place. Bombs both aimed and off-target will hit vital government installations, and some civilians will certainly be killed. But no systematic effort will be made to terrorise or inflict casualties on the Iraqi civilian population, because such strikes would damage the moral basis on which this war is being fought.' Amazingly, a few commentators were urging the use of nuclear weapons, deploying the argument advanced by some Americans forty years earlier, to justify nuclear action in Korea: 'Why should we forgo the huge advantage of our most devastating technology, in fighting a primitive enemy?' It seemed obvious to reasonable people that nuclear weapons were utterly unacceptable in the Gulf, but the hawks never give up. Nine years later, during the Kosovo confrontation, a well-known young right-wing historian rang me to offer an article, proposing that we should employ nuclear weapons in the Balkans. I told him that to run such a piece would damage our credibility as a newspaper almost as much as it would injure his own. He managed to find a platform for his views anyway, in a Sunday broadsheet. I have never thought much of his judgement since.

The *Telegraph* remained resolute in believing that when the Allied forces launched their ground offensive, they should not advance to Baghdad: 'It is most unlikely – and would be seriously mistaken politically – that Allied forces will seek to occupy Iraq. It is . . . desirable that Iraq's armed forces are destroyed wholesale in the course of the war, and essential that its chemical and potential nuclear facilities are eliminated. It would be absurd to flinch from the additional reality, that the future of the region will be far more comfortable if Saddam himself becomes a casualty of the conflict.' But it seemed one thing to hope that Iraq's dictator would be killed during bombardment, and another to propose occupying his capital. Since the war ended, many critics have denounced the Coalition's 'failure to finish the job'. I had several long conversations with Douglas Hurd about this, during January and February 1991. He lamented the absence of any credible Iraqi opposition leadership to supplant Saddam. I think now, as I thought then, that the British and American governments were right to decline to take responsibility for creating what must have been perceived as a puppet government in Iraq. Such action would have destroyed the Western Coalition with the Arab states, and could well have provoked a new Middle East crisis in the wake of the Kuwaiti one.

Among the most thoughtful and effective minds the *Telegraph* possessed on foreign affairs was our leader writer Simon Scott-Plummer, whom I had wooed from *The Times* back in 1986. Simon was in the best tradition of literate, thoughtful, highly disciplined foreign affairs analysts, of whom there are plenty in the world's foreign ministries, and too few in newspaper offices. It was Simon who wrote a perceptive editorial early in January 1991, in which he suggested that the West might inflict a devastating defeat on Saddam, and destroy his credibility in our eyes, while discovering that the Iraqi tyrant retained widespread regard in the Arab world, merely for having resisted American might. Simon shrewdly appreciated the paradox: many Arabs who accepted the need to join the Coalition against Iraq nonetheless retained a deep frustration about their inability to deflect American indulgence towards Israeli occupation of the West Bank.

I pursued Scott-Plummer's theme in a signed piece on 25 January, in which I criticized the British media for its relentless scepticism about the Coalition, when 'seldom in modern times has the American military displayed such confidence and evidence of competence ... I believe that on the day [the land offensive is launched], after weeks of air bombardment on the present scale, the Allied ground forces will achieve a relatively speedy victory. The grounds for serious concern, I suggest, are the immense complexities of the politico-military endgame after Kuwait is freed; and the danger that the mere fact Saddam has stayed in the ring against Allied forces for some weeks will lend him lasting heroic status in the Arab world.'

As the Allied air offensive pounded Iraq's defences through

February, the world remained in a state of daily expectation and tension about the launch of the ground offensive. There were repeated false alarms. Just before our first edition was due to go to press, at 9 p.m. one night in the third week of February, I strolled onto the newsroom floor to look at the front page. The back bench was in a state of fevered excitement and activity. David Ruddock glanced up: 'The ground war's started,' he said, as he set up a huge front-page banner with the news.

'Hang on a minute,' I said, 'how do we know?'

'The agencies are reporting that our tanks are advancing.'

'It doesn't feel right. I'm just not convinced that this is the real thing.'

'Oh, come on, Max. The tanks are moving. What more do you want? And we're past off-stone time already.'

'No, stop it. The risk's just too great.'

I was haunted by the potential embarrassment of prematurely putting out a paper with such a headline. Though David fulminated, I insisted on scrapping the front page and reverting to another lead story. Half an hour later, it was confirmed from Saudi Arabia that there was still no ground offensive.

I quote that episode simply as an example of how nerve-racking it can be for every editor to be obliged to make judgements of this kind in a few minutes. It is a blow to the morale of a newspaper's entire staff if they wake up in the morning and find they have missed a big story which every other title is 'splashing' on. That happens to us all, sometimes. But the bigger the story, the more disastrous it is to get it wrong. It would have been especially so in this case. In justice to David Ruddock, I should add that his judgement on these things was usually much better than mine. More than once, in the five years we had already been together, he had saved me from making serious blunders in our choice of 'splashes', and I was generally happy to defer to him. That tense exchange between us in the Gulf War still left the honours in matters of news judgement about 20–1 in his favour

against mine. But in the context of the war, because of my own
military credentials, I felt more confident than usual about over
ruling him.

Three nights later, the ground offensive against Kuwait started
in earnest. Like every newspaper in the world, we found ourselves
overwhelmingly dependent upon our roaming and unauthorized
correspondents in the desert – in the *Telegraph*'s case, chiefly
Patrick Bishop – for usable copy. The accredited correspondents
with the Coalition forces saw nothing of the fighting, and filed
little of value until the battle was over. The Gulf War experience
did much to discredit those – including me – who had argued
that the media should seek accommodations with the military
in the field during conflicts. Henceforward in the world's wars,
every responsible newspaper and broadcast organization would
seek to circumvent the official information net, rather than
allow itself to be dependent upon making bargains with Whitehall. Given the opportunity, even the governments of the great
democracies had proved unable to resist abusing censorship and
information management, to keep reporters as far as possible from
military action. Subsequent experience of American behaviour in
Haiti and Afghanistan shows that the US Government, especially,
has become more committed to stifling the reporting of conflict
since the Gulf, rather than less so. I am surprised that the
American media, incomparably more powerful in their society
than the British media in our own, has accepted official restraints
so passively.

The *Telegraph* gained more from my relationship with Douglas
Hurd in those days than at any other time. I met or spoke to him
regularly, gaining priceless insights about Washington's state of
mind – and of course, Washington called all the important shots.
Douglas was himself at the White House when General Colin
Powell made his controversial pitch to President Bush to halt the
fighting, 'because my men don't like running a turkey shoot'. Even
those of us who opposed a march on Baghdad were deeply
dismayed by the Coalition's failure to complete the destruction of

Saddam's armed forces. The military opportunity to do so was there for the taking. Washington's ill-judged outbreak of humanity caused the breach of a fundamental principle, that the objective of battle is the destruction of the enemy. The victors could have smashed Saddam's Republican Guard, his vital power base, without going anywhere near Baghdad. The consequences of that US failure of will in 1991 still lie heavy upon the world today, more than a decade later.

On 29 February, 100 hours after the battle began, a ceasefire was declared. Iraq's forces had been expelled from Kuwait at negligible cost to the Coalition. The sceptics – and there were many in Britain – who had questioned Allied military competence were confounded. John Keegan's faith in the Coalition's power and his contempt for Iraq's armed forces had caused him to be widely criticized in some left-wing media circles as a Whitehall stooge. Now, his judgement was vindicated and his contributions to the *Telegraph* were recognized by all those who knew their business as the outstanding media analyses of the war. Dear John, a man of strong emotions and sympathies, of which patriotism is not the least, allowed himself a crow of triumph on our leader page. He argued that the principal British broadcasters, with their relentless scepticism about the Coalition, had failed in their duty. He claimed that Jeremy Paxman and the Dimbleby brothers 'had betrayed their responsibilities to a contemptible degree'. He went on: 'I take no satisfaction in saying I told you so. But in an article I wrote on Christmas Eve last year I forecast that the Iraqi air force would be eliminated from the war without any significant loss to the Allied side, and that once the ground war began, with the Iraqi air force absent, the Iraqi army would run away.' John was awarded a well-deserved OBE in the Gulf War Honours List, but his achievement received fewer plaudits than it deserved from other journalists, who are more comfortable celebrating messengers of institutional failure than heralds of government success. When I suggested that he deserved one of those dubious annual prizes journalists award to each other amid riotous scenes, I was told that any professional bouquets were more likely to go to Robert Fisk, whose coruscating rudeness about America's conduct had captured Fleet Street's imagination. John indeed received no award from his peers in the media, despite plenty of applause from everybody else.

Although victory in the Gulf was overwhelmingly an American achievement, John Major found himself identified with the Coalition's triumph. We were full of praise for his conduct in those first months of his premiership: 'The war has demonstrated in conditions of crisis both the resolve of our new Prime Minister and the competence of his ministerial team. There is no reason to doubt his ability to turn these qualities to the government's advantage in tackling the domestic tasks ahead.' In the euphoria and relief of Gulf victory, we were not the only ones to allow ourselves a moment of indulgent optimism about the prospects for Mr Major.

On 4 March, I flew on an aircraft of the Queen's Flight with three other editors – David English of the *Daily Mail,* John Birt of the BBC and Stewart Purvis of ITN – as guests of Tom King, to visit 1st Armoured Division in Kuwait. It was a shameless piece of war tourism, but of course fascinating. It was nice of the Defence Secretary to include me, when the *Telegraph* had been brutally critical of his tenure of office, and especially of his *Options For Change* plan. But Tom, with the good nature which is both a virtue and weakness in politics, rose above all that, and found me a seat on his plane. Our first stop was in Bahrain. We visited a squadron of Tornados, the inadequacies of which had been painfully exposed by the war. Alongside American Stealth technology, all European military aircraft now looked primitive. The RAF's crews had suffered relatively severely for small military advantage. In the Operations Room, Tom delivered a stirring oration to the aircrew about what a splendid job they had done. Then, with the air of a man who knows he has said all the right things, he sat down and invited questions. A pilot at once rose to his feet: 'Please, sir, can you tell us: is *Options* still "on"?' Tom looked as discomfited as any politician can do, when he is pursuing one agenda and discovers that his audience is determined to address another. The unfortunate Tornado crews were overwhelmingly preoccupied, not with the war which had just ended, but with the brutal question of whether they had jobs to go home to, if the Tory government's planned cuts went ahead. Tom's media guests commiserated with the Defence Secretary about what an unjust world we live in.

Our little party flew on to Riyadh and thence, after a series of briefings, by Hercules to Kuwait with the British Commander-in-Chief, Sir Peter de la Billière. Helicopters took us for a tour of the battlefield. Beyond the vast palls of smoke enshrouding the sheikhdom, from the oil wells fired by Saddam, I was immediately struck by how few destroyed Iraqi vehicles we saw. There was evidence of massive destruction on the Basra road, but in many former Iraqi positions there were only empty tank pits. I have always been a sceptic about the limitations of air power. For most of the past century, its exponents have consistently overstated both what it can do and what it has done, from Trenchard and Harris to the Gulf and Kosovo air commanders. Its role in modern war is indispensable. It can achieve devastating results against vehicles on the move. Its aiming technology has vastly improved over the past thirty years. In 2001, it achieved remarkable success in Afghanistan with few civilian casualties, against a weak enemy (and with no journalists underneath, to describe the carnage to a squeamish world). But air-dropped high explosives remain imperfect weapons against guerrillas, bunkers, dug-in troops and vehicles. It was obvious in Kuwait that much of Saddam's army had escaped, as a consequence either of ineffective bombing or of Colin Powell's outbreak of pity for the vanquished. It came as no surprise a year later, when the official Congressional report on the war showed that initial US Air Force estimates had wildly overstated their 'kill' score against Saddam's forces.

By the time we reached 1st Armoured Division, leaguered in the desert, media controversy was already bubbling about an incident at the end of the war, in which the British suffered their heaviest casualties from a misdirected American air strike, which killed nine soldiers in two Warrior APCs. The media, ever eager to punish perceived American hubris, made much of this. British newspapers kept the story on the front pages for years, through successive inquiries, including a grotesque British civilian inquest, which found the Americans guilty of unlawful killing. I cannot say that the British troops in the desert in 1991 seemed minded to regard the Warrior bombing as any more than a tragic accident, of the kind inseparable from conflict. One of the greatest weaknesses in modern media reporting of war is that journalists impose upon conflict the same criteria and expectations of fault and blame, cause and effect, which obtain in peace. This difficulty is intensified when so few journalists who report wars any longer possess military knowledge. The reality is that in every war in which young men are entrusted with deadly weapons, mistakes are made which cost lives, sometimes civilian and sometimes from one's own side. In the Second World War, armies and air forces killed their own men in hundreds, most conspicuously in Normandy in 1944. Nobody made much of it. Today, the accuracy of bombardment is much improved, but mistakes are still made, and will persist as long as men go to war. That is why we campaigned vigorously in *The Daily Telegraph* for British soldiers who mistakenly killed people in Northern Ireland, such as Private Lee Clegg in 1994, to be court-martialled and subjected to military disciplinary action rather than to face civilian murder charges. The murder convictions of Clegg and others represented a shocking betrayal of responsibility by successive British governments. And that is why, in our paper, we refused to treat the deaths of British soldiers in the Warriors outside Kuwait as anything more than a ghastly mistake, of which it was surprising there were not more and worse.

The formal ceasefire in the Gulf was signed on 9 April. It was soon evident that a serious diplomatic mistake had been made, by the Coalition's failure to insist that Saddam should report to the desert rendezvous in person, to make his humiliation explicit in the eyes of his own people and of the world. Before many weeks were past, our reporters who had been filing from the Saudi desert found themselves in northern Iraq, in Kurdistan, describing the new crisis the Iraqi tyrant's actions had thrust upon the region. And our correspondent Charles Laurence was filing from Sarajevo, a place the world had scarcely considered since 1914, about the renewed threat to peace poised by the imminent break-up of Yugoslavia. In the wake of the collapse of the Soviet Union, there were those who supposed that war between major states, and especially conflict involving the Western democracies, had become an obsolete phenomenon. The last decade of the twentieth century, and the first years of the twenty-first, have shown us otherwise.

10

CONRAD

SOON AFTER CONRAD BLACK bought the *Telegraph*, he acquired a London house, in Highgate of all places. I teased him a good deal about this implausible location for Xanadu. He muttered something sheepish about having been talked into it by Andrew Knight. For a couple of years afterwards he came to London for a longish summer visit, but otherwise was more often to be found in Toronto or New York or Palm Beach, in all of which he possessed homes. In the early years of his visits to London he often seemed lonely, not least because his marriage to his first wife, Joanna, was unhappy. From 1989 onwards, however, as the *Telegraph*'s fortunes boomed, he spent increasing periods on this side of the Atlantic, enjoying his success. Conrad revelled in wealth and power. 'The deferences and preferments that this culture bestows upon the owners of great newspapers are satisfying,' he once observed complacently. He began to be lion-ized, as newspaper proprietors are, by some important people and some worthless ones. He moved first to Chester Square for a time, later to an enormous mansion in Kensington. I saw more and more of him, usually pleasurably. His company could be great fun. He is much readier to be teased than some of his critics allow. But I learned to dread his nocturnal telephone calls, sometimes from the other side of the world. Conrad loves to talk. He gives little heed to time if he is enjoying a conver-sation. He rises late, and is seldom much in evidence before mid-morning. His unpunctuality is legendary. He will think nothing of turning up half an hour late for a board meeting or a dinner, but might then linger for hours if he is enjoying the talk. Late at night, for those of us who like to be in bed by 10.30, he can be a menace. When I was his editor-in-chief, there were not a few occasions when the phone rang at midnight or after, London time. After a brief exchange of platitudes, Conrad would get to work: Why were we so down on Colonel Oliver North? What were we thinking of, writing leaders denouncing IVF treatment for women over fifty who desired to conceive children? Had we no sense of personal freedom of choice, a fundamental principle of every decent Conservative? What did I think of this new Labour man Tony Blair? Would these 'safe havens' in Kurdistan achieve anything? One was required to jerk oneself from slumber into instant fluency, and thereafter to maintain a conversation sometimes for an hour or more. My wife muttered at these moments: 'Think of the money, think of the money.' And so I did.

A year or two after I became *Telegraph* Editor, Conrad dropped me a note about a Canadian journalist of his acquaintance, one Barbara Amiel, a girlfriend of George Weidenfeld, who had moved to London and wanted to start writing for British newspapers. He proposed that I should see her. I had never heard of Barbara Amiel. It was obviously politic to indulge Conrad by meeting her, but there seemed no case for making implausible commitments. On the appointed day, a vision of fine cheekbones and huge deep, penetrating eyes surmounted by a mane of black hair swept into my office, swathed in furs. I have seldom been so discomfited. Like many middle-class Englishmen, I am not at my best dealing with glamorous and formidable women. Not to put too fine a point on it, I was terrified. My chief notion was to bluster my way through this, to spend long enough with Ms Amiel to satisfy courtesy, and then to get her out of the door. I blush a bit, recalling our conversation.

'What sort of journalism do you think you want to do here?'

'I'd like to write a column.'

'But nobody gets to write a column until they've shown us what they can do by contributing features for a while. How much do you feel you know about British life?'

'I was born in London, though I haven't lived here that much in recent years.'

'How much journalism did you do in Canada?'

'Quite a lot. I was even an editor at one stage.' Dazzling, gamine smile.

'Have you got any cuttings we could look at?'

'Frankly, no. But I suppose I could find some.'

'The problem, I think, is that it's hard to imagine being able to use you regularly in a British newspaper until you've been here for a while. Can I suggest that I put you in touch with our Features Editor, Veronica Wadley, and see if we can arrange to commission you to write one or two features, and see how we get on?'

The story gets worse. I sent a jolly note to Conrad, summarizing my exchange with his job applicant:

> I saw Barbara Amiel. I cannot say that I think it was one of my great performances, in that after a 45-minute chat, she told me she found me most frightening. I said that made two of us. She said that she thought I misunderstood her essentially sensitive and vulnerable nature. I said that I had perhaps been overhasty, in doubting that any friend of George Weidenfeld's could be overendowed with either characteristic. She said she feared that I was laughing at her, rather than with her . . . I do not think it was a great meeting of minds. She said she was concerned about continuity in the direction of the paper if she came, and asked how long I was likely to be around. I said that I had every intention of sticking around for 2–3 years, which is as far ahead as anybody can look, and which anyway discounted the possibility that you might have other views. She said she thought 2–3 years was not very long. I said that if one was in an office on the Isle of Dogs, it seemed a pretty long time to me.

... Perhaps I am just not good at dealing with these thugs.

In the event, in 1990 and 1991 I conducted further dalliance with Barbara about becoming a contributor to the paper. But by then, she had already established herself in *The Times* as a columnist. Our negotiations never reached fulfilment, though I would not suggest this was because Conrad cautioned me, memorably: 'I think it is quite in order to proceed with Ms Amiel, but don't feel that you are being urged to pay her more than you think she is worth.' The world knows the rest. Barbara Amiel became a successful columnist for *The Times*, then Conrad's girlfriend, then Mrs Black, and today Lady Black of Crossharbour, an increasingly formidable influence upon both Conrad's wardrobe and the conduct of his newspapers. I have always been grateful that neither of the two seemed to hold my early joust with her against me. In our subsequent encounters, Barbara treated me with generosity and sympathy. Our relationship even managed to surmount a fairly fundamental difference of opinion about the policies of successive Israeli governments. Much to my own surprise, I was invited to be one of half a dozen guests at her wedding to Conrad at Chelsea Register Office in 1992. I made a speech at the dinner afterwards at Annabel's, in which I felt obliged to confess the circumstances of my first meeting with the bride. Years later, when I no longer worked for Conrad and married my wife Penny after my divorce, I told friends that we were too old for parties and gifts. Barbara sent us a handsome wedding present anyway. I am not the only Englishman whom Barbara can alarm, but I have good reason to think warmly of her today.

*

CONRAD IS A DEDICATED international networker. It was through the Bilderberg conferences, after all, that he originally met Andrew Knight and went on to acquire the *Telegraph*. He packed the

'International Advisory Board' of his holding company, Hollinger, with such luminaries as Henry Kissinger, Lord Carrington, Lord Hanson, and others who provided him with invaluable introductions on both sides of the Atlantic. All the stars turned out for his grand dinners in London, Washington, Toronto. I never felt very comfortable at these affairs, but obviously it went with the *Telegraph* turf to attend them. Occasionally Conrad invited me to make a speech. I did not always shine. Lady Thatcher (as she had become, after her resignation) cannot much have enjoyed listening to me hold forth about the state of the Conservative Party on a summer evening at Spencer House in 1994.

Once Conrad gave a dinner, ostensibly in my honour, at his vast house in Toronto with its Grinling Gibbons fireplace, and cupola modelled on that of St Peter's. The city's business community turned out in force. I spoke, barely adequately, about the place of the *Telegraph* in British life. At the end of the evening, our host waved me into the limo of Charlotte Ford, no less, to share a ride back to the King Edward Hotel. Ms Ford and I made desultory conversation on the journey. Though she had sat through the dinner and my speech, it rapidly dawned on me that she had not the faintest idea who I was. I have always believed that the social radar of the very rich simply does not engage acquaintances worth less than, say, a hundred million dollars.

But for those of us who have our chippy moments socially, I witnessed one to cherish at a lunch of Conrad's in Washington, at which I was sitting between Henry Kissinger and Lord Hanson. I am an unabashed admirer of Kissinger, and have thoroughly enjoyed my encounters with him. We were talking on one of his favourite themes, early nineteenth-century Europe and the place of Metternich. James Hanson suddenly leaned across and asked a question. Kissinger contemplated him without great enthusiasm.

'Before I respond,' he replied, in that inimitable voice calling from a deep-sea diving bell, 'may I know to whom I am speaking?' I have seldom seen a man look as deliciously flustered as poor

James. I doubt whether he had been invited to identify himself for thirty years. 'Er, I am, er, James Hanson,' he said.

Kissinger: 'And may I ask what is your role?'

'Yes, well, I'm a businessman. I have companies here and in Britain.'

Kissinger gravely nodded acquiescence, and delivered an orotund response, as if he had been importuned at the rostrum to satisfy a somewhat banal enquiry from a student audience. James listened submissively, then retired hurt from the conversation.

In my first years at the *Telegraph*, we entertained regularly at the Conservative Party Conference, as do many newspapers. We organized dinners for senior ministers, which Conrad liked to attend, and a drinks party for the world at large. After some years' experience of these affairs, I insisted that we should drop the dinners. All entertaining should give pleasure to either hosts or guests. At party conferences, politicians are under immense social pressure. They attend dinners given by editors or proprietors with the deepest reluctance, goaded only by fear of what we might do to them in print if they stay away. It is far more profitable to meet politicians one-to-one in London. As for drinks parties at conferences, I became weary of seeing a throng of dedicated freeloaders drinking our profits in Blackpool and Bournemouth. I gave an annual drinks party at Brooks's in London, well attended by politicians, which seemed both more discriminating and more fun. Although the Chairman enjoyed our seaside parties, I persuaded him that no one else did. Party conference entertaining is merely an ego trip for media bosses. I do not believe any company ever gained the smallest political or journalistic advantage from it.

Once the *Telegraph* began to pour cash into Conrad's coffers on a scale his businesses had never known before, he became ambitious for more big buys. Many of the titles that came on to the market, however, were mere licences to lose money. 'I have no interest,' he observed characteristically, after a brief glance at the potential of the Manhattan-based *Daily News*, 'in coming to New

York to clasp my lips around an exhaust pipe.' In the spring of 1991, however, a far more promising prospect opened. Conrad formed a pact with the tycoon Kerry Packer to buy the Australian Fairfax Group, which had been brought to the brink of bankruptcy by the mismanagement of the young family heir, Warwick Fairfax. It was a marvellous opportunity, which needed delicate handling because of the potential Australian competition law problems, relating both to foreign investment and to Kerry Packer's existing media holdings. Packer invited Conrad to lunch in his permanent suite at the Savoy, to discuss the deal. Dan Colson and I were detailed to join the party. From the outset, the occasion defied parody. Packer was flanked by his son, a lanky youth whose head appeared to have undergone some bizarre longitudinal experience in a cider press, and who sat mute throughout the proceedings. I have always thought the service at the Savoy pretty moderate, but I assumed that a star guest such as Packer was granted better treatment. Not so. As we talked, we were treated to a performance of Fawlty Towers inadequacy. Waiters clashed china and dropped food around us in a fashion that would have dismayed Manuel. Finally, the exasperated Packer was driven to tell the waiters: 'Put the ****ing food down there, put the ****ing bottles here, and get your useless ****ing asses out of here.' The waiters beamed broadly, nodded amiably, and continued as before. They were apparently uninstructed in Australian or even basic English.

I had never listened to a big international tycoon discussing a deal before. Packer's share of the dialogue was borrowed from the script of *Dallas*: 'Right, Conrad. We're all agreed, then. I shall take a back seat on this one. You'll lead the band. I'll fix Canberra. I'll deal with the state government. I'll square the banks. All I want out of this one is to see certain people's heads so deep in the shit that the tops of their heads will only be visible through a powerful microscope!'

Legal objections eventually forced Packer out of the Fairfax deal, but Conrad triumphantly achieved control – though not a majority shareholding. He descended on Sydney in his customary outspoken mode, along with Dan Colson, who became his viceroy in Australia. 'You can see that I do not have cloven feet or wear horns,' he observed benignly on his first appearance at the Fairfax offices. 'Contrary to widespread rumours, it is not a plan of Mr Colson's or myself to erect a guillotine and move journalists through it on a random basis.' The new regime's first meetings with Fairfax staff proved tense affairs nonetheless. Dan rang my office and asked us to get together any personal information we could muster about the key Fairfax editors, and to fax it to him in his hotel room. With the aid of our Australian staffers and some hasty calls down south, we put together a brief markedly unflattering to several of the personalities concerned. Soon after my secretary transmitted this, Dan called back. It was midnight in Australia, his fax machine was out of paper. Could she retransmit the stuff to another number? She did so, and thought no more of it until the next day, when the roof fell in. Long extracts from our document were all over the front page of Rupert Murdoch's *Australian.* A pall of embarrassment descended on all of us, not least the hapless Dan. The number he had given my secretary was that of the hotel fax. Exhausted after a day of negotiations, Dan fell asleep without remembering to go down and collect our transmission. A mischievous employee in the hotel's switchboard room passed the papers to Murdoch's newspapers. As well as exposing our brutal strictures, the episode scarcely conveyed an impression of administrative competence on the part of the Anglo-Canadian team.

A few weeks later, Conrad suggested that it might be useful for me to make a visit to Fairfax. I demurred. Friends who knew Sydney well had already told me that my height, my accent, my accent added up to the sort of Pom Australians love to hate. After the fax fiasco, I would be lucky to get past the airport Arrivals Lounge in one piece. I stayed at home. Although Conrad made a healthy profit out of Fairfax, he eventually felt obliged to sell out, after becoming mired in political opposition to any increase in his shareholding, as a foreigner. 'I was under the delusion that I had become familiar with every known brand of political and commercial corruption, Max,' he once growled to me, 'but Australian politicians have discovered ways of playing crooked pool that would have commanded admiration in Tammany Hall.'

Most of my meetings with Conrad took place either over dinner, or betwixt the portrait of Napoleon and the bust of Cardinal Newman in his deeply upholstered brown study of an office on the management floor in the Canary Wharf tower, to which the *Telegraph* moved from South Quay Plaza in 1992. The Chairman possessed expectations of how movers and shakers should live, which often worked to my advantage. He was generous about my extravagances on the company's account. He was thus bemused by the austerity of my office. One evening, he wandered down for a chat, and gazed around without enthusiasm at the simple fittings and furniture, which were standard through our floors. 'You know, Max,' he observed, 'this company is not so impoverished that it would find itself unable to generate resources to house our Editor-in-Chief in somewhat more stylish circumstances, should you see fit to wish it.'

'That's very sweet of you, Conrad,' I said, 'but it wouldn't do much good for the troops' morale if they saw me here knee-deep in Colefax & Fowler while they're all working on steel and plastic.' I added that most colleagues regarded my office as the Editor's only concession to hair-shirtery, in what was otherwise a self-indulgent regime. From the moment the *Telegraph* began to make serious profits, Conrad rewarded me handsomely for my own contribution in both salary and share options – indeed, I became one of the best-paid editors in Fleet Street.

Like most tycoons, Conrad was seldom unconscious of his responsibilities as a member of the rich men's trade union. Those who have built large fortunes seldom lose their nervousness that some ill-wisher will find means to take their money away from them. They feel an instinctive sympathy for fellow multimillionaires, however their fortunes have been achieved. When one of the tribe falls from grace, they share the sensations of French aristocrats in the Reign of Terror, watching a laden tumbril lurch over the cobbles towards the guillotine: hairs prickle on the back of the spectators' necks. Not infrequently, adverse comment in our newspaper about some fellow-mogul provoked Conrad's wrath. Our excellent Art Critic, Richard Dorment, once wrote scathingly about the malign influence on the international art market of the vastly rich Walter Annenberg, who had been briefly US Ambassador in London. It took some days of patient argument to dissuade Conrad from insisting upon Dorment's execution for speaking unkindly of his old friend Walter. We had some similarly sticky exchanges about the paper's coverage of Gerald and Gail Ronson, before, during and after Ronson's stretch in Ford Open Prison for his role in the Guinness affair. Conrad felt that the law had dealt uncharitably with Ronson, a view disputed by most of our own pundits.

We experienced similar vexations over Chief Buthelezi, leader of South Africa's Zulus. Conrad allowed himself to be persuaded by his friend John Aspinall, the gambling king, that Buthelezi was South Africa's greatest statesman. Our correspondents on the spot disagreed. While they displayed a certain sympathy for Buthelezi's predicament, they believed that he must bear a substantial share of responsibility for the tempestuous course of negotiations between his Inkatha and the African National Congress. We were able to dissuade Conrad from seeking any dramatic change in our coverage. I stressed the importance of backing the judgement of the people on the ground. But I also suggested to the Foreign Desk that our people should tread carefully on this issue, simply to avoid wearisome exchanges of memos and telephone calls with the Chairman. He sometimes chose to ride bizarre hobby horses.

Mohammed Fayed harried Conrad energetically, in pursuit of his demand to be referred to in our newspaper as 'Al Fayed'. I sent the Chairman a note, explaining that this was a long-running saga: 'The Fayeds have been seeking for years to call themselves Al Fayed, just as a socially ambitious Frenchman might seek to style himself de Fayed, or a German von Fayed ... At one level, it is harmless if the Fayeds wish to call themselves kings of Sheba, but I always feel determined to demonstrate that we will not be threatened.' I had not forgotten the lack of subtlety with which Fayed sought to link our coverage of his business affairs with Harrods' advertising spend. After several exchanges of memos, Conrad acceded to my view about Fayed's title or lack of it, in a witty note addressed 'to Sir Max Hastings OM CH KBE DSO and Cluster MA (Oxon), from His Most Eminent Beatitude the Grand Mufti of the *Telegraph*'.

Coverage of Sir James Goldsmith required delicate handling, after Conrad put him on our board. I had always respected the size of Jimmy's bank balance, but regarded his forays into British politics as absurd. It was George Walden who discovered and pointed out in our newspaper that Goldsmith's book attacking Europe, which became so popular among British Eurosceptics, in its original French edition had adopted some entirely contrary and even sympathetic views about the prospects for a single currency. Goldsmith had a long history of seeking to bully journalists and editors – he even tried to persuade Lord Hartwell to sack Bill Deedes back in 1976, when the *Telegraph* published a sympathetic piece about *Private Eye*'s feud with Sir James. To the end of Goldsmith's life, I found myself receiving threatening – and invariably fatuous – communications from the tycoon and his lawyers, demanding more sympathetic treatment for his political crusade. There was a memorable moment at a party when Charles Powell's wife Carla, a pantomime dame who was also an ardent supporter of Goldsmith, danced up and down before me, warning with blazing eyes that if I continued to mock Sir James's political activities 'Jeemee will get you! Jeemee will get you!' I responded flippantly, I fear: 'Come off it, Carla, this isn't Palermo, you know.' At the *Telegraph*, however, I felt obliged to mute our mockery, as long as Jimmy was a director.

On the whole, however, the newspaper as well as Conrad benefited from the range of major British businessmen whom he persuaded to join the board. In addition to their commercial wisdom, which I sometimes found very helpful to our City coverage, several possessed arcane specialist knowledge. David Montagu suggested to me one of our most successful editorial appointments, that of Tony Forrester as Bridge Correspondent. David knew him as a fellow-member of the Portland Club. The company of Peter Carrington, that peerless raconteur, vastly enlivened board lunches. I valued the advice of Martin Jacomb, another director, with his encyclopaedic knowledge of City affairs. Martin was always supportive when our City staff came under fire from some special interest.

Occasionally, of course, in the paper we trampled on the cherished concerns of a board member who made a fuss. I received an enraged call from one director, about our treatment of an ailing company with which he was involved. I always kept Conrad informed about such goings-on. I sent him a note on this occasion, reporting the director's call and saying: 'I felt unable to give P— any comfort, and I believe his sensitivity is prompted by the fact that he is trying to ride a horse of which three legs are terminally diseased. But it seems right you should know when a director is cross with us.' On this occasion, as on most, Conrad simply let events – and our coverage – take their course, until the collapse of the company concerned.

John King, then Chairman of British Airways, also became one of Conrad's boardroom luminaries. I formed a warm affection for him. He possesses in the highest degree the gift of making people feel good by focusing the entire force of his personality upon them while he is in their company. John flatters brilliantly, by appearing to confide to each individual some morsel of intelligence that he has been saving for his or her ear alone. Passing in a restaurant one day, when a big report was due on an air crash, he took me by the arm, peered gravely over his spectacles and murmured: 'It was pilot error, you know,' before steaming on. Even when one knew that he was doing the same to fifty other people in a day, even when the remark, so weightily delivered, possessed no great substance, at the height of John's powers few people could resist his charm. I learned a lot from him.

In the late 1980s, all my energies were focused upon building a new team and restructuring the newspaper. In the 1990s, although of course we continued to recruit writers and to develop the titles, we were no longer engaged in running a bloody revolution. I felt able to travel in order to write for the paper – to South Africa, Hong Kong, Hungary, the US – which may have helped to remind our own writers that I remained an enthusiastic reporter at heart. I also found myself involved in occasional dramas as Conrad's representative, rather than as a journalist. In 1993, a considerable fuss developed when it became known that the Churchill family trust proposed to sell to the highest bidder the greatest Englishman's entire collection of papers, held at Churchill College, Cambridge. It was alleged that this was being done chiefly to provide young Winston Churchill, the Tory MP, with funds for his expensive divorce. I was approached by one of the good and great, who asked me to convey a message to Conrad: might our Chairman be willing to fund the purchase of the collection for the nation, on the assurance that he would receive a generous tax break, and an early peerage?

I replied that I would certainly pass on the message, but that I would advise Conrad strongly against such action. I believed the sale was a deeply unsavoury business, when many of the papers in the collection were former state documents, illicitly removed from Downing Street when Churchill left office. Obviously, no one had been troubled at the time, when the nation owed the great man such a debt of gratitude, and when the Archive was to be lodged at Churchill College. But if it was now to be sold, issues of law as well as taste were at stake. My own objections were reinforced when Lord Hartwell, who remained a *Telegraph* director, drafted an incisive memorandum on the issue. He said – and Hartwell was an unimpeachably truthful witness – that his father, Lord Camrose, had paid the former Prime Minister very large cheques in his lifetime. These were clearly understood to embrace the

Churchill papers, as well as the serial rights to his war memoirs. Camrose saw himself as a willing benefactor of a great Englishman, though in an age of gentlemen's agreements he had never sought to cement the details of the deal in writing. Hartwell added that he was one of the last survivors who had attended the official deposit of the papers in Cambridge, alongside Clementine Churchill. He said he could state unequivocally that Lady Churchill took it for granted that the deposit was permanent.

I discussed all this with Conrad. He never seriously contemplated buying the collection himself, but briefly flirted with causing the *Telegraph* to make the deal: 'It could significantly accelerate my peerage and your knighthood, Max!' Lord Gowrie, then Chairman of Sotheby's, who were handling the sale, came to see us at Canary Wharf, and painted a rosy picture of the possible commercial advantages to the paper of owning the Churchill archive: 'You could sell copies of historic documents to your readers!' I responded to this proposal with a resounding raspberry. I pointed out that all the documentation was already in the public domain, in Martin Gilbert's vast official volumes.

The controversy had now broken into the open, and was being publicly debated in the media. The mood grew nastier when one of those concerned with the trust put forward an ill-founded claim that the sale could be justified by the fact that the papers were not being properly looked after at Churchill College. I approached Robin Butler, the Cabinet Secretary, and urged that the government should take legal action to prevent the disposal of the Churchill state papers. Butler did indeed consult the lawyers. The government's eventual conclusion, however, was that the legal position was extremely confused, and that anyway ministers were politically reluctant to confront the Churchill trust in court. After a long discussion at a *Telegraph* board meeting, to my immense relief the company determined not to buy the collection, perhaps not least because the purchase would have cost some 20 per cent of the annual profits of a company that was by now publicly quoted. It later fell to Lord Rothschild, as Chairman of the new

Heritage Lottery Fund, to announce that the HLF would fund the purchase on behalf of the nation. Jacob somehow persuaded himself that this decision would be greeted with warm public applause. I told him I thought he was wrong – that there would be an immense outcry about a pretty shabby transaction. So indeed it proved, and though at least the right outcome was achieved – the Churchill Collection is now safe at Cambridge in perpetuity – no one felt good about it. I was merely relieved that the *Telegraph* had been steered out of any entanglement in the mess, which had taken up a remarkable amount of our time.

*

ONE OF THE MOST sensitive issues for many British newspapers is that of how they treat rival proprietors in print. There is a shameless, self-serving compact between companies, that the personal embarrassments of newspaper owners are not reported by competitors. Anyone who attempts to write about Rupert Murdoch's or his family's domestic arrangements for another publication is likely to receive a call (or, more likely, his editor or managing director will do so) from one of the great tycoon's senior stooges at News International, drawing attention to the proprietors' pact, and warning without much subtlety about the inevitability of retaliation if the convention is breached. The preposterous Barclay brothers ruthlessly assert their right to be spared personal publicity of any kind, even about the fortress they have constructed in the Channel Islands, and even though they have chosen to become newspaper owners. It always seems pretty rich, that titles which derive most of their income from laying bare the private lives of others should show no embarrassment about protecting their own proprietors from scrutiny, through what amounts to a system of social nuclear deterrence. The 'hands-off' agreement does not, however, extend to mere paid hands. When David Montgomery was Chief Executive of the *Daily Mirror* and his personal life was in some disarray, David English observed with relish: 'Montgomery keeps ringing up and asking for things to be left out of our papers, and I keep having to point out to him that he is not a proprietor!'

Conrad was among those who possessed a soft spot for the *Mirror*'s earlier owner, Robert Maxwell. I had been an unwavering enemy of Maxwell since Tom Bower and I made one of the first major TV films about him for the BBC, back in 1972. When Maxwell drowned in November 1991, Conrad called me from New York and said: 'Don't be too hard on Bob, Max. I know he was a crook, but he was a not uninteresting character as well. He had his moments.' I disagreed with Conrad's last sentence – in my view, Maxwell was an unredeemed scoundrel – but I, too, was inclined to err on the side of generosity in the first hours after the man's death, before the vast scale of his defalcations was known. I wrote a piece for the *Telegraph*'s leader page, in which I told a string of stories about Maxwell's ghastly behaviour, drawing on personal experience; but I concluded that those of us who had never experienced anything to match his journey from the basest childhood poverty in Czechoslovakia should not, perhaps, condemn him absolutely. I had never forgotten Tom Bower telling me, after writing his Maxwell biography, 'To understand that man, you have to realize that as a kid his family was too poor to put shoes on his feet when he went to school.' Much as I loathed the bouncing Czech, I could never escape a twinge of awareness of my own cosseted middle-class upbringing, an uncertainty about what any of us might be capable of doing, to escape from such poverty as that which Maxwell knew. Conrad complimented me warmly on the piece I wrote, but when the scope of the man's crimes became apparent, I felt cross with myself for having succumbed to an impulse of generosity.

After the departure of Andrew Knight in November 1989, I answered directly to the Chairman on all matters relating to his newspapers. Most of the time this was not onerous, not least because Conrad spent so much time on the other side of the Atlantic. But crises in the Conservative Party provoked spasms of concern about our coverage of the government. International issues periodically raised the Chairman's hackles. Any comment in our pages that was deemed anti-American was sure to cause trouble. As the years went by, he also developed increasingly strong views on the Middle East question, and thus on our coverage of it. Especially after his purchase of *The Jerusalem Post*, Conrad showed himself an energetic supporter of the Israeli cause against that of the Palestinians. I felt obliged decisively to reject a request to provide *Telegraph* credentials for some *Post* correspondents travelling abroad. The risk to our own people, if anything went wrong, was simply too great. Conrad and I had several sharp exchanges, after pieces appeared in the *Telegraph* which he deemed anti-Israeli or even anti-Semitic. One of Conrad's favourite terms of approbation was to describe a friend or colleague as 'giving me a high comfort level'. Conversely, when one of our writers erred in his eyes, I knew it was time to hoist storm signals when the Chairman declared – with only a nod towards irony or conscious extravagance – that 'This snivelling product of some pinko journalism school administered by the John Pilger–Christopher Hitchens Trust for the propagation of liberal mendacity does not give me a high comfort level, Max.'

It was ironic, therefore, when one of the major rows of our time together descended on Conrad because he was accused of publishing anti-Semitic material in one of his own organs. In November 1994, a Los Angeles 'stringer' for the *Telegraph*, William Cash, wrote a piece for *The Spectator* – which the *Telegraph* had purchased from Algy Cluff in 1991 – suggesting that Hollywood was a Jewish town. In the wake of its publication, the roof fell in. A long roll-call of Hollywood luminaries headed by Tom Cruise, Steven Spielberg, Barbra Streisand and Kevin Costner wrote letters to Conrad and an open letter to *The Spectator*, and delivered diatribes to anyone who would listen, denouncing Cash's piece as a disgraceful piece of journalism. 'We have seen it all before, from the Inquisition in 13th Century Spain to the Holocaust of 20th Century Germany,' ran one of the less hyperbolic passages of their *Spectator* letter. 'When, to the editors of magazines like the *Spectator*, racist cant becomes indistinguishable from thoughtful commentary, it should sound a loud warning that we have not progressed so very far after all.' I was sitting in Conrad's office while he took a call from an enraged Jack Valenti, speaking on behalf of the Hollywood Motion Picture Association, about Cash's piece. They were demanding space not only in *The Spectator*, but also in *The Daily Telegraph*, to denounce the author. It was one of the few moments in my time with Conrad when I saw him look seriously rattled. I did not think Cash's piece represented memorable – perhaps not even tasteful – journalism, but nor did I believe that it deserved the ludicrous overreaction of the Hollywood community. Their demands, especially for space in the *Telegraph*, seemed absurd. I urged that they should be given a right of reply in *The Spectator*, but otherwise told to take a running jump. Conrad said: 'You don't understand, Max. My entire interests in the United States and internationally could be seriously damaged by this.' The complainants eventually subsided. So too did the row, as I was growing to understand that all rows eventually do.

It sometimes caused me irritation that *The Spectator* was prone defiantly to assert its independence of its *Telegraph* parent company, at all moments save when it needed our help, or when I was asked to become involved in a row such as that with Hollywood. I exploded when, for instance, Dominic Lawson sought to sell to *The Times* his memorable interview with Nicholas Ridley, without offering it to us. Since *The Spectator* was heavily dependent upon *Telegraph* staff writers to fill its pages, it seemed not unreasonable that the magazine should occasionally return the favour. I was irked by the fact that my foes, such as Paul Johnson, were free to vent their spleen about the alleged political shortcomings of the *Telegraph* in the pages of a magazine we owned. Conrad was reluctant to intervene in these squabbles. He would rumble sympathetically about 'our team of embryo space cadets in Doughty Street', but generally left us to sort matters out between ourselves. Looking back, I think he was right and I was wrong. A small magazine like the *Spec* needs to be able to show that it plots its own course. If *Spectator* editors' demonstrations of independence were sometimes childish, the broadsides I delivered to them were often pompous. As the years went by, I learned to accept Jeremy Deedes' unchanging counsel, and to ignore petty slings and arrows in print. I wish I had done so sooner.

The novelist Anthony Powell, whom I admired prodigiously, reviewed books for the *Telegraph* for decades. By the late 1980s, his powers were flagging, but we continued to use him out of veneration. When a collection of his reviews was published between hard covers, Hilary Spurling reviewed it respectfully for our pages. In a mad moment, however, our Literary Editor, Nicholas Shakespeare, commissioned Auberon Waugh to review the book for the *Sunday*, before disappearing on holiday. Bron indulged himself, strewing poisoned apples broadcast in a fashion which reflected his commitment to sustain an undying feud with his father's old rival. Powell resigned next day as the *Daily*'s book critic, despite my supplications. This provoked predictable glee in other titles' gossip columns. A year or two later, Hilary Spurling contacted me: she had a problem. Having commissioned six casts of a bust of Powell, she could not place one of them, and was stuck with a bill for £5,000. Surely it would be appropriate for the *Telegraph* to buy one, given Powell's long association with the paper? I reminded her of the frightful row, but eventually succumbed. After some rumblings, Conrad and the management agreed that we should pick up the bill for the bust. It stands to this day on the *Telegraph* editorial floor. It came as a pretty bitter pill, however, when Powell later published his journals, in which he first passed withering comment on my alleged vulgarization of *The Daily Telegraph*, and then mocked my folly in buying the bust. Mercifully, I don't think Conrad is a fan of Powell, or read the journals.

For a man who had once spoken so disparagingly of journalists, it was remarkable how much the proprietor enjoyed their company. Not en masse, perhaps, and not indiscriminately, but he

loved to talk to the writers whose work he admired. John Keegan
was foremost among these, but Conrad's enthusiasm also embraced
political columnists who caught his fancy. I would have been
happier if these had not always been men and women of the
Right. He would admit to his parties a journalist such as Taki –
who seemed to some of us finally to have exiled himself from the
pale when he wrote a column in praise of General Franco –
because Taki was perceived to be on the appropriate side of the
fence politically, and possessed the additional merit of being rich.
Meanwhile, Conrad was often irritated by the louche, iconoclastic,
or maverick behaviour of talented journalists, especially those
whose wages he was paying, if their political objectives seemed
inimical, or positively anarchistic. We faced periodic spasms of
protest from staff members about the difficulties of working at
Canary Wharf, which the Chairman's instincts inclined him to
suppress with bayonets. I was never successful in convincing him
that the only criterion which counts in hiring people to work for
newspapers is that they should be talented. I once sent him a copy
of an article published in the *British Journalism Review*, by an
American journalist, Michael Kirkhorn.

'Virtuous journalism is a weedy growth,' ran the salient passage, which struck a strong chord with me.

> It tends to be weedily unsystematic. Virtuous journalists are
> much more likely to hang around ... than to practise any
> form of 'precision journalism' ... Journalism is not art, it is
> not science; neither is journalism scholarship, although the
> accomplishments of journalists, purposeful and accessible,
> often outdo the investigations of scholars ... Journalists ...
> are free to be amateurs, to be interested, to practise ... 'the
> art of the scavenger' ... They help us to remember, or
> remember for us, what we need to know to understand the
> workings of the world; they educate, first themselves and then
> each other (the newsroom has always been a school – one of
> the very best), then the rest of us.

Conrad believes that as a breed, journalists are prone to envy of the tall poppies about whom they write, 'especially when there is a drought in real news, the practice is almost universal of compulsively, almost rhythmically, building up and tearing down reputations,' he once observed to Nicholas Coleridge. 'It pleases the journalist . . . to think of himself as an underdog, a person with a cause, if not a mission. This condition is accentuated in this country by Britain's admirable, but sometimes perversely exaggerated, love of underdogs. And it is further aggravated by the penchant of many journalists to masquerade as a learned profession while behaving like an industrial union.' On the whole, Conrad achieved a 'satisfactory personal comfort level' with journalists whom he perceived to be on the side of life's 'haves', and not with those who inclined towards the 'have nots'.

It was good to possess a proprietor passionately interested in politics and international affairs, rather than one of the grey money men who had dominated much of the British newspaper industry for years. I found it frustrating, however, that Conrad cared so little for executives whose names were unknown to the public, yet whose contribution was critical to the welfare of the paper. I often remarked to him that the pool of talented writers in British newspapers was remarkably large, while the number of first-class departmental editors was sadly small. We needed to cherish the dedicated, extraordinarily hard-working group we possessed. One Christmas, I suggested that he should send cases of wine to our key people both in editorial and management. I said that I would arrange the delivery in Conrad's name, if he would merely approve the gesture in principle. In the event, come mistletoe time, he sent me a case of superb claret, but he would not endorse any wider largesse. I tried to explain that I had not been soliciting personal favours, gratefully though these were received. I was urging appreciation of some of the under-recognized talent at the coalface. In many organizations top people are extravagantly rewarded. But second-tier management, which can be so readily encouraged by modest gestures, remains neglected.

Once Conrad's relationship with Barbara had become firmly established, inevitably I saw less of him. The couple forged a life in the club of the international rich, which tends to make its membership at home everywhere, and yet nowhere. Unsurprisingly, Conrad's telephone calls began to reflect Barbara's views, as well as his own. After our Fashion Editor one day in 1994 proclaimed the death of the miniskirt and the impending descent of hemlines, the Chairman rang me to express his own and his wife's scornful dismissal of this prognosis. Short skirts would rule the world, said Conrad, and if our Fashion pages knew what was good for them they would renounce any long-hem heresy. We spent a good many hours pondering how to square Mrs Chairman's strong views with the contradictory ones of Kathryn Samuel and Hilary Alexander. Some sort of fudge resulted. On the point of substance, if one can call it that, I rather fancy that Conrad and Barbara were right, as skirts in every high street have continued to testify from that day to this. But the Features Department staff were understandably dismayed to find themselves under the grill from the Chairman on an issue of high fashion. 'Shades of Lord Copper again,' muttered somebody.

As his international interests grew, so his sense of the smallness, the parochialism of Britain increased. Yet we still shared moments of intimacy, not least when he invited me to comment upon a draft of his memoirs. I told him that he had left out all manner of things the world would love to know, such as how much money he inherited from his father, to give him his start in business. But while he could be touchingly indiscreet about some personal matters, on others he remained determinedly opaque. I don't think he changed a line of his manuscript in response to my criticisms: 'I'm publishing the book chiefly, Max, to set the record straight in Canada on certain things. I probably won't even sell it here.' And indeed, he did not do so.

Why did I go on liking Conrad, even when he often exasperated me, as I exasperated him? He was witty. He was never less than interesting. He possessed immense charm, when he chose to exercise it. I often remonstrated with him about his fantastic unpunctuality, pointing out that it was his own management team's time he wasted, by keeping meetings waiting for half an hour, an hour, or even longer. I believe he would have better served his own interests, had he been able to match a measure of self-discipline to his brilliant skills as a deal-maker. I moaned about his whimsical telephone calls from the other side of the world, questioning implausible aspects of the paper's doings. Yet, maybe because I have always been an enjoyer myself, I warmed to Conrad's relish for life, conversation, new people and old history. In one-to-one conversation with me, he was delightfully unself-conscious, not least about money: 'I have just been obliged to make some calculations about the current state of my own financial affairs, Max, and I must say that the numbers achieved a heart-warmingly satisfactory consummation,' said Conrad benignly at lunch one day. I could not imagine Rupert Murdoch having such a chat with one of his editors. After my marriage to Tricia broke up in 1992 and I found myself living for a time in extremely modest rural circumstances, Conrad would enquire with, I think, sincere curiosity: 'And how is life, Max, at Rose' – the word was spun out to create one of the English language's longer syllables – 'Cottage?' He found it bizarre that any relatively important figure in his life should be domiciled in, well, former peasant accommodation. When the time came at last for us to part, he expressed his regret that he had never seen the inside of Rose Cottage. 'But what would I have done with you there, Conrad? There's no library, no ballroom, only a vast armoury of equipment for things you don't do, like gardening, fishing and shooting.'

I often compared my role in Conrad's life, especially in our later years together, with that of the grand vizier to a medieval Turkish sultan. One was accorded considerable powers, but it would have been unwise to forget for a moment that few of one's peers retired by choice into a comfortable old age. The garrotte, the scimitar, the oubliette are domestic accessories of every newspaper proprietor. Risk, whim, hostile intrigue, the *lettre de cachet* are occupational hazards for their servants. Yet even when I felt most impatience towards our Chairman, I could never forget that if he had not come into my life, it would have been deprived of some of its most exhilarating moments.

11

ALARUMS AND EXCURSIONS

I MET JOHN MAJOR for the first time when he was Chief Secretary of the Treasury, and did not do so again until early in 1990, a few weeks after he became Chancellor of the Exchequer. He was in the run-up to his debut Budget. He squeezed under the opposite side of the table at Wilton's, grinned and demanded disarmingly: 'Well? What would you do?' It was a masterly opening, a classic demonstration of Major's famous charm. First, it was flattering to be asked my opinion. His predecessor Nigel Lawson would have found it risible to consult a teenage scribbler about a Budget, even as a matter of politeness. Second, Major's gambit threw me onto the defensive. For much of the rest of lunch I was struggling to remember Sarah Hogg's most recent observations about monetary targets, interest rates and mortgage tax relief.

Yet when Major became Prime Minister, it became apparent that his commitment to consultation could become a serious weakness. It was not long before I heard one of his Cabinet say: 'It's all very well, this going round the table asking everybody what they think we should do. But there comes a moment when you want to say: "For God's sake – you're the Prime Minister – it's time for *you* to tell *us* what we're going to do." After the long, weary feud between Downing Street and the *Telegraph* under Mrs Thatcher, I was happy to establish a less confrontational relationship with the new regime. For the first few months, it seemed plausible that we should be able to maintain this. Under Sarah Hogg's influence, the paper had endorsed Britain's entry into the ERM. Through 1991, despite mounting doubts and uncertainty,

Stop dithering, Prime Minister, do you want red or white wine?

Matt's drawing for internal circulation, after John Major came to lunch at the *Telegraph*, and made a less than decisive impression.

we continued to support membership, and Downing Street seemed appreciative. But from the beginning, there were disturbing signs of Major's sensitivity to press criticism. Once, at a dinner, he niggled across the table about a hostile piece of Noel Malcolm's on our leader page. I said I was impressed that he read *The Daily Telegraph* so thoroughly. 'I used to, Max, I used to,' said Major, wagging a finger. He got his round of laughter from the rest of the table, but the raw sensitivity underlying his little jest seemed troubling in a Prime Minister.

We gave his government broad support. We were bitterly critical of Mrs Thatcher's incessant political interventions. Winston Churchill had not ventured to interfere in the affairs of his party after his retirement, yet Thatcher reached out from the political grave to blight the Tories' affairs for a decade. Even Conrad acknowledged that the former Prime Minister's almost deranged intemperance exceeded the bounds of political decorum. Yet in John Major's administration, we soon found plenty upon which to comment adversely. There were some small matters, such as Kenneth Baker's Dangerous Dogs Act. Bill Deedes said: 'All laws made in haste in response to media hysteria about a single perceived ill are repented at leisure.' Other issues were more serious, such as the Tories' refusal to take seriously the mounting devolutionary pressures in Scotland. I suggested to Michael Heseltine that it would be unacceptable for the English to rule Scotland on a colonial footing if – as some of us expected – the Conservatives were soon left with no seats at all north of the border. He gave a theatrical shrug. 'The Scots will just have to put up with it,' he said. I strongly disagreed. 'It may well be that some form of Scottish assembly proves essential,' I argued in a leader on 3 February 1991,

> Mr Major must leave Scotland in no doubt of the essential corollary, that Scots representation at Westminster will be diminished. That is a matter of common justice. We shall all be losers, in some measure, if Scotland insists upon changing its relationship with England. But if the will of the Scots for some form of devolution is plainly expressed in a referendum, then few sensible Tories would wish to continue to rule Scotland by political *diktat* imposed upon a hostile people.

We were not inspired by the Citizens' Charter, a concept so dear to Mr Major's heart. Matt did a brilliant pocket cartoon, depicting a man sitting bolt upright in bed, saying to his wife: 'I couldn't sleep a wink, I'm so excited about the Citizens' Charter.' Even though our editorials often praised the Prime Minister, he soon made plain his sensitivity to barbs from our right-wing columnists. The old, familiar tensions with Downing Street began to reassert themselves.

It has often been said that John Major is a nice man. I would put it a little differently: he is one of the most naturally courteous men I have ever met. His manners, his thoughtfulness on public occasions, are remarkable. He always remembered my wife's name. On one occasion, he allowed me to bring my teenage daughter to a lunch at Chequers. He invited me to a lunch at Downing Street to meet President Gorbachev, then perhaps the most sought-after table companion in the world, and was at pains to draw me into conversation with the Russian leader. These were the sort of kindnesses Major showed to many people, who were as appreciative as I was. Yet beneath the veneer of good-natured blokeishness, it was easy to sense the tension, the anger, which became more pronounced with every year of his premiership. Once I invited him to give a dinner at Downing Street, which we would pay for, to celebrate Bill Deedes's eightieth birthday. He exploded: 'But Bill Deedes called me a dull, grey man the other day!' I said: 'Oh, come on, Prime Minister. First, I'm sure Bill never wrote anything so discourteous, and second, surely we can rise above all that.' Major eventually hosted the dinner, but I was disappointed that he made no speech.

It seemed odd to find such insecurity in a man who had achieved the highest political office in Britain, yet it was always there. Major's ministers were very conscious of it. One of his senior colleagues observed that he had never known another figure who had climbed so high, yet whose wounds remained so raw. Most men by middle age have grown comfortable with themselves. That is to say, they may not be complacent about what they are, but they are resigned to it. Major shared with the Prince of Wales a lack of ease with himself which contributed greatly to his unhappiness in office.

Especially in his early years in office, he seemed a lonely figure. His wife was often absent at their home in Huntingdon, while he was at Downing Street. There was some gossip that his marriage was unhappy, but we knew nothing of his recent affair with Mrs Edwina Currie, which must have intensified his private tensions and apprehensions of exposure. I suspected that, because he had

risen so far so fast, he suffered from the fact that he had known
no one very long. Most of us, especially when we are in trouble,
turn for support to friends of many years' standing. In John
Major's meteoric ascent, he had left behind his old colleagues of
the Standard Chartered Bank, of Wandsworth Council, of the
Commons back benches. He was utterly dependent on colleagues
and subordinates almost none of whom he had even met five years
earlier. It is not possible even – or, perhaps, especially – for a
Prime Minister to forge from scratch in middle age relationships
of the kind which sustain those who have shared them for many
years. At first, it baffled many of us that Major displayed such a
weakness for the companionship of Jeffrey Archer, an obvious
charlatan. Gradually, however, we came to understand how easily
a man as isolated as the Prime Minister could be seduced by
Archer's shameless flattery, his generosity with his time and
hospitality. Also, perhaps, Major sensed something of the same
outsider quality about the novelist that he possessed himself. When
he made one of his rashest gestures by rewarding Archer's friendship with a peerage, this seemed a deliberate act of defiance
towards all those who thought the man not good enough for polite
society, though Major might usefully have considered that much
of the hostility came from people who simply recognized a crook
when they saw one.

The Prime Minister was morbidly sensitive about what he
perceived as snobbery towards his own modest origins. One of our
writers penned an early piece, posing some unanswered questions
about John Major's picaresque account of his own family history.
I had not read it carefully before publication, and when I did so I
concluded that the piece was unnecessarily sceptical, and cast
gratuitous doubt on Major's truthfulness. Though at the time –
and contrary to Major's own belief – the paper had no hostile
agenda in publishing the article, I regret that we ran it. But the
intensity of Major's anger highlighted his sensitivity. It is interesting that he cites *The Small House At Allington* as his favourite

Trollope novel, when even many Trollopeans find the book arch. Its hero is the Petty Bag Office clerk Johnny Eames, a young 'hobbledehoy'; its theme is Eames's pursuit of the book's exceptionally tiresome heroine, Lily Dale. I have often wondered how far Major identified Eames's youthful loneliness and frustrations with his own.

Cabinet colleagues were puzzled by Major's personality, much more complex than his plain-man image suggested. 'Funny fellow, funny fellow,' Douglas Hurd would sometimes say, shaking his head. Douglas was utterly loyal to Major. When I criticized the Prime Minister across the dinner table, the Foreign Secretary would patiently catalogue his merits to me, above all Major's mastery of a brief and skill in negotiation. But most ministers acknowledged sooner or later that there was a dark side to their leader, where he became extraordinarily hard to reach. They displayed growing concern about the Prime Minister's difficulties in imposing his personality on his turbulent party. Everyone agreed that John Major was intelligent, personable, solicitous, witty, a first-class committee man. But was he a leader? Was he gravely handicapped, as Sarah Hogg had feared, by vulnerability and a lack of steel for the deadly struggle at the top? For all his charm, he was conspicuously lacking in presence. A civil servant who attended a big Whitehall party at Downing Street heard Major mutter to his press secretary, Gus O'Donnell, as he entered the room buzzing with 200 people's conversation: 'How shall I get their attention?' The guest who told me the story shook her head: 'Margaret Thatcher never needed to ask that question.'

Once when Major had been complaining to me about the lack of support he received from the press, and – by implication – from such alleged sympathizers with his European policies as me, I said: 'Prime Minister, I do understand how frustrated you feel, out there on the floor of the Colosseum, fighting the lions while we lounge in the dress circle eating grapes and taking bets about whether you will survive. You feel we ought to get down there with you in the ring, and help with the lions. The trouble is, that isn't our job. Even if we want you to win, we have to remain up there with the spectators.' He was underwhelmed by my response.

Until the ERM debacle came, we remained on civil terms. But I believed that he expected more from me than any journalist should deliver to any politician. More and more, Major found it comforting to fall back upon the company of the handful of media sycophants willing to express unflagging support for him in print, even if their titles enjoyed little regard. For this, too, one thought less of the man.

After six years at the *Telegraph*, I had learned something about government, and about the ways of ministers and their departments. Politicians who achieve office, of all parties, divide into three categories. A small minority – in the Tory era the likes of Tebbit, Howe, Lawson, Hurd, Heseltine, Clarke – decide upon an agenda and pursue it with purpose and energy. Most men and women in this group must ultimately be satisfied if they accomplish one big thing during their time in a given department. There is a second group, of whom Norman Fowler was a prime exemplar. Such men are adept at clinging to office for long periods, and make no trouble for Prime Ministers. As Trollope said of one of his country squires, however: 'He would leave this world having made small mark upon it.' Norman was an amiable man, but his achievements in office were slight, and his judgement poor. For instance, he remained an impassioned standard-bearer for Jeffrey Archer, even in the great novelist's last pre-conviction phase as Tory candidate for Mayor of London. Simon Jenkins once asked me whether I thought that Norman, if he had continued his early career in newspapers, would have risen to become News Editor of *The Times*. We agreed that it would have been touch and go.

The third and largest group of ministers in any government spends its entire time in office in a state of fear: fear of the Prime Minister, of the electorate, the *Daily Mail*, TV news, unexpected events. All transport ministers, for instance, exist in a permanent state of apology. We were regularly invited to take a team from the paper to lunch at the department, to hear excuses for failure successively from Cecil Parkinson, Malcolm Rifkind, Norman Fowler and so on, their hand-wringing tempered with varying degrees of defiance. On one occasion I took a group from the paper to the Department of Transport, to be told that the Secretary of State was running late. We lingered in the gloomy Stalinist lobby for twenty minutes, until I begged that we should at least be allowed to go and sit in the dining room. 'Nobody can go upstairs until the Secretary of State is here,' said a prim little civil servant. I removed our delegation to lunch at Brooks's, whither we were eventually pursued by the minister, pleading in vain with us to come back.

Perhaps one should add a further category of ministers, who find themselves chronically troubled by policy or conscience, and diminish their own stature among colleagues by voicing their doubts. Malcolm Rifkind, for instance, is a clever and likeable man, but in his years of office he undermined himself by frequent mutterings about resignation. John Major observed once, 'If I had a pound for every time Malcolm has threatened to resign from this government, Max, I'd be a rich man!'

Douglas Hurd trusted me with many confidences. The problems of Hong Kong were high on the agenda throughout his years as Foreign Secretary. In particular, the Hang Seng Index soared and plunged for months in accordance with the progress of negotiations on the colony's new airport. One night at Wilton's, Douglas said to me: 'Well, thank God we've got one bit of good news – on Thursday we shall be announcing that the Hong Kong airport deal has been signed.' I was touched that he did not trouble to add: 'and for Heaven's sake don't breathe a word about the biggest diplomatic and commercial secret in London this week.'

Even on evenings when he was visibly exhausted, and there were many, Douglas would sit for hours, fingers drumming restlessly on the table, talking about whither Russia, whither China, whither the Balkans. He harboured an enduring, rather touching delusion, common to almost all British Foreign Secretaries, that our relations with France were improving: 'I really believe that at last we are starting to work well with the French on the things that matter.' The big issues, the big challenges, fascinated him. He showed little interest in trivia, gossip, small talk, and this intellectual austerity weakened him as a politician. But he possessed a profound concern for the public weal which, in my eyes, marked him out as a great public servant. He was sometimes described as a cold man by those who knew him little. I found, on the contrary, that beneath the professional veneer he cared passionately about many things. In the early 1990s, he agonized relentlessly about whether Britain should commit troops to the Balkans. I applauded his caution, in the absence of any promise of American ground troops, and of clearly defined objectives. He was bitterly attacked in the liberal media – as was *The Daily Telegraph* – for alleged pusillanimity and indifference to the human suffering. Within our own office, the old Thatcherites were passionately advocating a policy of 'lift and strike' – lifting the international arms embargo and committing Western air strikes against the Serbs – initially to enable the delivery of munitions to the Croats. Later, when the Croats turned their fire upon the Bosnian Muslims, I could not resist reminding the 'lift and strikers' that if they had got their way, Croat atrocities would have been incomparably bloodier. Douglas, of course, was the focus of right-wing hostility on this issue. He had opposed the German Foreign Minister's successful campaign to recognize the new breakaway republics in old Yugoslavia because he believed that recognition without international guarantees was a formula for disaster. I believe history will judge that he was right in this. Subsequently, I warmly sympathized with his reluctance to see British forces committed, in the absence of the Americans. Yet so great was the humanitarian disaster which followed in the Balkans that Hurd's passivity was condemned by his critics as one of its causes. Later I think that he, too, came to regret that he remained for so long opposed to engagement. He believed that he had been slow to perceive an important change in public sentiment, and in the nature of international affairs. With the Cold War over, many of the old imperatives against foreign intervention were gone. Western opinion was no longer prepared to stand by while evil men perpetrated crimes against humanity in small countries relatively close to home. Yet it was always wrong to suppose that Douglas was unmoved by the issues. He believed, in my view justly, that in the new world as in the old one, foreign policy cannot be conducted in response to emotional pleas from television presenters who declaim nightly that 'something must be done'. One summer night after dinner, when we were staying in the same holiday house in France, Douglas suddenly said to me: 'I hope history does not judge that it was easier than it seemed to us at the time to intervene in the Balkans.' At that moment, it was plain how much he minded, and what anguish the dilemma had caused him. Afterwards, he was at pains to acknowledge regret about his own hesitations, and to pay tribute to John Major's personal decision to commit British forces.

One evening, some months after the first British troops had gone into Bosnia, the Foreign Secretary arrived for dinner looking a trifle irritable. 'I do wish your military friends would make up their minds whether they want to be in Bosnia or out of it,' he said. 'I've just come from a Cabinet Committee meeting at which the Chiefs of Staff went on and on about the difficulties, lack of clear objectives and so on. Finally I asked them if they wanted to pull out. Peter Inge said: "Well, er, actually no." What *do* they want?'

'Come off it, Douglas,' I said. 'You know perfectly well why the military are so equivocal. They don't like any part of the mess they're being asked to handle in the Balkans. Soldiers always ask the embarrassing questions politicians flinch from: "What are our objectives? Are they attainable?" But they also know that if the regiments out there were brought home, in five minutes the government would disband them in pursuit of its "peace dividend".'

From Douglas, I learned a lot about how public appointments

are made, or not, as the case may be. It is a common delusion in the outside world to suppose that there must be a host of plausible contenders for big jobs. In reality, ministers spend much time with their heads in their hands, asking desperately: 'Who on earth can we find to be Chairman of the BBC / Chief of the Defence Staff / Chairman of Railtrack?' In the early Major years, the government was much exercised about who should become Governor of Hong Kong, in the run-up to the 1997 handover of the colony to China. The incumbent, Sir David Wilson, found himself in the wretched position of being left in the job faute de mieux. The hapless Wilson was obliged to read constant newspaper leaks from Whitehall which suggested that he no longer commanded the government's confidence. When I visited Hong Kong myself to write an article for our magazine, I lunched with Wilson and found him pathetically anxious to know what on earth London wanted. I saw Douglas on my return, and urged that the governor should be either backed or sacked. 'Yes, yes,' said the Foreign Secretary. 'But who do we send instead? Where is the [Christopher] Soames de nos jours?'

I told Douglas that George Walden, an old China hand, strongly argued against sending a big man to Hong Kong, on the grounds that a big man would be expected to do big things, while no big things could realistically be achieved before 1997. Douglas demurred – he believed that Britain's last proconsul should be a heavyweight. We discussed the governorship again and again when we met, not because I had any answers to offer, but because the problem for Douglas would not go away.

A droll postscript: when Chris Patten was finally appointed to succeed Wilson after losing his Bath seat in the 1992 election, Douglas asked John Major: 'Just as a matter of interest, who would you have sent to Hong Kong if Chris had said no?'

PM: 'I thought David Owen looked a good bet.'

FS: 'I think that would have been a terrible idea.'

PM: 'Who would you have gone for?'

FS: 'Francis Maude might have made rather a good fist of it.'

18. Margaret Thatcher leaving Downing Street in December 1990:
the Tory leadership crisis provoked weeks of tension at the paper.
We supported Douglas Hurd for the succession, though the
Thatcherites were flocking to John Major.

19. Sharing a platform with Douglas Hurd in his days as Foreign Secretary. I was closer to Douglas than to any other minister. He said wryly that John Major always described me to him, without enthusiasm, as 'your Max Hastings'.

20. Receiving the Editor of the Year award in 1988 from Michael Heseltine, whom I liked and admired. Unfortunately, Michael remained anathema to Conrad and my right-wing colleagues at the *Telegraph*.

21. After almost five years of warfare between the *Telegraph* and Mrs Thatcher, I hoped for a less confrontational relationship with John Major as Prime Minister. Yet he proved an unconvincing occupant of 10 Downing Street– perhaps even to himself.

Royals and Reptiles.

22. Our admiration for the Queen never flagged, even in her annus horribilis . . .

23. . . . but the Prince of Wales's whimsy and self-pity increasingly made him seem an unsuitable prospect for the throne

24. I am the wrong height to be seen alongside any member of the Windsor family, but like everyone else I was captivated by the Queen Mother. She and Princess Alexandra, alone among the Royal Family, possessed the priceless art of making people feel good. Here, she was unveiling a Blitz memorial outside St Paul's with marginal assistance from the author.

25. This picture provoked much laughter among colleagues, who accused me of leering unbecomingly at the Princess of Wales, when she came to lunch at the *Evening Standard*, shortly after I moved from the *Telegraph*.

26 & 27. The Gulf War: one of the big news stories of the '90s, which gave the *Telegraph*'s news and foreign staff an exceptional opportunity to show their mettle.

Hardships of an Editor's life.

28. Inspecting the work of our Fishing Correspondent, David Profumo, on the Tweed.

29. Shooting in Yorkshire with inseparable companion Bill Anderson, my driver, who is loading.

30. Rupert Murdoch: our deadliest rival, willing to sell a cut-price *Times* at a huge loss, in the hope of breaking the *Telegraph*. I believed that, as a proprietor, Murdoch sooner or later tarnished every title he touched.

31. After it was all over: the three best leaders the Conservative Party never had. Michael Heseltine, Douglas Hurd and Ken Clarke on holiday with the author in the Galapagos in 2002. Michael dubbed this 'the cruise of the blue boobies'.

PM: 'Well – that's who it would have been, then.'

One other point about my respect for Hurd. Few ministers retain the regard of journalists if they are chronic complainers and ringers-up of editors, yet a surprising number continue to make this mistake. Politeness demands that one should always take a minister's call, but there is no reason either to listen to whingeing or bullying (a rash tactic which, in more recent times, has cost Alastair Campbell and Peter Mandelson much Fleet Street respect, and has made John Prescott the object of derision). Once, when a Tory minister telephoned me to protest about something, he said: 'I hope you don't mind me ringing you like this.' I answered: 'Not a bit. It's your job to try to bully me, and mine to tell you what to do with it.' Peter Mandelson once telephoned, to offer a personal assurance that a story our reporters were investigating was without foundation. I duly called off the hounds, but when I subsequently discovered that Mandelson had lied to me, I can't say that thereafter I felt much inclined to take notice of his assurances, or his complaints. Douglas never complained. He thought it beneath the dignity of a Home or Foreign Secretary to moan about newspaper stories. And, of course, he was right. At a press conference in Copenhagen during an immensely sensitive Danish EC referendum, our correspondent Boris Johnson trapped the Foreign Secretary into an indiscretion that featured prominently on next day's front page. The British government had to indulge in some tortured double-speak to extricate itself.

A few hours after the paper appeared, I was with our Foreign Editor, Nigel Wade, when my secretary told me that Douglas Hurd was on the line. Nigel grinned: 'He must be hopping mad about what Boris did to him this morning.' I said: 'I'll be surprised if that's it. It's just not Douglas's style to make a fuss.' Sure enough, Hurd simply asked if I could come round and see him at the Foreign Office that afternoon, to talk about the Balkans. I went, we spoke for an hour. As I left, I said I admired the fact that he had not even mentioned the Copenhagen story. Douglas shrugged: 'What would be the point?' Few politicians are so

forbearing. I was amazed when Geoffrey Howe once volunteered
to me, without evident embarrassment, that he had never allowed
the *Daily* or *Sunday Telegraph* into his house, after Perry Worsthorne's *Sunday* Comment section published a cartoon depicting
his wife Elspeth as Lady Macbeth.

Newspaper editors and many company bosses enjoy the luxury
of appointing congenial subordinates, some of whom are friends,
or become so. Prime Ministers must form governments from the
ranks of MPs, who often have little in common save their shared
quest for power. The world always perceived Michael Heseltine
and Kenneth Clarke as kindred political spirits, yet the two men
enjoyed surprisingly little personal intimacy. Ken once told me
how much he would like to go birdwatching with Michael, but
said that he did not think he knew him well enough to suggest it.
John Major actively disliked not a few of his colleagues. He
complained fiercely to me about Alan Clark, whose 'economy with
the *actualité*' had plunged the government into the Arms for Iraq
crisis which precipitated the Scott Inquiry. 'You gave him a job,
Prime Minister,' I said. 'No, I didn't,' said Major crossly. 'Margaret did.' 'But you kept him in it, and most of us wouldn't trust
Alan to wheel a pram across Hyde Park.' Archie Hamilton, as
Chairman of the 1922 Committee, observed bitterly: 'Why don't
people understand that Alan Clark isn't *pretending* to be a shit.
He's a *real* shit.' I was inclined to agree. I lunched with Alan from
time to time, never less than enjoyably. We shared an interest in
military history, though his claims to scholarship in that field were
somewhat exaggerated. But it seemed incomprehensible that any
Prime Minister should have given office to a man so constitutionally reckless, so preoccupied with the desire to épater les bourgeois,
who fantasized about urinating from his Whitehall office window
onto the masses beneath.

Geoffrey Howe observed memorably to the Scott Inquiry that
Clark 'couldn't see an apple cart without wanting to overturn it'.
The joke, of course, was that while Alan was obsessed with his
own role as gentleman and cavalier, in reality he was one of

nature's spivs. His grandfather had not merely bought his own furniture, he had bought his own castle – from Bill Deedes's family, as it happened. He deserves to be remembered for his incomparable diaries, but they should be enjoyed as fantasy, not historical record. The troubles he brought upon the Major government reflect the fact that no Prime Minister in modern times has been able to fill over a hundred government posts without resorting to some of parliament's known lunatics and delinquents to make up the numbers. Clark was part of the price the British electorate pays for government by its MPs. It was a nice irony, of course, that few men believed in the virtues of democracy less than Alan did.

*

EARLY IN 1992, my domestic life suffered a sad upheaval when I separated from my wife Tricia, and moved from Northamptonshire to the Berkshire downs. Initially, I bought our old family cottage from my mother, and soon afterwards I began a new life with Penny Grade, former wife of Channel 4's boss Michael. Penny and I had known each other since we were seventeen. We married a few years later. Amid the unhappiness inseparable from any domestic break-up, I had cause to be grateful that, if my life as an editor was never humdrum, it had settled into a familiar routine. This was not infrequently interrupted by crises, but we had created a formidably disciplined machine for running the paper, which operated as effectively (some thought more so) when I was absent as when I was in my office at Canary Wharf. I led the band when there was a big breaking news story, but on a normal working day my chief involvement in the paper was through its leaders and features. I continued to write as much as I could, partly because I enjoyed doing so, and partly because I believed that any authority I possessed over my staff stemmed from the fact that I could demonstrate the ability to compose a leader, create a Weekend front or rewrite a reporter's copy as well as most people in the building, and perhaps faster.

Some of the unscheduled dramas we confronted were of our own making; others, however, were thrust upon us. On the night of Sunday 16 November 1992, the IRA planted a bomb at Canary Wharf which caused the entire building to be evacuated. This is the worst misfortune that can befall a newspaper – to find itself at the heart of events it is unable to report. Our editorial floors stood empty for hours. I was desperately seeking to contact the Commissioner of the Metropolitan Police, to plead with him to do everything possible to enable the paper to be produced, at least by letting our vehicles through police roadblocks. To my fury, Scotland Yard refused to connect me to the Commissioner, or to any responsible officer. I have always believed that one of society's principal objectives in fighting terrorism should be to minimize the economic disruption terrorists are allowed to create. The police often impose draconian restrictions over large areas for many hours when a terrorist risk is identified. Plainly, a balance must be struck between public safety and the maintenance of vital services, but police overreaction often seems to represent the antithesis of the Blitz spirit. When the Canary Wharf bomb was at last defused, by tremendous efforts on the part of writers and production staff an 'Emergency Edition' of the paper was published and distributed. This contained great slabs of blank newsprint, not least on the front page, but we believed it was right to make the gesture of defying the terrorists. We received precious little help from the police to do so.

Newspapers spend a lot of time recording the embarrassments and difficulties of others. We are fortunate that more of our own do not get into print. One laughs about some of them now, but they did not seem funny at the time. We endured a long legal saga involving unethical behaviour by one of our specialist correspondents. British newspapers are not very corrupt, but there are murky areas in which some veteran correspondents behave in a manner which does not stand scrutiny. In this case, we found ourselves in possession of clear evidence that our man had received cash from a commercial organization for promoting its wares in our pages.

To my impotent fury – but as often happens – we were obliged to give the black sheep a severance payment to leave, because the legal complications of exposing him were so great.

Boris Johnson got himself into a considerable tangle over his relationship with his old Oxford friend Darius Guppy. Boris had joined the *Telegraph* after a brilliant career at Eton and Oxford (so often the precursor of a lifetime of obscurity) and a brief spell as a *Times* trainee. He became first a leader writer and then our much-admired Brussels Correspondent. In those days, oddly enough, Boris was not the rabid Eurosceptic he later became. I fear that it was the Brussels posting which made him so. In any event, from the outset he made himself much beloved as well as respected, concealing high intelligence behind his impersonation of Oofy Prosser of the Drones. I did my best to discourage Boris's occasional mutterings about a career in politics. Not only would this be a waste of his journalistic talents, I have always thought that a penchant for comedy is an almost insuperable obstacle to achieving high political office, which seems the only point of becoming a member of the House of Commons.

One day, I was dismayed to receive through the post a copy of a tape recording of a telephone conversation between Boris and his Oxford friend Mr Guppy, who was by then serving a term of imprisonment for an elaborate but imperfectly executed fraud; also in the envelope was a disingenuous letter from a media enquirer, demanding what, as his editor, I was going to do about this. Jeremy Deedes and I listened to the tape. Its highlight was a request from Guppy that Boris should assist him to find a hitman, to deal with an inconvenient witness. At no point in the conversation did Boris assent to Guppy's request, but neither did he explicitly decline.

Jeremy and I thought that it was impossible for the *Telegraph* simply to ignore an issue touching on the personal integrity of one of the staff. We flew our correspondent to London for a serious discussion. Boris easily persuaded us that he had never taken any action in pursuit of Guppy's proposal, nor had he intended to.

We sent him back to Brussels bearing only a strongly worded note from me, suggesting that he would be rash to make such an error of judgement again, or even to indulge such a man as Guppy down the telephone. As a virtue, loyalty to friends has its limits. The story got into print, of course. These things always do. The worst punishment Boris had to endure was years of subsequent teasing from Matthew Norman in *The Guardian*, who nicknamed our EC Correspondent 'the Jackal'. Today, of course, the MP for Henley-on-Thames and Editor of *The Spectator* has put such nugatory matters far behind him.

One day in 1991, Auberon Waugh asked me to lunch with him. Almost as soon we sat down he said: 'I'd like to write the Way of The World column for you. I think it could be my pension.' Having at last managed to retire Peter Simple as the column's author, it was now being written by Christopher Booker. I liked Booker, but I did not think he was doing the column well. I did not hesitate for a moment about accepting Bron's proposal, though it caused both of us to incur some odium from Booker and his friends. It is often hard for the boss of anything to admit his own mistakes. Unsticking appointments that fail, whether executive or journalistic, is one of the hardest parts of running a business. Nothing is more brutal than to give a job to a man or woman who then proves to have been overpromoted. The fallen angel's career often fails to recover, even back on a lower rung of the ladder. In Booker's case, of course, this was never an issue. His fanatical hostility to Europe increasingly distorted his journalism, but there is a flourishing Fleet Street market for Eurosceptic propaganda. Bron, after a shaky start for the first six months, proved an inspired author of Way of The World, too quirky and funny to be damned by a new generation of readers as a mere reactionary. He was a wonderful catch for the paper.

All newspapers are threatened with litigation at regular intervals. Most of us settle actions for small sums of money, in order to avoid the huge risks of going to court. If a paper decides to fight, this is almost invariably because an issue of principle is at stake. In 1993, we found ourselves being sued by the sheltered housing firm McCarthy & Stone, over a hard-hitting investigation we had published in our financial pages, detailing alleged abuses by the company. We believed it was essential to defend the writ. This was an issue of keen interest to our readers, and we stood by the findings of our investigation. We hired George Carman to represent us, and eventually found ourselves in court. The nervous strain of these affairs is enormous. The financial cost of defeat and the loss of face are painful to any newspaper. I turned up in the Strand myself for some hours a day, because in these situations it is important to show that the editor is personally engaged in what is being done in the paper's name. I watched with awed admiration as Carman cross-examined. If ever a lawyer earned his fees, that man did. Under a notably unsympathetic judge, however, the first days of the hearing went poorly for us. Then we had an unexpected break. A *Telegraph* reader, seeing our report of the hearing, telephoned to enquire whether we recalled that the Office of Fair Trading had formally warned the company about precisely the abuses our coverage of McCarthy & Stone complained of. This, of course, gave a new vigour to our defence. On the third day in court, Carman told us that a deal was on offer: McCarthy & Stone were willing to drop their case and walk away. Each side would bear its own costs. I was outraged. I wanted to fight to the end. Surely we could not let them off the hook at this stage? My reaction was that of every editor in such a situation. The reaction of Carman and our solicitors was that of any good lawyers. Take the deal, they said. This case is not over yet. With any court action, it is utterly impossible to be sure what the outcome may be. The risks of fighting on far outweighed the irritation of allowing the other side to quit the field undefeated. Reluctantly, I acquiesced. It was an unheroic ending. It left untarnished the credibility of the paper, our writers and the story we had published, but cost us several hundred thousand pounds. I tell the story here, not because it represented any media milestone, but because the case was typical of the ways of newspapers and libel actions.

I sought to maintain contact with as many of the paper's staff as I could through a rolling succession of departmental lunches. A dozen or so writers, subeditors and executives from a given area – Sport or City or Weekend or Features – would gather once every month or so in our upstairs dining room. I started by briefing them for five or ten minutes about the state of the *Telegraph* as I saw it, and about my hopes for the months ahead. Then I invited any questions they wanted to ask for an hour or so, which they did with varying degrees of nervousness or frankness. The experience was hard work, not unlike holding a ninety-minute press conference, with the same need to beware of bear traps, while being as honest as possible. I also gave occasional dinners at Brooks's for the younger journalists, most of whom I had recruited myself. The young turks represented our future. Three factors determine whether talented writers stay with a newspaper: money; space; and relentless stroking. I have seldom known a gifted journalist who was not 'difficult' in some way, prone to tantrums or extravagant behaviour. But, as I often reminded harassed executives weary of the eccentricities of the prima donnas, our docile and compliant writers were, by and large, our least effective. Every editor, every boss of anything, must play favourites. There simply is not time to indulge every reporter to lunch at Wilton's or even to one-to-one conversation. At the *Telegraph*, the best I could do for most of our staff was to hold a big family summer party on a July weekend out in the countryside, and to preside over a mulled wine party in the office one afternoon in the week before Christmas. If the humbler hacks sometimes envied the stars, the sensible ones recognized that without the top talent we had so painstakingly recruited since 1986, the resurrection of the paper could never have been achieved.

By the early 1990s, our stars represented an amazing group. The Sports Section bulged with personality columnists. If I was sometimes tough on other departments' budgets, I tried to give our superb Sports Editor, David Welch, anything he wanted within reason. In 1987, we possessed a Sports staff thirty-eight strong. By 1995, this had grown to sixty-seven. We had to defend our supremacy in this area at almost any cost. After some humps and bumps with our Saturday magazine, Emma Soames came from the *Evening Standard* to take over, and within a year had made it the best of its kind in the business. Emma's appointment was, above all, Veronica Wadley's inspiration. Veronica had to overcome some initial reservations from me. I remembered Emma as a somewhat dilettante member of the Londoner's Diary staff, when I ran the column back in 1976. Yet as soon as Ms Soames arrived, I fell in love with her professionalism and boundless capacity for fun. She is the most enchanting of colleagues.

For a happy year or two, Stephen Fry wrote a weekly column for our op-ed page. I liked as well as admired Fry, and I regarded him as a critical catch, to advertise to potential young readers how much the paper had changed. He showed himself a first-class journalist. Indeed, I believe his literary gifts are better suited to writing a column than to producing novels, best-sellers though they may be. I remember overcoming dreadful difficulties to find a reviewer willing to speak on the credit side of neutrality about one of Fry's books in our Literary pages, at a time when I was desperate to keep him as a contributor. But, in the end, like not a few writers, he convinced himself that contributing to newspapers was less fun, and less satisfying, than creating novels. We lost him. The trouble was, Stephen did not need the money. Cash is normally the surest means of securing the services of even the most principled scribe.

Tony Parsons, who contributed a column to our Arts page for several years, was another notable writer of a new kind for the paper. The former husband of Julie Burchill, Parsons represented a strand of British pop culture which the old *Telegraph* would never have trafficked with. Not only did he write very well, he revealed himself as a polymath. A couple of times, the *Telegraph* entered teams for charity 'Brain Games'. Our victories (unassisted by any significant contribution from me) owed a lot to Parsons' extraordinary reservoir of information on the most arcane subjects.

And he was very good company. Alas, no broadsheet newspaper can today afford the fees his writing has come to command.

Martyn Harris was a good example of a writer of the highest ability, who could make himself pretty charmless. Martyn's work first caught Don Berry's attention in *New Society* back in 1987. My own enthusiasm was fired by a piece Harris wrote, demonstrating the advantages of wet shaving over those of electric razors. I have never used the latter since. He contributed fine columns and even better features for us. I liked Martyn personally, but was often exasperated by his graceless behaviour. One day in 1994, he went to interview Lauren Bacall. Plaster was falling off the ceiling for days afterwards. In his usual blunt Swansea fashion, Martyn asked the screen legend whether she did not attribute her success to having got lucky with Humphrey Bogart, rather than to any notable acting talent on her own account. Harris wrote: 'Bacall is no great actress or intelligence, although she tries to conceal the shallowness behind a battery of hard-boiled mannerisms. It is what she leaves out of her self-account that tells you the most.' He described how Bacall said to him: 'You know, I don't really like your tone, mister. You have a hell of a nerve. You are looking for nasty unpleasant things. I am not gonna deal with that kinda crap.' When the piece was published, I found myself dealing with Bacall on the phone in person, raging. I wrote emollient ('I deplore the excesses of British journalism as much as anyone') and grossly flattering ('your eminence demands a reasoned response to your call yesterday') letters, sent flowers, abased myself, to scant avail. It was a situation familiar to all editors. One knows that a writer has behaved badly, but feels obliged to back him regardless. An incident such as that between Harris and Bacall helps to explain why many Hollywood stars now decline to be interviewed by any newspaper without a contractual promise of prior notice of questions and subsequent approval of published copy. This kind of restraint dismays us all, reflects what we call the '*Hello*ization' of journalism; but in considerable measure we have brought it upon ourselves. That day with Bacall, the only point which I felt unable to mention to the star in mitigation was that when Harris interviewed her, he had just started chemotherapy treatment for the cancer which later killed him. Awkward customer though he was, Martyn was a brilliant talent.

Every modern Fleet Street newspaper struggles to find good cartoonists. I was exultant when we won the 'Alex' strip and its creators from *The Independent* for our City pages. But the *Telegraph*'s greatest star was, as he remains today, Matt. Even now that he is nearing forty, Matthew Pritchett seems fated to go through life looking like an uncommonly sweet-natured member of the Lower Fifth, the kid who always has a twinkle in his eye and a bucket on top of the door for teacher. It was remarkable how soon after he started drawing pocket cartoons for us in 1988 that he developed his distinctive line, characters with huge eyes and big conks. He has mastered the art of being funny without a hint of cruelty, of putting into his work a warmth that brings a glow to the heart of every beholder. Matt's output is prodigious. He offers the Night Editor a choice of four, five, six cartoons, any one of which every other title in Britain would kill for. In the early days, we sometimes used several of his drawings in a single issue of the paper. Then we realized that we had a talent beyond price, and must not abuse it. One Matt a day is all that *Daily Telegraph* readers now receive, and supremely grateful they are. He is one of a tiny handful of stars for whom readers will buy a newspaper. Good cartoonists are very rare in Britain today. I don't know why this should be. Many editors trawl provincial papers and art colleges in search of new blood, as I did. Matt's achievement as a cartoonist comes close to genius. Most of his peers rely for their captions on other people, but his jokes are all his own. He maintains a much more consistent standard than even Jak or Giles achieved in their heyday. His modesty and charm are legendary in the *Telegraph* office. So is his loyalty. When I eventually moved to the *Evening Standard*, David English persuaded me to write to Matt, offering him a king's ransom to move to the *Daily Mail*. Tears trickled down my cheeks, because at heart I was convinced that Matt was

Peattie and Taylor sent me this drawing when the wonderfully awful Alex moved from *The Independent* to the *Telegraph*. Charles Burgess was the *Indie*'s Managing Editor.

*'It doesn't necessarily mean
his wife is trying to kill him'*

An archetypal Matt, following a woman's trial for an alleged
attempt to murder her husband with a lawnmower.

ideally suited to the *Telegraph*. But needs must. Don Berry said
gloomily, as well as blasphemously: 'It's like tempting Jesus Christ.'
Three weeks later, Matt's reply came back: 'Dear Max, even though
the *Daily Mail*'s offer is £150,000 more than I'm getting here, I
feel I have to say no, because I'm so happy at *The Daily Telegraph*.'
Don and I embraced each other. Matt had shown himself, as we
had hardly dared to hope that he would, the last unbribable loyalist
in Fleet Street. To know him is to love him, in print or in person.

In 1991–92, I was a founder member of the Press Complaints
Commission, which succeeded the Press Council as the self-
regulatory body of the British newspaper industry. Like most
journalists I oppose statutory regulation of the press. First, there
are the obvious free speech objections to curbs, coupled to the fact
that British journalists enjoy none of the constitutional protections
afforded to their American counterparts. Second, and perhaps
more important, the practical difficulties of wording and enforcing
a credible privacy law seem insuperable. Great villains such as
Robert Maxwell have used Britain's tough libel law as a club with
which to suppress press comment on their doings. There is every

reason to suppose that scoundrels would be able to exploit a privacy law in the same way, against the public interest. Today, the British press is sometimes grossly intrusive on trivial matters concerning people's personal lives. But even the existing libel law – so much tougher than that which prevails in the US – remains a damaging constraint on legitimate media investigation of crooks.

Yet, even if one argues the objections to further statutory press regulation, how convincing is the system of self-regulation funded by the newspaper industry itself? On the credit side, press mal-treatment of ordinary citizens has declined since the birth of the PCC under its first Chairman, Lord MacGregor. Newspapers are sufficiently fearful of a formal rebuke from the PCC that the worst excesses of the old days, when photographers casually stole family portraits off newly bereaved widows' pianos, have been curbed. It remains the case, however, that if the stakes are high enough, if material is available involving celebrities or members of the Royal Family, most tabloid titles will ride roughshod over privacy, in pursuit of commercial gain. Worse, the PCC sometimes appears to perceive that its function is to provide figleaves of justification for 'red-top' excesses. Those responsible for running British press awards have always argued that different standards must obtain for tabloid journalism from those applied to broadsheet entries, 'because otherwise the "red tops" would never win anything'. Thus prizes are not infrequently awarded to newspapers which have gained scoops merely by writing large cheques, or for doing things which would prompt the sacking of the journalists concerned from any broadsheet title. In the same fashion, it often seems that the PCC is prepared to assess the misdeeds of 'red-top' titles by the standards of their own swamp, rather than those of polite society. We all make mistakes – as an editor, I have been justly censured by the PCC on at least two occasions – but some British newspapers flourish on habitual indifference as to whether what they print might be true or not. And the editors of such titles, including that of *The People*, to name but one, are invited to take their turns as members of the Press Complaints Commission. The

PCC is better than nothing. Self-regulation is preferable to clumsy and stifling press laws – we can imagine the sort of legislation the present government might contrive, if it got down to drafting. But the PCC is diminished by the participation of journalists who should be perceived as beyond the pale.

Like media awards, the Commission would be held in more respect if lay influence upon its verdicts was seen to be greater. Over the past year or two, the PCC's standing has been further damaged by its byzantine relationship with St James's Palace, its involvement in brokerage between the Prince of Wales's staff and tabloid newspapers about what they can print. The Commission will never deserve much regard from the public, as long as it appears willing to justify obvious excesses by some of the newspapers which pay its bills. The PCC's most obvious difficulty is to find itself a chairman whose independence and integrity are not fatally compromised by a need to appease the commercial interests of the titles which afford him a handsome competence.

*

I BELIEVE THAT I was a better Editor of *The Daily Telegraph* than I was a Group Editor-in-Chief. It poses almost insuperable problems for the operational director of one title to bear responsibility for others also. It is impossible for such a figure convincingly to arbitrate, to weigh competing interests. I was not proud of my handling of any situation involving *The Sunday Telegraph*. First, of course, in 1989 there was the fiasco of the aborted merger of the titles. Then I sent Trevor Grove, who had been a brilliantly successful Assistant Editor of the *Daily*, to run the *Sunday*. Under his stewardship, the paper continued to languish in circulation and revenue – hardly surprising, when Trevor had scant resources, and no control over the Comment pages. Conrad always felt a special regard for *The Sunday Telegraph*. At intervals, he advanced proposals to make a big investment in the paper, to enable it to engage *The Sunday Times* head-on. I shared Stephen Grabiner's view, that extravagant spending would be mistaken, and I hope this was not from selfish concern for the *Daily*'s interests. We argued that as a target, *The Sunday Times* was beyond our reach; it was impossible to sketch any plausible business plan which would make *The Sunday Telegraph* significantly profitable, with or without big investment; and we were achieving brilliant success in outflanking *The Sunday Times*, by continuing to expand our Saturday product and build the *Daily*'s Saturday sale. In particular, we dissuaded Conrad from launching a Sunday colour magazine. Yet I believed that some investment in the *Sunday* was badly needed, and I was bitterly critical of management executives, including Grabiner, who seemed content to see the *Sunday* expire from malnutrition. I used a different figure of speech in a note to Conrad and the board on this issue in April 1991:

> There is a danger . . . that we sometimes talk ourselves into unnecessary crises. The management must sometimes feel that it owns two racehorses, one of which regularly wins big money races, the other of which is seldom out of the hands of the vet. Some of the company's senior executives privately believe that it would be kinder to send for the knacker. I believe that we . . . should look at the [*Sunday Telegraph*] from a different viewpoint. Almost anyone in the world in the media business would express admiration and jealousy, if told that a proprietor owned a paper with far lower costs than any of its rivals, which sells almost 600,000 copies . . . We should recognise that we have reached a plateau, where there is no significant scope for making further cuts in its editorial costs. The paper has an identity problem, resulting from a series of compromises which we made with our eyes open . . .
> I believe Trevor Grove is doing everything that any editor could, to produce a good product, given the limits of his own authority [at that stage, Trevor had no control of the Comment section] and the constraints upon his resources.

A year later, however, Conrad intervened decisively. He argued that Trevor was still not delivering a convincing newspaper, even after the final closure of 'Worsthorne College', with which the Chairman had become as disenchanted as any of us. I found it hard to dissent, though the decision to move Trevor caused me much pain. He was an old personal friend, as well as colleague. I remembered David Ruddock's words during the era of mass sackings in 1986, that I would find it harder when the time came to remove people who were my own appointments than those whom I had inherited. So it proved. But I endorsed Conrad's proposal that Charles Moore should take over the *Sunday*, and I brought Trevor back to the *Daily* as Deputy Editor.

Today, when *The Sunday Telegraph* looks a strong paper and possesses an excellent colour magazine, I look back and wonder whether I was plain wrong, in adopting a relatively pessimistic strategic view – albeit less so than our management. The *Sunday*'s 2002 circulation figure (730,000) is substantially inflated by its participation in the *Daily*'s seven-day subscriptions, introduced in 1997. The *Telegraph* looks a more impressive and substantial company because its second major title is a much more solid product than it was in my day. We were right to be sceptical about the money, however. I doubt that recent investment in the *Sunday* has been justified by increased profitability, or is ever likely to be. The *Daily* is the vital source of profit, and always will be, come rain or shine. Yet, as Editor-in-Chief, I could have done a better job in steering the debate about the *Sunday*, had I not also been the working Editor of the *Daily*. We muddled along for too long, attempting to compromise between competing management interests, pursuit of the bottom line foremost among these.

The last big change in the direction of the newspapers while I was at the *Telegraph* came in 1994. Conrad argued energetically to me that, following Charles Moore's departure, the *Daily*'s leader page and political comment remained weak. I agreed. The standard of serious debate on our pages had become visibly less impressive than that of *The Times*. Whatever our undoubted successes as a News and Features title, on the political side we looked less than assured.

A substantial body of Fleet Street opinion, especially of a liberal persuasion, respected the new *Daily Telegraph* for its break with the torrid right-wing past. I was pleased when Paul Vallely wrote in *The Independent* that I was a product 'of the old school of fair-minded, decent pragmatism that had once been the distinguishing feature of intelligent middle-England Conservatism'. That was the sort of school report I should have liked to write for myself. But others, especially on the Right, sharply dissented.

'Professional – that is the word that springs to mind', wrote Stephen Glover, reviewing the *Telegraph* in a 1993 column for the *Evening Standard*. 'But something is missing ... A great newspaper, even a properly successful one, must have a powerful and distinctive world view. By this measure the modern *Daily Telegraph* fails lamentably ... My quarrel is not with Mr Hastings's politics, insofar as they are discernible. The point is rather that *The Daily Telegraph* no longer has a strong character.'

Glover, of course, had his own agenda. He was a former *Telegraph* leader writer who deeply admired several of my old Conservative bêtes noires, above all T. E. Utley. After fulfilling an honourable role as a founder of *The Independent*, Glover fell out with his colleagues and eventually departed in some dudgeon after a brief spell as Editor of *The Independent on Sunday*. Thereafter, I was not alone in discerning a sourness in some of his media comment, especially towards perceived rivals. He seemed to nurse a bitterness that he did not himself occupy an editor's chair. I am doubtful about the wisdom of the Fleet Street custom whereby so many media columns are written by either failed or superannuated ex-editors. Yet I could not deny that there was an element of justice in what he wrote about the *Telegraph*'s political position. Our leaders, especially on Europe, reflected the interminable struggle to square my own one-nation Conservatism with Conrad's passionate Euroscepticism. As far back as 1991, when the *Telegraph* won a major industry award, another waspish commentator, Michael Leapman, observed in *British Journalism Review*: 'The judges would have more justification in naming Max Hastings

"Tightrope Walker of the Year", for his achievements in the field of acrobatics and survival have been more spectacular than his contributions to journalism.'

One day in January 1994, Conrad sent me a long handwritten letter from Palm Beach, following a difference of opinion down the telephone the previous day about a *Telegraph* leader, opposing the exploitation of new science to enable women over fifty to give birth.

Dear Max,

    I think you're a brilliant editor as well as friend . . . and absolutely pivotal to the past and future success of *The Daily Telegraph*. You have my entire confidence and support, but I'm afraid you don't have a great aptitude for ideology or the philosophy of public policy. As a Conservative newspaper, we must start from the premise that people are responsible and should exercise all liberties except those whose exercise impinges upon the liberties of others. The idea of contracting any officials, elected or unelected, with authority to decide what women are eligible to have children horrifies and nauseates me . . . You must realise that the application of scientific advances to this is not 'playing God' any more than heart transplants or sophisticated dental work . . . We must be faithful to a philosophical view, without being dogmatic or reflexive . . . I don't regard it as my job to instruct the leader writers, to write the leaders myself, or to respond to the leaders . . . Rather I look forward to discussing with you how to avoid these fates. If *you* put the right people into the leader conference with proper rules of engagement, I'm sure it will work out, but we must start with first principles.

    You put out the paper, Max, I know I'm a nuisance, but please indulge me,

    Yours Always

I replied in the bantering terms which I often employed in correspondence with the Chairman, likewise writing in longhand:

My Dear Conrad,

Thanks for your thoughtful and generous fax. No more need be said till you return, though I hope you will not mind my continuing to argue that an unborn child has rights as much as any mother. Speaking personally, at 48 I feel too old to cope with Lego and buckets and spades again,

Yours Ever,

My purpose, as always, was to avoid a retreat on the issue at stake, while seeking to maintain a measure of deference to the Chairman and principal shareholder. This was not an easy circle to square, and – recalling Stephen Glover's strictures above – I was never under the delusion that all right was on my side. I spent many hours brooding about who could be hired to add energy and edge to our political commissioning, of a kind acceptable to Conrad, without betraying all that I believed in. I approached one or two candidates, who turned me down, foremost among them the excellent Andrew Marr of *The Independent*. The working atmosphere in other areas of the *Telegraph* was generally perceived as happy and positive, which helped us greatly with our recruiting. But the political tensions within our building had become well known outside it. There was no widespread enthusiasm to clamber into the bearpit. In the end, after much heart-searching I accepted Conrad's proposal that Simon Heffer should come across from *The Spectator*, where he was Deputy Editor under Dominic Lawson, to run our leader page as Deputy Editor (Comment), while Veronica Wadley became overall operational Deputy Editor. With as bad a conscience as at any time in my editorship, I asked Trevor Grove to go. Not surprisingly, Trevor's confidence had not recovered from the move back from editorship of *The Sunday Telegraph*. Yet he had contributed so much to the resurrection of the titles that this decision seemed to me, as well as to others, a poor recompense for our eight years together. I thought of *Pickwick Papers*: 'It's over, and can't be helped . . . as they always says in Turkey ven they cuts the wrong man's head off.'

The *Telegraph* continued to prosper in the eighteen months that followed. An immensely talented team was running a superb editorial machine. But it would be deceitful to suggest that the atmosphere in the office was as it had once been. The 'band of brothers' was fractured. I continued to write most of the big political editorials myself, not least to keep them out of the hands of more strident Thatcherite pens, and to encourage the expression of a range of views. But some of our leaders, especially on Europe, represented what Douglas Hurd had called 'camels'. They attempted to express one view, without altogether alienating those who held others – not least Conrad. My senior staff were conscious of mounting political pressures. Simon Heffer displayed all the gifts we knew him to possess as a writer, but I remained sceptical about his judgement. I sometimes suspected that Simon had chosen to occupy the position in Christendom accorded to King James I by Henri of Navarre. His colleagues were irked that, in his preoccupation with politics, Simon left himself too little time to fulfil the mundane daily grind that falls to the lot of every newspaper executive. I wrote him a letter, expressing some of my own beliefs about what a newspaper, and its political commissioning editor and columnist, should be seeking to do:

> The first duty of any journalist, even a political columnist, is to inform his readers about what is going on, essaying a measure of objectivity. Some of our columnists make no attempt to do this, but merely offload the week's cargo of prejudices, with which readers are already very familiar. In the short run, there will always be an audience . . . for a Tory prepared to heap articulate scorn upon his own side. In the longer term, however, the most successful political commentators are those whose work is underpinned by the knowledge that governing is very difficult, that government is a hideously imprecise science, and that most Cabinets of any political complexion are largely filled by men and women of moderate talents . . . While I do not mind whether the government

thinks we are 'fair', I do mind greatly what rank-and-file Tories out in the country think. We cannot treat them as if they were shackled to our chariot wheels, as if we possessed some power to compel them to read any outpourings we choose to offer, rather than in reality requiring to woo them in keen competition with our rivals.

The *Telegraph* team had come so far together, and had shared so many happy times since 1986, that it was a sadness now to see shadows deepening around us. By late 1994, I was beginning to ponder my own future. I had already outlasted most occupants of Fleet Street editors' chairs. I believed that it would be wrong to continue to do my job – any job of such a kind – for much more than a decade. I grew increasingly sure of this, in the new circumstances in which we found ourselves working at the *Telegraph* by the end of that year.

12

THE TORY ECLIPSE·

WHEN JOHN MAJOR BECAME Prime Minister, for a good many months the *Telegraph* did its utmost to focus on the virtues of his government. I felt, a visceral desire to assist the moderate pro-Europeans to triumph over the Eurosceptics. I believed that Britain's ultimate destiny must lie with Europe; that we could not indefinitely remain on the periphery of the EC; and – in direct contradiction of Conrad's strongly expressed enthusiasm for British membership of the North American Free Trade Area – that no alternative relationship with the United States was credible. I was significantly influenced by a conversation around that time with the US Ambassador in London, Raymond Seitz, whom I admired. At one of our lunches, Ray observed: 'Always remember that the United States is only interested in Britain today, insofar as Britain is a player in Europe.' I was then, and remain today, convinced that he is right.

As far back as 1987, Bill Deedes warned gravely, at a leader conference, that he believed the Conservative Party could face terminal schism over Europe. At that time, to most of us, such a prediction seemed extravagant. Yet now, indisputably, such an outcome threatened. In 1991–92 there were three camps within the *Telegraph* on the pivotal issue of our membership of the European Exchange Rate Mechanism. The first was that which I myself represented, and which was reflected in our editorials. This maintained an uneasy optimism that the ERM experiment would prove successful. The optimism was Sarah Hogg's most substantial legacy to us. Uneasiness was generated by the attitude of our City

Editor, Neil Collins, and that fine City columnist Christopher Fildes. I liked and respected both men, though I christened Neil and always referred to him at conference as 'Mr Grumpy', because of his fairly sincere misanthropy. On all other economic and financial issues, our editorials took their cue from Neil and Christopher, and were often written by one or other. Yet they opposed fixed exchange rates. On such an important issue as the ERM, it troubled me to maintain an editorial position at odds with their deeply held convictions. Through 1991 and until the summer of 1992 Neil, however, was grudgingly minded to believe that Britain's ERM position might be sustained, even if he still thought entry had been a mistake. This qualified support helped to persuade me that the policy was still tenable. Our third camp was, of course, made up of resident Eurosceptics, whose hostility to almost all things European never faltered. Their chief standard-bearer was Charles Moore. Only Charles's unfailing courtesy enabled us to work harmoniously together when we differed on such a fundamental matter.

Very few newspapers can lay claim to consistency of political purpose over long periods. Those that do so may be guilty of tedious dogmatism. William Rees-Mogg is often perceived as the epitome of the intellectual as editor and commentator, yet his somersaults on the great issues of our time are legendary. Indeed, in 1991 the great sage published a book predicting the imminent collapse of Western capitalism. He urged his readers to liquidate all share and real estate holdings, pay off credit card debt and stop bothering to shop. No wonder newspaper readers do not take the utterances of pundits very seriously, however Olympian the tone of their pronouncements.

Nonetheless, I recall *The Daily Telegraph*'s wobbling on the issue of the ERM without much pride, even if other broadsheet titles shared the same experience. Here are some samples: on 5 September 1991, our City Comment observed: 'After a sticky start, ERM membership has indeed been remarkably successful. The fans will point to the 3.5% off borrowing costs . . . Inflation, however measured, is falling fast.' Likewise on 13 September: 'There are no danger signs at present; interest rates are not too low, the money supply growth is modest, and the outlook for inflation next year is encouraging.' Our front page on 14 September reported John Major's declaration that the government had 'licked' inflation, with a fall to 4.7 per cent, its lowest for three years. Yet on 30 September, Christopher Fildes was warning that the decision to join the ERM 'remains a gamble'. On 7 October, the former Chancellor Nigel Lawson contributed a leader-page article for us, urging that Britain should move to join the narrow band of the ERM as soon as possible after a general election. This provoked scornful comment from Neil Collins in his column. By late November, the pound was sliding. Collins observed gloomily that it would be madness to abandon the ERM, and politically difficult to raise interest rates. The government could only sit tight and hope for the best.

Meanwhile, intense political attention was now focused upon the forthcoming EC summit at Maastricht. Charles Moore was withering about the prospect. 'Monetary union will advance,' he wrote in October 1991, 'and European government, through majority voting and the stronger European parliament, will come nearer. Britain will sign. As a piece of politics, this will be very cleverly done, and the mind of the whip admires nothing so much as a piece of clever politics. Whether it will be the best thing for the country is quite another question.'

I wrote in an editorial on 9 December:

Few would deny that the British government, as much as the majority of the British people, wish that most of the political feast groaning on the Summit board was absent, and that Britain could depart after a token canapé. As it is, the government has to make the best it can of all the many courses. We have expressed our faith in the judgement of the Prime Minister and the Foreign Secretary. It is equally appropriate to declare that, given the strength of their known commitment to achieving agreement, they will deserve the full support of both their party and their country if they finally conclude that what is on the table at Maastricht is not acceptable to Britain. But, plainly, if a reasonable agreement can be achieved that enables us to remain in the long negotiating game that lies ahead, to check the extremists and put the EC on a sane and realistic path to the future, then that will be the best outcome both for the government and for this country.

On the eve of the Summit, Charles wrote an impassioned leader-page column denouncing the whole process and demanding that Britain should employ its veto to block a treaty. I spiked it – withdrew the piece from the newspaper an hour before the first edition closed. I hated to do this. Other than when a piece by a given writer failed to pass a quality threshold, this intervention was unique during my period at the *Telegraph*. I sought to give free access to the widest possible range of views in the paper. I told Charles that if he had simply been a political columnist, I would have allowed his piece to run. But he was also Deputy Editor of the newspaper. The *Telegraph*'s mixed signals would lapse into outright chaos if we carried his piece alongside an editorial written by me, supportive of Major's freedom to negotiate. It is a tribute to Charles that neither then nor later did he show ill-will over this episode.

The eventual Maastricht deal, with opt-outs for Britain from EMU and the Social Chapter, was widely hailed as a triumph for John Major's negotiating skills. Although the treaty's passage through the House of Commons was marked by constant cliff-hanging votes provoked by Tory anti-European diehards, the summit appeared to have bolstered Major's personal standing, and given him a modest chance of winning the 1992 General Election against the odds and the polls. Yet looking back, I find it hard to regard the government's presentation of Maastricht with much enthusiasm. Because of my close personal relationships with

Douglas Hurd and Sarah Hogg – and at that time, I was also still on relatively easy terms with John Major – I was better informed about what was going on at the summit of government during the Maastricht period than ever before or since. The attitude of the *Telegraph* was considered vital to preserving rank-and-file Tory support for a treaty. I was talking regularly in person or by telephone to members of the British delegation, before, during and after the summit. From John Major downwards, all of them repeatedly expressed the view that whatever our EC partners were signing at Maastricht, they had no intention of taking most of it through; there was no realistic prospect of Monetary Union coming to pass by the end of the century; much of the treaty was mere verbiage, to satisfy a few visionaries. I do not believe this was merely cant peddled by senior ministers to a newspaper editor, to gain my acquiescence. I think that it reflected the sincere view of John Major and his senior colleagues, that Britain's European partners were not serious about federalism, or about the early introduction of EMU. If I am correct, this was a huge misjudgement. Even those of us who continue to believe that we must make Europe work, with Britain as part of it, should not delude ourselves about past errors. The Eurosceptics, whose cause was so eloquently pleaded by Charles Moore in our pages, can claim to have had the best of the intellectual argument about Maastricht, even if many of us remain convinced that the Treaty was a politically necessary act for this country, and that British failure to sign would have represented a death warrant for our membership of the EC.

Bitter Tory post-mortems on the Summit coincided with new falls in sterling, and fresh fears about the sustainability of our ERM position. In an editorial on the last day of 1991, we acknowledged the danger that devaluation might become necessary, 'although it would give an appalling signal that Britain was incapable of tough financial self-discipline.' We urged against throwing away all the economic sacrifices of the past year to squeeze out inflation, merely for a short-term electoral advantage from devaluation. Charles Moore wrote in his column on 10 January 1992:

> Being in the ERM resembles driving a car with only one gear. In a way, the government is being incredibly brave, because it is the first government in modern times to go into an election while actively deflating. But the Tories do have one piece of almost unbelievable luck. Both the opposition parties are committed to a worse version of the very policy which is causing the government so much grief. The best economic argument for voting Conservative is that if you vote Labour you would dig us much deeper into the same hole. It is a perfectly good argument, if not an inspiring one.

It was Neil Kinnock who enabled the Tories, against all probabilities, to win the 1992 General Election. And it was Neil Kinnock who made it possible for the *Telegraph*, and the Tory Party, to fall in behind John Major during the campaign. Charles Moore wrote a 2,000-word op-ed page piece in March under the heading 'Nightmare on Downing Street', fantasizing about the first hundred days of a Kinnock government. Charles's grisly predictions of rising taxation and economic mismanagement were easily believed. Our own coverage was enlivened by a wide range of pundits and guest columnists. The novelist Sebastian Faulks contributed Sketches from key constituencies. Our columnist Stephen Fry wrote a leader page about why he would vote Labour, in pursuit of greater fairness and tolerance. On the eve of the poll, we predicted a photo-finish. Privately, I believed the Tories would lose. I joined the general euphoria, when John Major scraped home with a majority of twenty-one.

Conrad Black called up early in the campaign, and asked me to arrange an election night party for him. He obviously had it in mind to revive the tradition of Lady Pam Berry's get-togethers. I warned of the danger that this one might turn into a wake, if the Conservatives lost. Conrad told me to go ahead anyway. I booked a grand room at the Savoy, lobster and champagne and wall TV screens, and sent out 500 invitations to the good and great. The occasion turned into a riotous, unexpected celebration, though I did not see it until very late, because I was down at our office in Canary Wharf. Not a few Eurosceptics believed then, and have argued since, that defeat in 1992 would ultimately have worked to the advantage of the Conservative Party. They would have escaped the last five ignominious years of John Major's rule. The country would have tasted high-tax socialism under Neil Kinnock and John Smith. As it was, of course, Kinnock resigned to be succeeded as Labour leader by Smith, and our shrewd political commentator Anthony King wrote a piece headed 'CAN LABOUR EVER RECOVER FROM THIS?'. A wholly unexpected sense of reprieve swept through the Tory ranks.

Yet even while the election campaign was still in progress, we carried a leader on 7 April 1992 in which we said: 'It is becoming hard to avoid the conclusion that the government made an error of judgement when it decided to take Britain into the ERM in October 1990, just as Germany was entering an economic crisis.' Britain's least bad option, as sterling languished, seemed to lie in a remote chance that we might combine with France and Italy, which had problems of their own, in a joint downward realignment of currencies within the ERM. All through that torrid summer, the economic picture worsened steadily. 'The government is not facing an economic crisis', we said in an editorial on 30 June. 'But it is liable to find itself doing so disturbingly soon, unless hard public spending decisions are confronted and adopted.' It seemed fantastic and frivolous, at a moment when the Treasury coffers were under strain, that the government promised £4 million for Paul McCartney's Liverpool Institute for the Performing Arts. In small things as in large, the government's policies seemed muddled, even before taking account of the regular budget of Tory sexual and financial embarrassments which was now filling the front pages.

The economist Tim Congdon wrote on our leader page on 30 July that he saw no hope of economic recovery if Britain remained in the ERM. Yet the Chancellor, Norman Lamont, stuck to his guns. He rejected as 'fool's gold' the suggestion that devaluation would speed economic recovery. He said there was 'no such thing as a free lunch, devaluation would be disastrous', leaving the ERM would be 'the cut-and-run option'. In a leader on 27 August, we suggested that Lamont had now staked his political future on the government's commitment to the ERM, but we were increasingly doubtful whether our membership was sustainable. This piece was strongly influenced by Neil Collins. Throughout the year thus far, Neil had expressed the private view that though he had opposed ERM entry, the country had endured so much pain to sustain our position in the Mechanism for almost two years that it would be folly to abandon it. Now, however, he walked into my office after his summer holiday and said: 'Sorry. It won't wash any more. We're going to have to get out.' I believed him.

The government's desperate manoeuvres in the first days of September – borrowing to sustain sterling, offering defiant public statements and finally raising interest rates to crisis levels – became grotesque to onlookers. On Wednesday 16 September, Britain ignominiously withdrew from the ERM. The government's economic strategy lay in ruins. I wrote in our leader next morning:

> Within the next few days the Chancellor of the Exchequer must resign his office. If such a sacrifice seems in some measure an injustice to Mr Lamont, it is an essential public recognition of the failure of the policy for which it has been his misfortune to bear responsibility. If Mr Major seeks to retain Mr Lamont in his office he will not be praised for loyalty, but condemned for lack of judgement. It is impossible to deny that the Prime Minister's personal credibility is sorely shaken by these events. He has chosen to bind himself in chains to this policy, and now he must pay the political price.

That morning of 17 September, the Chancellor asked to see me in his office at the Treasury. We exchanged pleasantries. For years, Norman had been something more than an acquaintance, something less than a friend. 'I thought it would be helpful to have you in, Max,' he began smoothly, 'and to emphasize that our economic policy – monetary targets and so on – will remain unchanged as a result of yesterday's events.'

'Yes, Norman,' I said. 'But who's going to be in charge?'

'How do you mean – "in charge"?'

'Who's going to be Chancellor?'

'I am.'

'But you can't be.'

'Why not?'

'Because nobody's got any confidence in you any more.'

'The Prime Minister has expressed his full confidence in me.'

'But no one else will.'

'Nobody could have anticipated what happened yesterday.'

'Don't be ridiculous – scores of pundits including ours have been predicting this for weeks, months. When you raised interest rates to 15 per cent, Christopher Fildes said it was time to send for the men in white coats. Look, Norman – you and I have known each other quite a long time. This is your chance to show that you know what to do. When a disaster of this magnitude happens, you can have an argument about who walks the plank, but somebody has got to. If you go now, everybody will applaud and say, "Good old Norman, he's done the right thing." You can come back in a year with no hard feelings. But if you stay, you'll simply be hounded out sooner or later.'

'I am sorry if you take that view,' said Norman with a cool, oriental smile. 'I am sorry if Conrad Black takes that view. The Prime Minister and I take a different view.'

And so we parted, never to speak in amity again. Black Wednesday and its aftermath marked a decisive point in many people's view of Mr John Major and his government, and I was among them. Failure to recognize the absolute need for someone to take the blame seemed a huge moral as well as political lapse. From that moment until John Major's fall, while the *Telegraph* intermittently sought to make the best case for his faltering

"IT IS A FAR, FAR BETTER THING THAT I DO, THAN I HAVE EVER DONE ..."
(A TALE OF TWO CITIES)

Garland's *Telegraph* cartoon after Black Wednesday, when
Norman Lamont declined to resign.

government, my heart was not in the struggle, and the hearts of
most of my colleagues never had been. My advice to Norman
Lamont that Thursday was perhaps the only unequivocally wise
political counsel I ever tendered. We wrote again and again in the
Telegraph thereafter that the Major government was fatally flawed
by the continuing presence of a bankrupt Chancellor of the
Exchequer. 'Mr Kenneth Clarke, a superbly self-confident minister
of great experience and resilience, should succeed Mr Lamont
before the Tory party conference,' I wrote on 19 September.

I cared not a fig for Norman's subsequent personal embarrassments, the allegations about his Thresher's wine bills and suchlike,
except insofar as they reinforced the sense of ridicule surrounding
his occupancy of the Chancellorship. Our City Diary carried a
bitchy paragraph, reporting that Treasury insiders considered that
Lamont was too preoccupied with his personal problems (not
least evicting a 'Miss Whiplash' from a basement tenancy of the
Lamont home) to be paying proper attention to his Chancellor-

ship. I thought this piece a blow beneath the belt, and caused Neil Collins, despite his bitter resistance, to carry an apology in the paper and to write privately in contrition to Lamont. The embarrassment was all on my side later, however, when in evidence to a Commons Select Committee, Lamont's key adviser, Sir Terence Burns, confirmed the truth of our City Diary story. Our City Editor rubbed my nose in that one.

By both his political and personal behaviour, Lamont did more than any minister to translate John Major's government from the realms of inadequacy to those of absurdity. We campaigned relentlessly for his resignation until at last it came, more than a year afterwards, too late to save either Lamont or Major. An embarrassing *placement* soon after the Chancellor's fall put me one away from Norman at a grand dinner table. He began to tell the woman between us, a tycoon's wife who was obviously bewildered by the hostile vibrations darting across her front, that he was writing his memoirs in order to set the record straight, to undo all the wicked canards against himself put about by evil newspapers such as *The Daily Telegraph*. 'Oh come off it, Norman,' I said. 'The best thing you can do is to let the past be, and say nothing.'

'No, I'm going to do the book because I've had enough of all the lies,' he said with unconstrained bitterness. 'You don't run a newspaper. You're running *Pravda*.'

Lamont has often asserted in the past decade that he never believed in the ERM policy. He supported it only because he was told to. If true, this seems to makes his conduct of his office even less admirable. Charles Moore was one of those who wrote during the summer of 1992 that the Chancellor did not believe in ERM membership, perhaps as a consequence of private briefing from Norman. Yet I could not forget an embarrassing evening early in 1992, when I was obliged to accompany Conrad to a dinner for Norman at Woodrow Wyatt's house. The sole purpose of the occasion was to lobby our Chairman about the virtues of the Treasury's ERM policy. Twice later that year, the Chancellor called me in to the Treasury, to assert with private energy what he was stating with public eloquence – that we had to stick it out with the ERM, and that the policy was working. Whatever one's interpretation of the Chancellor's conduct, it was unimpressive. The root problem, most of us believed, was that Norman was a clever, witty, engaging lightweight who had been grossly over-promoted to the Chancellorship, merely because he ran John Major's leadership campaign. Lamont paid a humiliating price for his own elevation, and John Major's reputation suffered lasting damage for his folly in promoting a mere personal cheerleader to the stewardship of the nation's finances. Lamont's only lasting contribution to British politics was the devastating denunciation of Major's government in his resignation speech as 'in office, but not in power'. But we are told even that line was inspired by Woodrow Wyatt.

A footnote to Black Wednesday: after my tense, angry exchange with Norman on the Thursday morning, by chance I found myself keeping a date later that day to lunch with Kenneth Clarke, who had also been one of Major's 'War Cabinet' which sat through the nightmare the previous day, when interest rates were raised 5 per cent within a matter of hours, in a vain attempt to stave off disaster. Ken is among the most robust politicians of modern times. He never allows himself to appear rattled, even when others are shinning down falls into the lifeboats. He ate an exceptionally hearty lunch. 'You know,' he said, as an oyster disappeared down that unfailingly cheery hatch, 'a lot of the accounts of our day yesterday in the bunker at Admiralty House get the mood wrong. It wasn't all gloom and doom. At times there were some quite good jokes.' It was hard to decide whether this made the story better or worse. His words reminded me of Theodore Roosevelt at the Battle of San Juan in 1898, struggling for the mots justes to comfort a desperately wounded friend who was dying before his eyes. 'Well, old chap,' Roosevelt finally essayed, 'isn't this splendid?'

*

EARLY IN 1993, Roy Jenkins penned for us a magisterial assessment of John Major's flagging administration.

> Presiding over this theme of government weakness and popular despair is the Prime Minister. No one suggests that he has committed any single act which would call for his resignation, but the criticism of him must nonetheless be deep. Last week, I came across a quietly damning remark of the Duke of Bedford of the day about Goderich, who was head of government, happily only for five months in 1827. Bedford simply said that Goderich was 'a good-natured and good-humoured man, but totally unfit to be Prime Minister'. Nothing is easy, when confronted with the mess we are in today. But almost anything would be better than the weak and whining progress from improvisation to improvisation which has recently passed for an economic policy.

Lamont's belated sacking in the spring of 1993, to be replaced – as we had strongly urged in the paper – by Kenneth Clarke, could not alter the fundamental fact that the Tory administration was led by a man who commanded scant respect from his own party, and had shown himself conspicuously to lack the gifts of leadership essential to any man or woman who aspires to rule the country.

Like most newspaper proprietors, Conrad overestimated the political power of his titles. By early 1994, heavily influenced by Margaret Thatcher and her acolytes, he had had enough of the Prime Minister. 'My patience with John Major is exhausted,' he wrote, in a memorable note to me. He was increasingly eager to see *The Daily Telegraph* lead a charge to depose the Tory leader, probably in favour of Michael Portillo. I was unwilling to accede to this, partly because I do not believe it is the business of serious newspapers to try to bring down Prime Ministers – whatever my own private view of John Major's shortcomings – and perhaps also because newspapers appear so foolish if they fail. The day after a lunch with Conrad late in February, I wrote to him:

I still think the armaggedonists underrate [Major's] chances of survival, if he himself has the bottle to stick it out . . . Even Major's most bitter critics would rather he went quietly than that he had to be dragged out kicking and screaming, and his stubbornness may yet surprise us all . . . My own view of Major has not changed since 1990. He is a small man who was never suited to the premiership . . . [but] I believe we have done the paper's reputation nothing but good by refusing to join the various hunting packs which have sought to bring him down.

I described my own unwillingness to support Portillo.

The *Sunday* would be expected to do this, because Portillo fits in the tradition of quirky right-wingery it has made its own. But the very people who are now urging Portillo's claims are those who made such a huge misjudgement about John Major. I admire Portillo's intelligence, but still have grave doubts about his judgement, heightened by some recent silly speeches . . . We cannot possibly know whether this man is prime ministerial material until he has been tested in a frontline job. I have no prejudice against him – indeed, I rather like him. But today I don't see how we could possibly take another huge flier with such an unknown quantity.

I remained an impenitent admirer of Ken Clarke, but I expressed concern about his 'insouciance, carelessness, call it what you will', when considering his claims to the leadership. One Monday after Ken had become Chancellor, he arrived late for lunch with me: 'I had trouble finding anywhere to park.'

'Surely you've got a driver.'

'Oh, it's been a hell of a day. My car wouldn't start at home in Nottingham, and in the end I drove myself straight here.'

'Couldn't you have rung the office on a mobile?'

'Never switch it on. I like to listen to a bit of jazz on the M1.'

When we emerged from lunch and Ken went off to feed his meter, I found desperate messages waiting on my own car telephone, beseeching the Chancellor to telephone the Treasury. It was typical of the man, it was wholly endearing, but I was never entirely sure that any front-line minister in modern government could live as Clarke did, least of all if he possessed aspirations to the premiership. At root, Ken no longer even liked or respected most of the Tory colleagues he aspired to lead, as the party's parliamentary membership lurched ever more sharply rightwards.

Douglas Hurd was plainly no longer a candidate for the leadership, and I found no difficulty in dismissing Michael Howard's pretensions. Michael Heseltine was hampered by his party enemies and fears about his health, following a heart attack. In my note to Conrad, I concluded that I doubted whether any new leader could 'reverse the climate of deep public weariness with the Tories, which they themselves sometimes seem to share'.

Yet Portillo remained the Right's – and Conrad's – white hope. Late in March 1994, Michael himself telephoned and asked me to meet him as soon as possible. A drink at Brooks's was frustrated when we arrived to find the club closed for the Easter weekend. We moved up the road to the bar of Brown's Hotel. After a brisk exchange of courtesies, Portillo stared coolly into my face and said: 'I believe John Major is going to fall this year. I want his job. I hope you'll help me get it.' I was stunned by the sheer recklessness of his remarks. First, as a matter of judgement, while my own view about Major's prospects wobbled several times in 1994, I thought it was most likely that the Prime Minister would survive, unless he lost his nerve. Indeed, I won several bets on this issue with Simon Heffer and other right-wingers. Second, and much more significant, I was amazed that Portillo should so far stick out his neck to a newspaper editor who was no more than a professional acquaintance. Perhaps he had received some encouragement to do so from Conrad, or from *Telegraph* colleagues. I still don't know. But his remarks crystallized all my own unease about his political judgement. At Brown's, I temporized. I acknowledged that I had no more time for Major than he did, but I thought that it was by no means certain the Prime Minister would fall. If he did, we would certainly give sympathetic coverage to a Portillo run. But I offered no promises, and we parted on an equivocal note.

At lunch years later, Portillo suddenly hesitated before answering a question and said: 'How can I talk to you about that, when you're editor of a newspaper?' I said: 'Think back, Michael, and you'll remember that if I was going to embarrass you by revealing something you said, I would have done it after that evening at Brown's Hotel.' He thought for a moment, then grinned: 'Maybe.' He answered my question.

In 1994, even if I was unsure about the Tory succession, it remained as difficult as ever to muster much sympathy for John Major, a Prime Minister under siege from his own party. One evening late in May, I was called in for a drink at Downing Street. We met in the Cabinet Room, Major's Press Secretary, Chris Meyer, sitting in the background: 'Hope you don't mind being in here, Max,' said the Prime Minister. 'Norma's upstairs in the flat getting sorted out after the weekend.' Yet several visitors had noted that the old informality of encounters with the Prime Minister in his office or flat was often now replaced by meetings in the Cabinet Room, a venue which Major or his advisers seemed to suppose would fortify his dignity.

He started with more bounce than he had shown of late, asserting that the economy was looking good, and so were prospects in Europe. The new EC president would be less important than Jacques Delors. Germany was now committed to enlargement of the Community and to reform of the CAP, he said confidently. The new Italian government was much more helpful to Britain. The Spanish and Portuguese were feeling far less centralist. I asked why he did not give an immediate promise that he would hold a referendum on the single currency before there was any question of British membership, as we had been urging in the paper. 'I'll tell you why, Max. Because for dozens of Tory MPs, that would be a concession too many to the Right. They'd be on my back, simply furious.' He was scornful of Paddy Ashdown's proposal that Britain should abandon its EC veto – 'if Ashdown had his way, British troops could be sent to Bosnia whether we liked it or not.'

He talked surprisingly freely about his next reshuffle, which he said would take place in July 'so that the people who go will have the summer holidays to get over it. It's more humane.' His tone sharpened as he began to talk about his colleagues, for whom he betrayed little enthusiasm. 'Some days, Max, I look around this table and ask myself how so many promising ministers of state could have become such old deadbeats. How many of them should I sack, do you think?'

'You haven't got a lot of room for manoeuvre.'

'But if I don't have many sackings, you'll all say I'm a wimp. You said in a leader the other day that some of the candidates for the party chairmanship simply aren't credible. Who were you thinking of?'

'Well, David Hunt, for one.'

'He's a very good man.'

'I had lunch with him the other day. We think he's a trimmer.'

'Like me, you mean? I think David's just the man to cheer up the party. You must have caught him on a bad day. I know what he was trying to do. What about promoting Jonathan Aitken?'

'He's undoubtedly able, Prime Minister, but you must have better sources of information than we do about which of the innumerable skeletons in Jonathan's cupboard is liable to jump out and bite you.'

Brief silence, then: 'It may be a bridge too far to make Jonathan Defence Secretary, but he certainly deserves promotion.'

As we began to talk of the Tory Right, his asperity increased perceptibly. 'They're always briefing, always planting stories that this or that thing isn't being done because I won't make a decision, or agree to it. I'm fed up with being accused of short-termism – there was even something in the religious column towards the back of your paper the other day – Sacred and Profane, was it? We *do* have a long-term vision. We *do* know where we're going.'

He complained bitterly about a *Sunday Times* article questioning a claim he had made in an interview with *Farmer's Weekly* that
his father had done some farming: 'They're always trying to show
I'm a liar.' He exploded at the mention of a controversial adviser
to Michael Portillo at the Defence Ministry. 'He [the adviser] is a
bad man. I knew nothing about that. Everybody always thinks I
know about everything, but I knew nothing at all about that.
Christopher, we must do something about it.'

We came to Portillo himself. I suggested that he might one
day be Tory leader, but was not yet a mature politician. 'Max,'
said the Prime Minister, leaning towards me, 'I will bet you the
best lunch the Garrick Club can produce, on our eightieth
birthdays, that Michael Portillo will *never* be leader of the Conservative Party.' Towards the end, he demanded in familiar terms:
'Well – what do you think I should be doing?' I reminded him
that he had asked me the same question when we met at Wilton's,
as he prepared his 1990 Budget.

After an hour and a half (Bill Deedes once observed that
'no sensible Prime Minister has more than forty-five minutes for
any journalist, however distinguished') I came out into the fading
spring sunshine of Downing Street flattered, as one always was, to
have been granted a privileged glimpse into the heart of power,
yet deeply dismayed by the man himself. I felt a batsqueak of
pity for Major in his loneliness. But no man who attains the office
of Prime Minister should routinely seek to exploit the sympathy
of those around him as a tool of governance. I had no wish to
assist the Right in dispossessing John Major, but like so many of
his own party, I no longer retained any belief in his fitness for
office.

Not a few of the government's problems stemmed from the
failure of its pro-Europeans to fight their corner. Between 1992
and 1995, I argued repeatedly to Michael Heseltine, Douglas
Hurd, Kenneth Clarke and others that they needed to assert
themselves far more, both in Cabinet and out in the country.
Again and again in private conversation, they simply denied the

existence of a problem that seemed glaringly apparent to most of us. Confident that the Europeans still dominated the government, they refused to notice how swiftly the ranks of their supporters were thinning, how the balance of power in the Conservative Party was tilting away from them. At lunch with me towards the end of 1994, Kenneth Clarke belatedly accepted the mistake: 'At the time of Maastricht,' he said, 'the Tory Party was still broadly pro-European. Today, it isn't. We've lost the argument by default.' John Major must bear the principal responsibility for what took place, but it is impossible to exonerate his closest colleagues for failing to discern the shift of the Tory political tide against Europe, and the urgency of the need to fight back. By late 1994, the anti-Europeans dominated political debate within the Conservative Party. The pro-Europeans had lost the battle, almost before they had noticed that it was taking place.

Through the remainder of that year, Conrad became increasingly sensitive about both the shortcomings of John Major and criticism of Michael Portillo, the Right's heir apparent. Late in August, Allan Massie wrote a leader-page piece critical of 'the darling of a Right-wing coterie . . . Thatcher's favourite son,' as he called the Employment Secretary. Massie criticized Portillo's headline-grabbing attacks on welfarism, and mocked his constituency party's proposed rally at Alexandra Palace to celebrate his decade as an MP – a modest enough achievement, some thought. Massie concluded: 'The battle is on for the centre ground, and he is far to the Right of where the real fight is taking place.' The piece provoked a sharp note to me from Conrad, attacking it as 'banal and ill-informed. If we want to be critical of Portillo we should do it in an intelligent and judicious way, but we should bear in mind that he is the only visible hope the Party has of [against?] a rather mediocre incumbent. Massie strikes me as a rather unintelligent Majorite.'

Conrad enclosed with his note a copy of a letter from a Wiltshire Tory, expressing dismay at the piece. Disgusted of Downton, as I shall call her, wrote to our Chairman:

I am a District Councillor and everyone I talk to is bored to
death with the middle ground, and are desperately looking
for a champion to lead the Conservative Party out of that
territory. Many of us in the Conservative Party realise you
cannot burn your boats completely with the present PM, but
after reading *The Daily Telegraph* for many years editorials
and articles such as yesterday's might well drive my family to
the *Times*. I will continue with the *Sunday Telegraph*, because
its editorial thrust has more direction and offers a way out of
the quagmire this country is in with its high taxes, the EU
and lack of vision.

A letter such as the one above interested me, for the opposite
reason that it caught Conrad's fancy. It reflected the growing
determination of some of the Tory faithful to turn their backs on
the real world, the battleground on which the next election would
be fought, and to fortify themselves in a stronghold of principle
which might not enable their party to win power – perhaps never
again – but would offer the comfort of like-minded company and
a passionate belief in their own rectitude. It was Disgusted of
Downton and her kind who were to give birth to the leaderships
of William Hague and Iain Duncan Smith, and drive some of us
away from Toryism altogether. Who knows? Such people may yet
be able to claim that they were in at the birth of a movement
which finally destroyed the modern Conservative Party. Back in
1994, I felt myself more and more strongly obliged to oppose
them. I also believed that such Tory flat-earthers were by now far
too few in number to merit consideration in formulating the
Telegraph's commercial strategy. I replied robustly to Conrad's
note about Massie, and to a subsequent exchange in which he
suggested that we should not lose sight of the likelihood that
Michael Portillo would eventually be the *Telegraph*'s candidate to
succeed Major.
Yet it would be wrong to create the impression from the
political exchanges between Conrad and me that our personal

relations were deteriorating. The Chairman ended his note to me about the Tories with a friendly comment about circulation, and observed that the newspaper was 'looking very good'. Socially, he was under growing pressure from the Tory Right to use his newspapers against Major. These people were his friends, and of course his admiration for Margaret Thatcher remained unstinting. But he also enjoyed argument for its own sake. Looking back on our correspondence over the years, I was often more intemperate than he was. He had plenty to forgive me for, even if he sometimes underestimated the relentless strain that I felt, balancing the political pressures from the Right against what I perceived to be the commercial imperatives for the newspaper's future. The attacks on the Tory leadership by some of our pundits – especially in *The Sunday Telegraph* – dismayed some readers close to home. In December 1994 David Montagu (by now Lord Swaythling), one of our directors, wrote me a strong letter copied to Conrad, urging that both *Telegraph*s should appear less critical of the Major government, the only Conservative administration we had got. I wrote back recognizing his concerns, but concluding: 'In many ways Conrad is the most enlightened of chairmen. It is scarcely surprising that, when the political atmosphere is so febrile, he finds himself tempted by siren voices who wish to see the *Daily* and *Sunday Telegraph* employed as a battering ram to achieve political objectives of their own.'

*

As JOHN MAJOR's political authority ebbed, his personal spleen increased. The image of 'Mr Nice Guy' was always mistaken. Beneath Major's admittedly remarkable natural courtesy, there was anger and even spite. I was often surprised by the manner in which Major made barbed, bitchy observations in my presence about ministers whom he knew were personal friends of mine, notably Michael Heseltine and Douglas Hurd. Both men could have made a vast amount of trouble for Major, had they chosen to do so. Yet each, as I knew better than most, was impeccably loyal. One day, the Prime Minister was complaining about the absence of first-division public performers to make the government's case. I asked: why didn't he use Michael Heseltine more?

'Oh, we want to keep Hezzie for the big occasions,' said Major – for some reason, he always referred to Michael as Hezzie rather than the usual Hezza. 'We don't want to overstrain him on routine things, do we?' A glint of mischief – no, perhaps malice – lit his eye as he thumped his own chest: 'The old ticker! The old ticker, you know!' Douglas Hurd remarked that Major always referred to me without enthusiasm as 'your Max Hastings', apparently attributing a share of blame to Douglas for the *Telegraph*'s misdeeds: 'The Prime Minister doesn't like you, because he feels he never knows what you're going to do next,' said his Foreign Secretary.

'But that's my job,' I said.

'I understand that. He doesn't.'

At Christmas 1994, I received a cold Christmas card from Downing Street, signed formally 'John Major'. The years of 'John and Norma' were over with a vengeance. A similar missive from the new leader of the Labour Party was signed 'Tony'. And after her years in office, when I never received any communications at all from a chronically angry Prime Minister, suddenly in my new guise as a critic of John Major, I was astonished to receive a seasonal greeting signed by 'Margaret and Denis'. By such trifles did we read the runes.

*

THE LAST TWO YEARS of John Major's administration provided an experience of decay and political failure from which many Tory ministers recoiled in as much dismay as did the British people. The contrast between the Prime Minister's efforts to appear buoyant and purposeful, and the reality of a government sliding into the sand, became ever more embarrassing. At leader conferences, Bill Deedes strove manfully to dissuade John Major's most virulent critics from their view that the Prime Minister was presiding over the worst Tory government in living memory.

'These are Mr Major's news-papers – I'm cutting out all the bits that might upset him'

Matt's vision of the duties of John Major's staff.

'Come, come,' Bill would say sensibly, deploying his extraordinary powers of personal recollection, 'are we seriously proposing that Michael Howard is a less impressive Cabinet minister than Sam Hoare, or that Sir Thomas Inskip was the superior of Malcolm Rifkind?'

Yet while I discouraged hyperbole among our writers, my own spirits were scarcely lifted by personal encounters with the Prime Minister. It became increasingly difficult for both of us to maintain a charade of good fellowship, though we struggled manfully. One evening at the end of January 1995, I was reading in the Downing Street waiting room when Major came in with Chris Meyer and Sarah Hogg. The Prime Minister was exuding affability, putting a warm arm round Sarah's shoulder.

'How about swapping my Teresa Gorman for your Simon Heffer?' he enquired cheerfully, as we walked through to the Cabinet Room. 'What's the exchange rate, do you think, what's the exchange rate?' He slipped in a cross word about a column of Boris Johnson's in the paper. What an assiduous, masochistic reader of newspapers he was! Then he declared confidently: 'At last, we have a clear policy for Europe that we can unite behind.'

He said he was sure of having the Tory rebels back under control within a few weeks: 'I can't say more, but they're under a lot of pressure from their constituency chairmen.' I suggested that the government still faced a huge problem of hostile public perception of Europe. Maybe, admitted Major, but we can overcome this. What about the latest fiasco, I asked, with the Spanish apparently walking all over our fishermen? 'Yes, well, of course that's the direct result of Thatcher signing up for the Common Fisheries Policy fifteen years ago.'

'But you can't expect the British public to find that an adequate explanation. The Tory rebels are in an almost euphoric mood, because they believe the whole Europe debate is going their way.'

'I would delete the word "almost",' said Major drily. But he insisted that he remained confident of winning the European argument. He embarked upon a long exposition of his own conviction that there was little danger the EC Single Currency project would come to fruition, and certainly not according to Chancellor Kohl's ambitious timetable.

A week or two earlier, Downing Street had unveiled its grand plan to revive the government's popularity – privatizing the railway system. I wrote a leader myself in the *Telegraph*, condemning the scheme as politically suicidal. Sarah Hogg turned up for lunch and plumped down on the seat opposite me at Wilton's. She demanded crossly: 'So now we have to assume, do we, that *The Daily Telegraph* no longer believes public services are better administered by private enterprises?' I told Major about that conversation. I asked why a government in as much trouble as his own had embarked upon a project as dangerous as rail privatization. 'Because we want an efficient rail service, that's why.'

'But all the predictions are that services will fall off steeply.'

'That's nonsense. And it isn't as if the railways were working very well at the moment, are they?'

I mentioned widespread concerns about how matters were going in Ireland. Major complained about all the leaks on the peace process that came out of 'bloody Dublin – excuse my French, Max.' Then he leaned across, smiled dazzlingly, and patted my knee: 'It'll all come out all right, Max, it'll all come out all right.'

The trouble was, that in order to believe that the Prime Minister's confidence was justified, one needed to discount the daily horror stories we were hearing, from every corner of Whitehall. Only a few days earlier, I knew that Major had discussed Europe with Douglas Hurd and the Chancellor, Ken Clarke. Douglas asked: 'If we joined a single currency, could we still present a national budget?' The Prime Minister immediately responded: 'No.' The Chancellor said: 'Yes.' Douglas observed in despair: 'If we can't agree upon something as fundamental as this, then where are we?' A senior minister told me privately: 'The trouble is that on every issue, the Prime Minister can always be moved, and even if he can't be, people think he can.'

Conrad now found himself the focus of intense agitation from the Tory right – and from some of their representatives inside our building – to employ *The Daily Telegraph* to unseat the Prime Minister. On 11 April 1995, I wrote at length to our Chairman, setting out the situation as I saw it:

> I believe the foremost [political] objective of the *Daily Telegraph* must remain that of being perceived to be a supporter of the Conservative Party, albeit dismayed by the conduct of the present government. If – as I think – the Tories are to lose the next election under any leader, there will be a great search for scapegoats. It would be a bad day, if the *Telegraph* was to be perceived as partly responsible for 'letting Blair in' ... I do not think a Blair government would necessarily, or even probably, be a one-term wonder ... I still find it desperately difficult to decide what is in the Tories' best interests about the leadership. Before we support dumping [Major], we need to be clear of our subsequent objectives ... Major may yet survive, precisely because the Tory ranks are as uncertain as I am about the merits of deposing him. I

remain convinced that it is strongly against the *Daily Telegraph*'s commercial interests to be at the front of any charge to ditch Major, partly because the public dislikes overmighty newspapers, and partly because if we move too soon, we would be in danger of looking foolish if he survives. You may remember that some colleagues were eager to lead a 'ditch Major' movement as long ago as a year or two. We would have looked pretty red in the face, had we gone that route. No newspaper is alone powerful enough to undo a prime minister, probably fortunately for democracy . . .

I did not present to Conrad, therefore, a moral proposition that his newspapers should not unstick John Major. I argued on pragmatic grounds that they could not do so. It would be disingenuous of me to pretend that I was always, or even often, privately frank with the Chairman about my own political views. Against the background of our deep divergence on fundamentals, I sought to present tactical arguments most likely to convince him of a course for his newspapers which I could live with.

Douglas Hurd told me early in April that he believed that John Major would force an early leadership election, to bring about a showdown with his party opponents. The Foreign Secretary had spent an hour privately with Michael Portillo, late one night in the House of Commons, seeking to persuade him to moderate his hostility to the government's European policies. Portillo, he said, was perfectly civil, but immovable. Douglas was still havering about whether to leave the government. I urged him to do so. I could see no possible advantage in his continuance in office. After so many years of public service, he owed it to himself and his young family to make some money. It is often underestimated how deeply many ministers are troubled by money worries throughout their years in office, and Douglas was no exception. He spoke with admiration for the Prime Minister's continuing robustness under fire, but he remained troubled by the man's loneliness, the fact that Major seldom seemed to confide in anyone, least of all his colleagues. He was certain, he said, that Major would never willingly abandon the premiership.

Douglas was right, of course. On 22 June 1995, the Prime Minister stunned Westminster by walking into the garden of Downing Street and announcing that he was resigning as Conservative leader, to offer himself for re-election. He was 'sick and tired' of speculation about his leadership. Boris Johnson wrote that 'for the first time since Maastricht, he has achieved genuine tactical surprise'. Simon Heffer declared acidly: 'After a rule characterised by drift, indecision and weakness, nothing became John Major's leadership so much as his leaving of it – he would say temporarily ... It was a courageous and, above all, correct decision.' Bill Deedes wrote: 'His stag at bay response to [the Tory rebels'] behaviour is rash, but nobody in their senses could call it unreasonable.' My own editorial said: 'The lack of an obvious and widely acceptable successor provides Mr Major's best chance of pulling off his gamble. For all his shortcomings, supposed and real, he may well see off his critics and gain re-election.'

After so many months in which even many of John Major's Cabinet colleagues despaired of his surviving – or deserving to – the rich irony of the days after 22 June was the absence of serious rivals to challenge him. Norman Lamont introduced a note of absurdity, by briefly offering himself as a prospective leader. Douglas Hurd took the opportunity to announce his retirement from the Cabinet. John Redwood – 'the Vulcan' – launched his own leadership campaign flanked by a parade of Tory grotesques headed by Teresa Gorman, Edward Leigh and Lamont. The great absentee, however, was Michael Portillo. Even as his closest supporters arranged telephone lines for his campaign headquarters – a badly kept secret – the man himself flinched. He declined to stand. Most of his old right-wing admirers never forgave him. It remains uncertain whether he could have won, but when his biography is written, that June moment is likely to be perceived as decisive for his political fortunes. For so long, he had been the Major government's foremost critic-in-residence. Yet he could not bring himself to stake everything on a grand throw against the Prime Minister. Nor, of course, could Michael Heseltine. This was plainly the President of the Board of Trade's last chance to seize the leadership. Even some Eurosceptics conceded that Michael was the only star who possessed a slender chance of averting disaster for the Conservatives. Richard Ryder, the Chief Whip, told me over a drink that Heseltine was now favourite among the cognoscenti, though Portillo could run him close: 'So many of the Heseltine people left parliament at the last election.'

My wife Penny and I lunched with Michael and his family at Thenford, the magnificent Heseltine home in Northampton-shire, on the Sunday before the first ballot. We felt as if we had descended on Colombey-les-deux-Eglises circa 1960. The Tory Party's saviour-in-waiting looked relaxed in designer sports shirt and white slacks. I failed one test on arrival – Michael was contemplating five roses on his desk, and invited my help, as a professed gardener, in identifying them. I couldn't manage one. We sat under close, threatening skies outside the Quinlan Terry poolhouse while the butler distributed barbecue fare. We dreamed, in the full flood of excitement. Everything turned on the first ballot. If Major could be checked by Redwood, Michael's hour would come. We believed that he would be unstoppable. The pundits at Westminster, not to mention senior ministers, were predicting Major's defeat. The entire Conservative press had turned against the Prime Minister. Now Major had vacated his office, I no longer felt inhibited about expressing his unsuitability for it.

That Sunday at Thenford, Michael anticipated that if Major failed to gain victory in the first round, Gillian Shephard, Ken Clarke, Michael Portillo would all throw their hats in the ring along with himself. I told him it remained doubtful that Conrad would tolerate my giving him the *Telegraph*'s direct support if Portillo was also a contender. But nothing was impossible. One day that spring, our Chairman had amazed me by declaring that if Major was forced out, 'we shall just have to shut our eyes, hold our noses, and go for Heseltine', on the grounds that only Michael might be able to deliver a general election victory. Now, at Thenford, I could at least assure my host confidently that I would deny the *Telegraph*'s support to Portillo – whatever difficulties this course might provoke. He said gleefully: 'That would really get me in – if you were sacked in the middle of all this because of a political disagreement. We could have a wonderful row about the independence of the press.'

What about his health? Michael responded gaily: 'Don't ask me. Ask the doctors. They opened me up, and they say that I have the arteries of a forty-year-old!' We talked much about Europe, and about how he would handle the issue if he became Prime Minister: 'I have a plan,' he asserted confidently – though he was also entirely realistic about the difficulties facing any leader in resurrecting his party before a general election. I surmised from his conversation that if he was victorious, he would offer no olive branch to the defeated Right. His messianic enthusiasm for Europe was as powerful as ever, yet he said: 'While I have always been a European, I have always also been a nationalist European. I want us to win. Why otherwise would my book have been entitled *How Britain Can Win In Europe?*'

We weighed the likelihood that Paul Dacre's *Daily Mail* would come out for Redwood or Portillo rather than for him, despite the personal enthusiasm of Sir David English, the *Mail*'s Editor-in-Chief, for Heseltine.

'Should I talk to English?'

'Yes. It may be your only chance there.'

We were two days off the first ballot. Michael said he had prepared no speech, would give no off-the-record briefings to lobby correspondents, 'because if I suddenly unveiled all that sort of thing on Wednesday morning, everyone would say: "He's just like the rest of them."'

I felt intense affection for Michael that day, and cherished high hopes that this last great Tory star might yet save his party, even if I could offer him only modest personal assistance in achieving this. We parted from the Heseltines on their drive just as rain began to fall. All of us were convinced that the prize was almost within his grasp. Yet still there was that worm of uncertainty, which I reflected in a leader: 'The great drawback of this two-handed contest is that other serious contenders have been forced to remain mute. MPs will have to vote on Tuesday largely in ignorance of what several potential leaders might decide to offer if Mr Major is forced to step down.'

We argued unequivocally, as did almost every other newspaper, that it was 'time for a change of leadership ... It is time for Mr Major to go, and give another leader the opportunity to save the Tories, not least from their own divisions.' The *Daily Mail* ran a front-page Cummings cartoon showing Major on the bridge of a sinking ship. Major's fall seemed assured, even if the succession was not.

In the event, of course, the vote among MPs gave the Prime Minister 218 votes to Redwood's 89, with 8 abstentions and 12 spoiled papers. Jeffrey Archer's last great service to Major was to rush out of the count and declare triumphantly to the assembled media that the Prime Minister was safe. It was a notable tactical manoeuvre. The media immediately acknowledged Major's victory. If the political journalists had paused to think, if some more muted herald had emerged from the count, the mood might have been very different. It was scarcely a wonderful result, for the Prime Minister to have been unable to maintain the support of more than a hundred of his own MPs, against a comic-opera opponent. But it sufficed to keep John Major in his job. We observed bleakly next day that the Tories had gazed over the precipice, and flinched from the uncertainties beneath. Bill Deedes said that Major had retained power, but he doubted that he would enjoy party peace for long. Boris Johnson wrote a rueful and astute piece, declaring that the real vote was Major 1, Hacks nil. The power of the media to dictate political events had been exposed as far smaller than some people, including editors and proprietors, liked to suppose. For exactly that reason, while the outcome represented a sorry verdict for the Conservative Party, I thought it a good one for democracy. MPs had shown a welcome willingness to defy the urging of the press and the pundits. Michael Heseltine became Deputy Prime Minister. We shall never know whether he could have attained the Tory leadership, had he been willing to wield the dagger. He himself remains convinced, after his experience in November 1990, that the assassin of a Conservative leader could never hope to gain his crown. Simon Heffer suggested that Heseltine did not want the job because he recognized that under any leader, the Tories would lose the next election 'so spectacularly it would make Hiroshima look like a minor eructation'. That is far too Machiavellian. Michael wanted Major's job, right enough. But he could not see the tactical path by which he could achieve it. I believe that, had Heseltine gained the leadership, the job would have killed him, given his past heart trouble. But I shall always regret that three good men whom I liked and admired – Michael Heseltine, Douglas Hurd and Ken Clarke – were denied the leadership of the Conservative Party, while the sorry figure of John Major was allowed to drive doggedly on, flicking the reins towards Tory nemesis.

A few days after the June ballot, the Deputy Prime Minister rang me. He enquired whether I would consider coming to work for him, on the presentation of government policy, for which he had now become responsible. He wondered if Conrad might like to give the Conservative cause a little help by continuing to pay my salary while I did so. Touched though I was that Michael should want me at his side, I could think of few roles for which I would be more wildly unsuited. Restoring the fortunes of the Major administration in the eyes of the British public was a task which would have defeated even a man who believed the objective a worthy one. And, of course, I loved what I was doing. I declined, and thus missed my first and probably last opportunity to work in government. Many journalists occasionally flirt with offers of this kind. It can seem momentarily attractive to abandon a lifetime on the touchline in favour of a spell on the pitch, to use Michael Portillo's analogy. The consequences, for those who succumb, are almost invariably disastrous. Think of the price in popular derision Lord Birt, to name but one, has paid for entering service in Downing Street.

Not long after Major's re-election, I was summoned to lunch. This began with a moment of comedy, when I rang the bell of No. 10, and was startled to find it opened by a workman in overalls who announced cheerfully: 'I'm not the Prime Minister, you know.' The building was being refurbished. Up in the Majors' flat, the man himself delivered a confident exposition of his policies for the months ahead, a few of which seemed plausible. Yet the pinpricks of bitchiness persisted, even after his victory in June: 'When Michael Heseltine came in here after the result, he spent an hour with me discussing the reshuffle – then two hours with Robin Butler discussing his office.' Why could Major never be at peace with himself? Why could he not leave pettiness to his enemies? Hurd, Clarke, Heseltine were big men, whatever their weaknesses. For all Major's intelligence, politeness, charm, decency, there came a moment in every conversation with him at which the mask of high office slipped, to reveal the angry little bank manager beneath. I found it impossible to respect him, even though I shared more than a few of his political beliefs.

The Major government staggered wretchedly on for almost two years, an embarrassment even to most of its own supporters. I was grateful that by May 1997, as editor of the *Evening Standard*, I could declare unequivocally that it was time to put the Tories out of their misery, and to welcome New Labour, whatever subsequent shortcomings the party revealed.

13

ROYALS AND REPTILES

NEWSPAPERS NEED ROYALS and royals need newspapers. In some respects I was well to the left of *Telegraph* man. In others, however, I was an old-fashioned Conservative. Early in 1986 when we reviewed every aspect of the newspaper, I concluded that on both principled and pragmatic grounds, there should be no change in the *Telegraph*'s traditionally loyal, even deferential, coverage of the monarchy and the Royal Family – though I always resisted the appointment of a dedicated 'Royal Correspondent' to join the shabby ranks of the Fleet Street 'ratpack'. Through the late 1980s, we carried a steady stream of supportive leaders and features, many of them written by Hugh Massingberd or Bill Deedes. 'Rupert Murdoch', wrote Bill in a characteristic piece in January 1987, attacking News International's coverage of the Royal Family, 'has widened the frontiers of bad taste, allowed some of his editors to undermine newspaper ethics, and driven his closest rivals to imitate him . . . He has no particular regard for our Royal Family, save as adjuncts to his newspapers' circulations.' We praised the Queen's steadfastness and sense of duty. We applauded the Prince of Wales's commitment to causes, though we argued that he should have a proper job – perhaps the Chairmanship of the British Council – both for his own self-respect and to learn the discipline of work. We ran his big speeches on architecture, the environment, the prayer book at length in the paper. We carried as many pictures as any title of the Princess of Wales. We dismissed early rumours of troubles with the Wales marriage, quoting 'a friend' in a news report of May 1987 about the Prince's frequent absences from home: 'The marriage ... is fine – the Prince is simply enjoying a couple of days with the Queen Mother, while the Princess carries out long-planned public engagements in London.' In October that year, we asserted in a leader that 'the Royal Family deserves not special protection, but common decency and good manners, which is currently being denied them'. We stifled our dismay about the behaviour of the Duke and Duchess of York, though I heard Andrew Hutchinson murmur between clenched teeth at the time of their wedding: 'Hanoverian white trash!'

Early in 1991, on the occasion of a television film about the monarch, we wrote in a leader:

> It is impossible to think of an occasion when Elizabeth II has made a serious mistake ... when she has displayed greed or vanity or neglected her duties. In all her actions, she has shown a love of her country and a conscientious wish to serve its people which we would be tempted to call unique, were it not so carefully modelled on the conduct of her own father. We have been incredibly lucky.

We ran a sympathetic leader in June 1991, after there was a media witch-hunt at Ludgrove School to discover the identity of the boy responsible for hitting Prince William with a golf club. 'The fact that obsessive and brutal comment on the Waleses has become familiar in the tabloids does not make the additional pains imposed under these circumstances any more bearable. If sooner or later the media do not drive one or more of the Royal Family mad, it will not be for want of trying.' Some of our younger staff chafed for a more sceptical – they would have argued, realistic – approach to the Royal Family. Yet as late as 1991, I remained sure that it was right to maintain our existing policy.

Even as Editor of the most traditionally loyalist British newspaper, I had little personal contact with the royals, which seemed a good thing. The monarchy's best defence lies in a Trappist silence on the part of its principal ornaments. Everybody loved the Queen Mother, though she never expressed a public opinion, and was privately rather less enthusiastic about the public than the public was about her. Soon after my appointment, I was invited to one of the Queen's regular London lunches, with the usual varied little group – a Whitehall permanent secretary; the Director of the Wallace Collection; Joan Hickson, the actress who played Miss Marple. I exchanged a few platitudes with the monarch about fishing, shared ninety minutes' bromide exchanges about nothing in particular, and went home clutching my menu as a souvenir, like any slightly upmarket tourist. That was the sum total of my encounters with the Queen as an editor, discounting an evening at a Buckingham Palace state banquet, among a cast of hundreds. A few months after the 1986 lunch, there was a considerable row when Peregrine Worsthorne recycled in print some remarks made by the Prince of Wales at a private lunch. Perry shrugged off the fuss, observing that if his host invited newspaper editors to lunch and told them things, presumably he wanted his views broadcast. I encountered the Prince at a charity meeting at Highgrove soon afterwards. 'What should I do?' he demanded. 'I'd like to go on seeing editors, but it's difficult when this sort of thing happens.' I replied by quoting Bill Deedes's wise observation on the Perry row: 'Journalists are, by their nature, unsuitable confidants for princes.' The point was subsequently highlighted, when it proved necessary to sack Bruce Anderson from *The Sunday Telegraph* in 1990 for repeating in print, in defiance of direct instructions, an alleged disobliging remark made privately by the Prince to a journalist about Andrew Knight. Charged with the offence, 'the Brute' cheerfully pleaded guilty, asserting that 'shafting Andrew Knight was an objective that transcended any other consideration'.

I myself only met the heir to the throne again when he was deep in his marital troubles. As an editor I was sure that it was right for him, and indeed for all the Royal Family, to keep us at arm's length. I had lunch occasionally with Palace staff, and formed an affection as well as respect for Robert Fellowes, who became the Queen's Private Secretary in 1990. It was widely believed in Fleet Street that the loyalist *Telegraph* must be deep in

Palace counsels, yet in truth I neither knew, nor wanted to know, royal secrets. David English observed ruefully: 'I hate to say this, but the most reliable source of Royal gossip is *The Sun*, because News International have got so many Palace lackeys on their payroll.' Then as now, the Murdoch papers were, of course, the scourge of the Royal Family – especially Andrew Neil's *Sunday Times*. Yet the two palaces, and especially the Prince of Wales's office, seldom discriminated between friendly and unfriendly news-paper titles in feeding occasional crumbs to the jackals. At a time when *The Sunday Times* was already making it hot for the Waleses, I was galled to learn that the serial rights of a book written by the Prince had been sold to Andrew Neil's organ without the *Telegraph* being invited to bid. I complained to the Prince's staff. The *Telegraph* did not expect any special favours for playing goody-two-shoes, I said, but it seemed bizarre to discriminate in favour of the Murdoch press and against us when marketing a product of substantial commercial value to our rivals. St James's Palace was impenitent.

By 1992, gossip and rumour about the state of the Wales marriage was mounting steadily. Almost alone among national titles, the *Telegraph* took no part in the speculation. Among my colleagues, impatience grew. Veronica Wadley said fiercely: 'Max, you can't pretend this isn't happening. Everybody knows the Waleses are scarcely on speaking terms. You've got to start treating this as a story.' No, I said: 'This is all still tittle-tattle. Our readers won't thank us for joining a stampede to break up the great fairy-tale romance.' It is worth emphasizing just how much unsubstan-tiated gossip about royals, politicians, tycoons circulates routinely in newspaper offices, is accepted as true by supposedly intelligent journalists, yet is never thereafter substantiated. Week after week, rumours fly that 'the *News of the World* is going to break the big one about X's gay lovers on Sunday'. In the event, not infre-quently, nothing appears. A game of grandmother's footsteps is played between rival titles, which often causes one tabloid to rush into print with its own version of a given rumour, as a 'spoiler' ahead of a competitor's supposed scoop. One of the most familiar lines in Fleet Street, uttered with grave nods of assurance after some titbit of sexual scandal has appeared, is: 'There's a lot more to come out about this.' Very often, there is not.

It was against this background, long experience of how wildly unreliable the newspaper industry can be, especially in matters pertaining to the Royal Family, that I continued to hold back on the story of the Wales marriage. The issue became more difficult, however, when a friend who was close to the Prince of Wales asked to come and see me urgently. When he arrived in my office, he did not waste words.

'The truth has got to be told about that woman,' he said. 'Diana is a monster. She lies about the Prince, she lies about herself, she is briefing journalists against her husband, she is going to bring down the monarchy if she goes on like this. You have got to expose her in your newspaper.'

'What on earth good would it do to print all this?' I demanded. 'Most of our readers wouldn't believe it, and it certainly wouldn't be any help at all to your friend. If the two of them start a blood row in public, the damage to the monarchy will be ghastly.' We argued the toss for an hour. He left without receiving any encouragement. A couple of weeks later, a version of what he had said appeared on the front page of the *Daily Mail*. I assumed that, after I disappointed him, he had turned elsewhere.

In July 1991, the *Telegraph* ran a big three-part feature series under the heading 'The Monarchy & Society', written by Bill Deedes, Margot Norman, Hugh Massingberd and Allan Massie. Massie wrote of the Waleses: 'Let it be said that the state of the marriage now discourages the Prince's friends ... Let it be admitted even that it may be in difficulties. It would be surprising if it was not, given the strains to which the Prince and Princess have been separately subjected. Constitutionally, it does not matter whether they are happy together or not.' Massie suggested that, if the couple were not getting along, they should live separate lives, while keeping up appearances in public: 'They would be ill-advised to do otherwise. A divorce would for a time divide the nation far more sharply than Edward VIII's abdication did, and such a division would damage the monarchy. It would also damage the Prince and Princess. She would be condemned to a life of insipid and tedious celebrity. He would grow old, lonely, embittered and eccentric.'

Matters became much more serious in May 1992, when *The Sunday Times* launched its stunning serialization of Andrew Morton's book *Diana: Her True Story*. I had never respected the royal 'ratpack' of tabloid reporters, of which Morton had been an apparently undistinguished member. I dismissed without serious thought the notion that the Princess of Wales might have trafficked with such a man, far less told him her secrets. In the office, I said that we would simply ignore the Morton tale in the *Telegraph*. Veronica Wadley argued passionately with me. Don Berry raised a quizzical eyebrow. We were damaging the *Telegraph*'s reputation as the paper of news, they said. We simply could not ignore the reality of this huge row, and the shattering blow to the Royal Family. Yet, serenely contemptuous of Morton's book, I kept digging my hole. I wrote a dismissive article for *The Spectator* about the behaviour of News International towards the Royal Family. On *World At One* with Andrew Neil, I expressed scorn for his claims that the Morton version was authentic. Could one seriously believe, I demanded, that the Princess of Wales had poured out her heart in such a fashion to such a man? Neil stuck to his guns. I stuck to mine. And of course I was utterly wrong.

Fortunately for me and for the *Telegraph*, the truth filtered through slowly, over many months and even years. Only those who knew the inside story understood that I had blundered. Andrew Knight, by now Chairman of News International, told me crossly: 'If you saw the unpublished stuff we have in the safes here about the Waleses, you would realize what is happening. *The Sunday Times* would never have printed the Morton stuff without absolute proof that it was authorized by Diana.' In 1996, Andrew wrote me a letter in which he detailed the defence of his own and News International's conduct at this period:

> ... Public confidence in the monarchy was hurt not because the story was wrong, but because it was correct. Indeed, we often understated it ... Mr Murdoch and Kelvin Mackenzie personally buried the 'Squidgy' tape, though it was clearly authentic, for two years before the *Sunday Express* started publishing extracts from a second version of it; I personally dissuaded Patsy Chapman [editor of the *NoW*] from publishing the James Hewitt story for almost as long. There are other examples. The *Sun* and *NoW* were repeatedly scooped through managerial (not editorial) inhibition. The *Mail*, the *Mirror* and the *Sunday Express* were far less inhibited. Decades hence, some earnest researcher will doubtless pore over the actual dates of events and the cuttings, and bear me out.

Throughout this period, however, the British public remained unsure what to believe, amid the blizzard of sensation and allegation. One of my own relations, at a dinner party deep in the Shires countryside, castigated me when I said gloomily that both the Wales and York marriages appeared to be on the rocks: 'Come off it, Max – that's typical of the sort of nonsense you journalists like to put about.' In middle England, even at this late stage, a royal divorce remained unthinkable. It was precisely because, in the early 1990s, there remained a deep reservoir of unswerving loyalty to the monarchy among the middle classes, that the shock of disillusionment was so great, when it came. A host of traditional monarchists felt betrayed, to a degree that is still not fully understood by some members of the Royal Family.

Predictably, however, the successive Wales scandals provoked a fine flood of middle-class hypocrisy. Angry voices muttered about the disgraceful behaviour of *The Sunday Times* in publishing such stuff, just as they did later when *The Times* ran a serial which included mention of Prince Philip's alleged extra-marital affairs. They all bought it, however. The Morton book, and the ensuing marital carnage in the Royal Family, left me as one of its minor casualties. It exposed the folly of my own policy, in breaching the normal rules of journalism. The mistakes which I made at that period probably did not do me much harm in the eyes of *Telegraph* readers, but they certainly did so in those of Fleet Street colleagues and rivals. While sharing few of Andrew Neil's values, I had always respected him as a journalist. As a middle-Englander myself, I hated what Morton had done. Yet I had to recognize that one could no more blame a member of the royal 'hackpack' for his behaviour than a fox invited into a hencoop, and likewise Neil's *Sunday Times*. Responsibility for what had happened lay squarely within the Royal Family. As an editor, Neil emerged triumphant from the bitter controversy surrounding the Morton serialization. The 'new Britain' of which he saw himself as standard-bearer decisively saw off 'old Britain', whose advocate I had rashly chosen to be. I look back on the whole episode with chagrin.

By 1993, the Queen's '*annus horribilis*', like the rest of the country *The Daily Telegraph* was obliged to acknowledge that the monarchy faced a crisis of public confidence. John Major described to me his amazement, after the Windsor Castle fire in November, on beholding the tide of public anger which followed the government's announcement that it would pay the bill to repair the damage: 'That really shook me,' said the Prime Minister. 'I thought the fire would produce a great outpouring of sympathy, with the public demanding that we should pay everything. Instead, there was this terrific row. Was it envy, or what?' Another senior minister described the Prince of Wales 'becoming odder and odder . . . self-indulgent and spoilt . . . When it comes to self-pity, it's a remarkably similar experience dealing with John Major and the PoW.' He expressed concern that no one at Buckingham Palace seemed capable of gripping the situation. 'You've no idea how little that family talk to each other. One day the Queen remarked that she was wondering whether she should scrap *Britannia* and the royal train, but she had no idea what Prince Charles's view was. I kept wanting to say: "Why don't you ask him, ma'am?"'

I suggested to the same minister that sooner or later Prince Charles would have to have another woman in his life, to possess any chance of retaining a grip on his sanity. My friend disagreed crossly: 'It is an entirely modern idea that men need to be having sex all the time. The Victorians got along very well without it.' He described the difficulties created for the government by Princess Diana's periodic forays abroad, with neither Downing Street nor her foreign hosts confident of whether she should be greeted with official courtesies. The minister believed she needed a structure in her life – a job – to prevent her succumbing to relentless narcissism.

Our writers were still striving, in the face of mounting difficulties, to make the case for treating the Royal Family with some measure of mercy. Bill Deedes wrote, late in 1993, that while it was possible some future political decision might be taken to make Britain a republic, 'it seems to me, there is a more immediate risk of losing the monarchy by accident, as it were. And this could come about by allowing a mixture of half-truths, innuendo, lack of charity, ignorance and pure mischief to bamboozle us.'

I continued to think that the only credible way forward for the entire Family was to pursue a policy of silence. Early in 1993, I had a conversation with the Prince of Wales's Private Secretary, Richard Aylard, about the embryo proposal that Jonathan Dimbleby should be authorized to write an official biography of the Prince. I said: 'It's bonkers. All anybody will care about is the marriage. Another book will simply give the whole story new legs.'

'But we've got to do something,' said Aylard.

'Why? The only sane policy is: say nothing, say nothing, say nothing.'

I wrote to him much later:

Throughout the ages, favourites have been dangerous to monarchies, whether the marks of favour which they receive amount to lands, shares in naval dockyards or (in contemporary terms) access to highly marketable journalistic information. None of us, even princes, can expect to write our

'My wife doesn't understand
Prince Charles'

Matt on royal tribulations.

own school reports. It also becomes difficult for some of us
to defend the Royal Family's right to privacy, if the Prince
and Princess of Wales decide selectively that they will trample
all over their own privacy.

I argued that it was ipso facto impossible for the interests of
the heir of the throne to coincide with those of any journalist,
however sympathetic. When, at last, in October 1994 the Dimbleby book was published, laying bare a royal orgy of self-pity, it
was serialized in the same *Sunday Times* which had earlier fired the
devastating Exocet into the monarchy by publishing Andrew
Morton's book on Princess Diana. Once again, the Prince of
Wales appeared untroubled by conceding commercial advantage
to enemies of the monarchy by allowing the book to be sold to
Murdoch interests. The *Telegraph* persisted with a policy that we
would not unilaterally publish material damaging to the Royal
Family. But we would not again withhold news or comment on
royal issues in the public domain. We carried a banner headline
on 30 June, 'I CAN DIVORCE AND STILL BE KING', reflecting the
Prince of Wales's assertions to Jonathan Dimbleby. It was no

coincidence that Prince Philip granted an interview to the *Telegraph* at the same time, on the eve of a foreign visit he was making. I was invited to undertake this myself, at Windsor Castle. But I suggested to those concerned that, if the *Telegraph*'s Editor met personally with Prince Philip at such a moment, the encounter would be perceived by the world as the reflection of a direct confrontation between the old Royals in the blue corner, in alliance with *The Daily Telegraph*, versus the Prince of Wales in the red corner with the Murdoch press. The point was taken. Our reporter Robert Hardman conducted the interview in lieu of me. We gained a banner headline anyway from Prince Philip's remarks, which made plain his deep distaste for his son's decision to lay himself bare before the world.

The morning after the film which accompanied the Dimbleby book was screened, I wrote of the Prince of Wales in a leader:

> Last night's documentary, which was intended to relaunch his image after its fearsome battering in recent years, at best did him little good, and at worst may have done him much harm. There are no public relations 'quick fixes' for the problem of low public esteem. The remedy, almost always, lies in a life of unostentatious dignity and decency. This does not mean retreat to a monastery, but it requires the rejection of cheap exposure. Fly-on-the-wall television is the enemy of dignity. The Princess of Wales's attempts to 'tell her side of it' have already cost her dearly, and may do more grievous damage yet, unless she changes tack. The Prince possesses a relatively large staff, who would dissuade him from a policy of ill-judged activism, if they were doing their jobs properly.

By a nice irony, a few weeks later the BBC contacted me, to enquire whether I might be willing to become presenter for a new television series on the monarchy. I felt obliged to decline, for a host of reasons. I had no stomach for expressing any frank personal opinions on camera about the monarchy's crisis. And it would be absurd to produce a television series which attempted to rebuild a fantasy image of the Royal Family. The Prince of Wales's efforts to revive his own fortunes by laying bare his miseries seemed disastrously misconceived. If the Royal Family cooperated with such a series as the BBC proposed, the likely outcome seemed more of the same. When I wrote to the producer to explain why I felt I could not make the programmes, I added a few personal thoughts, about why I believed further exposure would be mistaken, above all for the Prince:

> He makes the classic error of hoping to be judged for what he *does*, whereas in reality . . . he will be judged for what he *is*, a subtly but importantly different matter. The monarchy cannot be and should not seek to be other than ornamental and constitutional. Its future must hinge upon remaining a thing of beauty and illusion. The moment ugliness creeps in, then it is in deep trouble, as we all see . . . Even those who expressed support for the Prince after the [Dimbleby] film were moved, I believe, by feeling sorry for him. I don't think this a desirable emotion for the heir to the throne to evoke. Lying on one's back and kicking one's legs in the air like a naughty spaniel does not, in the long term, contribute much to one's own dignity.

By now, events were moving at alarming speed. In November 1994, it was announced that the Queen would henceforward pay income tax. So low had the Royal Family's standing sunk that the most common popular reaction appeared to be irritation that she had escaped for so long without doing so. It was obvious that public sentiment would demand the scrapping of such extravagant symbols as the royal train and the royal yacht *Britannia*, a move which we argued in the paper had become inevitable and right. On 9 December, the separation of the Waleses became official. 'Divorce is ruled out, but Royalty faces its greatest crisis since Abdication', proclaimed the *Telegraph*'s front page. Our editorial, while sympathetic, raised for the first time my personal view, that the best future outcome for the monarchy might be the renunciation of the throne by the Prince, in favour of his son William. The Prince could then be free to make a life with Camilla Parker-Bowles, which no one would grudge him, if he accepted the necessity for a choice.

A courtier observed at lunch with me, a few months after publication of the Dimbleby bombshell, that the Queen had suffered deep, long-term hurt from the book, and its version of her son's judgement upon her: 'If anything, the whole thing looks worse now than it did when the book first came out.' He described the petulant anger of the Prince of Wales, whenever he saw a photograph of his wife prominently published: 'He's simply got to learn to grow up some time.' It was plain that relations between Buckingham Palace and St James's were at rock bottom. All my own sympathies lay with the former.

Despite the *Telegraph*'s bitter criticism of the media treatment of the Waleses, our trade could scarcely be held responsible for the breakdown of their private relationship. There seemed a good case, however, for suggesting that relentless media pressure had made it impossible for the couple to maintain a public facade, even had they been willing to do so. A measure of hypocrisy has been an essential ingredient of all societies and many relationships through-out history. In former times, however much the Prince and Princess of Wales disliked each other, they could have maintained the appearance of their marriage, while leading separate lives. But in the 1990s, in an age when self-revelation had come to be perceived as a high virtue, and evasion of personal disclosure as a grievous vice, this was no longer possible.

The Prince of Wales's camp by now perceived the *Telegraph*, and its Editor, as hostile forces. This was not unjust, since although I would have sought to defend our motives, I could scarcely deny that both privately and in print I had been strongly critical of the Prince's behaviour. If it had become publicly known that some other rich eccentric such as Howard Hughes had taken to carrying his own towels and lavatory paper to every house in which he stayed, as well as specifying in writing the texture and dimensions of the sandwiches he expected (both of which had become princely practices), it would be assumed that medical supervision could not be far off. It seemed dismaying that any man should so often use such a word as 'holistic' without a hint of self-parody. He appeared never to have learned the self-discipline which is so prominent among the virtues of his mother. His taste for subordinating, even enslaving, himself to a chosen mentor or adviser of the moment (even if the revolving cast of charlatans was prone to whimsical and ruthless dismissal in a fashion which recalled the fate of Stuart favourites), threatened more disturbing consequences. I had one long private meeting with the Prince at about this time. He seemed consumed by self-pity. I suggested that he should not succumb to despair. He should recognize that, for all the burdens of his position, he remained an immensely privileged person. It was a time to show some moral courage. The public had great sympathy for his predicament, but this would not be increased by any overt appeal for support. He was unimpressed, and indeed angered. His fist banged on the table, rattling the silver: 'Nobody but me can possibly understand how perfectly bloody it is to be Prince of Wales.' I have never met him since, and have sought to sidestep social encounters, to avoid embarrassment for both of us. Douglas Hurd, who in his government role saw a good deal of the Prince, rebuked me for my attitude, and attempted to persuade me that some sort of reconciliation, or at least contact with the heir to the throne, should take place. I declined. I continue to believe in the wisdom of Bill Deedes's observation, that princes should keep their distance from journalists. In any event, a consistent strand in the Prince's behaviour over the past decade has been a refusal to heed any counsellor whose views do not accord with his own perception of his comfort.

I was obliged to acknowledge, however, that like others of my kind, I found myself unable to keep my distance from princesses. Diana was now living alone at Kensington Palace. She had become a masterly media lobbyist. Selected journalists and editors were regularly invited to see her. Most of us deluded ourselves that we were offering her advice. In reality, I am not aware of any instance in which she acted upon any of the sage words that were offered. But of course, she charmed us brilliantly.

> Dear Max [ran a not untypical billet-doux from Kensington Palace]
>
> I read the Editorial about me in today's *Telegraph* with interest (as you might imagine!) Though in many ways doubtless a model of good sense, I feel it suffers for being based inevitably on incomplete knowledge.
>
> While unable entirely to correct this shortcoming, I nevertheless wonder if you might find it useful to come to Kensington Palace to talk to me privately. Your next pronouncement on the subject might then be even more authoritative!
>
> Yours Sincerely,
> Diana

Who could resist such an appeal, and such a barrage of exclamation marks? I went, listened, talked, and went back for more. My dealings with Diana were far less frequent than those of say, Richard Kay of the *Daily Mail* or some more surprising figures such as Paul Johnson – not to mention Andrew Morton. But I assume that our conversations, when I was editing the *Telegraph* and later the *Evening Standard*, were not untypical of those she conducted with other journalists. I had moved from Northamptonshire to Berkshire after my 1992 separation from my wife Tricia. One day, I received an invitation to dinner at Peter Palumbo's house near Newbury, on a Friday evening. Sorry, I said, I never go out on Fridays. Yes, well, quite, said Peter. I'll be frank. Diana wants to see you. I went, of course. The four of us dined. Then Hayat Palumbo did her tapestry and Peter read a book, while the Princess and I talked for a couple of hours in the sitting room at Bagnor Manor.

Her size was the first thing many people noticed. I am so absurdly large that most people simply seem to me small. Diana, for all her magnificent proportions and features, was a big woman. She curled up on the sofa, wearing a long dark blue-and-white-spotted dress, those huge eyes gazing earnestly, sympathetically, into mine, not infrequently over her lashes. She asked about my children, whom she had met. This is always an endearing gambit. A notable social characteristic of the Royal Family – the Queen Mother and Princess Alexandra being the exceptions – is an inability to display even polite interest in other people's lives. 'I'm so grateful the *Telegraph* has been so sympathetic, Max,' she said. 'I'm not bitter. I don't want to "win". But I am absolutely determined to see William succeed the Queen. I just don't think Charles should do it. I don't want a divorce. I don't even want a formal separation, because that would suit Them – They would love to marginalize me. If that happens, I think it will hurt the children.

'I asked Charles directly at Highgrove three weeks ago if he knew what he wanted. He said, "I think so," but then he wouldn't say what he meant.'

She took me aback by asking what I knew about a scheme funded by the Canadian gold tycoon Peter Munk of Barrack Mining – an acquaintance of mine – to hire the public relations man David Wynne-Morgan 'to get rid of me at any price'. I answered truthfully that I had never heard of this one.

'What I would really like,' continued Diana, 'is to sit round the table with the Royal Family and work out what I can do to give service to my country. But they won't do it. It's always the same thing – this hopeless lack of communication and indecision among themselves.'

We talked of the Queen Mother, who was said to be a much tougher proposition than the public understood: 'That's music to my ears.' She expressed her hostility to the Duke of Edinburgh, and glee about the forthcoming Kitty Kelly biography, allegedly exposing him: 'He's got away with murder for years.' I asked: 'Are things generally getting a bit better with the Royal Family?' No, said Diana. 'My mother-in-law has been totally supportive, but it's

'Fire, police, ambulance or
the Princess of Wales?'

Absurdly hysterical tabloid press coverage followed a
report that the Princess of Wales lent marginal assistance – literally,
from the lakeside – when a man was saved from drowning.

so difficult to get a decision out of her.' She professed sympathy
for her husband, but in reality her contempt for the man pierced
every sentence of her conversation. She said that her relations with
Prince Charles had grown marginally more amicable since their
separation, 'but the marriage was hell from day one.' I asked:
What do you want? She said: 'Whatever is best for my children.
The Royal Family would just like me to disappear into some
desert somewhere and leave the children to them. I won't do it.'

She said she thought Robin Janvrin, then the Queen's Assistant
Private Secretary, by far the best of the royal courtiers. I said: 'You
must feel you're helped by knowing how enormously popular you
are with the public?'

'Yes,' she answered, 'but I go on an official visit to Wales and
talk to all these people, then I come home and cry for two hours
because of the strain that so much is expected of me. People want
to touch me, to put crosses on my head. When we were skiing,
the photographers did leave me alone after I gave them a facility
for fifteen minutes, but the Palace was furious with me for granting

any facility at all.' She talked about her passion for health, and said she'd like to do more in that area. She spoke with some complacency about the manner in which 'countries are queueing up to be visited by me'. She claimed not to read newspapers much, but mentioned a Mary Kenny article in the *Daily Mail*, criticizing her for a speech she had made about mental health. She expressed great warmth toward Ludgrove School, and to the Barbers, who ran it. I said that Buckingham Palace was remarkably frightened of her, and of what she might do. She laughed heartily: 'How can they be frightened of *me*, after all these hundreds of years?'

Her directness and frankness, her easy laughter, were hard to resist. Always, however, one perceived oneself in the company of a brilliant performer, appealing shamelessly to the audience's sense of her vulnerability, deploying the semblance of candour as a weapon. We gossiped about tennis players. She spoke of her dislike for Navratilova and Becker. She had just paid her fourth visit to *Les Misérables*, but it was hard to discern any other evidence of cultural interests. She plainly revelled in her own power to charm and to draw crowds. She had 'adored' a recent trip to Nepal. She was keenly interested in what Buckingham Palace was or was not saying about her, and quizzed me closely. She said she had urged the Prince of Wales not to spread himself so widely, to focus on fewer interests: 'I so much want to see him happy and fulfilled.' Well, maybe. I did not mention Camilla Parker-Bowles, though I am sure that Diana would not have hesitated to respond had I done so. She was relatively well informed about politics and politicians. She enjoyed gossiping about personalities: 'God, I was so grateful to [David] Mellor last summer for taking the heat off us for a fortnight with his bonking troubles.' She spoke warmly of Douglas Hurd. I sensed her pleasure in her own power to turn people on, to play the icon. She returned again and again to the theme of the importance of touching people – including her own children. I said I thought that the Andrew Morton book had been a great mistake, and had done much harm. Hayat Palumbo made a rare intervention, to agree decisively. For a moment, Diana seemed at a loss. She made no comment. I said that my own advice to anyone in her position was to keep silent. Once again, she did not respond. I asked: what did she now want from the Royal Family? A divorce, or an official separation? No. A role? Yes. Did she feel hounded? Yes.

She returned again and again to the theme of her children and their interests, of her desire to serve her country. She mentioned the funerals of two children in Liverpool, who had died under terrible circumstances in a case which attracted massive national publicity. She said the Palace had made no plans to send anyone until she telephoned and asked if she could go. She marvelled at their insensitivity. I asked if anyone these days could marry from outside into the Royal Family and make a success of it. She shrugged: 'I told Charles again and again: together, we can be a great team.'

We both signed the Palumbo Visitors' Book in the hall, then walked out onto the drive, amid a warm, clear, starry night.

'What are you doing tomorrow?'

'Watching Wimbledon on telly, then going down to Windsor on Sunday.' She glanced at my Range Rover. 'We've got the same car.'

'I'm flattered you've driven all the way down here, just to bend my ear.'

'I want people to get the story straight.' She glanced up at the sky. 'Full moon tomorrow night.'

'How on earth would you know?'

'Well, it affects most of us, doesn't it? What's your star sign?'

'Capricorn. For God's sake – surely you don't believe all that kind of thing?'

'Well, let's say I'm interested.'

I drove the few miles home thinking the sort of thoughts most men indulged about that divinely beautiful, lonely, bewitching, almost wholly duplicitous woman. It was like coming back from a great evening at the National Theatre. I had witnessed a consummate feat of dramatic art.

Despite Diana's strong contrary views, the *Telegraph* continued to argue that she and her husband should be divorced, for the sake of both. This provoked another coy little note from Kensington Palace, and an invitation to lunch, this time with her Private Secretary, Patrick Jephson, sitting in. She patted me onto the big sofa beside her in the sitting room, quizzed me as usual about my own life and family. She was wearing a light grey check suit and black stockings, looking dazzling as ever. We sat down in the absurdly large dining room, and began to pick at a delicate lunch dominated by marginal morsels of lamb, and claret in very small glasses. 'I assume, Max,' she launched straight in, 'that you think I should be responsible for starting the divorce. But it wasn't me who wanted even the separation, you know.'

'Yes, ma'am – I didn't mean to imply that you should have to bear the odium of starting proceedings, simply that we feel – I feel – that sooner or later there has got to be a divorce, and you've got to be able to start having your own life.'

'I'm perfectly prepared to go on living as I do now. I think it's essential to put my duty – especially to the children – before anything else.'

'Yes, ma'am, but surely it's in the best interests of everybody, including your children, if you have a life of your own and a legitimate relationship with somebody. Everybody needs companionship in their lives, including you. Unlike some of the Royal Family, you have some of the outward attributes of a normal human being.'

She said there had still not even been any discussion of divorce, less still about money. 'All this stuff about me asking for ten million pounds is absolute rubbish. Charles,' she said scornfully, 'still hasn't the remotest idea what he wants.'

'How are you finding life at the moment?'

'Well, I suppose surviving would be the best way of putting it, after all the Carling business.'

'You could hardly be surprised by all the publicity, if you get into any sort of relationship with an airhead like Will Carling.'

Crossly: 'I used to see Carling mostly for the children's sake.'

'Surely at some point you must want to be in a position in which you can have a recognized relationship with someone?'

Giggle. 'It'll have to be someone whose wife's dead – safely six feet under. Or again, I like a challenge. Maybe I should marry a queer and convert him.'

Patrick Jephson: 'Well, you know plenty of them.'

MH: 'I gather Douglas Hurd has been very helpful in sorting out a role for you – we had some talk about it a few months ago.'

'Douglas has been marvellous, and Malcolm Rifkind's carrying on. What I really want to do is to travel abroad as an ambassador for Britain.'

'Who do you hobnob most with, these days?'

Giggle. 'I see quite a lot of Fergie.'

'God Almighty.'

More giggles: 'Well, she does know her way around that family.'

'Most of us would think it was a disaster if she came back to it.'

'Oh, that won't happen. But it suits her and Andrew to do things together for the children's sake.'

'Does she have to flog her wares around the world the way she does?'

'She needs the money.'

Diana said that in her own life, all that really mattered was the children: 'They really are pretty OK, you know.'

'Well, I don't know many children who aren't pretty deeply affected by marriage break-ups. Mine certainly were. It's very difficult not to let a competition develop between parents in handling the children.'

'William's really happy at Eton. He's so sweet – going to his first real party at half-term, very anxious about whether I've remembered to get his dinner jacket for him. At least I don't have to worry about what happens to him, with a large detective just behind him.'

I suggested that all she needed to maintain public support was to avoid scoring own goals: 'Surely it's best to leave it to the Prince of Wales to make the mistakes by wheeling out Mrs Parker-Bowles, which I'm sure he will do?' Somehow, the subject of animals crept into the conversation. I said: 'You've never been much into animals, have you?' Giggles and lowered eyelashes: 'Well, I did once win the prize at school for Best-Kept Hamster.'

She asked what I would do if I was making a plan for the monarchy over the next five years. I suggested that the Royal Family needed to recover the art of making people feel good, which the Queen Mother alone possessed. Nobody expected the Queen to change, but the younger ones – especially the Prince of Wales – had to learn how to relate to people, how to become less self-obsessed. I also thought that the Royal Family had to focus more on things in British life which relate to the present and the future, rather than forever to the past: 'The only time they look really lively is when they go racing.'

She came out into the courtyard to say goodbye. Mawkishly, I said: 'If Pavarotti is allowed to kiss you, may I?' She assented with another giggle, then peered into the back of my Range Rover in some dismay: 'You're going fishing!' She had been through all that before, in the life from which she was struggling to escape. 'You weren't supposed to see all that,' I said.

I saw her several times more before her death, and indeed she came to lunch with my senior staff at the *Standard* shortly after I moved newspapers ('It was a great thrill to meet so many famous people!' she wrote in a memorably arch thank-you note. 'I hope I passed the exam, although you must forgive me if some of the answers lacked the detail necessary to satisfy the examiners completely!'). I suppose I can claim the distinction of having had my worthy words of advice, such as they were, rejected by both the Prince and Princess of Wales.

Months after my last lunch with her, I experienced a irresistibly comic moment, on the way to the West End from the office. My driver, Bill Anderson, suddenly said: 'Look, sir! Look! Princess Di's waving at you!' I glanced out of the car window. There indisputably, alongside in her Rover, fluttering a hand as well as her eyelashes, was the princess. I beamed back, amid much giggling from a woman colleague in my car. Princesses make fools of us all. It was the last time I ever saw her.

The criticism is often made that the Royal Family's troubles are brought upon them by poor advice. In my time as an editor, the Queen's successive Private Secretaries Robert Fellowes and Robin Janvrin seemed to possess admirable good sense and judgement. The obstacle in the path of private secretaries is the manner in which their current role is defined. They possess influence without power. The Queen needs a top-class chief executive, who enjoys the same scope and authority as a Whitehall permanent secretary. The Royal Family professes to see itself as 'the family firm', yet it has done nothing to impose upon the conduct of its own affairs the disciplines that are essential to any successful business, never mind a key element of the nation's constitutional framework. It is hard to overstate the difficulties caused for the monarch's staff by the fact that there is so little communication, never mind harmony, among her family. Towards the end of 1994, I was lunching with a courtier. I mentioned that the impending divorce between Brigadier Andrew Parker-Bowles and his wife Camilla seemed likely to cause him some headaches. His plate almost cascaded to the floor. I said that I was not absolutely sure the divorce was going ahead. I had published nothing about it in the paper. But I had been told on the social grapevine, some weeks earlier, that proceedings were imminent. My companion said bleakly: 'We'd be at Ipswich Crown Court on October 27th 1935.' He was thinking of Mrs Ernest Simpson. A month or two later, when the divorce was indeed announced, he rang me and said: 'I don't want you to think I was holding out on you when we had lunch. I was told nothing until a week ago.' This was a matter which plainly had vital implications for the monarchy, yet he had been wilfully kept in ignorance of it. No adviser, however skilled, can work effectively in such a climate. Senior Palace figures urged the Queen to stop shopping at Harrods, and to avoid further contact with Mohammed Fayed at the Windsor Horse Show, but for years she declined to heed them. Advisers and friends warned the Prince of Wales that it was inappropriate for him to borrow the vast yacht of such a controversial figure as the Greek tycoon John Latsis, but summer after summer he ignored them, in pursuit of his free holidays. If the Royal Family is inadequately advised, it is their own fault.

By the time I abandoned editorship, I found that my own attitude to the monarchy mirrored that of much of the public. My respect for the Queen was undiminished, and very great. A courtier told me one day that debate in the media about the monarch's possible abdication was well wide of the mark: 'Some of your lot don't understand,' he said, 'she *likes* being Queen.' I was relieved to hear it, because I had become one of those doubtful of the fitness of the Prince of the Wales for the throne, a scepticism undiminished in recent years by the ruthless and undignified campaign of media management conducted from St James's Palace under the auspices of Mr Mark Bolland. I cannot believe that the interests of monarchy are best served by marketing the Prince, and his relationship with Mrs Parker-Bowles, through undeclared pacts with selected newspapers. It seemed extraordinary that a royal servant was in 2001 allowed to accept a prize from the public relations industry, for successfully promoting the lover of the heir to the throne. The Prince's self-indulgence, his financial extravagance and egotism are no worse than those of many other rulers in history, but if he becomes king these weaknesses will be displayed at a far more dangerous period for the monarchy. That the man who wishes to be king should so far have abandoned touch with reality that he declines to read any newspaper, lest he discover something disagreeable to himself within it, suggests an increasingly tenuous connection with planet Earth. His impulsive correspondence with ministers about issues that excite him, such as foxhunting, seem to reflect a dangerous naivety about the perils of royal interventions in political issues. In theory, a single ill-suited incumbent of the throne neither could nor should risk making his people republicans. But public support for the monarchy, and for the Royal Family, has become so precarious that events could move at remarkable speed in the wrong direction, if a new ruler behaves unwisely, or misunderstands his function within the constitutional framework. The Queen's historic success in occupying the throne has been achieved by doing very little. The Prince of Wales's eagerness to be seen to *do* things, to pursue policies often founded on undisciplined thought and ill-informed sentiment, seems perilous for the future of the monarchy. To be well-intentioned is not enough.

George Walden once shrewdly pointed out at a *Telegraph* leader conference that the greatest problem for the monarchy today is not public animosity, of which there is very little, but public indifference, of which there is a great deal, especially among the young. The great success of the Golden Jubilee in June 2002 highlighted public goodwill towards the Queen, but does not negate the validity of Walden's observation. The Royal Family remains highly vulnerable to follies by its younger members, especially the heir to the throne. Many of those who shrug about a possible marriage between the Prince of Wales and Mrs Parker-Bowles – 'Why not just let them do what they like?' – are people who care little about the future of the monarchy. 'Just remember,' a senior courtier once said to me, wagging a finger, 'all the media speculation about morganatic marriages is nonsense – if Charles marries Camilla, she will be queen. And I don't think the country will like it.' The newspapers which are today pressing for the Prince to remarry are motivated solely by the commercial lure of a new chapter in the royal soap opera.

It would be foolish to dispute that relentless media scrutiny of the Royal Family has contributed to the unhappy state of some of its principal members today. Most of us take for granted a measure of privacy, even – or perhaps especially – when we are enduring family crises and personal tragedies. Yet in the case of the Royal

Family, as I wrote in a leader in the *Telegraph* in 1993, 'One day as a society we may awaken and find that we have committed an act of cannibalism: having relentlessly devoured whatever portions of the Royal Family are set before us in the public prints, we shall profess amazement when a breakfast comes at which the plate, and the crown, are empty.' Ignorance of the truth caused me – and thus *The Daily Telegraph* – to misread the behaviour of the Princess of Wales when her marriage began to collapse. Of course she acted foolishly, but our trade must share with the Royal Family some responsibility for her fate – not for her death, but for her descent into folly. Her experience seemed to demonstrate that no commoner, even a member of an aristocratic family, can any longer support the burden of being cast into the vast, terrifying soap opera of modern monarchy. To join such a masquerade possesses appeal only for ambitious young members of the public relations industry. I once made a remark to the National Theatre's director, Trevor Nunn, about the manic behaviour of many screen and stage stars. He said: 'Unless one has experienced it, it is impossible to understand what it is like to live with the highest degree of fame.' The Prince of Wales would no doubt endorse his words. I lament my own errors of judgement in the *Telegraph*'s coverage of the Royal Family at the height of their crisis. I do not, however, regret the paper's attempt to hold back from the assault on the surviving tatters of the Family's privacy, which the British media has sustained ever since.

Lord MacGregor, then Chairman of the Press Complaints Commission, denounced press treatment of the Waleses and the Morton saga back in 1992, by accusing newspapers of 'dabbling their fingers in the stuff of other people's souls'. He was made to appear ridiculous, soon afterwards, when indisputable proof was offered of the Princess's complicity in publication. Today, if only through his appointed staff, the Prince pursues an activist media policy whose consequences are not dissimilar: the heir to the throne can no longer promote a convincing claim to his own privacy. If only as citizens, and as purchasers of tabloid newspapers, we all share some responsibility for the pass to which the Royal Family, and the monarchy, have come. But the journey to the present state of affairs has reflected the ugliest aspect of the media industry's behaviour during my time as a journalist.

14

BATTLING WITH MURDOCH

By the summer of 1993, I had been editor of *The Daily Telegraph* for more than seven years. Our commercial position in the market place was formidably successful. The paper had more than doubled in size since 1986. When *The Independent* was launched six years earlier, it was widely predicted that it would critically wound, perhaps even destroy the *Telegraph*. Yet now we were still selling comfortably over a million copies a day, more than the *Times* and *Independent* combined. The company was heading for an annual profit of some £60 million, against a £12 million loss in the year I took over. Since 1987, our editorial staff had increased in numbers only marginally, from 305 to 319, but the quality of the journalists had improved immensely. The editorial budget had soared from £17 million to almost £35 million. Likewise, *Sunday Telegraph* staff numbers had risen from 65 in 1987 to 80 seven years later, its budget from less than £5 million to more than £9 million.

At last, we were edging towards the major colour capability for which we had waited, lagging behind rivals, for so long. Our Monday Sports section was the envy of Fleet Street, even more so was our Saturday publication with its own TV, Arts, Weekend, Motoring and Children's sections. All these elements are now taken for granted in Saturday packaging throughout the industry, but the *Telegraph* led the field. Our response to any breaking story, from both News and Features, was envied throughout the business for speed and quality. The policy with which we had persisted since 1986, of steadily developing and modernizing the paper,

Matt on the Newspaper of the Year Award.

rather than adopting a 'big bang' approach which would have
appalled our traditional readers, had paid off handsomely for
Conrad, for the company, and for me. I resisted calls from our
Marketing Department for a fresh visual makeover every year or
two. I took to heart Don Berry's dictum that redesigns are the last
resorts of scoundrels. Newspaper design, Don often observed,
must be content-led, and not allowed to become a self-fulfilling
device to create change for its own sake, every time circulation
hiccups. Managements of ailing titles often fall into this trap, and
do not fool their readers. We aimed to make small incremental
changes only when these seemed worthwhile.

Political tensions within the paper remained irksome. My
scepticism about Simon Heffer's suitability as an executive
remained undiminished by experience, but our team was strong
enough to carry him. That year, the *Telegraph* won the industry's
Newspaper of the Year Award. These prizes are normally decided
by a show of hands among managing editors, but in 1993 the

award was presented after a ballot among the editors of every British newspaper and magazine. We valued it accordingly. Stephen Glover speculated almost weekly in the *Evening Standard*'s media pages about how long such as an unconvincing Conservative thinker as myself could keep my job. I knew that Conrad's right-wing friends continued to urge a change of editorship upon him. Yet for all our spats, he was remarkably loyal. He would remain so, I believed, unless I showed signs of failing him commercially. I had set myself a private target of completing ten years at the *Telegraph*, then moving on – to what, I was unsure, though most likely back to writing books and broadcasting. Among the paper's senior team there had been few changes since 1986, save on the Comment pages. I felt cheerfully comfortable with all our top people – Veronica Wadley, Don Berry, Nigel Wade, Jeremy Deedes, Neil Collins, George Jones. More than that, I felt a warm affection for them. In my younger days, I had been thought a poor team player, yet working with this group had proved among the happiest experiences I had ever known. We were professionals, with minimal interest in ideology, merely a passionate commitment to producing a great newspaper. I tried to distribute both praise and blame generously. I often remarked that my objective was to make our good people happy, and to make our bad people feel sufficiently unloved to go away. Above all, I sought to make working for the paper seem fun. I perceived my principal role as that of transmitting energy, ideas, laughter. Jeremy Deedes and Don Berry saw their jobs as being to dissuade me from my extravagances, and to 'hose Max down' as necessary. There was a notable occasion when we published reprints of 1939 *Daily Telegraph* issues to commemorate the first days of World War II, which proved popular with readers. I conceived the demented idea of continuing the facsimiles for every day of the succeeding six years, until the fiftieth anniversary of VE Day. Don and Jeremy mopped their brows after dissuading me from that one. Our relationship represented a vital balancing act.

We had built up a remarkable stable of top-class writers: Paul

Hayward, Henry Winter, Robert Philip, Michael Parkinson, Christopher Martin-Jenkins (as well as that extraordinary old evergreen, E. W. Swanton) on Sport; Gillian Reynolds on radio, Stephen Pile on TV; Cassandra Jardine, Liz Grice, Martyn Harris and many more in Features; I welcomed every contribution we could extract from Matt Ridley on science, and we regularly featured Steve Jones and Lewis Wolpert, as well as our excellent Technology Correspondent, Christine McGourty, and Science Editor Roger Highfield, who had become a star; Clifford Longley wrote on religion; Norman Lebrecht on music. Alex Chancellor, Oliver Pritchett, Boris Johnson, Stephen Robinson, Claudia Fitz-herbert, Lesley Garner, Jonathan Porritt, Oz Clarke were among our best by-lines. When a paper has built up a bank of talent as strong as that, it is not difficult to maintain a further influx of recruits to reinforce it. My only substantial regret about staffing was that we had failed to recruit journalists from minority com-munities – a major shortcoming of most British newspapers. Later, at the *Evening Standard*, I introduced a modest training scheme specifically for black and Asian journalists, because I had come to believe that only 'affirmative action' would produce results.

Our *Telegraph*'s most significant weakness was, I think, that it generated fewer scoops than I would have liked. We spurned the use of the label 'exclusive' so much favoured by rivals, because so few alleged 'exclusives' are, in reality, either new or true. I often discussed with Don Berry how we might break more big stories, and get more credit for those which we did produce. Back in 1986, I had thought of creating an investigations team on the lines of the old *Sunday Times* 'Insight'. From his own long experience, Don dissuaded me. While he believed strongly in investigative journalism, he argued that if investigations groups are institution-alized, they become expensive, inbred, and not infrequently end up by suffering collective nervous breakdowns, brought on by an excessive diet of villains, real and imagined. I am sure Don's judgement was correct. Because the *Telegraph* does not trumpet its scoops, small and large, the paper gets less credit than it deserves for the number of story it breaks first. Don pointed out to me how often our pioneering efforts were followed up across Fleet Street next day, without attribution to us. But looking back, I wish our paper had been seen to lead the pack more often.

The other criticism of which I was conscious was that the paper had grown more trivial, had moved downmarket under my editorship. Today, I occasionally meet old readers who bemoan the 'Hurleyization' of the *Telegraph*, and say comfortingly they are sure that it would never have happened in my day. I am afraid that it would, and it did. The evidence is overwhelming, and had already become so in 1994, that middle-market newspaper readers possess a mounting appetite for trivia about showbusiness, celebrities, royals. Personality journalism needs to be dressed in more respectable garb for *The Daily Telegraph* than for the *Sun* or *Mirror*. But Veronica Wadley was foremost, rightly, in urging upon me the need for change in this direction. If we were to hold our position in the struggle against *The Times* – which had been moving visibly and consciously downmarket – and the *Mail*, we needed more glamour pictures, more gossip, more women's features, more showbusiness and television coverage. A title which does not respond to market pressures of this kind is threatened with the kind of atrophy that has befallen *The Independent* over the past decade. Veronica deserves much of the credit for the *Telegraph*'s new-found sensitivity to women, to the young, to all manner of new minority groups and special interests. When our environmental coverage won prizes, when our health and food and drink coverage gained attention and admiration, I knew we were getting somewhere. It may be argued that a public which becomes preoccupied with such issues is hedonistic and narcissistic, that its interests reflect the absence of an external threat to the nation, a commitment to trivia unworthy of a responsible society. But it is the business of any successful newspaper to reflect the world as it is, rather than to attempt the impossible task of changing the values of a generation.

It was almost always senior executives, rather than me, who

originated the ideas about new sections, recruits, special coverage. My job, that of any editor, was to make sure that I was listening, and acted upon their advice. My overwhelming claim upon Conrad's support was that I delivered commercial success. Our management had felt able to maintain the *Telegraph*'s cover price above that of *The Times*, and thus to produce record profits, at the cost of a circulation loss they considered acceptable. We were feeling triumphalist towards News International. *The Times* was in the hands of its third editor since I took over the *Telegraph*. Our circulation lead over Murdoch's title had widened by 40,000 copies since 1986. There was no sign that any of our rival's revamps, stunts, recruiting drives had borne significant fruit. All Murdoch's threats to break us had proved to be Australian wind.

How rash can one get? It was now our turn to see hubris punished. Even as we basked in complacency that *The Times* posed no serious editorial threat, Murdoch struck. On a Monday morning in September 1993, without warning, he reduced the cover price of *The Times* from 45p to 30p, against our 48p. This represented a headlong assault on *The Daily Telegraph*. If *The Times* could not defeat us editorially, Murdoch proposed dramatically to change the commercial odds. Poker-faced, he declared that he considered British newspapers overpriced. In some countries, what he did would have been illegal under competition legislation. He began to use his vast profits in the tabloid sector to cross-subsidize the sale of *The Times* at a loss – which our informed guess estimated at £30 million a year. It might even be argued that the British taxpayer was underwriting his assault. Murdoch had contrived tax arrangements for his international operations which ensured that his British companies' profits yielded a negligible dividend to the Exchequer. Our titles, meanwhile, possessed no other source of revenue from which to draw subsidy. Indeed, Conrad's British newspapers were the principal cash generators for his interests around the world. We faced serious trouble.

Before 1986, the success of the *Telegraph* had been achieved by the first Lord Camrose's genius, in producing a quality newspaper which sold on the streets at a price which undercut all its rivals. When Camrose bought the *Daily* in 1929, he began by cutting the price from 2d to 1d. Thereafter, its price remained significantly below that of *The Times*, and never much greater than that of the *Daily Mail* and *Express*. Even when Conrad took over in 1985, the *Telegraph* was selling for 20p, against *The Times*'s 23p. In the face of desperate financial necessity, the price of our paper was quickly raised to 30p, in exchange for a modest loss of circulation. By 1989, however, the *Telegraph was* charging 32p – 35p on Saturdays – against 22p for the *Mail* and *Express*, 30p for *The Times*. Thereafter, the differential in *The Times*'s favour persisted. Our management, and especially Joe Cooke, who became Managing Director in 1989 after Andrew Knight's departure, argued that if we produced a strong enough news-paper, we could charge a much higher price for it. 'A premium price for a premium brand' was Joe's slogan. For four years, his policy delivered astonishing financial results. The cover price was increased twice more, first to 35p, then to 40p, and finally in February 1993 to 48p against *The Times*'s 45p, and the *Daily Mail*'s 30p. And still we seemed to be getting away with it. The *Telegraph* suffered only modest circulation losses for huge revenue gains, and held our market share. By the summer of 1993, despite our latest price hike we were selling 1,030,000 copies, against *The Times*'s 373,000. I warned repeatedly at management meetings about the dangers of 'trying to milk the cow three times a day'. The 'premium price' argument seemed a spurious justification for taking a huge market risk. Our final price hike, to 48p, represented not the pursuit of a healthy profit, but undisguised greed. It was the negation of the historic and hugely successful Camrose policy of selling a broadsheet newspaper at a tabloid price. We were now marketing the *Telegraph* at a stiff premium to all our competitors, for no better reason than that we supposed that we could get away with doing so. Some media pundits commented unfavourably on our circulation performance in the early 1990s. They appeared to fail to notice – or anyway did not mention in print – that between

1986 and 1994 the *Daily Telegraph* shifted from being the cheapest broadsheet in the market, to becoming significantly the most expensive save the *FT*.

Joe Cooke had done our company great service in 1986–87, through his influence as a management consultant on our move out of Fleet Street, the change to new technology and consequent mass redundancies. Since then, however, I had not been an admirer of his policies, which seemed to be driven exclusively by pursuit of the company's bottom line. He would have argued, no doubt, that this represented his mandate from Conrad Black. In any event, there had been no love lost between the two of us since Cooke became Managing Director. I believed then, and would maintain now, that his siren song about the merits of making *The Daily Telegraph* the most expensive title in our market represented an almost fatal stroke of commercial arrogance for the company. As far back as May 1990, I had written to Conrad warning that I believed Cooke's 'premium pricing' strategy was highly dangerous:

> We need to look to the perils ahead for the whole industry, in which we shall share. We have to consider the strengthening City view of British national newspapers, which is that having leapt ahead on the back of the new technology, we are once more approaching a plateau, on which revenues and profits are in danger of stagnation over say, a ten year span. The overall newspaper market in this country is likely to continue its gentle, but inexorable, slippage.
>
> I strongly believe that we underrate the extent to which even prosperous newspaper readers are influenced by price, out of all proportion to the real influence on their pockets. I am struck by the fact that all my middle-class friends in Ireland read the *Telegraph* chiefly, they avow, because as a result of a freak of local pricing, it is the cheapest quality title there. My acquaintance in England – even those who own racehorses – complain bitterly about the price distinction between the *Times* and *Telegraph*, to our disadvantage.

Nearly a year later, in another note to Conrad in February 1991, I returned to the charge: 'I believed we have pursued and are pursuing incompatible pricing and marketing strategies. The *DT*'s great historical success . . . was achieved through a pricing policy that persisted for almost half a century, of charging the same as the *Mail* and *Express*, significantly less than other "qualities". The paper was, in other words, priced as a "popular quality", a true alternative for *Mail* and *Express* readers.' I urged that we should adopt a policy of offering identifiable young readers, for whom pricing was especially significant, a heavily discounted paper at 25p or even 20p.

The problem, of course, was that our own 'premium pricing' policy could only continue to work, laying the *Telegraph*'s golden eggs, for as long as our 'quality' rivals were willing to play the same game. Now, in the autumn of 1994, Rupert Murdoch had torn up the rule book. The question for the *Telegraph* was: could we afford to hold our course, and what would the rest of our competitors do? *The Independent*, always struggling financially, was in no position to cut its cover price. The *Financial Times*'s specialist market was so secure that it had no need to do so. *The Guardian* was too remote politically to be considered a direct rival for our readers. But after years in which *The Times* seemed unable to match the *Telegraph*'s editorial performance, it was characteristic of Murdoch to strike ruthlessly and unexpectedly in a new direction. The self-serving doctrine cherished for so long by proprietors and managers, that broadsheet newspapers were not price sensitive, was to be put to the test.

For the first few months of the *Times* price cut, our circulation seemed only moderately affected. Our sale for the first six months of 1994 was down only by 9,000 on the second-half figure for 1993. *The Times*'s circulation rose by 72,000 in the same period, to 485,000. Conrad himself wrote defiantly on our leader page: 'It does not seem to us that Mr Murdoch's formidable strengths lie in the field of quality newspaper publication . . . *The Daily Telegraph* is unafraid.' Thereafter, however, *The Times*' sale began to climb relentlessly, and our decline accelerated. Anecdotally, I was dismayed almost daily to meet rich men who told me laughingly that they had switched to *The Times* because 'your newspaper is so expensive'. The odd thing was, they meant it. Like everybody else, they loved a bargain. In a long memo to Conrad and our directors, I wrote:

> The success of [Murdoch's] price-cutting operation has clearly demonstrated that newspapers *are* price sensitive. He has openly and ruthlessly sought to seize *The Daily Telegraph*'s traditional ground, as a low-price popular quality newspaper, closely mimicking our own editorial approach and style. The *Times* has improved as a product, to the point at which *The Daly Telegraph* may remain superior, but is certainly not 60% superior. The *Times* today offers a better-printed news-paper, with consistently fuller coverage in a wide range of areas, more open lay-out because of lower ad-ing on key early pages, some better columnists than the *Telegraph*, and a Saturday package which offers a real alternative to the *DT* at a much lower price . . . I can think of a good many things to be done to improve our marginal position . . . but I find it difficult at present to conceive any editorial improvement which will satisfactorily dispose of the long-term threat.

I concluded that in the short term, we must pursue all possible forms of disguised discounting of our titles, to sustain circulation. But we could not rule out the need overtly to cut our cover price, if the *Telegraph*'s haemorrhage of readers continued. The financial pain of such a course would be bitter indeed. Neil Collins remarked tartly: 'There must be something better you can do with £40 million than hand it to your customers.' In the months that followed, we continued to send brave noises from Canary Wharf, but we were paddling furiously underwater to find a way out. The company made both formal and informal enquiries among the competition authorities and the government, to dis-cover whether Murdoch might be prevented from running *The*

Times as a loss-leader. I drafted a long note for Michael Heseltine, as President of the Board of Trade, setting out the issues as we perceived them. But British law seemed to offer no scope for deflecting Murdoch, and anyway no politician felt inclined to confront News International on such an issue, merely to serve the interests of Conrad Black and the *Telegraph*.

By June 1994, it seemed plain to us that we could not maintain our price. It was not merely the headline circulation numbers which convinced us – *The Times'* 545,000 against our 1,041,000 – it was the accelerating trend against the *Telegraph* and in favour of Murdoch's title. This was the point our Advertising and Marketing directors emphasized. If we delayed action until, say, October, our own circulation could have fallen to around 900,000, while theirs would be above 600,000. We were not convinced that even a big marketing push – there was talk of £10 million worth – could match the impact of *Times* discounting. Our readership figures – the measure by which advertising agencies decide their spend – were also falling. The Advertising Director told us that he did not believe he could maintain our tremendous rate premiums – between 200 per cent and 300 per cent of the page costs charged by other broadsheets – unless we halted the circulation slide. We seemed overwhelmingly vulnerable on Saturdays, by far our strongest sale day. Our Saturday circulation was around 1.2 million, and we charged 70p for the paper. Yet *The Times* was now offering its own Saturday package for 30p. Readers were chasing the bargain.

Conrad was in Palm Beach on the June morning when Joe Cooke, our Advertising Director Len Sanderson and Marketing Director Stephen Grabiner sat down at the table with Jeremy Deedes and me to discuss the crisis – for crisis it had become. A friend who saw Murdoch in Los Angeles at this time gave me a personal insight into the man's mood. News International's boss believed he had delivered a knockout blow. In Los Angeles, he expressed ebulliently his conviction that the *Telegraph* could not afford to respond to *The Times'* discounting campaign, that at last he had found the means to break us. My friend's account intensified my own determination to prove Murdoch wrong.

After an hour of debate, Joe Cooke proved to be the only one of those around the table who did not favour an immediate cut in our own cover price. Joe was gracious enough to confess afterwards that his own resistance was partially influenced by knowledge of what a discounting war was bound to do to our company's share price. In that respect, all of us around the table were in the same boat. We held options on shares which, at the market price then prevailing, promised to yield me (to name but one) some £500,000 in capital gains the following year. Those hopes would disappear out of the window, along with our profits, if we began discounting. With bitter regret, yet confident that there was no choice, we called the Chairman in the US to deliver a recommendation which, belatedly, Joe made unanimous. We should cut the week-day price of the paper to 30p with immediate effect. I do not think Conrad was surprised to hear this view, yet it was indeed our advice to him and in no sense his own unilateral decision which prompted the launch of *The Daily Telegraph*'s discounting campaign three days later.

The latter point is important, because a big City row followed our announcement. Just a month before, those self-consciously blue-chip brokers Cazenove had handled the sale of some £30 million worth from Conrad's personal shareholding in the company, to British institutions. The purchasers paid a price which I, for one, thought remarkably generous, in view of the fierce battle with Murdoch in which we were engaged, which was bound to cost us a lot of money – and which the City was watching intently. Now, as *Telegraph* shares slumped, the buyers of Conrad's stock vented their spleen. Two days after our announcement Cazenove announced, in their customary fastidious fashion, that they wished to do no further business with our company. Those of us on the inside track were disgusted, not because of loyalty to Conrad, but because of our knowledge of the facts. In May, when Conrad placed his shares, no decision had been made to cut our cover price. We were still hoping to avoid such desperate measures. A month later, it was our own management team in London who rang Conrad to recommend drastic action, not the other way around. I recollected that a Cazenove representative had been in our building that day. He gave no hint of concern that a price cut would create an ethical problem for his firm's partners. Above all, those of us who had knowingly accepted a painful personal financial hit, offering advice for the company's welfare which blew to pieces the value of our own stock, felt bitterly irked that the move should now be interpreted as a piece of financial chicanery by Conrad. Everything that had been done was driven not by secret intelligence, available only to *Telegraph* executives, but by publicly available circulation and readership data. Anyone in the City who could not see in May that, if the *Telegraph* management was behaving responsibly, we should be obliged to take some expensive action to respond to *The Times* was not reading his newspapers intelligently. I believed then, and I still believe today, that Cazenove dumped Conrad as a cynical gesture to appease its angry clients, rather than because anything had been done which represented an affront to City ethics. This affair did nothing to diminish my own scepticism about the behaviour of City institutions, on which I had received an early education twenty years earlier, when I made a BBC TV film about Robert Maxwell. Never go tiger-shooting with a banker in an Old Etonian tie, even if he is a close personal friend of the Queen. He will turn out to own a minority stake in the tiger.

Our price cut from 1 July did not stop the march of *The Times*, whose circulation was climbing towards 700,000 and beyond. Murdoch's response to our initiative was to reduce *The Times'* price once more, from 30p to 20p. But the *Telegraph's* action checked the fall in our own sale, and indeed this rose 60,000 in the weeks after we began discounting. We dug into our trenches for a long, bitter campaign of attrition. Cost savings were the order of the day. I told our staff that we had entered a struggle in which every copy counted. We must pull out all the stops. We were confident that *The Daily Telegraph* as a product had never been better – but we also knew that *The Times* had raised its game. Murdoch's paper was accepting additional cash losses in order to run more pages than us in almost every key area – Home News, Foreign, Politics – regardless of cost. It was a nerve-racking business, seeking to compete on such a lopsided battlefield against a man prepared to throw everything into the struggle in order to destroy his opponent. This was capitalism red in tooth and claw.

Slowly, however, through the latter months of 1994, our nerve strengthened. We gained confidence that Murdoch's assault might continue to bleed our company, but could not destroy us. It seemed increasingly grotesque, that both the *Times* and *Telegraph* were spending tens of millions in a struggle which benefited the consumer in the short term, but threatened to diminish quality severely in the longer run, as the cash cost made its inevitable downstream impact on editorial budgets. It was Murdoch's objective also, of course, to diminish consumer choice by destroying *The Times*' principal competitor. In reality, such a dramatic outcome never seemed plausible to anyone save the News International boss in one of his more megalomaniacal moods. The price war, it was soon apparent, would not end in decisive victory for either rival. Yet Conrad was deeply dismayed by the drain on his resources. He sought through backdoor channels to persuade Murdoch that the campaign of mutual attrition should stop. But Rupert, as ever, was in the game for the long haul. He was impressed by the big *Times* sales gain on the back of price-cutting. He knew – and Conrad hated to acknowledge this – that he possessed deeper pockets than we did. The *Telegraph* team settled down to run our newspapers in a new world, in which roles remained unchanged, but the rewards for our company were vastly diminished.

15

GOING

BY EARLY 1995, my personal difficulties in supporting the Conservative government were mounting. I admired individual ministers, in particular Kenneth Clarke as Chancellor of the Exchequer. But even that relentlessly ebullient soul was becoming ground down by the shortcomings of John Major, the relentless and debilitating leaks from within the Cabinet, and what the Chancellor perceived as the impossibility of conducting serious political debate amid a hostile and frivolous media. I had several meetings with Tony Blair, Labour's new leader, and was always impressed. I had first encountered him as a fellow-panellist on *Any Questions?* at King's Lynn, back in the days when he was Home Affairs spokesman. I was amazed by how little he said on the air with which I, as a Tory, could disagree. He exuded common sense.

Even in Blair's early days as leader, there was a powerful sense of stage management about our encounters, not wholly dissimilar from that which prevailed when meeting the Princess of Wales. The bustling family atmosphere in the Blair household at 1 Richmond Crescent in Islington, with cafetière coffee, the Leader of the Opposition in shirtsleeves, Cherie and the children coming and going, was charmingly normal, but in somewhat the same fashion as an exceptionally skilfully directed television sitcom. Blair asked me what he could do if he found himself dealing as Prime Minister with the same rabidly Eurosceptic press as John Major. I answered that it was a misfortune of the times that almost all the ablest polemicists of the day seemed to come from the Eurosceptic stable. The devil had the best tunes. But I believed that the Right's real influence on the electorate was much smaller than most people believed. I suggested that a government with a strong message to deliver, which contrived the right political circumstances, could prevail – in a referendum, for instance – even in the face of right-wing media hostility.

Blair's directness and decency were very attractive. He seemed a man comfortable with himself, carrying none of the sorry baggage of personal anger which crippled John Major. I made a mistake one day, by taking the Leader of the Opposition to lunch at Wilton's. It was not at all Blair's kind of place. He looked ill at ease, and glanced around without enthusiasm at the customers of that overwhelmingly Tory upmarket canteen. I was accustomed to the ways of Conservative ministers who ate and drank heartily, even before a big Commons performance. Blair nursed only a glass of water with his plaice and chips, a gesture to austerity which we were to discover was characteristic of New Labour, however striking its self-indulgence in other respects. The Leader's views on every big issue, however, seemed so enlightened and sensible, after all we had known of the Labour Party for twenty-five years, as almost to defy credibility. That day at Wilton's in February 1995, he spoke of a 50 per cent top limit on taxation. Sceptical, I pressed him. He held firm. I would have laughed had he suggested that under his government, the top rate of tax would remain at 40 per cent. He asserted his confidence that the old Left was in terminal eclipse, though he said he needed at least another six months to achieve complete control of the party before being ready to take office. He expressed scorn for political correctness and determination to introduce wholesale welfare reform. I was personally sympathetic to his commitment to devolution and constitutional reform, above all removal of hereditary peers from the House of Lords, and his commitment to the long-term unemployed, whom the Tories had so shamefully neglected. He said he was confident that the new global economy made a return to large-scale industrial unrest impossible. I said that if his party abandoned its commitment to abolish foxhunting, I would vote for it myself. This was only partially facetious, because foxhunting has always seemed to me a touchstone of personal liberty, rather than an issue of animal welfare. I sensed that Blair, like Peter Mandelson and others, was bemused that any intelligent person could care a fig about such a matter, one way or the other.

Neither in 1995 nor afterwards did I ever pretend to Tony Blair that I was a convert to New Labour. Rather, like millions of others, I was a one-nation Tory who no longer found it possible to support the Conservative Party. By the summer of 1995, influenced not least by three long meetings with the Opposition Leader, I was convinced that he should become the next Prime Minister, and that he was incomparably more fit to hold the office than John Major. Yet where would that leave me, as Editor of *The Daily Telegraph*, when a general election came? Even in my most extravagant moments, I did not suppose that the paper could come out for Labour. Leave principle aside – the shock to our readership would be intolerable.

Meanwhile, the pressure on Conrad from the Tory Right was intensifying, and widely discussed throughout Fleet Street. 'The conflict within the *Telegraph* is well known,' wrote Bryan Appleyard in his *Independent* column that July of 1995.

> On the one hand there is an old, one-nation Tory editor, Max Hastings; on the other his new-right deputy, Simon Heffer, and a highly moralistic editor of the *Sunday Telegraph*, Charles Moore ... Above them all is the hard-right proprietor, Conrad Black. They are united in their contempt for John Major, but divided about solutions. Hastings wants a centrist Tory government that is, unlike this one, capable of shame and the honourable resignation. Heffer and Moore want a rightist, Euro-sceptic party.

I felt a growing unease about whether my editorship deserved any longer to be tenable, if the gap widened yet further between my own political perspective and that of our Chairman.

Late in June 1995, I was touched when Barbara Amiel took the trouble to invite me to lunch, and to assert the confidence of Conrad and herself in my regime. She said that they had been dismayed by rumours that I was thinking of moving on, perhaps to work for my close friend Michael Green of Carlton Communications. I told her I would rather have Michael as a lover than an employer. I said that I had no plans to move for a year or two, but it seemed hardly surprising that there was some jockeying for position going on, when I had been *Telegraph* Editor almost ten years.

As I said yesterday [I wrote to Barbara next morning], a significant body on the Right would love to wrest control of the *DT* from me, and into the hands of someone more committed to their own cause. It is scarcely surprising, given Conrad's known personal political views, that they should continue to nurture hopes in that direction, which people like Stephen Glover voice [in the *Evening Standard*]. Glover . . . wrote some while ago that he would like to see T. E. Utley back here . . . I remain resolutely convinced that if the nostalgics in that direction ever got their way, it would be commercially disastrous for the paper.

Conrad has been generous in making a public commitment to me. Where would journalists be, without relentless intrigue and melodrama? It remains a pleasure and a privilege to do the job, and I hope neither of you will ever doubt the durability of my gratitude to Conrad for all the fun we have had together since 1986.

I have just been re-reading Gibbon with much pleasure, for the first time in 30 years. I am enchanted by many of his phrases, but was especially taken by his account of the young Persian nobleman 'who never left the Sultan's presence without satisfying himself that his head was still attached to his shoulders.' Walking out of Wilton's yesterday, you never even saw me twist my neck, did you?

Yet circumstances change. On 31 July 1995, the Editor-in-Chief of Associated Newspapers, Sir David English, asked me for lunch at Mosimann's. I met David occasionally, to gossip about the industry. I had known him since we were both correspondents in the United States in 1968. In more recent times, that master of flattery and intrigue had always been nice about the *Telegraph*, and about what I had done with it. The only severe criticism he had made in recent years was to assert that we were mad to have followed Rupert Murdoch in discounting. He was proud of the fact that the *Daily Mail* had held its price – at 30p – together with its circulation. I told him what I believed then and believe now: we had no choice. In the mid-market, the *Mail* faced no very formidable competition, while *The Times* was the *Telegraph*'s head-on challenger. The strain of fighting the battle with News International was very great for all of us at Canary Wharf. A few weeks earlier, Conrad had summoned the top management team to the boardroom and addressed us in uncompromising terms: 'Right,' he said. 'I do not want any of you to speak until I have finished. I wish to make plain my absolute determination to adopt measures of sufficient gravity to convince our rivals of our intention to prevail in this ridiculous and costly contest with News International. I am determined to end this price war nonsense now. I intend to take steps that will make Rupert Murdoch see that he can gain nothing by persisting.' Conrad's proposal, which stunned us, was that we should cut the cover price of *The Daily Telegraph* still further, and give the *Sunday* away free. Mercifully, after protracted discussion the notion was dropped. A few weeks later, both the *Times* and *Telegraph* increased their cover prices by 5p, which somewhat eased the strain on our creaking balance sheet. Conrad said he believed that the struggle was in sight of a conclusion. The rest of us were less confident. We had lost some 4 per cent of our share of the quality market, while *The Times* had gained 10.4 per cent. Fighting a war of attrition against an opponent as rich and ruthless as Rupert Murdoch was a grim business, although I made light of it to David English.

I also felt conscious that I was running short of big new ideas for the paper. We had done so much, and come so far. We had built a marvellous team, which was producing good things every day. But whereas a few years before, I had a long shopping list of new plans and fresh faces, now I was chiefly in the business of managing what we had got. Was this good enough, when our rivals were keeping us under intensive bombardment? Could somebody else, another editor, bring new thinking to the paper? These doubts increasingly troubled me, amid relentless pressure from the management floor to come up with an editorial formula that would turn the tide against *The Times*, without costing us more money.

Over coffee that day at Mosimann's, David English suddenly said: 'Stewart Steven is going to retire at the end of the year as Editor of the *Standard*. Is there any chance you might be interested in taking it on? The gossip is that you're not getting on too well with Conrad. You've been doing the *Telegraph* a long time.' I was amazed, and immediately interested. I had always loved the *Evening Standard*. I was halfway through my tenth year at the *Telegraph*. A decade was a lot longer than I had ever imagined myself editing the paper. I had been thinking more and more about moving on. Sooner or later, I intended to return to writing books. But it would be wonderful fun, first to have the chance to run another newspaper for a few years. For me, who had seemed the unlikeliest of editors a decade earlier, the idea of being given a second Fleet Street title seemed exciting. I told David I was flattered. I asked the question every journalist asks at these moments: 'How much?'

David took pride in the fact that Associated never flinched about money. 'More than you're getting now,' he said. 'How much is that?'

'275k, a bonus, and quite a lot of share options. But don't you want somebody younger, like Dominic Lawson?'

'All we know about him is that he can edit a small weekly.'

'Sarah Sands?' I asked. Sarah was the highly regarded Associate Editor of the *Standard*.

'Her whole background is in Features. She knows nothing about News. We've got lots of people who might be up to it in a few years, but nobody who I think can do it now. You're a *Standard* man – you came from there, it's been part of your life. I think you'd have a terrific time doing it for, say, five to seven years, then you could do what you like. You know Associated never fires ex-editors – you'd be very well looked after. Of course there are other people we could ask, but frankly you're top of the list. I've told Vere Rothermere I think you're the right man, if you want it.'

I asked David how long he planned to stick around himself as Chairman – he was already sixty-five. He said he would carry on until the end of the century – 'though of course one can never be sure what might happen if Vere died. His son might have other ideas.' I said that I would consider his offer very seriously. David said I need not make up my mind until the autumn at least. I drove back to Canary Wharf thinking hard. I went on thinking through the weeks that followed.

It was an unexpected twist in a complex puzzle. One of the only two colleagues in whom I confided about English's offer laughed heartily at its ingenuity: 'He gets a double whammy – you away from the *Telegraph*, and you to the *Standard*. Don't under-estimate the attractions of running a monopoly title from an office in Kensington.' My friend, like all of us, loathed Canary Wharf. It would be frivolous to suggest that I was tempted to the *Standard* by the location of its offices, but I would not have thought of moving to another newspaper based in Docklands. What of the big issues, however? I loved the *Telegraph*. I believed that we were producing a great newspaper. But I also felt that I had done as much there as I ever would. All successful newspapers need to live in an almost constant state of revolution. To go on and on, merely because one did not want to abandon a gilded chair, seemed feeble, even irresponsible. A serious political difficulty loomed ahead, with the prospect of a general election at the latest by the spring of 1997. The *Telegraph* must always be a Conservative newspaper, yet I anticipated great difficulty in endorsing John

Major again. I thought the Tories had exhausted their policies, their energies, and their claims to rule Britain. Privately, many ministers felt the same.

Within the *Telegraph* building, amid the huge tensions of the price war, Conrad and the management executives were pressing me hard to 'freshen up' my own senior team, which had been largely unchanged since 1986. I accepted that there was a good objective case for new blood, but I also felt strongly that I could not start sacking men and women who had done a wonderful job for me, merely to make way for different faces. It had never troubled me to fire people who seemed incompetent, but if I began to dispense with those who had shown themselves both talented and loyal, what claim would I have on the respect or loyalty of those who stayed? In particular, Conrad was enthused by the notion of removing Veronica Wadley as Deputy Editor, in favour of the rising star Dominic Lawson. He was minded to transfer Simon Heffer back to *The Spectator*, in one capacity or another. I respected Dominic as a journalist, but I was doubtful that he would prove a convincing team player. A close confidant put it to me that summer: 'If you bring in Dominic, he will have only one idea in his head, which is how quickly he can get rid of you.' Meanwhile, I was devoted to Veronica Wadley, whose contribution to the *Telegraph* had been priceless. She was a supreme professional, who understood many aspects of newspapers and modern life which I did not.

Intense discussions of strategy and tactics for the *Telegraph* Group occupied much of our time through the late summer and early autumn. I made up my mind that I would not use English's offer of the *Evening Standard* as a bargaining ploy with Conrad. Even if this succeeded in the short term, it would poison our relationship. If Conrad was obliged to concede on either policy or salary merely to prevent my defection, the only enduring legacy would be his resentment. Life would become intolerable for both of us. I would play out the hand at the *Telegraph* for a month or

two longer, and see how the cards fell. I would then decide either
to stay, or move to the *Standard*, without engaging in any
negotiation.

Early in September, I lunched with Dominic Lawson. Nothing
that was said reassured me about the prospect of working closely
with him. He did not know much about newspapers. 'What is the
back bench? I don't think a lot of your magazine. I find nothing
to read in it. Couldn't you send Veronica Wadley off to edit it?
I'm not sure I'd want to do a lot of Sunday editing. Rosa likes to
go to the country at weekends. Couldn't I do the preparation for
Sunday, and leave someone else to do the actual editing on the
day? Can't we make Rebecca Nicolson, the *Spec* Features Editor,
Features Editor of the *Daily*?' I told Conrad afterwards that what
we needed at the *Daily* were not more ambitious heirs apparent,
of whom we had a surfeit, but professionals prepared to do the
hard daily grind of getting the paper out. Conrad pressed the case
for Dominic: 'Aw, what he needs is a couple of years being licked
into shape by you.' I had always considered that the Chairman
overrated the value of the Conservative polemicists on our payroll, and undervalued the superb, non-ideological executives and
journalists who made the paper what it was. At that moment, I
thought so more than ever.

Joe Cooke had by now left the company, much to my relief.
Stephen Grabiner, the former Marketing Director, had become
Managing Director. He was the second of the two colleagues with
whom I discussed David English's offer. He urged me to take it
seriously: 'I don't think there's going to be a lot of fun to be had
here in the next couple of years.' He thought the difficulties of
maintaining the price struggle against *The Times* very great. Our
promotion budget was running at £6 million, against *The Times*'s
£15 million. He argued that if I continued to resist Conrad's
demands for executive changes, while circulation slipped, my own
position would become vulnerable. Dan Colson, who sensed that
I was growing restive, sought to reassure me: 'It would be a disaster
if you left here in the next couple of years. And you know Conrad

never fires anyone close to him.' But Grabiner also told me that
Colson had been privately dismissive of any danger of my quitting:
'It's not as if Max had anywhere else to go.'

I spent the second week of September fishing in Scotland, and
thinking. Colson rang me at the lodge. He said that he and
Conrad believed Dominic should come to the paper, and that he
would insist upon the sole title of Deputy Editor. The day I
returned to the office, Conrad asked to see me. He suggested that
we should make an arrangement by which I was paid more money,
received an annual bonus, and signed an agreement to continue as.
Editor for at least the next two years, after which we could review
the position. But he added: 'It seems that you are in line for the
Andrew Knight–Joe Cooke award for avarice.' I sensed very
strongly that Conrad was making this new offer reluctantly, and
only because he thought I was on the brink of quitting. I asked
for a few days' grace. Stephen Grabiner told me that Conrad had
rung him, suspicious of my prevarication, and asked what was
going on. Grabiner answered that he thought I was considering an
offer, but he did not know from whom.

The following night, I dined with David English at the Savoy
Grill. He confirmed his offer, and agreed to match everything I
was given at the *Telegraph*, with an increase in salary. Next day,
I was lunching in the *Telegraph* dining room with a friend,
Annabel Astor, when Conrad came in to join us. He was at his
most charming and seductive. Afterwards, he asked me to come
and see him. He could not have been kinder or more flattering
about my editorship. He enquired when I would sign my new
contract. I mumbled, and suggested we should meet again in a day
or two. Conrad was so engaging that when I left his office all
my affection both for him and for the *Telegraph* had reasserted
themselves. I passionately wanted to stay, to carry on with my
wonderful team and this peerless newspaper.

Next morning, however, I had a long heart to heart with
Veronica. The more we talked, the more sure I was that there was
no way of reconciling Conrad's desire for change at the top with

my own loyalties and convictions. Stephen Grabiner came in as
she left. I told him that there were no circumstances in which I
felt willing to move Veronica to make way for anyone else. He
said: 'Now you've made your decision, I can tell you that if you'd
sacked Veronica, I for one would never have thought the same of
you again.' I rang David English's office. We settled various details
of my contract with Associated Newspapers. We agreed that I
would come to his office the next day for a meeting with Vere
Rothermere, and a signature on the deal. On Thursday morning,
28 September 1995, I muddled with difficulty through the business of editing the paper, then drove to Brooks's where I had a
drink with Bob Ayling, Chief Executive of British Airways. At
2 p.m., Bill Anderson took me on to Barker's in Kensington,
citadel of Associated Newspapers. David English's secretary showed
us the way into the underground car park, and thence by goods
lift to the Editor-in-Chief's wonderfully over-the-top office, apparently designed by the man who conceived tycoons' quarters for
Dallas. David, who adored conspiracy, was loving every moment
of this one. 'You'll like it here,' he said gleefully, in that engaging
gravel voice, 'the journalists run the place, and the managers do
what we tell them.' Then we walked down the corridor to the
office of Vere Rothermere, for a formal kissing of hands. We
chatted with Vere for a few minutes, then I disappeared once
more into the goods lift, to keep an appointment with the dentist.
Conrad rang me in the car, deeply suspicious that something was
afoot. I mumbled indistinctly, and arranged to meet him at 11
a.m. next morning. At 6 p.m., still full of novocaine after a painful
filling, I fulfilled one obligation that I thought was due. Charles
Moore, in open-neck shirt on a day off, turned up at the Royal
Lancaster Hotel for a drink, baffled about my purpose in seeking
an urgent and obscure rendezvous.

Though we disagreed profoundly about politics, Charles had
always behaved to me with punctilious loyalty. Now, I thought I
owed him a warning that I was going, so that he had a few hours
in which to gather his own thoughts, and to marshal his ambitions,

before the news became public. Charles was suitably amazed. After twenty minutes, I left him and went home. I sat limp, emotionally exhausted, while Penny cooked supper and we played a ritual game of Scrabble. I felt a little Lear-like, giving up a kingdom where I had been so happy, and which meant so much. Part of me wanted to put back the clock, to undo the events of the past few days. But at root, I was sure that the decision was right – for me, for Conrad, and for *The Daily Telegraph*. For almost ten years, I had edited the paper despite the gulf between my personal political views and his own. I found nothing unreasonable about the man who owns a newspaper wanting it to reflect, in substantial measure, his own world view. If I had not conducted editorial policy in accordance with Conrad's wishes, I had sought at least to avoid trampling upon his most sensitive convictions. It had proved possible to accommodate Simon Heffer in our executive ranks, at one remove from the operational chain of command. But Conrad now wanted to impose his own appointment at the heart of the paper. It was time to move on. Our respective visions could no longer be reconciled. The two of us could have muddled along together for a while longer. Perhaps we should have done so, but for David English's offer, and the knowledge that in the *Evening Standard* I could express freely my own convictions.

At 11.40 on the morning of 29 September, I walked into Conrad's office at Canary Wharf for the last time. He was standing by the window, looking wary and bleak. I sat down and said: 'Conrad, I'm going. I've had a very good offer from Vere Rothermere and David English, to edit the *Evening Standard*. I've done virtually ten years here. I think it's enough. I shall always be grateful to you for giving me the chance to run the *Telegraph*. It's been marvellous, but now it's time to give somebody else a go. Who knows? They may have a lot of ideas I haven't even thought of. I am editing the paper as well as I know how, but if I go on for a year or two, you'll be getting more of the same. You're almost certainly right that we need some new blood near the top. But I'm not the right person to introduce it.'

Conrad was incandescent. He spoke witheringly of Vere Rothermere and David English: 'How could they do this to me, given our relationship? Is it too late to discuss an alternative?'

'I'm afraid it is, Conrad, I've signed with Associated. I've always thought that nothing could be worse for our relationship than for me to sit here and extract terms from you at pistol point.'

'This is scarcely promotion for you, Max.'

'It depends on how you look at it. For me, it's a great new challenge. Nobody should go on doing any of these big frontline jobs for more than ten years.'

'Your timing is hardly convenient for us. The price war isn't over yet.'

'If we didn't have this conversation now, in a year or two I would be sitting here sobbing and asking what on earth would happen to me, because you would have decided it was time that I went. The chance to edit a second title in a career doesn't come twice.'

'Can we keep this quiet for a few days?'

'I think it's almost impossible. English has no reason to do any favours by shutting up. You'd have to ring him yourself.'

A decisive headshake: 'I won't do that.'

I left him gazing fiercely out of the window upon the torrid glories of the Isle of Dogs. It was the last time we spoke for two years, until time persuaded him that I was right, that he and *The Daily Telegraph* benefited as much as I did from my decision to go.

There was a long-arranged lunch for some of our financial journalists in the dining room that day. I felt obliged to go through with the occasion, after the group had travelled to Canary Wharf from the City. At 2 p.m., the statement of my resignation was issued, accompanied by some generous public words from Conrad. I broke the news to my bewildered lunch guests, then went down to talk to staff in the Newsroom, and to see senior executives one by one. Curiously enough, very few had possessed even the smallest expectation of my going. *The Guardian*, reporting the story, called it 'one of the newspaper world's best-kept secrets'. My colleagues had believed I would remain for at least a year or two. The pain of parting was very great, the goodbyes to people with whom I had worked so closely for so long.

At Westminster, some senior Tories hastened to convince themselves that I was leaving simply because I had fallen out with Conrad over Europe. Michael Heseltine telephoned on the afternoon of the announcement of my resignation, full of suspicions; so too, more surprisingly, did the Prime Minister. I was at pains to assure both men that it was not simply some ideological clash which had prompted my going. It was a career decision. *The Guardian* was not far wrong in asserting that 'an attractive salary offer from the *Standard* and weariness with the in-fighting are thought to have prompted his decision'. John Major remained sceptical: 'I know more about it all than you might think, Max,' he observed darkly. An emotional *Telegraph* colleague said: 'But the paper's never been better.' I hoped she was right, I answered. That surely made it the right moment to go. My right-wing critics were, of course, delighted by my departure. But I cherished some kind words. *UK Press Gazette*, the industry paper, said that since 1986 the *Telegraph* 'has become younger, politically less aligned, and has stayed at the top of the quality market despite the fierce cover-price battle with the *Times*'. *The Observer* said that I had moved the paper 'from loony right to eccentric centre'. *Private Eye*, so often my scourge, criticized Conrad: 'Thanks to his ham-fisted interference, he has lost a successful editor who will be hard to replace.' This was a trifle hard on our Chairman.

The last issue of the paper for which I was responsible carried a Saturday Column I had written for the leader page, contrasting television's charming picture of rural life in the age of Jane Austen with a somewhat harsher reality. If this was a whimsical parting shot, it also reflected one of the great pleasures of writing for such a newspaper as the *Telegraph*. There is almost no topic across the range of human affairs which it is impossible to find an excuse to address somewhere in its pages.

There were no farewell dinners for my close colleagues, as I should have liked. Too many thunderclouds hung over the Chairman's floor to make such an occasion politic. But we held an impromptu drinks party for the editorial staff upstairs at Canary Wharf. 'If, as I think we all believe, this is a marvellous newspaper today,' I said in my speech,

> it is not because of anything I have managed to do, on odd days between fishing and shooting. It is because of what all of you have done. This is an extraordinary gathering of journalists, without doubt the ablest, most brilliant team any newspaper in Fleet Street possesses. Almost every one of our specialist correspondents is recognized as supreme in his or her field. Between us, we've moved this paper a long way in the past decade. We've learned how to entertain readers as well as to inform them, how to reach out to women and to the young, how to package and design a modern broadsheet. We've achieved absolute dominance of our field on Saturdays.
>
> Whatever spats we have had with our management, through all these years we have never been significantly underfinanced, and nobody should undervalue the support we have had in that direction from Conrad, Dan Colson and Stephen Grabiner. I'm leaving now, not because I want to abandon *The Daily Telegraph* and all of you, which is probably the greatest wrench of my life, but because most people in every walk of life spoil everything by staying too long. *The Daily Telegraph* must never stand still, must never grow complacent. It's time somebody else brought a new mind to bear on this wonderful creation. The time to go is when you've given it your best shot, when the paper is at the top of its form, and when one has the chance of a new challenge. I haven't had a wholly uneventful life, but by far the most thrilling, rewarding, fulfilling years of it have been those I have spent here, with all of you. Even today, most of our readers are barely aware who is the Editor of *The Daily Telegraph*. In a year or two, my tenure will have been forgotten. What matters to them, and

what matters to us all, is that this is a great newspaper which will never be destroyed by Rupert Murdoch or any other predator. To all of you who will be carrying on the torch, thanks for everything from the bottom of my heart.

Then I drove away from the building for the last time, leaving Jeremy Deedes as Acting Editor in my stead, while Conrad debated who should succeed me. That evening, one of my oldest friends said abruptly over a drink: 'So now you're richer, but less important.' I was momentarily wounded, but of course he was right. The Editor-in-Chief of the Telegraph Group was a much bigger fish in Fleet Street than the Editor of the *Evening Standard.* Nothing in life stays the same in our business, however, and if it does so, it should not. I had been granted a wonderful opportunity, to start over again at the *Standard.* A few days later, I sat down at my new desk in High Street Kensington and looked around at the unfamiliar furniture.

And now it would all be different, I thought.

AFTERWORD

CHARLES MOORE became my successor as Editor of *The Daily Telegraph*. I may have exercised a marginal influence on this outcome, by warning David English within days of my move to Associated that Conrad was dallying with Paul Dacre, Editor of the *Daily Mail*. I was reliably informed that a deal was imminent. 'It doesn't sound very likely to me,' said David thoughtfully, 'but perhaps I'd better go and have a word with Paul.' A few hours of frenzy followed, before Paul signed a new and extremely lucrative contract with Associated.

Dominic Lawson took over *The Sunday Telegraph*. Simon Heffer resigned after Conrad declined to grant him the executive role he coveted. Jeremy Deedes became Managing Director of the *Telegraph*, when Stephen Grabiner departed soon after me. I wrote to Dominic before the new appointments were announced, explaining that my own hesitations about recruiting him to the *Daily* had not been prompted by any doubts about his abilities:

> I am confident that you are going to be a great newspaper editor, but as I wrote to Conrad, just as I would have been unsuited to play any subordinate executive role in a newspaper office, so I suspect you would have been ... It may well be that, after a decade, some changes in the upper executive ranks are needed. But I simply didn't feel that I could be the one to make them, if this involved throwing overboard people who have done a lot of good things for me. I have always said that ten years was a landmark, at which

one should think again about one's own life . . . along came
. . . the prospect of a whole new challenge which should keep
me busy for at least five years, by which time I shall be more
than happy to go off and do other things in the country. I
have always liked to keep the initiative in my own life, and it
seemed far preferable to make a bold decision now, rather
than to have everybody wondering when I would slink out of
here, a year or two down the line.

Both the *Daily* and *Sunday Telegraph* look better now than
they did in my day. The process of evolution and change, in
design and content, has continued in a fashion that I doubt I
could have contrived. A marketing ploy was introduced, which
I lamented that no one conceived in my time: cut-price subscription sales. The cost to the company's bottom line has been fierce,
and some people in the newspaper industry believe it was a serious
strategic mistake; but the discount subscribers who now make up
some 40 per cent of the paper's purchasers have sustained its
circulation close to the 'magic million'. Ironically, therefore, many
Telegraph readers now get the paper for less in real terms, by
comparison with the price of a tabloid newspaper, than they did
in the first Lord Camrose's day. By a back door, his pricing
formula has been restored. Conrad is much happier with the
political tone of the *Daily* than ever he was under my regime,
though of course I regret that the attempt to make the *Telegraph*
a one-nation Conservative newspaper ended with my editorship.
I spent six happy years at the *Evening Standard,* building a new
team to run a completely different kind of newspaper. Don Berry
went with me from the *Telegraph* to become the *Standard*'s
Associate Editor, along with several other old colleagues. It proved
a wonderfully exciting experience, to work as hands-on editor of a
tabloid, writing headlines and engaging in every aspect of five
editions a day, after running the *Telegraph* from the relative
remoteness of a lofty bridge.

At the 1997 General Election, I wrote the *Standard*'s full-page editorial, declaring the paper's support for Tony Blair. It was a piece I could never have written, nor have expected to write, for the *Telegraph*. A few weeks before the 2001 election, I was lunching with our Chairman, Lord Rothermere. He asked: 'Who do you think the *Standard* will support?' I said we would come out for Labour again, as indeed we did. This was a conversation that reflected the freedom editors are granted at Associated Newspapers, and which I valued very much. One of my abiding memories of Jonathan Rothermere's father, Vere, is of a conversation during the 1997 election campaign. We had been tormenting in the paper Sir James Goldsmith, whose Referendum Party seemed a mischievous rich man's indulgence. Sir James responded with a barrage of lawyers' letters, and a call from one of the great democrat's henchmen, who said: 'Sir James has asked me to make clear to you that he is not sending legal letters as a matter of form. After the election, he intends to destroy you and the *Evening Standard*.' One of the Goldsmith lawyers' missives included the memorable line: 'We draw your attention to the fact that our client is a close personal friend of your proprietor.' In my reply, I said that while I embraced the carpet at the mention of our proprietor, Lord Rothermere's relationship with Sir James did not change the *Standard*'s view of the Referendum Party. I sent copies of both sides of this correspondence to Vere Rothermere, who responded with a note a few days later: 'It is absolutely true that Jimmy Goldsmith is a very old friend of mine. But I see no reason why this should prevent him from being teased in the *Evening Standard*.' That is the sort of note from a proprietor which any newspaper editor cherishes.

To my surprise and delight, Paul Dacre appointed my old *Telegraph* deputy Veronica Wadley to succeed me as Editor of the *Evening Standard*. I am once more an author of books and a mere contributor to newspapers. To be a journalist is an inherently conceited activity, because one is obliged to offer to the public Olympian verdicts upon a range of issues that would daunt Socrates, from the future of the National Health Service to the merits of engagement in Sierra Leone. It is a relief no longer to be required to produce a relentless bombardment of opinions, month in and month out, at an hour's notice. Now that the strain has gone, I realize how great it was. Even on holiday, an editor can scarcely run a box on the front page dissociating himself from anything published in his absence. But I miss the company of colleagues whom, in many cases, I loved as well as respected, together with the opportunity each day to work among clever people, whose brains one could pick about everything from Proust to the future of Africa.

There are few thrills to match that of running a great newspaper when a big story is breaking somewhere in the world. The buzz of excitement across the newsroom rises audibly as off-stone time comes near, and scores of men and women rattle out the words, peering intently into their screens, making up pages, scanning half-tones, communing with each other in muttered shorthand. No one could spend long in our business who fails to embrace a sense of romance about it, however spurious this might seem in the eyes of the outside world. On a daily newspaper, the fruits of triumph and disaster are laid before one's eyes within hours. It is an old cliché of our trade, that you – the writer, and above all The Editor – are only as good as your last edition.

Our team felt a great sense of achievement, that between 1986 and 1995 we revived the fortunes of *The Daily Telegraph*, and transformed it into a modern newspaper. We sought to marry the paper's traditional virtues with new skills, fresh talent and contemporary presentation. We were committed, above all, to a belief that our chief business was to convey accurate, objective, non-partisan information. If this sounds banal, consider the number of titles in the British press today which possess no such aspiration.

I have no regrets about the new political spirit with which I sought to infuse the *Telegraph*. I believe now, as I believed then, that we were right to reach out to a constituency of the future, rather than to one of the past. Eurosceptic, right-wing Conservatism has no message for the vast majority of the British people. I am only one of a vast number of former Conservatives, who today feels unable to support the party, above all because of its stance on Europe. But it would be foolish to suggest either that the political aspect of my editorship of the *Telegraph* was wholly successful, or that I left any political legacy behind me. Today, the paper's policies are far closer to those of the *Telegraph* in 1985 than those of, say, 1992. The critics – including Andrew Knight – who suggested that I lacked an embracing political vision were probably right. I certainly did not possess one which could have been expressed with frankness in Conrad Black's *Daily Telegraph*. The difficulties of marrying my own one-nation Toryism with the convictions of its proprietor were, ultimately, insuperable. Above all, it was impossible plausibly to reconcile my belief that Britain's future must lie in Europe, with that of Conrad – and of most *Telegraph* readers – that the European Union remains an anathema. Some readers of this book will conclude that editorial independence was not much in evidence during my years at the *Telegraph*. The story I have told sometimes sounds more like a ten-year diplomatic negotiation, than a saga of high journalism. Yet one of my purposes has been to describe, as frankly as I can, the detail of the relationship between an editor and a proprietor. My own experience represents no universal truth about the media, but merely illustrates the reality that absolute editorial independence is a rarity. The sort of debate which took place at the *Telegraph* in my day is more commonplace in our industry than some of my peers are willing to concede, if only to preserve their own amour propre. Michael Kirkhorn, an American journalist, has written: 'The editor of any newspaper owned by a chain or group will say with absolute assurance that overt corporate restraint rarely if ever reaches the news-room – but, then, that editor's intuitive understanding of what is permissible is so keen that overt restraint will never be required'.*

There is a further point. I never considered that my relation-

* *BJR* Summer 1990.

ship with Conrad ended in a miscarriage of justice. At any time, if I disliked the terms upon which I was editing the newspaper, it was open to me to resign. I am a free-marketeer. I accept the principle that a proprietor is entitled to publish the sort of newspaper he chooses. It seems more remarkable that Conrad continued to support me as Editor for almost a decade, when the paper frequently espoused policies from which he dissented, than that a parting finally became inevitable. In the long run, Conrad might have served his own international commercial interests better had he eschewed the temptation to pursue political objectives as well as financial ones. But he could argue today that the state of his bank balance demonstrates that it is possible to have it both ways. Two years after I left his empire, Conrad came to dinner at my home in Berkshire. He peered curiously about the drawing room for a while, before observing magisterially: 'Nice house you've got here, Max – *but it would have been twice the size if you'd stayed with us!*'

If my time at the *Telegraph* commands any respect – and all newspaper editors are swiftly and justly forgotten – it will have to be for what our team achieved as professional news-gatherers. As a boy, and as a young reporter, I never dreamed that I should become Editor of a great national title. Even now a warm glow persists, that the experience cannot be taken away from me. On 5 October 1995, I wrote to Conrad Black: 'I shall always owe you a debt of gratitude for giving me the opportunity to edit the *Telegraph*, and for much good fun and good company over the past decade. If I ever emulate you in writing my memoirs, my memories will almost all be fond ones.'

Back in the Canary Wharf days, when I moaned across the lunch table about the strains and pains of running *The Daily Telegraph*, our long-suffering City Editor Neil Collins would listen, then dismiss my protests laconically: 'Yeah, but it beats working.' You were right, Neil. I loved it.

INDEX